THE END OF THE WORLD?
THE UNOFFICIAL AND UNAUTHORISED
GUIDE TO SURVIVORS

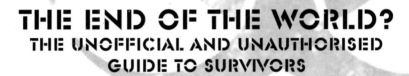

THE END OF THE WORLD?
THE UNOFFICIAL AND UNAUTHORISED
GUIDE TO SURVIVORS

RICH CROSS AND ANDY PRIESTNER

First published in England in 2005 by
Telos Publishing Ltd
61 Elgar Avenue, Tolworth, Surrey, KT5 9JP, England
www.telos.co.uk

Telos Publishing Ltd values feedback. Please e-mail us with any comments you may have about this book
to: feedback@telos.co.uk

ISBN: 1-84583-001-6 (paperback)
The End of the World? © 2005 Rich Cross and Andy Priestner
Foreword © 2005 Pennant Roberts

Internal design, typesetting and layout by Arnold T Blumberg & ATB Publishing Inc.
www.atbpublishing.com

Printed in India

1 2 3 4 5 6 7 8 9 10 11 12 13 14 15

British Library Cataloguing in Publication Data.
A catalogue record for this book is available from the British Library.

ACKNOWLEDGEMENTS

There are many individuals to whom we would like to extend our thanks and without whose help and support this book would have been so much the poorer. David Howe and Stephen James Walker at Telos for backing the first professionally published work on *Survivors*. For their willingness to be interviewed and share their memories with us: Tristan de Vere Cole, Stephen Dudley, Peter Duncan, Denis Lill, Lucy Fleming, June Hudson, Lorna Lewis, Hazel McBride, Ian McCulloch, Julie Neubert, Delia Paton, Pennant Roberts, Tanya Ronder, Carolyn Seymour, Don Shaw, Angie Stevens and Heather Wright. Throughout the writing of this book, Pennant – in particular – has been a constant source of encouragement, and a mine of information on the making of *Survivors*. For allowing us the opportunity to include as illustrations personal behind-the-scenes photographs from the production of the series, we are extremely grateful to: Anne Christie, Lucy Fleming, Lorna Lewis and Denis Lill. We are also indebted to those *Survivors* fans (website editors, location hunters and fanzine contributors) whose efforts over the years have done so much to extend our collective knowledge about the making of the programme. For their assistance with this book, we would like to express particular gratitude to Adrian Hulme and Bob Meade, for helping to confirm many of the filming locations recorded here. Additional thanks to Adrian for allowing us to reproduce several of his location photos and sourcing others. We also wish to acknowledge the help of: Colin Higgs of DD Home Entertainment (formerly DD Video); Dave and Julia of *Shoot That Tiger!*; *Action TV*; the articles and research of Andrew Pixley; Jonathan Bignell; *The Hereford Times*; Dave Rice; Solveig Tucker for finding 'that' film reel under her bed; Kevin Marshall for putting together the crucial first *Survivors* tome; Frances David for taking us up to Callow Hill and Juliette and Emily for showing us around while we were there; Brian Bowen for his insightful comments on earlier drafts of the book; and finally Marisa Priestner for proofing the whole darn thing.

Naturally, any errors of fact and all elements of description, analysis and criticism remain the responsibility of the authors alone.

Dedicated to Chris Skeats and Marisa Priestner,
who both survived the writing of this book.

CONTENTS

FOREWORD

We must have known from the start that we were on to a winner because we brazenly reserved a table in Waitress Service!

The Restaurant Block at BBC Television Centre in Wood Lane had in the '70s an established pecking order. Waitress Service on the second floor was the first that you reached as you crossed the Bridge from the Main Block: table reservations were *de rigeur*. (Even though thirty years have elapsed, I can't help slipping back into the jargon and Capitalisation of the day.) Where the other canteens in the block were self-service, this restaurant was staffed by the more senior biddies of the catering staff in their fading black and white uniforms. Because the service was excruciatingly slow, it was almost exclusively the province of the nabobs of Programme Planning and the Costume Department who had sufficient time for a Long Lunch. Even if you possessed the talent to catch the correct waitress's eye, it was advisable to allow a full two hours – mere mortals with work to be getting on with were rarely seen in such exalted company.

Terry Dudley felt that his new series deserved special treatment, and the three lead actors were invited to meet the series directors to break the ice (wisely as it transpired, because shortly afterwards *Survivors* was deferred for four months, and it proved a very long time before we could all get together again.)

Industrially speaking, 1974 was not a happy year at the Beeb. The production assistants of the Drama Department (amongst whose number I had toiled until the previous year) had long nurtured a grievance about their status within the scheme of things. Officially graded B1-, they believed that since they were doing the work of at least three individuals, they should be better recompensed. Nowadays their responsibilities are shared amongst production executives and their assistants, location managers, first and third assistant directors and a few more besides, so they probably had a strong case. After four months of aggro, normal service was resumed. The PAs were regraded B1+ and production lines restarted. I returned to Glasgow to resume work on *Sutherland's Law*, the series I had been obliged to abandon the previous April. Because *Survivors* was new, its production schedule was put back; rather than start shooting in September, it would now have to be in January.

In some ways the delay was a blessing in disguise, in that it gave the writers more time to complete their scripts, an advantage that didn't begin to unwind until midway through the second year. The downside was that we were committed to start filming in chilly January, when daylight hours were short and morning frosts thick on the ground. The weather wasn't particularly felicitous for Abby Grant's tennis scene at the start of the opening episode, or Carolyn's body temperature when she was required to wash herself in a Herefordshire stream on the very first day of Gerry Blake's shoot. Of course the bleak country landscapes ideally suited the drama of the early episodes.

The degree to which practical considerations governed content is not widely understood. Quite self-evidently in terms of a continuing soap opera, the production turnaround must match the transmission schedule on a weekly basis, or else chaos swiftly ensues. The vogue in the '70s was for thirteen-part series rather than the six-parters we generally watch today. Programmes were planned with the same supply chain management techniques that keep supermarket shelves stocked, and transmission dates dictated production, the paramount consideration being that the last edit day preceded the last scheduled transmission.

The Outside Broadcast units of the day had limited mobility, and nothing could be recorded

8

in camera. All pictures were routed back to the 'scanner', and even with 1,000 yards of cable on the wagon, locations had to be easily accessible. Each episode was recorded in 4.5 days, so that a scheduled unit move for the 'short' day was tolerable, but time lost in unloading and loading vehicles constituted a powerful disincentive against split-location days. When greater camera mobility was an absolute story priority, such as on the early episodes of Series One and "Lights of London" in Series Two, we reverted to the established combination of filmed location sequences and videotaped studio scenes, which was still the BBC norm.

Episodes were edited in a day and dubbed in four hours, ruling out the use of any specially composed music. The vast majority of the scenes were recorded on two cameras to accelerate the shooting process. A by-product of this cross-shooting technique was that it firmly placed the audience amongst the ring of characters, enabling it to become fully

Pennant Roberts with Ann Faggetter and Chris Green. ©Anne Christie

involved in the drama. Is this the significant factor that still weds viewers to soaps, and the reason why '70s TV is recollected as a 'golden age'?

Such a rough and ready approach would scarcely be tolerated nowadays, when location managers meticulously scour the countryside for the most ideal backdrops. The constant demand for higher production values and technical standards creates more specialisms, and larger crews working unacceptably longer hours. Pulling the production teams' strings are flocks of executive producers, poring over nuances of dialogue and niceties of clichéd casting, and wanting significant input at the very last moment. From reports that still filter back to me from the coalface, much of the buzz we directors enjoyed when shaping our storytelling, relating to the perceived needs of our audience, has been hugely diluted. The cost per broadcast hour has become vastly inflated, and the significant benefits are not always readily apparent.

For my money, the Waitress Service lunch saw the true birth of *Survivors*, when Carolyn, Lucy and Ian first met each other and their directors, and started to establish the relationships between their various characters. We may have believed we had something good going for us that day, but not one of us could have foreseen the publication of this book thirty years on. Within the following pages you'll discover much of the fun and frustration the cast and crew encountered in making *Survivors*. It has been meticulously researched by the two authors, and provides a fascinating insight into the making of *Survivors* both for fans of the series, and for anyone interested in the way a drama series reaches the screen.

Pennant Roberts
January 2005

INTRODUCTION

Survivors is one of the finest 'speculative' dramas ever produced by the BBC. Between 1975 and 1977, primetime British television audiences were drawn to a series shaped from a 'what-if' premise both horrifying and all-too plausible: what would happen if a global catastrophe all but destroyed the human race, laying waste the pillars of modern civilisation, and condemning the few survivors to life in a country plunged back into the dark ages? Devised by the prolific TV scriptwriter Terry Nation (one of the early writers on *Doctor Who*, creator of *Blake's 7* (1978-81), and contributor to numerous adventure drama series from the sixties, seventies and eighties including *The Saint, The Champions, The Baron, The Avengers, The Persuaders* and *MacGyver*), *Survivors* follows the travails and adventures of a group of British survivors who emerge unscathed from a deadly biological pandemic – unleashed by a laboratory accident that wipes out more than 95% of the world's population – into a desolate and almost empty world.

These isolated survivors flee the ruins of urban industrial civilisation and, searching each other out, begin to establish new agricultural settlements in rural enclaves. These scattered remnants of the human race must establish new ways of living – both self-sufficient and interdependent – that do not rely on modern technology, if they are to secure a future for themselves and their offspring. For some, these new communities must serve as the catalyst, and the foundation stones, for a new social order. Others, more pre-occupied with avoiding starvation, cold and isolation, struggle to see beyond their immediate plight. Around them emerge gangs determined to steal and horde the stores of civilisation, and would-be feudal barons anxious to restore order and impose new forms of serfdom. The post-apocalyptic world quickly proves itself to be a threatening, dangerous and unforgiving place.

Ian McCulloch and Tanya Ronder. © Anne Christie

Making maximum use of this compelling and frightening setting, *Survivors* provides diverse and compelling human drama of the highest quality. Intelligent, thought-provoking and – at its best – brilliantly written and performed, *Survivors* explores the terrain of its terrible new world through stories that combine high adventure with the exploration of critically important cultural, political and social themes. *Survivors* scriptwriter Don Shaw contends that the series was of a distinctive dramatic calibre: 'Originally there was a very marked delineation between series drama and single plays. Series drama was regarded as down-market. *Survivors* lifted it to the level of the play, in that it dealt with serious subjects in a serious way.' In setting aside the simplistic shoot-'em-up sensibilities of much of the post-apocalyptic canon, *Survivors* effectively reinvented the 'end of the world' genre on the small-screen, and became a touchstone and continual reference point for other 'speculative' dramas that followed it. Almost twenty years later, Nation was to reflect that, within his long and varied writing career, *Survivors* 'may be my only real "message" television show.'

Lucy Fleming, who played Jenny Richards in all three series of *Survivors,* is often surprised at how strongly the show resonates with viewers nearly thirty years after its original transmission: 'People do still mention it a lot. I get recognised, even nowadays ... and people talk to me about it and they remember it very clearly. Looking at the episodes now, some elements feel old-fashioned compared with modern television, but I think the stories were very strong.' Ian McCulloch, who played Greg Preston, also concedes that he's 'astonished that people still do remember it,' and while he too agrees that, technically-speaking, *Survivors* sometimes shows its age, he's equally certain that 'the stories are generally good, and the acting is, actually, very good.' He also recalls that for at least one woman viewer 'this programme changed her life – she became a microbiologist because of *Survivors.*' Stephen Dudley, who played their adopted son John, meanwhile comments that: 'I am constantly struck with the fact that the clothes may be dated but the issues and dilemmas are not ... That *Survivors* is still compelling with its dreary sets and miserable muddiness, without spacemen, fashion or fast cars, is because it is drama in the true sense. We care about what happens to the characters; that is the result of good writing, powerful acting and taut direction.'

The implicit and the explicit 'politics of *Survivors*' are fascinating. Scriptwriters, actors and directors all had to deal with the contentious social and political issues that lent the series' storylines such credibility and relevance. The different preoccupations of those involved in shaping and delivering *Survivors*' narrative produced a series with a surprisingly diverse set of political undercurrents. The characterisations and storylines of *Survivors* dealt with issues of class and of gender, of race and ethnicity, and depicted infirmity, disability and competence in the post-Death world. The chaos that immediately follows The Death, and the new social order that gradually emerges from it, highlight some fascinating – and often controversial – political and philosophical suppositions on the part of the series' makers. It can be judged that the series expresses both a pessimistic, even nihilistic, view of the human condition, and a belief in the imperatives of mutual aid and co-operation. It was this sort of mature dramatic complexity that helped to make *Survivors* such compulsive viewing.

Producer Terence Dudley. ©Anne Christie

Broadcast in a primetime weekday slot on BBC1, *Survivors* attracted healthy ratings from the outset, and retained its audience as each series unfolded. The narrative focus of each

11

John Abineri as Hubert Goss. © Denis Lill

series, and the ensemble cast that fleshed out its stories, changed considerably across *Survivors'* three-year run. The series – which began with the immediate aftermath of the devastating plague – concluded with the establishment of a new federation of trading communities across southern England and the switching on of the first revived hydroelectric power plant in Scotland: the first tentative steps on the road to a new society. This provided a satisfying, though far from uncontroversial, denouement – and one that the series' creator disliked intensely.

Survivors is today widely recognised as a 'cult' television classic – both by those who embrace it as 'science fiction', and by those who celebrate it as pioneering work of contemporary drama. Although – to the evident exasperation of its cast as well as its directors and producer – the series was never repeated on terrestrial television, popular interest was rekindled in the 1990s by its transmission on the satellite station UK Gold (albeit with edits to some of the episodes), and by the release of the first series on sell-through video by BBC Worldwide. A small but dedicated *Survivors* fanbase slowly emerged, organising events, publishing fan magazines and journals, and setting up specialist websites. The successful release of all three series of *Survivors* on DVD between 2003 and 2005, in box sets crammed with special features, has further enhanced its critical reputation. The DVD releases have provided the first opportunity since 1977 to see the series as it was originally transmitted, allowing viewers old and new the chance to reappraise it.

This work is the first commercially published book to scrutinise *Survivors* in depth and in its entirety. *The End of the World?* offers a guide to the production of each of *Survivors'* three series, and the characters who populate its storylines. It provides summaries of each of *Survivors'* 38 episodes, alongside a detailed appraisal of the themes, production mechanics, and behind-the-scenes developments. It is illustrated with a mixture of never-before-seen and classic photographs of the production, and incorporates new interview testimony from many of those involved in the making of the show – both in front of the camera and behind.

The End of the World? also re-examines some of the relationships between the key creative players whose talents together shaped how *Survivors* came to be realised on-screen. In particular, it sheds fresh light on the combative relationship that developed between Terry Nation and producer Terence (Terry) Dudley which, over the years, has come to dominate the history of *Survivors*.

The authors have discussed and debated each of the 38 episodes reviewed here repeatedly and at length. In the main, their positions have been very similar, but inevitably, and quite properly, there have been points at which their assessments of particular storylines have diverged. Sometimes one author has been able to convince the other of the rigour of his argument and changed his colleague's mind. But at other times their – entirely subjective – opinions have remained unreconciled. Fans reading this guide are certain to have similar reactions to the ideas they find expressed here – sometimes emphatic agreement; at other times vigorous dissent from what appears on the page. For that reason, the authors concluded that readers might like to know which author was responsible for which episode reviews – so that continuities, recurring ideas (and apparent contradictions) in that writer's opinions might be more easily identified! Both authors have had extensive input into each and every element of the book, but the initials of each author have been appended to episode reviews for which they take final responsibility.

The End of the World? provides the ideal accompaniment and reference work to this groundbreaking and extraordinary drama series – for the dedicated *Survivors* enthusiast, for those coming across the series for the first time, and for those interested in the history of one of the defining programmes from what is increasingly recognised as a classic era of BBC TV drama.

Lucy Fleming as Jenny Richards. © Denis Lill

13

SERIES 1 (1975)

Series Creator
Terry Nation

Producer
Terence Dudley

Main Cast
Abby Grant: Carolyn Seymour
Greg Preston: Ian McCulloch
Jenny Richards: Lucy Fleming
Tom Price: Talfryn Thomas

Writers
Terry Nation (1.1-1.3, 1.6, 1.10, 1.12, 1.13)
Jack Ronder (1.4, 1.5, 1.7, 1.11)
M K Jeeves (pseudonym for Clive Exton) (1.8, 1.9)

Directors
Pennant Roberts (1.1, 1.4, 1.7, 1.9, 1.13)
Gerald Blake (1.2, 1.5, 1.8, 1.11)
Terence Williams (1.3, 1.6, 1.10, 1.12)

Title Music
Anthony Isaac

Production Assistants
Ann Faggetter (1.1, 1.4, 1.7, 1.9, 1.13)
Michael Bartley (1.2, 1.5, 1.8, 1.11)
Derek Nelson (1.3, 1.6, 1.10, 1.12)

Production Unit Managers
Landon Revitt (1.1-1.8)
Jane Massingham (1.9-1.13)

Designers
Austin Ruddy (1.1, 1.4)
Val Warrender (1.1)
Ray London (1.2, 1.5)
Robert Berk (1.7)
Richard Morris (1.3, 1.6, 1.8-1.13)

Film Cameramen
Nat Crosby (1.1, 1.4)
Keith Hopper (1.2-1.6)
Colin Deehan (1.2, 1.4, 1.5)

Film Sound
Simon Wilson (1.1, 1.4)
Graham Bedwell (1.2-1.6)

Film Editors
Chris Wimble (1.1, 1.4, 1.6)
Bernard Ashby (1.2, 1.3, 1.5)

Studio Lighting
Peter Winn (1.1-1.6)

Studio Sound
Alan Fogg (1.1-1.4)
John Delany (1.5, 1.6)

Lighting (VT)
Hubert Cartwright (1.7, 1.9, 1.13)
Harry Thomas (1.8)
Bill Jones (1.10, 1.12)
John Mason (1.11)

Sound (VT)
Ian Leiper (1.7, 1.9, 1.13)
Robin Luxford (1.8, 1.11)
Vic Godrich (1.10, 1.12)

Videotape Editors
Stan Pow (1.7)
Sam Upton (1.8)
Peter Francis (1.9)
Edward Wooden (1.10)
David Hambleton (1.11)
Terry Bennell (1.12)
Neil Pittaway (1.13)

Assistant Floor Managers
Chris Green, Michael Morris,
Carolyn Southwick, Robert Gabriel

14

Director's Assistants
Mary Holdsworth, Diana Baldwin, Winifred Hopkins

Grams Operators
Michael Bartley, Andy Stacey, Martin Ridout

Technical Managers
Bernard Fox, Norman Brierley, Malcolm Martin, John Mason, George Jakins, John Wilson

Cameramen (VT)
Frank Hudson, Paul Harding, Stan Bale

Senior Cameraman
Peter Ware

Vision Mixers
John Barclay, Shirley Coward, James Gould, Vic Melaney, Sue Thorne

Costumes
June Hudson (1.1, 1.3, 1.5, 1.7, 1.9, 1.11, 1.13)
Al Barnett (1.2, 1.4, 1.6, 1.8, 1.10, 1.12)

Costume Assistant
Ros Ebbutt

Dressers
Janice Booth, Alice Gilbert, Dennis Brack, Steve Pokol, Richard Blanchard, John Atkins, Joyce Atkins, Pip Bryce

Make Up
Lisa/Susan Rothwell

Make Up Assistants
Judy Cain, Jane Boak, Lyn Clarke

Floor Assistants
Geoff Posner, Val Birch, Sandra Maeers

Graphics
Dick Bailey

Visual Effects
Jim Ward

Scene Crew Supervisor
Don Evans, Frank Sadler

Property Buyer
Roger Williams

Crew
13

Artists' Contracts Assistant
Angela Heathcote

Armourers
Alf Trustrum, Des Stewart

Animal Trainer
John Holmes

SERIES 1: PRODUCTION

The 1970s post-apocalyptic BBC TV series *Survivors* has long enjoyed a mixed reputation amongst television aficionados. Its status as a classic amongst 'end-of-the-world' dramas is rarely in doubt, and yet the lack of any repeat broadcast until the era of satellite television, has meant that memories of the show have remained hazy. This has encouraged the spread of some popular misconceptions about *Survivors*, with many of its strengths under-appreciated and some of its weaknesses over-emphasised.

Survivors' first series richly deserves to be considered as one of the finest drama series yet broadcast by the BBC. From a distance of nearly thirty years, it reaches out to audiences of today, honing in on important issues (and popular neuroses) that are still strong. The premise for *Survivors* was both chillingly stark and simple. The series explored the repercussions of a worldwide viral catastrophe that had decimated the population of every country on the globe. In preparing his outline for *Survivors*, creator Terry Nation recalled that he: '… researched the Black Death from the Middle Ages. In those days, The Death travelled through Europe and Asia at the speed of a man on a horse because that was the fastest form of locomotion.' By the 1970s, a similar pandemic would: '… travel at the speed of a jet plane. In 24 hours it would be in every major city in the world.' The compelling first series of *Survivors* depicts – through the experiences of a handful of disparate individuals – the terrifying aftermath of civilisation's collapse, and the coming together of the first communities that must begin the battle for survival.

The look and feel of *Survivors* may be dated by the flared trousers and haircuts on show, and by some of the techniques through which the series' storylines are told, but the series has lost none of its dramatic potency. Despite this, *Survivors* remains intimately bound up with the

Filming a scene from "Starvation". © Hereford Times

life-and-times of the era in which it was produced, and its concern to reflect many of the then dominant cultural and political preoccupations is frequently evident on screen.

In the mid-1970s, British society was wracked by social conflicts of all kinds. Strikes and stoppages by workers in the industrial and public sectors had become so commonplace that such unrest had come to be known as 'the British disease'. Head-on confrontations with organised labour had led to the fall of successive Conservative governments, and Labour's efforts to broker a new 'social contract' with trade union leaders were coming under increasing strain. Pay claims chased spiralling inflation, as prices on the supermarket shelves soared with every passing month. There were sudden, unexpected shortages of basic consumer goods, and as coal supplies dwindled, the first power cuts led to city-wide blackouts. Soon after, the Government issued petrol ration books to all citizens in anticipation of an impending fuel crisis. As the country's mood darkened, the political atmosphere grew more tense, and both the far-left and the far-right found new audiences ready to listen to radical solutions to the compound crises. In Northern Ireland, the first bloody years of 'the Troubles' had proved to be the precursor to an even darker and bleaker period of armed conflict. Britain's own problems were exacerbated by the international situation. Huge hikes in the price of oil had impacted dramatically on the economies of all countries in the northern hemisphere, and added to the mood of uncertainty. The Cold War standoff between the nuclear arsenals of the world's two superpowers, which was premised on the belief that MAD (mutually assured destruction) would deter the outbreak of hostilities, permeated all aspects of international relations. As the proclamations of world leaders increasingly came to resemble scenes from the film *Dr Strangelove* (1964), growing 'nuclear anxiety' was everywhere in evidence.

The 1960s had been a decade in which optimism about scientific, industrial and human progress appeared unchallengeable. Prime Minister Harold Wilson had promised that British society would be reforged in the 'white heat of new technology.' Such confidence about the future reached its zenith in the first manned moon landings in 1969. And yet the 1970s had quickly become marked by uncertainty and a growing unease with the march of progress and its attendant risks. Voices were raised that questioned the value of continual industrial growth and the production of limitless supplies of consumer goods, and highlighted the issues of pollution, waste and industrial blight. There were criticisms too of the collective preoccupation with material things and 'keeping up with the Joneses' and all of the compound pressures of an accelerating and increasingly atomised urban society.

Survivors was able to tap effectively into so many of the concerns of the hour – social upheaval, ecological instability, the spectre of global war – and give its drama immediate contemporary resonance.

If the apparent unravelling of society gave *Survivors* the necessary 'negative' context from which the series could project itself forward, there was a parallel 'positive' context from which it also sought to draw. From its roots in the hippie movement of the 1960s, a vibrant counterculture persisted in the Britain of the early 1970s, intrigued by the ideas of self-sufficiency, ecology and sustainability. There were sprawling networks both of communes and of smallholdings, supplemented by convoys of itinerant travellers, which tried to present 'living alternatives' to the drudgery of the nine-to-five treadmill and the urban 'rat race', and whose kibbutz-style ethos stood in sharp contrast to the semi-detached suburban existence of the traditional nuclear family.

Terry Nation was intrigued by the dramatic potential of an intersection between such powerful contemporary themes – the fragility of the modern world; and the challenges that would face refugees from that world if they were forced to start again amidst its ruins. But while Nation was keen to draw on some elements of 'alternative' and 'eco-thinking', his intention was not to condemn the modern world around him, nor to suggest that the sceptics who warned that 'the end is nigh' were right. His interest was in the drama that could be generated by plunging characters who were at home in the modern world into a new medieval present, one in which all the conveniences they had relied on for their whole lives were lost forever. For that reason, Nation resisted the temptation to populate his series with figures that came ready equipped with survival skills. In most cases, the characters who emerged unscathed from the plague were those who would find the challenges of the new world daunting, and their predicament bewildering. He was right to recognise that viewers would find more interesting the struggles of those who had no idea how to plough or keep livestock or tend to sickness than those who already possessed such skills in abundance. Indeed, Nation was keen to show how some professional skills would completely lose their relevance in a post-plague environment – whether those of the investment broker, the civil engineer, or the city secretary.

Above all, Nation was intrigued by the vulnerability that underlies the complex web of social and economic relations in modern society, and how much each individual is reliant on the skills, expertise and labour of thousands of others – people with whom they have no direct contact, and about whom they are often unaware. Writing in the *Radio Times*, Chris Dunkley suggested that to Nation this complex network of co-operative human relationships resembled: '... a battered skittle ball upon which an ingenuous and moody child has constructed an elaborate up-ended pyramid of dangerously swaying bricks.' Everything from refrigerators to footwear; from tools to car parts; from medicine to telecommunications – all are services that require the specialised inputs of thousands of different workers, who are in turn reliant on raw materials and support services traded and made available for them. Nation recognised the power of the drama that could be unleashed through the unravelling of that web of relationships.

By the time that Nation had developed his outline for *Survivors*, he was already an accomplished scriptwriter for both television and radio, with an extensive and impressive list of programme credits to his name. He had begun his writing career in the 1950s, producing material for comedians as well-known as Peter Sellers, Frankie Howerd and Ted Ray, for classic radio series such as *The Goon Show*, and television programmes such as *Friday the 13th*, *The Jimmy Logan Show*, *The Idiot Weekly Price 2d* and ATV's *Hancock*. In 1962, Nation began to diversify, writing three scripts for the *Out of This World* sci-fi anthology series ("Impostor", "Botany Bay" and "Immigrant"). The following year, he created the Daleks for *Doctor Who*; and in penning a story about the survivors of a nuclear war, which gave rise to his most infamous creations, Nation helped to assure the success of the new series almost overnight, despite behind-the-scenes concerns over introducing 'bug-eyed monsters' into what was originally intended to be a more realistic and educational adventure series.

Not all of Nation's pitches to the BBC were as successful. In 1960, he submitted the one-off drama *Uncle Selwyn* to the Light Entertainment Department. Set in the 1920s, this comedy recounted the exploits of a group of Welsh radicals who plot attacks on electric power lines to protect their uncle's failing lamp-oil business. The rejected script was sent on to the BBC's Script Department, where it was again turned down. (A revised version was, though, later bought by Associated Rediffusion, and broadcast in 1964.) Nation also had an outline for another intended one-off drama, *The Thousand and Several Doors*, which the BBC decided to take no further.

Despite his early success on *Doctor Who*, it is far from certain that Nation had planned to develop his career through a concentration on science fiction television. Indeed, in parallel with his sci-fi work, Nation scripted episodes for cult adventure series such as *The Saint* (1962-69), *The Baron* (1966-67), and *The Avengers* (1961-69). As Jonathan Bignell, who co-authored a 2004 study of Nation's screen-writing career, observes: 'He was interested in the possibilities of science fiction, but it seems he didn't plan to move in that direction at first. In some ways he was a writer who would take on all sorts of work to make a decent living, but once his name became associated with science fiction he was happy to keep on writing it.'

In his work on *Doctor Who*, Nation had explored several themes that would resurface in his work on *Survivors*. "The Survivors" had actually been one of the early working titles for the Daleks' introductory story, and was retained as the episode title of its second instalment. The story introduced not only the Daleks, but also the Thals – the human survivors of the nuclear war on the planet Skaro, who had for many generations been attempting to adapt to life on the surface of a ravaged world. His 1964 adventure "The Keys of Marinus" centred on an extended quest – a key component of the first series of *Survivors* – while in 1974's "Death to

the Daleks", a virulent space plague formed the backdrop to the narrative. Arguably, Nation's most notable *Doctor Who* contribution was the highly-regarded 1975 story "Genesis of the Daleks". The latter adventure concerns the Doctor's presence on Skaro, prior to both the onset of the Dalek menace and the planet's devastating nuclear war, and introduces one of *Doctor Who*'s most enduring and popular villains – deformed Dalek-creator Davros. During the story's fifth episode, the Doctor poses a question to Davros: 'Davros, if you had created a virus in your laboratory, something contagious and infectious, that killed on contact – a virus that would destroy all other forms of life. Would you allow its use?' Davros, of course, being a maniac of the first order, responds in the affirmative. Less than two weeks after this episode was broadcast, Nation's first *Survivors* episode would be transmitted – depicting the (accidental rather than criminal)

Carolyn Seymour. © Lucy Fleming

19

Hana-Maria Pravda (Emma) and Stephen Dudley (John) during filming of "Revenge". © Anne Christie

release of a virus of just such devastating power. It was the culmination of a dramatic theme that had clearly been preoccupying Nation for many years.

And yet, if *Survivors* was the extension of ideas that Nation had explored previously, it still came to be recognised as an innovative series, in part because it was so unlike anything else being produced under the banner of either sci-fi or drama on TV at the time. Its content matter and its overall sensibility were strongly adult in tone, and while its end-of-the-world premise was easily identifiable as 'high concept' science fiction, its narrative reach was more often in the direction of realistic drama than of fantasy.

Of course, the contention that *Survivors* is a 'distinctive' series is not intended to discount the many earlier influences that helped to shape the vision of its creators. In the field of literature, post-apocalyptic and dystopian themes had long found reflection in the works of diverse authors. The genre includes such reflective works as Nevil Shute's *On The Beach* (1957), excitable and testosterone-fuelled adventure romps such as John Christopher's *The Death of Grass* (1956), Cold War morality tales including *Alas, Babylon* by Pat Frank (1959), and the more considered J G Ballard catastrophe novels (*The Drowned World* (1962), *The Drought* (1964), *The Crystal World* (1966)) and John Lockley's *After the Fire* trilogy (1994-98). In *The Death of Grass*, as in *Survivors*, the pandemic has its origins in a Chinese laboratory – the culprit in Christopher's book is named the 'Chung-Li' virus. Two works that had an undisputed influence on Nation are George R Stewart's *Earth Abides* (1949) and John Wyndham's *The Day of the Triffids* (1951). *Earth Abides* is an expansive and sophisticated end-of-the-world novel, the plot of which ranges across the American continent and unfolds over the course of many decades. As well as appearing to take from it the inspiration for several specific plot developments, *Survivors* shares with *Earth Abides* a close concern with the strengths and weaknesses of human nature. *The Day of the Triffids*, like *Survivors*, examines the myopia of science and the corrosive consequences of human greed. It also unfolds within a recognisable and realistically evoked English landscape.

As well as post-apocalyptic fiction, the other main body of literature on which Nation and the other scriptwriters drew was the burgeoning number of books concerned with self-sufficiency, alternative technology and communal living that were published in the early 1970s. The most significant of these was *Self Sufficiency* (1973), written by John and Sally Seymour and subtitled *The Science and Art of Producing and Preserving your own Food*, which proved to be a persistent bestseller for Faber and provided an invaluable reference source on the practicalities of husbandry, agriculture and retro-technology. Nation himself put into practice his enthusiasm for self-sufficiency at his home in Lynstead Park in Kent where, together with his wife Kate, he produced much of his own food – growing various crops and keeping a number of farm animals.

In the television field, the clearest antecedent for *Survivors*, and one that provided both personnel as well as dramatic inspiration, was the techno-sceptic eco-thriller series *Doomwatch* (1970-72). The recurrent villains of the *Doomwatch* drama were blinkered scientists, profit-hungry industrialists and inept politicians, who together were steering society towards catastrophe through reckless experiments carried out in the name of 'progress'. With *Survivors*, Nation would take such scientific risk-taking to its deadly conclusion – with humankind's own biological obsessions ending in the destruction of the world. (For more on the relationship between the two series, see the Appendix '*Doomwatch and Survivors: Connections and Continuities*'.) As well as Nation's own explorations of post-apocalyptic settings in *Doctor Who*, other small-screen influences are evident. The fantasy-based children's drama *The Changes* (1975) which was transmitted on British TV screens as production got underway on *Survivors*, provided further evidence of contemporary dramatists' interest in the end-of-the-world formula. Adapted from the Peter Dickinson trilogy of novels, *The Changes* shares with *Survivors* a profound suspicion of unrestrained technological progress and of endless consumer consumption – which in producer Anna Home's drama triggers a collective psychosis, that brings about social collapse and renders cities uninhabitable.

In the early 1970s, Terry Nation developed a number of proposals for the BBC's *Drama Playhouse* slot. The BBC's Drama Department was keen to use *Drama Playhouse* as a forum to broadcast what were in effect 'pilot' episodes of potential new series. If the initial one-off play proved successful, a full-length series might then be given the go-ahead. This was the route through which both *The Onedin Line* (1971-80) and *The Regiment* (1972-73) developed into successful BBC drama series. Aware that this was a proven means to secure full series commissions, Nation approached Andrew Osborn, then Head of Series at the BBC, during the summer or autumn of 1971, to pitch two story outlines – *The Incredible Dr Baldick* and *Beyond Omega*. Robert Baldick was to be a Victorian gentleman crime investigator, whose adventures would involve him in mysterious and unnatural goings-on. *Beyond Omega* was a 'post-apocalyptic' tale of human survival. Impressed by Nation's work, Osborn commissioned both pilots, and set a deadline of 31 January 1972 for completion of the scripts. When Nation later reported that he was running into time trouble, Osborn told him to prioritise work on *The Incredible Dr Baldick*. The finished drama, ultimately retitled *The Incredible Robert Baldick* ("Never Come Night"), which starred Robert Hardy as the titular hero, was broadcast in the *Drama Playhouse* slot in October 1972, but no series was forthcoming.

The producer of *Drama Playhouse* was Anthony Coburn, who had joined the BBC as a staff writer in 1960 and who wrote the first ever *Doctor Who* story "100,000 BC", broadcast in 1963. Nation and Coburn discussed the potential of the *Beyond Omega* outline, and in May 1972 agreed that Nation should begin to draw up additional scripts for an ongoing post-apocalyptic drama, on which Coburn would serve as producer. In late 1973, Nation presented an initial batch of scripts (together with character profiles and support material) to Osborn with the hope of securing a full series commission for a show he was now calling *The Survivors*, without the need for a *Drama Playhouse* pilot. Osborn's interest was immediately engaged, and initial transmission dates in the winter of 1974 were agreed for a thirteen-episode first series. Inevitably there was some initial concern that it might not be possible to realise an end-of-the-world drama effectively within the budget and time constraints by which all BBC TV productions of the day were limited. Discussion and negotiation clarified the scale and budget that could be invested in the series' production. Nation agreed, firstly, that the spread of the apocalypse would not be depicted directly on screen, but evoked in the reaction of a core of characters and in a series of emblematic and metaphorical sequences; and, secondly, that the drama would focus on the aftermath of the calamity, depicting the reactions of a small group of British survivors to the catastrophe that had befallen them.

A development that would quickly curb Nation's enthusiasm for the new series was Osborn's decision to hire Terence Dudley as the producer, instead of Coburn. Nation had enjoyed an effective working relationship with Coburn and was confident that he shared his vision for the series. Coburn had served as a producer on shows such as *The Borderers* (1968-70), series one of the downbeat private investigator drama *The View From Daniel Pike* (1971-73), and the first two series of Royal Navy drama *Warship* (1973-77), alongside his *Drama Playhouse* duties. As *Survivors'* creator and lead scriptwriter, Nation was disappointed not to have been consulted about the decision to appoint Dudley, but Osborn was clear that the choice was not part of Nation's remit. With both Nation and Dudley possessed of strong personalities and clear, but often conflicting, ideas about how the show should develop, the relationship between them quickly became fraught. As Nation set his mind to questions of plots and dialogue, new producer Dudley came to exert an equally powerful creative influence over how the show would appear on screen. Nation would later assert: 'It was my show and I should have had greater control over it … and should have had him removed there and then. But the emotional level of a point like that is tremendous. The programme was already in production, and it is an exhausting battle to fight against the producer, who was actually there every day.'

Before landing his first job in television, Dudley had worked in the theatre, where he had become the Director of Production at the Grand Theatre Swansea. Dudley enjoyed both writing and producing, and had his first script (for a whimsical comic drama entitled *Song in a Strange Land*) accepted by the BBC in 1959. This was the start of a long and distinguished career at the BBC, producing a variety of successful series. In 1962, Dudley conceived and wrote all six episodes of *The River Flows East*, a weekend teatime serial for BBC1, produced and directed by Brian Bell. Notable for its reliance on a high proportion of location filming around the banks of the River Thames, this family-orientated thriller focused on the efforts of a blind scientist – who had been working to devise a cure for world famine – to find those responsible for kidnapping his daughter. The serial featured performances from John Bennett and John Rolfe, both of whom would later appear in *Survivors*. Other early scriptwriting successes for Dudley included *Moonstrike* (1963), *Detective* (1964) and *Boy Meets Girl* (1967), followed by – in the guise of scriptwriter, script editor and producer – five episodes of *Doomwatch*. However, Dudley – like Nation – did not get the go-ahead for all of his pitches at the BBC. In 1971, he developed a treatment for a new episodic drama entitled *Elizabeth*, which was to explore the emotional and relationship entanglements of its titular heroine. BBC bosses judged that the format would be too restricting and turned the proposal down. Dudley was also unsuccessful in his attempts to get approval for *Piece of Resistance*, a comic drama set in the Channel Islands about the exploits of two soldier friends who are sent on a mission to Jersey. This meant that both Nation and Dudley, each of whom had experienced successes and rejections as scriptwriters for the BBC, approached *Survivors* with a determination to enhance their reputation as wordsmiths, from a position of existing credibility as writers for the small screen. The fact that Dudley came to *Survivors* as an established *writer-producer*, rather than simply as a seasoned *producer*, would come to have significant consequences for the evolution of the show.

His writing ability aside, Dudley's work on such shows as *The Regiment* and *Doomwatch*, for which he had overall production responsibility, proved him to be a series handler of high calibre. At the same time, it demonstrated that he had a firm sense of conviction and vision of his own. The strength of

John and Lizzie as first seen in "Gone to the Angels". © Anne Christie

Dudley's own dramatic perspective made him determined to press his own view on the direction a series should take and the strengths and weaknesses of particular scripts – views that, in the case of *Survivors*, would come to contrast strongly with those of the series' creator and individual scriptwriters. It is possible that the conflicts that arose from Dudley's hands-on and proactive approach might have been avoided or ameliorated if the *Survivors* team had included a script editor to act as an intermediary. Director Pennant Roberts is clear that had Dudley 'wanted a script editor he could easily have been given one, since they were already very much in vogue at the Beeb,' but instead 'he remained convinced he could do all the editing himself' given that 'he was a writer in his own right.' Interestingly, Martin Worth, who would write for *Survivors*' second and third series, remembers that Dudley avoided having 'a script editor foisted on him' on the final series of *Doomwatch* by employing Anna Kaliski – who was already working for him as a researcher – as a nominal script consultant.

Prior to Dudley's confirmation in the producer's role, Nation and Coburn had already approached writers whom they hoped to recruit to the series' writing staff. Other than Nation himself, these included Clive Exton and Michael J Bird. Bird was an accomplished scriptwriter who had recently contributed to the BBC dramas *The Lotus Eaters* (1972-73), *Brett* (1971) and *The Onedin Line*, as well as to Thames's *Special Branch* (1969-70, 73-74) and HTV's *Arthur of the Britons* (1972-73). Clive Exton's first television script, *No Fixed Abode*, had been produced in 1958. He had worked with Nation previously on the *Out of This World* TV anthology, and was closely involved in the discussions that preceded Nation's original pitch for *Survivors*. Exton and Nation were long-standing friends and close collaborators on a number of projects for the small and big screen. In 1973, for example, the pair had co-authored the screenplay for the comedy-horror *The House in Nightmare Park*, which starred Frankie Howerd and Ray Milland, and for a time the two writers ran a production company called ExtoNation. Exton also had an impressive string of solo film script credits including *Entertaining Mr Sloane* (1970), the chilling *10 Rillington Place* (1972) and the spin-off *Doomwatch* movie (1972). By October 1973, Nation had completed the script for *Survivors'* debut episode, "The Fourth Horseman". It was a busy time for him as, in the same month, Osborn had also commissioned him to write two scripts for a new series entitled *No Place Like Home* that was to focus on an American and British couple that had taken early retirement and emigrated to Ireland. The series never entered production. On 2 November, Nation was commissioned for his second

Ian McCulloch. © Lucy Fleming

Survivors script, which became "Genesis"; Exton was commissioned to produce a script entitled "The Spark" (subsequently abandoned); and Bird, a script that would later be renamed "Enter the Soldier" (also eventually abandoned), which was intended to introduce a new character by the name of Jordan Neve. Around this time, Nation also appears to have taken on a temporary role of script consultant to the series, and in this capacity looked over Bird's and Exton's work. Pennant Roberts suggests that because Nation '... was streetwise, the probability is that he negotiated a special arrangement over Dudley's head as script consultant ... to bring in a few more pounds, certainly, but also to give himself a say in the direction the series was taking.'

Dudley took the helm as producer in the new year, and for a time, both he and Nation were asserting final authority over the selection of scripts for *Survivors'* first series, with Osborn attempting to mediate the conflict. On 18 March 1974, alongside three further scripts from Nation – which included "Gone Away", "Birth" (which later became "The Future Hour") and "The Serpent" (probably an early version of "Garland's War" and not "Revenge" as has sometimes been assumed due to the latter's serpent allegory) – Bird and Exton were both awarded further commissions. Exton was assigned "Promised Land" (which would later become "Spoil of War"), "Capital Punishment" (which evolved into "Law and Order") and "Shopping List" (which was subsequently dropped). Alongside a reworked outline for "Enter the Soldier", Bird was commissioned for new episodes entitled "Requiem" and "Flight from Tyranny". Some time later, Nation found that two of his own submitted scripts had been rejected outright as unusable by Dudley; while his work as a script consultant on "Enter the Soldier" proved insufficient to prevent its later cancellation in June 1974. Bird subsequently left the writing team before even beginning work on his other two scripts. Despite Dudley's rejections, Nation submitted an invoice for the consultation work he had undertaken.

Following Bird's departure, it was not until 30 July 1974 that a new writer joined the *Survivors* team. Jack Ronder, a talented scriptwriter with an impressive credit list, including work on *The Borderers* and *Hunter's Walk* (1973-76), would prove to have an acute interest in the human predicament angle offered by the series' premise. Prior to his television work, Ronder had also penned a number of successful stage plays, including *This Year, Next Year* and *Confessions of a Justified Sinner*. Ronder's initial commission was "Starvation", the seventh episode and a turning point in the storyline of the series. The final first series *Survivors* scripts were not commissioned until production was underway. On 24 January 1975, Ronder was contracted for the script that would become "Revenge", and Nation for "Something of Value" and the series finale "Directions", which would evolve into "A Beginning".

Nation's deal with the BBC allowed him to write the 'framing' episodes at either end of the first series, something that he hoped and expected would effectively secure him full control over its shape and tempo. This also made sound economic sense for him in terms of potential repeat fees, as when series were repeated it was generally accepted that the first and last episodes would always be re-run, but not necessarily all the shows in between. Nation was keen to keep the drama adventure-driven and to focus on the competition for control in the new post-apocalyptic setting. Jonathan Bignell observes that Nation '… kept returning to ideas about the exercise of power, and who can and should wield authority.' In practice, things proved far more complicated. While neither Ronder nor Exton clashed with Nation over his vision of the show, they each sought to bring out particular themes that interested them – each in their own way different from the character-driven adventure

Terry Scully (Vic Thatcher) during filming of "Law and Order". © Anne Christie

25

The crew queuing up for lunch on location at Hampton Court. © Anne Christie

romps that were Nation's own forté. In Ronder's case, the contrast with Nation was particularly marked. For him, the attraction of *Survivors* was the opportunity to explore the terrible dilemmas that its characters were confronted with. Ronder was less concerned with the clash of armed gangs and the squeal of Land Rover tyres than he was with exploring themes that were both more intellectual and more practical in scope. Such stylistic and thematic differences proved much less problematic than the issue of script editing. Both Exton and Ronder – like Nation himself – soon found themselves in conflict with Dudley over his reluctance to consult with them over changes to their scripts. It is likely that time constraints reduced Dudley's ability to refer back to his writers, but also probable that he frequently considered such negotiation unnecessary. Although this method certainly expedited the script-editing process, all three writers would come to find Dudley's robust approach difficult to accept. Looking back on his father's motivations today, Stephen Dudley remembers: 'He could be challenging and demanding, but he was tortured by a perfectionist's obsession with the art of television drama. If he occasionally frustrated writers and directors with a long screwdriver it was because he had vision, not because he lacked it.'

As initial scripts were written and the first few episodes entered pre-production, the show's working title remained *The Survivors*. This name appeared on script drafts, including that for the opening episode "The Fourth Horseman", and production paper work. Then the decision was taken to drop the redundant prefix. It was a simple change but it served to invest the series with a more evocative and edgy feel.

The BBC agreed to a production method – a mixture of film, studio and on-location Outside Broadcast (OB) work – that was relatively new, demanding a sharp learning curve from all involved if the series was to be completed on time and under budget. However, production was immediately threatened by other unforeseen events. A series of technicians' strikes at the BBC delayed work by several months. This setback had two significant, and positive, repercussions. First, it gave Dudley and his team some additional, and badly needed, set-up time – without which *Survivors* would certainly have struggled to be ready for the cameras. Secondly, it shifted the seasonal setting for the action, which would now, perhaps more fittingly, open in the chill of winter and conclude in the warmth and sunshine of late spring. The rash of technicians' strikes were eventually settled, but a potentially much more threatening challenge remained. Writer Brian Clemens (with whom Nation had collaborated on such shows as *The Avengers* and *The Persuaders!* (1971-72)), claimed that the original idea for *Survivors* was his, and mounted a legal challenge claiming infringement of 'intellectual copyright'. It appears that after his work on *Beyond Omega* had stalled at the BBC, Nation had worked with Clemens on modifying the original proposal for consideration by ITV. In addition, Clemens asserted that in the 1960s, whilst working on *The Avengers*, he had developed a pitch for a post-apocalyptic series entitled *The Survivors* that he hoped would develop into a British-American co-production with adventures on both sides of the Atlantic. Other writers with whom Nation had worked, including Clive Exton, backed up his insistence that the idea for *Survivors* was his own. Clemens explained to *SFX* magazine in May 1999 that: 'I took him to court, but nothing came of it. I suddenly realised both he and I were spending money on lawyers so I just dropped the action.' The case was withdrawn from the London High Court on 3 March 1976, less than a month before transmission of the second series began. Clemens reports that, prior to Nation's death from emphysema in March 1997, the two writers had reached mutual agreement to put the matter to rest.

Dudley recruited a team of three directors to helm the thirteen episodes of the first series, each of whom had worked with him on earlier projects. Pennant Roberts remembers that Dudley first '… offered me work on *Doomwatch*. After that I worked with him on *Colditz*. When I went freelance at the beginning of 1974, *Survivors* was about the first thing that came along, and Terry started to set that up during the summer, and offered me the series along with Terence Williams and Gerald Blake.' Roberts had begun his television career in 1962, joining the staff of Westward Television, before moving to BBC Wales the following year. He had gone on to direct episodes of *Doomwatch*, *Softly, Softly: Task Force* (1969-76), *The Regiment* and *Sutherland's Law* (1973-76). Early in his career, Blake had worked as a stage actor and director, before beginning work in television in 1962. He had directed episodes of *Coronation Street*, *Doctor Who* and *Dr Finlay's Casebook* in the 1960s, and instalments of *The Onedin Line* and *The Edwardians* in the 1970s. Williams also had a theatrical background, and had first worked with the Dundee Repertory Theatre as both a stage manager and director. Joining the BBC in 1956, he went on to work on episodes of *Maigret* (1960-63) and *Z Cars* (1962-78). He also set up *Emmerdale Farm* in 1972 for Yorkshire Television.

The task of auditioning and selecting the first series' cast was shared between Dudley and his three directors. As Roberts recalls: 'The convention of the day was that the producer was responsible for selecting the principal personnel … but then after that … the other parts of the casting the director would have been responsible for, rather than Dudley.' Dudley had also to bear in the mind the need to recruit actors with whom TV audiences were not overly familiar, so that the series' end-of-the-world premise might appear as credible as possible, and viewers not be distracted by the presence of well-known faces.

For the three main characters, Dudley selected Ian McCulloch for the part of Greg, Lucy Fleming for the role of Jenny, and Carolyn Seymour for the series' lead, Abby Grant. When asked his opinion of McCulloch's casting by Dudley, Roberts recalls: 'I said, "Yes, he sounds like an excellent idea." I certainly would have known of Carolyn, but I don't think I knew much about Lucy prior to our meeting up.'

Seymour had studied at the Central School of Speech and Drama before joining the company of the Theatre Royal in Windsor. She soon graduated to stage appearances in the London West End productions of *On the Rocks* and *My Darling Daisy*. Prior to *Survivors*, Seymour's major small screen appearance had been the role of Jenny in the final two series of *Take Three Girls* (in 1970-71). Just before *Survivors*, she also guest-starred as Lady Brooke in the major TV serial *Edward the Seventh* (1975). Her film career remained in its infancy, with early though memorable roles in *Gumshoe* and *Unman, Wittering and Zigo* in 1971, and *The Ruling Class* and *Steptoe and Son* in 1972. So taken was she with the potential of the role of Abby Grant, that she was willing to consider a TV role that would inevitably interrupt her big screen career. She remembers: 'I'd wanted to work for the BBC. I knew Abby was going to be the pinnacle of the leading triangle, and she was a great character. It was also just going to be one series at that point.' Negotiations were tough, but Seymour's agent brokered a deal acceptable to all sides. Seymour recalls that, as a result: 'I was supposedly the highest paid actress at the BBC at that time.' Another of the actresses shortlisted for the part of Abby was Wanda Ventham, who had previously appeared in such programmes as *The Prisoner* (1967-8), *The Troubleshooters* (1966-72), *The Lotus Eaters* and *Doctor Who*, yet Dudley apparently rejected her because she looked 'too well-fed' to appear convincing as a post-apocalyptic survivor.

Nation provided a detailed character outline for each of the series' three leads. Abby Grant was described as living a 'life of considerable privilege.' After a short career in publishing and interior design, she had settled for a happily married domestic life in which she juggled 'entertaining their friends and her husband's business contacts' with other many other interests 'that seem to keep her always short of time.' Abby was to take centre stage as a middle-class woman thrown from a comfortable background into the horrifying post-Death world, who would find reserves of strength and fortitude that would make her into a leader and figurehead of a new settlement of survivors.

Lucy Fleming's background had been primarily as a stage actress, with numerous appearances in a variety of classical dramas. After training with the English Stage Company, she appeared in productions of *The Voysey Inheritance* and, in London's West End, *When Did You Last See My Mother?* Her performance as Isabella in *The Tragedy of King Richard II*, opposite Ian McKellen, was one of several early roles that had drawn critical praise. Her film career was less developed, but had included a small role in the 1966 big-screen Russian historical drama *Rasputin: the Mad Monk*. In addition to a guest-starring role in the 1969 *Avengers* episode "Invasion of the Earthmen" (which Terry Nation had scripted), two of Fleming's more substantial TV appearances had been in adaptations of theatrical productions. In 1968 she had appeared as the young Sorell Bliss in Thames Television's version of Noel Coward's celebrated *Hay Fever*. In 1973, she had starred alongside Peter Eyre and Ben Kingsley in Ken Loach's adaptation of Anton Chekhov's classic short story *A Misfortune*. For Fleming, her role in *Survivors* was a significant small-screen career advance, and something of a change of direction. Nation described Jenny Richards as '... a good looking modern girl ... very trendy without being outrageous ... a capable and independent spirit.' She was also someone who appears vulnerable, which meant that '... her friends tend to be protective towards her.' In the post-Death world, Jenny would reveal the vulnerable and courageous sides of her personality in equal measure, and would often provide the emotional core of the relationship between the series' original leading characters.

Ian McCulloch's own film career was on the rise, with a starring role in the 1975 gothic horror *The Ghoul*, as a dashing adventurer who comes to a gruesome end – one of a number of attention-grabbing performances. Alongside other smaller movie roles in *It!* (1966), *Cromwell* (1970) and *I, Monster* (1971), McCulloch had made a number of television appearances. In 1968 he had co-starred in the historical six-part Scottish Television series *Flight of the Heron*, playing the role of the young Highland chieftain Ewen Cameron. Set against the backdrop of the Jacobite Rebellion of 1745, the series centred on the relationship of grudging respect between Cameron and the English army officer Captain Windham (played by Jon Laurimore). McCulloch had also made guest-starring appearances in *Man in a Suitcase* (1967-68), the BBC's *The Borderers*, and, in 1974, the LWT spy drama series *The Aweful Mr Goodall*. Perhaps McCulloch's most memorable small-screen performance prior to *Survivors* had been in the acclaimed six-part 1971 BBC period drama serial *The Search for the Nile*, in which he had co-starred as James Grant. McCulloch's growing reputation on both the big and the small screen was as a rugged, and often enigmatic, leading man – attributes that the character of Greg epitomised. McCulloch was also a singer-songwriter and had had a number of his songs released on the Decca recording label. Dudley opted to see McCulloch for the part of Greg after recalling his guest-starring role in the 1974 *Colditz* episode "Odd Man In", which Dudley himself had directed. Nation described Greg as 'slightly introverted' and 'something of a loner.' After suffering 'various emotional hurts' Greg has become 'guarded about new relationships but his natural compassion tends to involve him with people, even when all his experience warns against this.' Greg would find his fiercely independent nature tempered by the challenges that follow The Death. While always capable of being heroic, Greg would also discover that his commitment both to Abby and to Jenny

Talfryn Thomas, Ian McCulloch and Julie Neubert. © Anne Christie

revealed other aspects of a complex personality.

The interplay between these three leading characters would dominate the drama of *Survivors'* first series, yet in their adventures they would encounter a growing number of fellow survivors. Regular characters included: agricultural expert Paul Pitman (Chris Tranchell, cast by Gerald Blake due to his performance as Daniel Spencer in the 1965 drama *The Legend of Death*); Jewish matriarch Emma Cohen (Hana-Maria Pravda, who had appeared in the television serials *Napoleon and Love* in 1972 and *Dracula* in 1973) and her young companion Wendy (Julie Neubert, cast by Pennant Roberts who had previously worked with her on the 1972 *Doomwatch* episode "Waiting for a Knighthood"); veteran businessman Arthur Russell (Michael Gover, who had also appeared in *Doomwatch* in an episode called "The Logicians", as well as in numerous editions of *Z Cars* and *Softly, Softly*) and his faithful former secretary Charmian Wentworth (Eileen Helsby, who had guested in the *Doomwatch* episode "Tomorrow, The Rat", and had also made appearances in *Fall of Eagles* in 1974 and *Looking for Clancy* in 1975). They would be joined by crippled Vic Thatcher (Terry Scully, best known for his portrayal of King Henry VI in the classic Shakespearean serial *The Age of Kings* in 1960); mentally-impaired Barney (John Hallett, cast by Roberts, who remembered his performance as Private Hodge in *The Regiment*); and disreputable down-and-out Tom Price (played by peerless Welsh character-actor Talfryn Thomas, who had at that time just finished a run in *Dad's Army* (1968-77) as Private Cheeseman, and whose performance would deliver some of the most memorable comedic – and some of the most chillingly menacing – moments in *Survivors'* first series). The first series also boasted a wealth of notable guest stars, including: Peter Bowles, George Baker, Myra Frances, Nickolas Grace, Peter Miles, Peter Jeffrey, Richard Heffer and Glyn Owen. New Zealand-born actor Denis Lill, who had worked with both Dudley and Roberts on *The Regiment*, was cast in the one-off guest-starring role of Charles Vaughan in the fourth episode "Corn Dolly" – after Gareth Thomas (who would go on to star as the titular hero of Terry Nation's next BBC genre series *Blake's 7*) declined to be considered for the role. This casting decision, which was initially seen as a relatively minor one, would have major repercussions for *Survivors'* second and third series.

Director Gerald Blake. © Anne Christie

Nation's outline for *Survivors* had also included two recurring child characters, who would be effectively 'adopted' by Greg and Jenny and later join the community established in the second half of the series. Dudley proposed a practical solution to the need to recruit two child actors, who would be based on location for large parts of the production, by awarding the role of John Millon to his own son Stephen and the part of Lizzie Willoughby to Tanya Ronder, the daughter of scriptwriter Jack Ronder. Tanya, who was already interested in a career as an actress, was delighted at the opportunity to act in a primetime BBC drama. Stephen Dudley, on the other hand, had few acting aspirations, and was far more ambivalent about the

Scriptwriter Jack Ronder and his wife Anne. © Anne Christie

experience. Dudley had previously employed Stephen's talents on two episodes of *Doomwatch* ("Tomorrow, The Rat" and "Waiting for a Knighthood").

As cast and crew were being recruited, the production team sought imaginative solutions to the need to find numerous suitable 'post-apocalyptic' filming locations; wrestled with the restrictions that this filming method imposed on the shoot; and pored over the unforgiving production timetable that was required to get the show ready to air. Roberts recalls that for each episode: 'We had two-and-a-half days to rehearse it in, and often you'd spend a day of that walking around all the various locations. So the actors had to be extremely disciplined.' Initially, rehearsals were held at the BBC's Acton rehearsal studios prior to location filming, although Roberts remembers that these were not always as productive as they might have been. When preparing the scene from "Starvation" where Wendy first encounters Tom fishing, Roberts was worried that: '... Talfryn kept stepping over the rehearsal room tape into the "river". And then I realised that my concern was totally pointless; that once he was on location all would be well.' It became apparent that, given the pressures of time, it would prove '... much more satisfactory to rehearse *in situ*. The actors were able to take the real surroundings into consideration and make constructive suggestions, and it gave the production team an opportunity to work out the mechanics beforehand.'

June Hudson was assigned as the series' initial costume designer. Due to her seniority at the BBC, she was often chosen to start off series (she had previously been responsible for the first costumes for *Till Death Us Do Part* (1966-68, 72-75), *Are You Being Served?* (1973-85) and *The Fall and Rise of Reginald Perrin* (1976-79), and would later provide striking new directions for *Blake's 7* and *Doctor Who*) because: '... they knew I would fight for what I wanted and get the look and feel of a show right.' Hudson recalls that Carolyn Seymour was 'very thin and slim' and 'super to design for as she looked wonderful in everything' and that 'she had to look upper middle-class.' She purchased Jenny's blue fun-fur coat at C&A for £7.50 in a sale. In fact she bought two, as duplicate clothing for the principals was considered a necessity in case of damage or loss. One of the coats would later turn up as a numnah (fabric placed under a saddle to lessen strain on a horse's back) in the final series. Hudson remembers: 'The last time I went to the BBC in the '90s, I saw one of those blue coats on the 'tramp rail'!' Back in 1975, Talfryn Thomas's costume came from this particular rail. According to Hudson, Thomas 'revelled' in both the role and the money he received for playing Tom and 'liked the dressers to make a fuss of him' – leading to regular complaints from her team ('He wants me to help him put his boots on!'), which she chose to ignore. When it came to putting Ian McCulloch's costume together, Hudson remembers running into several problems. She visualised Greg as 'a he-man adventurer, hard and lean in denim' and wanted him to 'look like a hero.' The anorak that Greg ended up wearing throughout the series was bought from a ski shop in Notting Hill; again, two were purchased, the second often being worn by the series' stuntmen. Hudson recalls that when her BBC boss discovered how much the anorak and its duplicate had cost, he 'was absolutely furious,' but she argued that, as McCulloch was going wear it for the whole series, then the expense was actually quite reasonable: 'I felt that coat did everything for Ian.' The same argument arose when she came to purchase Greg's boots which, given the location-based format of the series, she knew would have to last and also protect McCulloch's feet. The metal-soled boots she selected were once again considered to be 'a ridiculous price,' despite the fact that this time only one pair was purchased. However, the boots did indeed wear well, and Ian wore them for the entire series

Lucy, Ian and Carolyn relax during a recording break. © Anne Christie

and actually bought them from the BBC when *Survivors* finished!

As the first scripts for the series were being finalised, it was evident that the issue of the principal filming location remained one of critical importance. It was recognised that both the premise of the narrative and practical production considerations required that the series took place in rural locations in the under populated English countryside. It was also agreed that filming sites had to be in places where unwanted soundtrack noise could be avoided. Roberts was impressed that: 'Terry Dudley was quite astute in establishing precisely where it might be quietest. He didn't want aircraft noise. We couldn't mask out industrial noise. So we settled on Herefordshire, Monmouthshire, Gloucestershire, Worcestershire and the Welsh borders region as being within a stone's throw of London but quiet, to enable us to film as "quietly" as possible.' Proximity to the production's London base was important, to avoid any delays in getting started on post-production work and to facilitate the quick turnaround of film units.

The first scene to be filmed on *Survivors* was shot in late 1974 at a junction of the London Westway, under the direction of Roberts. Shot using a single mute camera, the brief sequence from "The Fourth Horseman" featured Lucy Fleming's Jenny picking her way through growing traffic jams, during the evening rush-hour, on her way to the hospital, as the contagion takes hold of the capital. On 6 January 1975, principal filming on the series began in earnest, as teams began to shoot at sites around Herefordshire and Worcestershire for a new April transmission date. For the first six episodes, the process involved a combination of on-location film work – using 16mm film stock, in icy and inclement weather at a time when useable daylight was in short supply – and in-studio video recording – the first studio session, for "The Fourth Horseman", taking place at BBC Television Centre on the evening of 19 February 1975. From episode seven onwards, even the series' exteriors were shot on videotape, using the BBC's groundbreaking OB unit. Conditions were basic throughout, and creature comforts few. In Seymour's memory: 'The discomfort of it was the primary thing – being constantly tired and constantly cold. But the friendships I had with Lucy and Ian made for a great time. Despite everything, it was enormous fun.'

The production was constantly on the move, and the time pressures remained relentless. Roberts remembers: 'Gerry Blake and I started out simultaneously on episodes one and two, but I remember Terence Williams (who would have been working on "Gone Away", the third episode) turning up in his camper van when I was filming scenes for "The Fourth Horseman" at Great Comberton.' Despite the speed and logistical complexity of the production, Lucy Fleming cannot recall there being 'any accidents at all' during the first series' filming, although she does 'remember Gerry Blake falling in a ditch once!' Roberts remembers how closely that first production cycle was choreographed: 'I ended up with episodes one, four, seven, nine and thirteen. And then the other two directors were working around that sequence ... We were literally filming around each other.' It was the one time on the show that two film crews worked in parallel at different locations in the countryside around Hereford and Monmouth. Roberts recalls that '... because the transmission dates were so close, it meant that we had to take two filming units out, side-by-side, in that first month, in January.' Working under considerable time pressures, each of the directors 'would hope to get at least eight or nine minutes' filming, because that meant you only had to do forty minutes in the day-and-a-half in the studio.'

Ranging across Gloucestershire, Herefordshire and the Forest of Dean, the locations in which the exteriors for *Survivors*' first series was shot were both memorable and evocative. From "Starvation" onwards, the storylines required the use of a large country house or stately home, ideally one with extensive grounds, that had not been extensively modernised. In the summer of 1974, the production team settled on a large, empty and dilapidated manor house near Hope-under-Dinmore named Hampton Court. The cavernous, empty interiors of the house and its numerous rooms, corridors and stairwells were judged ideal, and there was also a large library and a dining room in which scenes involving the whole community could be comfortably staged and recorded. Julie Neubert (Wendy) remembers: 'The building was spooky… and it comes across as spooky – which is good. It's meant to be spooky. But the glorious outside! The absolutely magnificent trees! I do remember sitting underneath one between shots one day – during "Spoil of War" – and the most gigantic bumble bee I've seen in my life was buzzing around my feet! It was lovely to watch the episodes again recently and see the wonderful grounds.' Stephen Dudley also has fond memories of the location: 'The house was crumbling and damp and full of places to explore and intriguing junk. It is the sort of house one might fantasise about having … The scent of wisteria (which I love) can still transport me back thirty years, where one whole wall of what was, I think, a derelict orangery was smothered in the vine.' Although the many acres of the Hampton Court estate did not include the kinds of cultivated, arable fields to which several of the scripts made reference, they did include a large walled garden that could be used to depict the settlement's efforts to grow their own food. The shift to Hampton Court afforded the directors a stable production base, which helped them to meet the rigorous deadlines required. Roberts remembers that: 'For the back-end of the first series, we were shooting a fifty-minute episode on location in four-and-a-half days. They wouldn't even attempt to do that now.' The OB units relied on twin cameras attached to the mobile control booth by lengthy 'umbilical cables'. These imposed major constraints on the way that episodes could be shot, and could involve lengthy setting-up times. Directors had either to watch scenes on the screens in the control booth (which might be many hundreds of yards from the action) or to arrange for temporary monitors to be set up 'out in the field,' where both they and cast could watch playback. The recording method also encouraged directors to rely on longer than average scenes that could be recorded in a single continuous take. Neubert recalls that she found the process completely absorbing: 'The nice thing about the fact that it was being done on video was that you could see it being played back and [the director] could point out what was wrong with the scene … I found that very helpful … but I was really eager to learn … It was a bit intimidating, but quite a learning experience.'

Despite the constraints of time and technology, production on *Survivors'* first series proved to be a triumph of economy and efficiency. However, partway through the recording block at Hampton Court, one major problem did arise: Terry Scully – who had appeared in the role of Vic in a total of four episodes – fell ill, and was unable to continue. Scully had prepared for his next – and starring – episode "Revenge", and travelled to Hampton Court to begin the shoot, before he was taken sick. Hugh Walters was recruited to take on the part, with almost no preparation time. Scriptwriter Jack Ronder was keen for a simple voice-over to be added at the episode's transmission, announcing the recasting of the role, but Dudley rejected his request and instead demanded changes to the opening sequences that might temporarily 'disguise' the change of actor and so smooth the process of transition.

As the series progressed towards its finale (with recording on the final episode "A Beginning" being concluded on 16 June), the central members of the cast were experiencing the shoot in very different ways. While for some the work was relaxed and conflict-free, Carolyn Seymour had found herself at loggerheads with producer Terry Dudley from day one.

Series creator Terry Nation also found his relationship with Dudley was deteriorating past the point of no return. Probably the main factor that reduced Nation's 'hold' over the way the show came to be realised was the distance he kept from the production process. Author Jonathan Bignell did not 'find any evidence of Nation attending filming days on *Survivors*, so he did seem to stand back from production in that sense.' Roberts concurs, suggesting: 'He was basically quite a shy man, who kept himself very much to himself down in Kent.' Nation's unhappiness was doubtless increased by Dudley's practice of sending him letters outlining his criticisms of the 'shortcomings' of his work, and urging him to accept Dudley's own 'improvements'. Bignell and O'Day quote from correspondence in which Dudley presses Nation to abandon plans to make the aristocratic explorer Jimmy Garland a regular character, insisting the viewers were identifying much more strongly with the less-privileged Greg, whom they saw as both 'fallible and recognisable.' Dudley clearly felt himself as having the best interests of the show at heart, while Nation came to see his interventions as intrusive and unwarranted.

When "The Fourth Horseman" was broadcast on 16 April 1975, audiences had the first chance to see the series' title sequence, since celebrated as an outstanding example of the form – communicating so much, so economically, through such a simple montage of images and film techniques. The finished version of the titles differed quite significantly from Nation's original outline treatment, which read: 'We open on a totally white background. We hear the soft whirr of an electric motor and the gentle, efficient meshing of gears. After a moment of sound only there appears from the side of a frame a remotely controlled mechanical hand. It grips what appears to be an empty test tube. The hand projects slowly into the centre of frame.

Richard Heffer (Jimmy Garland) with the two greys hired for "A Beginning". © Anne Christie

The grip falters and the tube starts to fall. We go to extreme slow motion ...' From this opening, the progress of the virus across the globe would be depicted through the spread of blood red dots across a map, as travellers from Peking acted as unwitting carriers of the plague. This would begin with a 'red dot effect on [the] Chinese Official boarding the plane' with the picture in negative, and continue with: '... names of cities on departure boards. Planes and red dots. All washed over with red.' It was to conclude as the contagion reached London and the title was 'superimposed over the glowing red' that engulfed Britain.

Although the revised version retained the essence of Nation's concept, there was one outstanding difference – the guilty party responsible for unleashing the catastrophe was changed. Nation had pinned the blame on a piece of faulty technology, but Dudley instead chose to implicate a human scientist, so that the hand from which the deadly vial slipped was not mechanical but flesh and blood. It was a small change, but shifting responsibility from machine to man helped to emphasise the extent to which humanity was culpable for its own demise.

One of the most notable elements of the series was the complete absence of incidental music of any kind, and the reluctance to include any extraneous sound effects. This helped to reinforce strongly the series' sense of engaging naturalism. Not only did it prove that the drama of the piece did not need the additional support of soaring strings and booming chords, it showed the series dispensing with the mechanism most often used when telling an audience how they ought to respond to dramatic situations. In fact, the decision to do without incidental music was not a creative one but a happenstance: a pragmatic calculation based on questions of cost and time – it was simply impossible to consider adding to the edited programmes in the time available. The supremely effective title theme, devised and written by Anthony Isaac, was recorded by a twenty-strong orchestra on 6 December 1974, one month before the first block of filming on the series began. As the studio sequences of each episode were recorded, the theme music was played as the cast waited on the set to begin their scenes. The actors remember this greatly adding to the atmosphere of the occasion.

The first series was transmitted on BBC1 on Wednesday evenings between April and July 1975. Despite a distinct lack of publicity, the series recruited a dedicated audience that averaged 7.7 million viewers per episode. The British press were divided as to the series' merits. It was variously described as 'gripping'; 'pretentious rather than portentous'; 'fourth-rate'; and 'atmospheric'. Nevertheless, the BBC were clearly convinced that they had a success on their hands, having commissioned a second series before production on the first had even finished.

1.1 THE FOURTH HORSEMAN

UK TRANSMISSION: 16 April 1975: 8.10pm – 9.00pm
VIEWING FIGURE: 7.07m
WRITER: Terry Nation
DIRECTOR: Pennant Roberts
REGULAR CAST: Carolyn Seymour (Abby Grant); Lucy Fleming (Jenny Richards); Talfryn Thomas (Tom Price)
GUEST CAST: Peter Bowles (David Grant); Christopher Reich (Dr Andrew Tyler); Peter Copley (Dr Bronson); Margaret Anderson (Mrs Transon); Callum Mill (Dr Gordon); Blake Butler (Mr Pollard); Elizabeth Sinclair (Patricia); Giles Melville (Kevin Lloyd); Len Jones (First Youth)
UNCREDITED CAST: Paul Carter (Doctor); Maureen Niel, Dotlyn Kidd, Nicole Lee (Nurses); Patrick Nono, Terry Sartain (Auxiliaries); Ernest Blyth; Eden Fox; Paul Phillips; Geoffrey Brighty; Fred Davis; Charles Stuart; David Wilde; Jackie Bristow; Eve Aubrey; Annette Peters; Sylvia Lane; Martine Holland; Rosa Gold; Audrey Searle; Graham Tonbridge; John Tucker; Fred Bourne; David Pike; Gary Lean; Bill Lodge; Alan Gibbs; Paddy McQueen; Frances St. Barbe West; Amanda Carlson; Anna von Karina; Jackie Blackmore; Barbara Burnell; Iris Fry; Edward Brett; Ashley Keech; Huntley Young; Jules Walter; Jean St. Louis; Kathy Thomas; Tony Harris
FILMING: December 1974, January 1975 (starting 6 Jan)
STUDIO RECORDING: 19 February 1975
LOCATIONS: Westway (A40), London W12; Elmley Castle, Worcs; Little Comberton, Worcs; Great Malvern train station, Worcs; Pitville Circus, Cheltenham, Gloucs; Ross-on-Wye, Herefs; A449 between Ledbury and Great Malvern, Worcs; Llanarth Court, Raglan, Mons

SYNOPSIS: Well-to-do housewife Abby Grant enjoys her comfortable domestic life, as news spreads of a growing flu epidemic. Arriving at the railway station, Abby learns of the chaos now engulfing the transport network. Her husband David eventually returns late from London, with tales of worsening conditions in the capital. At their home, the electricity fails. In London, bright young secretary Jenny Richards searches for the doctor boyfriend of her ailing flatmate. She too learns of the seriousness of the contagion. Returning to her flat they discover that her friend has died. The doctor speaks of a 'natural immunity' that has allowed just a handful of survivors to recover. Jenny reluctantly agrees to leave London. Abby falls seriously ill, and David rushes to find the family doctor. David learns of the catastrophe now overwhelming the world. Abby wakes after days of feverish sleep to discover the dead body of her husband and the corpse-strewn village beyond her door. Out in open country, Jenny encounters itinerant vagrant Tom Price. He is sanguine about the plague, but refuses to let Jenny share his hilltop shelter. On seeing a photo of her son Peter, Abby races to his boarding school to find him. Peter's dormitory bed is empty, but she discovers the elderly and deaf science teacher Bronson. She learns that Peter and others had left with another master – although their fate remains unknown. Bronson describes the terrible realities of their new world, and illustrates how much technology and know-how has been lost. If humanity is to survive then it is imperative, he insists, that the survivors 'learn again.' Abby returns home alone.

Loading up her estate car, and setting fire to the family home – a funeral pyre for David Grant and her old life – she sets off into an unknown and frightening future.

ANALYSIS: "The Fourth Horseman" must rank as one of Terry Nation's finest single scripts, and sets an incredibly high standard for the drama that will follow. The opening episode of a new drama series imposes multiple challenges for the television writer: the series' premise must be established; key characters introduced; and audience interest in the fate of the programme's central characters secured. In the case of *Survivors*, Nation is required to achieve all that, whilst at the same time evoking a plausible picture of a global catastrophe using only the personal experiences of a few disparate individuals. In doing so, as Anthony Brown observed in *DWB* in 1993, he 'avoids all the clichés of disaster fiction.'

Nation uses his familiar technique of parallel storytelling to intertwine the different narratives on screen, and to isolate two of his central protagonists in this frightening new world, and set in motion their subsequent meeting. It is a testament to the confidence of his storytelling that the third central character of the series does not even make an appearance in this opening episode.

The setup in "The Fourth Horseman" works extremely well. From its opening sequences depicting the cosseted everyday life of the well-to-do suburban housewife, calamity gradually overwhelms the lives of the series' heroes through a series of small events that cumulatively have their devastating impact – a phone that slips out of order, a series of delayed trains, a minor flu epidemic, a power cut, and then an unexpectedly high number of sudden deaths …

A recurrent theme in the episode is that of denial and underestimation. There is reference to the Government 'downplaying' the scale of the epidemic to avoid a panic, but that process is reinforced by the reluctance of so many of the characters to acknowledge the full implication of what is happening. What Nation realises so well is the scale of interconnection and dependency in modern human society, and the fragility of social organisation. In the early stages of the epidemic, things are already approaching overload – overflowing hospitals, gridlocked city streets, collapsing public transport, a backlog of the unburied dead. As the support systems begin to buckle, the conveniences and comforts of the world unravel – an image evoked by Abby's discussion of the city as a 'big baby', being cared for by the continual labour of thousands of others.

While it would be easy to criticise the absence of an on-screen description of the plague's spread, and the cheapness with which it is realised, Nation's attention is focused elsewhere. It is a sense of restraint that actually helps to intensify the power of the drama. Nation's concern was to explore the aftermath of the plague, referred to as The Death, rather than to document the contagion. It would certainly have been beyond the budget of the BBC to have attempted to depict the disaster on any sort of scale, and it is a huge relief that the temptation to intercut stock footage of chaos and calamity between scenes is resisted.

One of the dramatic innovations of *Survivors* was the decision to move the depiction of the spread of the virus across continents to the memorable montage of images in the title sequence. Not only does this give the viewer an insight into the origins of the apocalypse denied to all of the characters in the series, it also communicates effectively the sense that this will be a drama about 'what happens next'. The sequence has a unique role in this opening episode – revealing to the viewer the nature of the calamity that is about to happen before a single character has been introduced, and raising the critical question of how many 'survivors' might be left at the episode's conclusion. It seems entirely fitting that the catastrophe engulfing the world is documented only second-hand – revealed in snatches of conversations, and overheard in the headlines of radio news broadcasts.

What "The Fourth Horseman" does very effectively is to establish perhaps the most important motif of the series: that although this is a global catastrophe, its repercussions are to be explored through the struggles and adventures of a small number of British survivors. Nation's work on his later *Survivors* novel, where a small nomadic group set out for a better life in Mediterranean Europe, suggests that he was interested in a larger dramatic canvas for his work. Yet although the tightness of focus in *Survivors* might have been driven by budgetary calculations, Nation does make the most of the dramatic constraints: through well-rounded characters, strong dialogue and effective protagonist conflicts.

There are a series of excellent switch-arounds, where unexpected characters fall ill and the survival of different people is nowhere guaranteed. The casting of Peter Bowles (an actor whose face was well known from numerous appearances on British television) is intended to misdirect the audience into thinking that David Grant, whose lifestyle Nation suggested 'makes him a natural candidate for a heart attack,' will be a major character in the series. It works especially well that he and Dr Gordon discuss the seriousness of the situation in the last scene in which they are seen alive on screen, while Abby battles with the virus alone in bed at home. There is an appropriate undercurrent in Bowles's performance; he is clearly more disturbed by the chaos he has seen than he is willing to let on, and Abby is slow to recognise the growing sense of unease in his voice. Abby's truism about 'foreign' deaths having less meaning is one that resonates uncomfortably truly, and is something that continues to inform news standards even in the present day. As the power supply is cut, the failing of the lights beautifully undercuts David's hollow assertion that, out in the commuter belt, 'We'll be all right.'

As Abby tosses in feverish sleep, her bedside clock counts out the passing of hours and then days. Anticipating an obvious question about its power source, Nation's script notes explain that this 'is a battery operated radio and digital clock.' Interestingly, although the on-screen clock displays only the days of the week, Nation was much more date specific: 'Shows the date as November 29th when we first see it. It is on December 1st when we see it again.'

The episode's theme of the total collapse of civilisation is eloquently framed. The opening shot of an indolent Abby being interrupted by her housekeeper, contrasts so well with the closing image, of a white-faced Abby turning away from the burning ruins of her redundant home. Much has been made of the class politics and apparent social snobbery of *Survivors*, yet in "The Fourth Horseman" it seems entirely fitting that the series' lead character should come from so privileged and sheltered a background, making her plunge into the new nightmare world that much more striking. It is also possible to read these class politics in a rather different way – akin to the survival rate of the Titanic, perhaps? Who might be more able to survive the chaos and terror of The Death: the privileged living in the leafy suburbs, or the urban poor, whose life expectancy and health were diminished to begin with, and who exist crammed into high-rise blocks able to travel only by public transport?

Much has rightly been made of the presence of two strong female characters in this opening episode. It is hugely significant that Abby becomes the hero of this drama, and that she and Jenny are so prominent in the adventures that will follow. The near-misses that continue to keep them apart are poignant and harrowing, rather than frustrating or irritating. Jenny's conflicts in the streets of London, her encounter with Tom Price, and her night-time meeting with a dying robber are moments that suggest the dichotomy between frailty and resolve that define her character in subsequent episodes. Seymour's brilliantly delivered line, 'Oh God, please don't let me be the only one,' as Abby stares forlornly to the heavens outside the church, is rightly recognised as one of the most powerful and iconic moments of the episode. This was actually a revision of Nation's original line as it appears in the camera script: 'Dear Christ, don't let me be the only one' – arguably a much less effective dramatic plea. In many respects, the moment when Jenny allows now-useless five pound notes to fall to the floor, and then walks away from the dead body by the fireside, is just as powerful and telling a reflection on the passing of the old order.

Tom's appearance, confirmation of the truly random nature of the survival lottery, also provides evidence of those who have yet to comprehend the true reality of what has befallen the world. The scenes between Tom and Jenny in this episode and those that follow are a brilliant clash of experiences and expectations.

What rightly permeates the episode is an atmosphere of fear, dread and foreboding – there is little light and no hint of humour in the collapse of the old world, and Nation does not dilute that sense of profound menace. Most of the characters who appear on screen in "The Fourth Horseman" are unquestionably dead by the episode's conclusion, whether seen on-screen or not.

Inevitably, the necessities of plot require one or two contrivances. The hospital doctor's speech to Jenny about survivors' 'natural immunity' is a coincidence that has to follow on from Jenny's second-hand friendship with a doctor. Similarly, Bronson's speech to Abby at Peter's school, delivered with great skill by Peter Copley and giving voice to Nation's own preoccupations that inform his drama, somewhat heavily signposts the plot and the importance of the ideas being communicated. It is in these exchanges that the absence of grief and loss seems most evident. Abby engages enthusiastically with the exchange of ideas at a moment when, in reality, the pair of them might most likely have been weeping, disconsolate, and incapable, feeling the initial effects of post-traumatic stress disorder. Instead they talk coolly and rationally about a future, which – so soon after the calamity – feels premature and forced. As one viewer noted in a BBC Audience Research Report for the episode: 'The survivors seemed to take it all very calmly.' In fact, Abby is later seen to crumble emotionally in "Gone Away" and "Gone to the Angels". Grief is not fully realised as a theme until series three, although the question of loss is touched upon in series two episodes such as "By Bread Alone".

It seems odd that schoolmaster Bronson should think his deafness automatically dooms him, but even more strange that Abby should agree to leave him behind. This is the first other survivor she has met after pleading not to 'be the only one,' yet rather than crave his companionship and support, she leaves him to an uncertain future and returns home alone. In fact, Dudley gives Bronson an unexpected payoff in the series finale "A Beginning", where it is revealed that he has survived and been reunited with other survivors from the school, including Peter Grant – although the very obvious implication (that Peter knows that his mother is alive and that she has been searching for him) is left unexplored.

Carolyn Seymour has suggested that it takes Abby too long to register memory of her son, yet this is perhaps more credible than she allows for. It is the hunt for Peter that will provide the central narrative drive for the early part of the series, and here the desperateness of Abby's longing is well evoked. Although the sequence in which Abby checks through the dormitory of corpses to find Peter's (empty) bed is shot without any lurid graphic content, it is still an acutely emotionally distressing 'image' for a pre-watershed (shown before 9pm) broadcast.

The brief scene where Abby's naked body is glimpsed in the shower is anything but salacious. As Nation's script notes make clear: 'This is a ritual washing away of the past. It is the end of something and a cleansing to begin again.' The moment signals Abby's separation from the old world. Her acceptance of the new, terrible realities, the cutting of her hair and the loading up of supplies, are powerful indicators of a strength of personality that will repeatedly become apparent in the episodes that follow. Despite the devastating losses she has endured, and the unimaginable horrors, dangers and uncertainties that await, Abby refuses to collapse – she has moved towards a sense of acceptance and realism. Instead she ends her connection with the old life of domesticity and sets off alone to meet what may come. Such stoicism is remarkable, and ends the episode with a brilliant counterpoint to the powerlessness and hopelessness that have preceded it. *RC*

1.2 GENESIS

UK TRANSMISSION: 23 April 1975: 8.10pm – 9.00pm
VIEWING FIGURE: 7.3m
WRITER: Terry Nation
DIRECTOR: Gerald Blake
REGULAR CAST: Carolyn Seymour (Abby Grant); Ian McCulloch (Greg Preston); Lucy Fleming (Jenny Richards); Talfryn Thomas (Tom Price)
GUEST CAST: Myra Frances (Anne Tranter); Vic Thatcher (Terry Scully); George Baker (Arthur Wormley); Brian Peck (Dave Long); Edward Brooks (Colonel); Peter Jolley (First Man)
UNCREDITED CAST: Eric French, Colin Taylor, Alan Davidson (Men)
FILMING: January 1975 (starting 6 Jan)
STUDIO RECORDING: 1 March 1975
LOCATIONS: Clenchers Mill Ford, Bromsberrow, Nr Ledbury, Herefs; Lydney, Gloucs; Harewood End church, Harewood End, Herefs

SYNOPSIS: Greg Preston returns home from Holland by helicopter. Finding his wife dead, he gathers a few possessions and sets off in his car. Jenny is still travelling alone and, once again, just misses Abby in her car. Greg is flagged down by a woman called Anne Tranter. She pleads for his help with her partner, Vic, who is trapped beneath an overturned tractor in a nearby quarry. Greg frees Vic and attempts to set his badly damaged legs with splints. Anne tells Greg how she and Vic have been stockpiling foodstuffs in the quarry from the surrounding area. Meanwhile, Abby encounters former trade union leader Arthur Wormley, who tells her about the national situation as The Death took hold. She also learns that he is intent on imposing law and order on the new situation. Abby imparts her views on the need for the survivors of the plague to become gradually less reliant on the hardware of the old world and to start again right from the beginning. After a roast beef supper, she takes a hot bath. Once dressed, she is horrified to witness Wormley sentencing a man to death. After he is killed, Abby flees into the night in a state of distress. Greg decides to leave Anne once he learns about her unrealistic and self-serving plans for survival in the new world. While fetching drugs for Vic in a nearby town, he meets Jenny for the first time and takes her with him. Anne abandons Vic and, upon meeting Greg and Jenny at the quarry entrance, tells them that he is dead. That night, while sheltering in a barn, Jenny notices a fire that has been set by Abby to attract the attention of other survivors. Leaving Anne behind, she and Greg set off towards it and meet Abby for the first time.

ANALYSIS: "Genesis" succeeds admirably in building on the considerable promise of the opening instalment, through the strong introduction of enigmatic engineer Greg Preston and an initial examination of the ideas and worldviews formulated in response to The Death, which will form the backbone of the series. The episode opens with an evocative depiction of Greg's return home by helicopter. A deserted shoreline, an empty street and a flock of sheep roaming freely on a motorway all serve to emphasise the stark fact that the old world is gone forever and that the few survivors of the plague are definitely an isolated minority, who therefore may not have been so lucky to survive after all. This theme of isolation is further explored through Jenny, who is depicted as the least able to cope with her new-found existence as she continues her lonely travels through the countryside.

Both Jenny and Abby take something of a back seat for the first half of the episode, allowing the new character Greg room to breathe. Ian McCulloch gives a confident performance as Greg and sensibly elects to underplay this satisfyingly complex character, with a subtle and restrained portrayal in line with Greg's controlled demeanour. Several years later, McCulloch would be considered for the part of Avon in Nation's *Blake's 7*, who shares several notable personality traits with the cynical engineer. Although Greg would never demonstrate the psychopathic tendencies of his space-age counterpart, there is clearly some substance to the view that Nation was thinking of his earlier creation when conceiving Avon (who, like Greg, would also be introduced in the second episode). We learn a great deal about Greg from his opening line – 'I was wrong, Jeannie, I thought you were the kind who'd survive just to spite me' – which demonstrates that he is embittered and world-weary even before the privations of the post-Death world have begun to kick in. During the aftermath of Vic's accident, Greg also proves to be practical and, unlike Anne, capable of enduring Vic's screams of pain. Nation's original character sketch explains that 'various emotional hurts have made him guarded about new relationships but his natural compassion tends to involve him with people, even when all his experience warns against this.' He is certainly guarded with Anne, but then she is clearly unpleasant and may remind him of Jeannie. However, when he meets the vulnerable Jenny he is similarly reluctant to be drawn on his future plans.

"Genesis" is not only the start of Greg's story but also the beginning of a trilogy centred on the ill-fated Vic Thatcher and his seemingly inextricable link with the self-serving Anne Tranter; her callous actions in this episode have repercussions that are depicted in "Spoil of War" and that ultimately lead to a dramatic climax in "Revenge". Thankfully, Gerald Blake was assigned to direct all three episodes to ensure that this continuing storyline was developed coherently. Myra Frances (the wife of actor Peter Egan) gives a believable performance as spoilt 'rich-bitch' Anne, whose particularly loathsome take on the new world includes an assumption that she will be able to turn the new situation to her advantage through the graft of other survivors: 'There'll be plenty of people who will be glad to work for a good meal or a warm coat.' She is also deluded as to the permanence of the new world. Greg points out that normality will not return 'in our or several other lifetimes,' and in so doing confirms the premise of the series: life will never be the same again.

Further foundations for the series are laid down through Abby's conversations with former trade union leader Arthur Wormley. Like Anne, Wormley is motivated by a desire to build on the lifestyle he previously enjoyed. He believes that the survivors will need leadership and guidance and that he is the man best equipped to provide it. He also considers the imposition of law and order to be a vital component of the way forward, expressing the need to keep out those whom he considers to be 'undesirables' and the importance of meting out justice in its severest form when necessary. Although his views may seem extreme to Abby – whose priorities are entirely different at this early stage – it will later become apparent, principally in "Law and Order", that she and her fellow survivors will not be able to ignore these issues, however uncomfortable they may be to embrace.

The meeting between Abby and Wormley also allows Nation to use another character as a mouthpiece for his views on the need for the survivors to start again from scratch. This time it is Abby's turn to hold forth on the subject, although she rather surprisingly claims that she reached these conclusions herself rather than acknowledging that she heard the majority of them verbatim from Dr Bronson. While Abby concedes that those who have survived cannot become self-sufficient overnight, she puts forward the view that in time their ultimate aim should be 'to become more and more self-reliant.' However, this idea of a gradual process is superseded first by Paul, and later at the Whitecross community, where it appears to have been agreed from the outset that they should never rely on anything that they cannot replace themselves. The extent to which the survivors would be self-sufficient was a matter of constant behind-the-scenes debate. Pennant Roberts always felt that the survivors abandoned the 'hardware of civilisation' too soon and that the series would have benefited from a researcher who could have calculated just how long materials such as foodstuffs would have lasted.

Despite Abby's growing confidence, particularly evident in her discussion with Wormley, she has not yet become hardened to the realities of the new world. When she witnesses Wormley ordering the man's execution, she is shocked and terrified, and although she objects to his decision, she quickly runs away from the situation rather than indignantly standing her ground as the fearless Abby of later episodes would have done.

Of the three leads, Jenny is portrayed as the least well equipped to survive. Her isolation and insignificance are beautifully symbolised in the sequence in which her tears fall into the fast-flowing stream, which also serves to contrast her personal grief with that of a whole world. Such is her loneliness that she even pleads to go with Tom when she sees him again, despite the fact that he is by no means an appropriate companion. After meeting Greg, she admits: 'I just want to be with people.' In sharp contrast, Tom has no interest in hooking up with other survivors and is intent on occupying his time experiencing those material things previously beyond his reach. His choices of a Rolls-Royce and what is presumably a high-fashion suit are as impractical as his take on the new world. These preoccupations prove to be temporary and serve to emphasise, as Abby later points out in "Starvation", that he is no good on his own.

Although both the Wormley and quarry storylines rely on dialogue-heavy sequences, the latter is the stronger of the two because far more is left unspoken, such as: Anne's decision to abandon her partnership with Vic in favour of Greg, who is a better prospect; and Greg's obvious distaste for both her personality and her ideas, to which Anne appears to be oblivious. The performances of Frances and McCulloch are electric throughout. Although the means by which the action switches between these storylines is maybe a little trite, it nevertheless highlights the difference between Wormley's charade of old world living (carving roast beef and serving tea in a china cup) and Anne and Greg making do with scavenged goods (slicing up luncheon meat and pouring warm champagne into a mug).

Several powerful moments arise from the Anne and Vic storyline: Anne's desperate pursuit of Greg's car – 'You've no right to leave me!' – and her subsequent scream to Vic to 'Shut up!' are cleverly counter-pointed by Vic's pleading to a departing Anne: 'You can't leave me!' Whereas Greg has every right to leave Anne behind, her leaving the helpless Vic – whom, through the accident with the tractor, she was responsible for crippling in the first place – is morally indefensible.

The script appears to have undergone few significant changes between initial and final drafts, although the opening scenes were originally intended to feature views of the desolate countryside filmed from the helicopter cockpit, and Vic Thatcher was initially conceived as a 'burly man.' Terry Scully hardly fits this description, but is nevertheless effective in the role. Interestingly, Nation chose to preface his script with dictionary definitions of three words: pandemic, survivor and hope.

"Genesis" maintains the high standard set by the opening episode and concludes with what feels like the inevitable coming together of Abby, Greg and Jenny. Their meeting attains a greater significance because of the commendable restraint that has been shown in not uniting them before now. More than any other theme, the episode demonstrates that their like-minded unselfish outlook will always be threatened by self-serving antagonists. *AP*

1.3 GONE AWAY

UK TRANSMISSION: 30 April 1975: 8.10pm – 9.00pm
VIEWING FIGURE: 9.39m
WRITER: Terry Nation
DIRECTOR: Terence Williams
REGULAR CAST: Carolyn Seymour (Abby Grant); Ian McCulloch (Greg Preston); Lucy Fleming (Jenny Richards); Talfryn Thomas (Tom Price)
GUEST CAST: Brian Peck (Dave Long); Barry Stanton (Reg Gunnel); Robert Gillespie (John Milner); Robert Fyfe (Phillipson); Graham Fletcher (Small Boy)
FILMING: January 1975
STUDIO RECORDING: 12 March 1975
LOCATIONS: Harewood End church, Herefs; Supermarket, Withington, Herefs; Suspension bridge, Hole-in-the-Wall, Nr Ross-on-Wye, Herefs; Mordiford, Herefs; Hoarwithy, Herefs; Hampton Bishop, Herefs

SYNOPSIS: Tom Price is scouring the countryside looking for provisions. Picking his way across an abandoned farm, he finds nothing edible in the kitchen. Breaking open a cupboard, he discovers two shotguns and cartridges. He kills a chicken, but before he can claim his prize, a young boy races in and picks up the bird. Tom chases him back to the fireside of the house, where he and an older man are sheltering. They plead with him, but Tom insists the meat is his – until the man reveals that the pair may be carriers of typhoid. At her church headquarters, Abby discusses plans with an enthusiastic Jenny and a cautious Greg. Arriving at a supermarket, they discover the corpse of a looter, and are apprehended by a unit of Wormley's militia. The gang claim the authority to control rationing and movement, but Abby is defiant. In the middle of an armed standoff, Greg takes charge, and Abby's group flees. Overcoming self-doubt, Abby is shocked to find herself seen as leadership material. Arriving back at the church, the group disturb a dozing Tom Price. Tom is soon revealed as a teller of tall tales and a reluctant worker, but he shares news of his encounter with the man and young boy – who Abby hopes might be Peter Grant. Jenny, Abby and Greg set off to investigate, but Abby is devastated to find only two corpses and no sign of her son. Wormley's men raid the church. The resourceful Tom renounces his hosts, and throws his lot in with Wormley. Milner – a reluctant gang member – helps draw his compatriots away, but when Abby returns, she discovers that the group have ransacked and set fire to the church. Amidst the chaos, Abby announces that she cannot found her new settlement until the search for Peter has been concluded – one way or another …

ANALYSIS: Such was the confidence of the series' creators that, having brought together the leading protagonists at the close of "Genesis", "Gone Away" spends its first nine minutes in the company of someone who had previously been a recurring supporting character: Tom Price. In sequences in which dialogue is sparse, Tom picks his way gingerly across the landscape of a rotting farm settlement, unflinchingly realised on screen. The animal carcasses, the sheds full of decomposing livestock, the farmhouse in which animals have taken shelter – all this has a nasty, feral, unclean feel. Thomas is superb in these sequences: even a gag over the cigarettes (a cliché even in its day) is nicely judged, and shows that the scriptwriter was willing to allow time for such character touches. When Tom cracks open and guzzles down the raw chicken eggs, the image is suitably repulsive.

Tom's ineptness with a new prize possession – the farmer's shotgun – is well handled, and makes his claim at the episode's end that he's a 'crack shot' all the more transparent. After the closely-focused attention on Tom's scavenging at the farm, the long-shot of him chasing the boy down the hillside, bellowing his protest at the theft someone else has carried out on him, evokes an incredibly powerful image of an otherwise deserted rural landscape. The mud and squalor of the campsite again reinforces the image of a fetid environment. Tom's crude self-interest and lack of compassion are revealed here in their darkest colours. It is not pity that convinces Tom to leave empty-handed, but concern for his own well-being. It seems right that the danger of typhoid should loom so large so soon in *Survivors*. It is first referred to as an imminent threat in "The Fourth Horseman", and "Gone Away" brings home starkly the fact that survival of the plague is no guarantee of a lasting existence. When the young boy slams the chicken carcass down in the mud at the feet of the retreating Tom, the poignancy of the moment is emphasised by the fact that we never see his character alive again.

The switch from the colour-muted on-location film sequences to the brightly-lit studio set of Abby's church base is far from seamless and, in an earlier draft of his script, Nation had originally included a short bridging film sequence in which Greg emerges from the woods having returned from looking for Anne, to find Abby cooking outside on a fire. Yet the studio-bound character exchanges that follow, as the group settle into each other's company, are skilfully realised by writer and cast alike. Important aspects of all three main protagonists are revealed, as they share their first full scene together. Jenny, who has been desperate for the company of others, here appears more relaxed and beginning to think about the future. Abby is both confident and forward looking, yet preoccupied with the search for her son. Greg appears keen to retain his independence and is reluctant to burden himself with new obligations. And yet Abby seems able to see that beneath his gruff exterior Greg may be less certain about leaving their company than he suggests. In the original script, Greg's description of the fires he left behind in Holland was even more chilling: 'It must have started in the oil refineries … Probably the best thing … It was the Great Fire of London that cleaned out the plague before, wasn't it? Maybe somebody should try and fire the cities again.' In that earlier version, Greg had also questioned the wisdom of Abby's own fire signal: 'It could have been attracting a whole lot of trouble too … a woman on her own,' to which Abby forcefully replied: 'There's no good hiding away.'

The sequences at the abandoned supermarket are some of the most chilling of the episode – an image of the strung-up looter swinging by his neck from the rafters is genuinely shocking on first viewing. These scenes appear to have exercised a major influence on a similar set-up in the 2003 post-apocalyptic big-screen drama *28 Days Later*. The fact that the patrol, which arrives to intervene, are from Wormley's militia is another strong indicator of the interest in continuity that many of the series' scriptwriters shared. All three of the series' heroes demonstrate their strength in different ways in these sequences – Abby, in open defiance of the Wormley directive; Jenny, in finding the courage to seize the shotgun; and Greg, in stepping in to take charge as Jenny's resolve falters. The moment when Greg seizes the shotgun is a defining one in the relationship of all three characters. It marks the point at which his commitment to the group and to their plans is irrevocably made. Moments before, he has said that he doesn't 'want any hassle about it', but here he risks his life to defend Abby and Jenny and to see off the militia. Even though Greg later confides to Tom that he wants to avoid a 'whole pack of responsibilities' and not 'get tied down,' the reality is that Greg knows that his future is now intertwined with those of Abby and Jenny.

One of the criticisms of series one, sometimes voiced by those involved in the production as well as by viewers and reviewers, is that there was too great a reliance on 'three men in a Land Rover with shotguns' turning up to threaten the protagonists. Even if "Gone Away" might be seen as the archetype of this plot device, the three characters in the Land Rover are well differentiated as well as suitably villainous.

As Abby, Greg and Jenny flee from their pursuers, there comes further confirmation of the degree to which the landscape of *Survivors* is opening up. This is an episode with numerous highly-effective on-location sequences, with carefully selected camera setups helping

Ian McCulloch outside Harewood End church. © Lucy Fleming

to give an expansive feel of a desolate and empty countryside. Abby's crisis of confidence could occur back in the church (although the original script direction suggested simply a roadside setting), but is here made all the more effective by its setting in the winter chill of a suspension bridge, above the running water and beneath the barren trees. The sequence, including Abby's disbelief at being cast in the role of leader, is excellently played – although there was barely time for any rehearsal. Rising river water brought forward the date of the shoot, to avoid the risk of flooding making it impossible, and the principals had almost no time to learn their lines. The scene is given an effective understated conclusion as Greg acknowledges in an offhand remark, 'You're the boss,' and Abby momentarily pauses.

The twin themes that dominate the episode are those of property and of political power. At the farmhouse, Tom sees no contradiction between his own acts of looting and his insistence that the young boy has stolen 'his' property. Tom however has few aspirations beyond his immediate wants. Wormley, in contrast, has laid claim to property of a different order, asserting the right to control its circulation and distribution. In other circumstances, it might seem appropriate to ration out scarce resources amongst those that need them, but Wormley's claims to be preventing profiteering and ensuring fair access are obviously bogus. In "Genesis", Abby observes that scavenging is only a stop-gap solution – something that Wormley seems not to have recognised – and that survival will require the creation of new produce, not simply seizing control of abandoned warehouses and storerooms. The conflict between Abby's sense of how new settlements might organise and what Wormley intends is well drawn. Abby's surprise that conflicts exist, that politics is continuing and that others might have different ideas of their own, is easily seen as naïve, but emphasises again how ill-prepared for the role of leadership she actually is. Is it not likely that, apart from the village pantomime and summer fête, Abby Grant's previous experience of leadership is likely to have been painfully thin?

What reinforces the sense of the challenges that Abby will face in this unexpected new role, is the fact that her 'first recruit' should turn out to be the hopelessly inappropriate Tom. His insistence to Wormley's men that he'll 'work like a dog' contrasts sharply with the sequences where he settles down in front of the fire while Greg unloads the supplies. It takes Greg no time at all to see through him. Tom is, naturally, oblivious to Greg's sarcastic observation: 'I can see you're a pretty useful fellow to have around.' Because of a fault on the soundtrack that occurred during the filming of this scene, Talfryn Thomas had to later redub the 'needed it more than me' line of dialogue during the recording of the episode's studio sequences – the sudden brief switch in audio quality is quite apparent.

The scenes in which Abby follows up on Tom's lead on the young schoolboy he met emphasise again how strong the emotional texture of the series will be. In describing their meeting, Tom exonerates himself entirely, but as Abby and the group set off to investigate, he must surely remain anxious that the truth of his heartlessness might yet be exposed. As they reach the man's and young boy's dwelling, Greg tries his best to temper Abby's over-eagerness, reminding her that the only description Tom has provided is of a boy of around ten wearing a school blazer. Greg also gets her to wait while he goes ahead, and when he discovers the bodies, he and Jenny support Abby as she goes to check on the identity of the dead boy. Abby's distress at the discovery that the corpse is not Peter is heartfelt, while Greg's actions highlight a tenderness on his part, and a concern for his new companions, not much seen before.

Robert Gillespie puts in a suitably understated performance as the reluctant gang member

John Milner. It seems very credible that many survivors might opt for a life under Wormley's patronage, not because of a conviction in his ideas, but because of the safety, food and shelter it might afford them. (Gillespie would return to *Survivors* in the third series to take on the new role of Sam Mead.)

Abby's announcement that the search for her son Peter must take priority over her plans to found a settlement in some respects clashes with her acknowledgement of the leadership role that she has now accepted. It might seem a reasonable maternal reaction to the shock and trauma she has endured since The Death, but it seems in some ways a step backwards for Abby. What is different now is that she has the confidence that – whatever their doubts – Greg and Jenny are committed to accompanying her. If she must continue to search, she will not do so alone.

As the closing titles roll, the episode – which concludes back in the same studio set – is given an unnecessary religious codicil, as the credits appear over the stained glass window of the church while our heroes busy themselves unseen below. Nation's script had originally specified that the episode should end on a mid-shot freeze-frame of Jenny and Greg gazing at one another. There have been no earlier spiritual references in an episode that is rather defined by very Earthly and material concerns (in which even the church itself is an operational base and make-shift dormitory). If the storyline had to conclude back in the studio rather than on location, there were probably few alternatives, but it does stick out as a glitch in an otherwise skilfully handled episode. *RC*

1.4 CORN DOLLY

UK TRANSMISSION: 7 May 1975: 8.10pm – 9.00pm
VIEWING FIGURE: 8.08m
WRITER: Jack Ronder
DIRECTOR: Pennant Roberts
REGULAR CAST: Carolyn Seymour (Abby Grant); Ian McCulloch (Greg Preston); Lucy Fleming (Jenny Richards)
GUEST CAST: Denis Lill (Charles Vaughan); Annie Hayes (Lorraine); Yvonne Bonnamy (Isla); Keith Jayne (Mick); June Bolton (Tessa); Maureen Nelson (Woman)
UNCREDITED CAST: Timothy Page, Kevin O'Leary (Boys); Margaret Pilleau (Woman); Kelly Varney, David Melbourne (Men)
FILMING: January 1975
STUDIO RECORDING: 22 March 1975
LOCATIONS: Llangarron, Herefs; Bernithan Court, Llangarron, Herefs; Llangrove, Herefs

SYNOPSIS: Abby, Greg and Jenny are driving back to Abby's village when their car runs out of petrol. Nearby, a woman named Lorraine is busy posting notices with directions to Maredell, a settlement set up by former architect Charles Vaughan. Charles is systematically gathering together tools, food and people for this venture. While exploring a house, he and Lorraine meet a boy called Mick, who agrees to join them. Outside the house, Charles spots and catches a piglet. Abby has been looking for petrol and fetches Greg and Jenny to a garage where she has spotted one of Charles's Maredell signs. Greg constructs a hand pump to retrieve petrol from the garage's tanks. Charles arrives and offers to share a roast pork supper with them at his nearby caravan. During the meal, Charles details his views on the survival prospects of the human race and the many problems that lie ahead of them. The trio agree to accompany him to Maredell to decide if they want to join him. On their arrival, a woman named Isla tells them that two people have died and everyone else is extremely ill after having eaten fish caught in the river. Although nothing can be done for the sick, their pain is eased with some morphine obtained by Charles. Isla believes that their problems derive from Charles having hung up a corn dolly. While threshing corn, Greg and Jenny share their first kiss. That evening, Charles propositions Abby, telling her that she must have his child. After she refuses, it transpires that both Isla and Lorraine are already pregnant by him. To Charles's dismay, Jenny and Greg elect to leave with Abby, who is keen to resume her search for Peter. Before they go, Greg helps Charles carry the bodies from the house to a funeral pyre.

ANALYSIS: Jack Ronder's "Corn Dolly", the first episode of *Survivors* not to be penned by creator Terry Nation, is a redolent and compelling treatment of the linked themes of fertility and rebirth. The tale is significant for its introduction of former architect Charles Vaughan, a passionate and persuasive man – convincingly played by Denis Lill – who is destined to become one of the series' central protagonists.

The episode's most effective motif is that of the persistence of nature in spite of The Death. As Jenny tells Greg: 'That thrush doesn't care what you do.' Spring is shown to have arrived again but, given what has befallen the human race, optimistic notions typically associated with this change of season are startlingly absent. The sequence in which Abby breaks down after noticing some snowdrops and a chaffinch illustrates this beautifully, and is sensitively directed by Roberts. Ronder noted in his original script: 'Abby can't equate the promise of life around her with the human catastrophe.'

The writer's keen interest in folklore and superstition is further explored in series two – principally in "The Witch" – but is here confined to Charles's figurative corn dolly, a pagan symbol of fertility that is, as Isla says, traditionally hung up 'when the harvest's home … not when you're threshing to get a few handfuls of corn for bread.' However, Charles is far more preoccupied with its representation of human fertility than with its significance in agricultural terms. During the episode, he is gradually revealed to have an almost fanatical interest in the idea of repopulating the new world; as such, he is one of the few protagonists we meet who appears to over-react to The Death. In the short time that the small community has existed at Maredell, Charles has already caused four women to conceive, and he views Abby and Jenny as having the same potential. This scenario is made all the more unsettling as the episode is constructed in such a way that the viewer is put in the position of both liking and trusting Charles before his obsession becomes apparent. Although the same charisma and persuasive abilities that the settlement's women found so convincing also initially work on the viewer, one ultimately has to share Abby's and Jenny's view that cold logic concluding that humanity urgently needs to procreate is one thing, but Charles's attempt to take responsibility for this so personally is quite another.

His fixation with reproduction aside, Charles is the first survivor we meet who has devised a systematic way forward that appears to be attuned both to nature and to the realities of the new world. This is presumably because he and his family practised a life of self-sufficiency before The Death, although this is rather unfortunately expressed by the line, 'I was devoted to the good life,' which today makes it sound as though Charles was a fan of the popular Surbiton-based sitcom. Charles's conception of the non-threatening slogan 'You need us, we need you' crystallises his general approach, which centres on expansion on the basis of mutual need; it later transpires that mutual survival is actually his expedient definition of love. Charles is also portrayed as having the foresight to envisage the future threat from rats ("Lights of London") and dogs ("Starvation" and much of the third series), the importance of hydroelectricity ("Power") and the need to survey Britain from the air ("New World"), thereby anticipating many future storylines.

As Greg considers himself to be both practical and capable, the battle lines are immediately drawn when he becomes acquainted with the equally confident Charles. Prior to this meeting, Greg is seen to scold himself for 'not getting organised' and for just wanting 'to keep the cold out,' so when he learns that Charles is already several steps ahead, his pride is unsurprisingly hurt and the tenor of their subsequent relationship is all but set. The tangible competition between these two characters – whom a TV critic would later describe as 'like stags about to fight' – would later dominate the second series. Costume designer June Hudson recalls that she was mindful that there had to be a vastly different image for the two characters. For this reason, in this episode and for Charles's return in series two, in contrast to Greg's denims, she dressed Lill in soft brown and beige wools and corduroy so that he would look 'like a sort of country gentleman.'

Greg's and Jenny's developing relationship is nicely handled, especially as their arrival at such an obviously natural affection is a strong counterpoint to Charles's survivalist agenda. Although Jenny is portrayed as vulnerable – particularly when she asks Greg 'Can I hug you?' and really means 'Can you hug me?' – she is just as capable as Abby of standing up for herself; as she says, 'Survival can wait for a bit.' Abby herself comes over as irritated during much of the episode, which is no doubt as much to do with her new role as gooseberry as it is to do with her anxiousness about Peter. The presence of Mick – played by Keith Jayne (who later made notable appearances in *Stig of the Dump* (1981) and *Doctor Who* (1984) and was undoubtedly one of the best child actors of his generation) – who for the sake of the narrative is employed as a substitute for Peter, serves to emphasise Abby's feelings of fear for her son's well-being. Abby asks Mick about his experiences with a view to learning what Peter might feel like if he too has survived; when she later places the coat about his shoulders, she is once again clearly thinking about her son.

A dismissive attitude towards death and the dead is an inevitable development of the *Survivors* narrative. To emphasise this, Ronder elects to make the occupants of the house that Charles and Lorraine explore as anonymous as possible by calling them Smith. When disaster befalls the Maredell settlement, Charles almost downplays the many deaths, describing them as a 'heavy blow'; and although the scenes in the sleeping room are undoubtedly upsetting, the overarching shadow of The Death does, whether intentionally or not, diminish their emotional effect. There is a terribly dark irony in Charles's initial suggestion that they hold a big bonfire at Maredell to celebrate the arrival of the trio, given that they are ultimately forced to build a funeral pyre to burn the dead. This horrendous turn of events could almost be interpreted as a mystical act of retribution on nature's part, countering Charles's single-handed attempts to accelerate repopulation. Whether he interprets the tragic events in this way or not, Charles does appear to have mellowed when he returns to the series in "Birth of a Hope", and has even settled down to a monogamous existence with Pet. However, his views on the subject – which is clearly key to the long-term survival of the human race – are given an inevitable second airing in Martin Worth's excellent "Over the Hills", in which he warns once more: 'If you don't believe in having children, there won't be a world.'

The only scene from the original "Corn Dolly" script not to be filmed was to have shown Charles braving entry into a small town to retrieve some drugs for his suffering flock. Presumably this scene was abandoned due to pressure of time and the fact that it would have added little to the plot; it would also have repeated Greg's similar mission on behalf of Vic in "Genesis".

Isla and Lorraine are interesting and unusual characters, both of whom add depth to the narrative. The actresses playing them would both later appear in the popular hospital drama *Angels* (1975-83). June Bolton (who later changed her stage name to Emily) appears briefly in the role of Tessa; she would later become a 'Bond girl' in *Moonraker* (1979) and be cast by Roberts as Christina Campbell in *Tenko* (1981-84), appearing in all three series and its 1985 sequel, *Tenko Reunion*.

"Corn Dolly" is one of many stories determined to prove just how hard survival in the new world will be, and it exhibits the series' typically unremitting lack of optimism. The Death is presented here not as the final tragedy, but as an event that has actually increased the opportunity for suffering, because of the type of world it has left behind. Those that prefer more action-orientated *Survivors* may find the episode somewhat lacking, as – with the notable exception of the piglet chasing scene – the story is true to Ronder's predominantly dialogue-based style. However, the tale ably demonstrates how well-suited the writer was to the subject matter, and also the unique and considerable value of his contribution to the series. *AP*

1.5 GONE TO THE ANGELS

UK TRANSMISSION: 14 May 1975: 8.10pm – 9.00pm
VIEWING FIGURE: 7.52m
WRITER: Jack Ronder
DIRECTOR: Gerald Blake
REGULAR CAST: Carolyn Seymour (Abby Grant); Ian McCulloch (Greg Preston); Lucy Fleming (Jenny Richards); Tanya Ronder (Lizzie Willoughby); Stephen Dudley (John Millon); Ben (Ben the dog)
GUEST CAST: Peter Miles (Lincoln); Frederick Hall (Jack); Nickolas Grace (Matthew); Kenneth Caswell (Robert)
FILMING: January 1975
STUDIO RECORDING: 2 April 1975
LOCATIONS: Great Malvern train station, Worcs; Llanarth Court, Raglan, Mons; Broad Oak, Herefs; Ripple, Worcs

SYNOPSIS: Abby, Greg and Jenny have spent the night at Brimpsfield railway station. Abby is still determined to search for Peter and suggests they split up for a while. However, all three agree to go together to Peter's school. *En route* they find an abandoned minibus. While Abby goes on alone, Greg and Jenny meet two children called John and Lizzie. The pair have been living in John's grandmother's house. Abby finds no sign of life at the school; even Dr Bronson has gone. She rings the school bell to signal to Greg and Jenny, who join her there with their new charges. The children tell them about some boys who were going to find three 'angels' – religious hermits – on a mountain in Derbyshire, whose story they had read in a newspaper. The group, now travelling by minibus, stops off for food and shelter at a seemingly deserted house, where Greg is shot in the arm by an unstable man called Lincoln who thinks they are members of a group who are calling themselves 'The British Government.' Abby goes on alone to look for the angels and succeeds in finding them. She debates the existence of God and the onset of The Death with Jack, their leader. Greg and Jenny reach the conclusion that the house they are staying in is unsuitable as a permanent base and decide to set off after Abby. Lincoln attempts to stop them from going by snatching Lizzie. The children's dog, Ben, attacks him and Lincoln is left behind. Shortly afterwards, Greg, Jenny and the children are reunited with Abby; however, it soon becomes clear that they are still carriers of the plague as, one by one, the angels fall ill. Abby and the others are unable to help, but remain with them until they die.

ANALYSIS: "Gone to the Angels" sees *Survivors* continue in Jack Ronder's philosophical and reflective vein with a storyline that poses insightful questions about God and religion in the face of the tremendous human catastrophe of The Death. Ronder's title refers not only to Abby's new lead on Peter, but also to the state of death itself.

The episode notably introduces children John and Lizzie, who for reasons of convenience as well as ability were played by the son of producer Terence Dudley and the daughter of director Jack Ronder respectively. Both youngsters perform well and bring a much needed lighter tone to the series. Presumably, the decision to write children into the show as regular characters was not taken lightly, given that it would have proved almost impossible to subsequently kill them off – even for an inescapably doom-laden programme like *Survivors*.

Tanya and Stephen join the series. © Anne Christie

Dramatically, their inclusion not only allows for a child's eye view on proceedings or for their regular use as hostages by the 'villains of the week', but also causes Greg and Jenny to adopt parental roles, adding an interesting extra dynamic to their fledgling relationship. During their debut episode, John and Lizzie display a disturbingly casual, but wholly plausible, attitude to the dead and the dying. On first meeting Jenny and Greg, the pair are matter-of-fact about it: 'Everyone's dead – didn't you know that?' Later, as the 'angels' begin to die, John is shown to be simply uninterested ('Let's play cards then') and when Jack lies on his death-bed, he calmly tells him, 'You'll be dead soon. Goodbye.' His statement is all the more sinister as it is quickly followed by a smile. At the episode's close, he and Lizzie are at play again, seemingly unmoved by the recent tragedy. Living through the plague promises to be an experience that may have irrevocably desensitised and brutalised the pair, particularly John – who is slightly younger than Lizzie, aged seven to her nine.

Faith and religion are the two central themes of the episode. The somewhat hokey angels claim to have 'the Word of God' and have no problem reconciling The Death with their beliefs. However, Jack's arguments in particular are rather glib and unconvincing, especially his view that nothing has really changed as 'half the world was trying to survive before the plague,' which fails to account properly for the scale of what has actually occurred. Although Abby is clearly questioning God's existence – earlier greeting Lizzie's question in the school chapel ('Where God is?') with silence – she is portrayed as more interested in seizing the opportunity to spend her time with the angels clearing her mind and reflecting upon her survival, rather than engaging in a heated religious debate. She also appears curiously immune to their undoubted condescension, and her passive acceptance of their manner does seem a little out of character. Abby's considerable tolerance is perhaps explained by the fact that she is at her lowest ebb here.

The angels are given – perhaps deliberately – some rather contrived lines, with Jack's question 'Would you believe I was a carpenter?' and Robert's discussion with John about 'little miracles' standing out as particular examples. Their status as angels, although verbally denied by the three men, is reinforced by the biblical dialogue used: the line 'And one taken and one left' is from Daniel's vision of the future given to him by an angel in the Old Testament; Jack's 'Please don't be afraid …' appears to be missing '… for I am the Angel of the Lord'; and, after their death, Abby reads from Psalm 103: 'Bless the Lord ye his angels that excel in strength that do his commandments, harkening to his word.' Ultimately, however, the fact that they are just as susceptible to the plague as everyone else serves to underline their humanity, although the angels themselves embrace their deaths as vindication of their faith. In direct contrast, when the series next returns to the issue of religious faith (in "By Bread Alone") we learn that cleric Lewis Fearns saw The Death as the refutation of his faith and initially abandoned it as a result. Fearns finds his faith again only through observation of the renewal of life.

Director Gerald Blake ensures that religion saturates the episode's memorable visuals as well as its dialogue. At Peter's school, Abby's signal to Greg and Jenny is a tolling bell. In the chapel, there is a prominent statue of the Virgin Mary, the eternal mourning mother, perhaps intended to parallel Abby. Finally, the scenes with the angels themselves are dominated by an ostentatious Bible.

A strong element of the story is the guest appearance of Peter Miles as the unhinged Lincoln. As in his other cult television roles, Miles makes far more of the part than is down on paper and, despite his character's many unpleasant characteristics, succeeds in engendering some empathy from the viewer. Abby, Jenny and Greg are unnecessarily dismissive of Lincoln, seeming to take advantage of his instability. In failing to give him the comfort and protection he clearly craves, they appear to exacerbate the situation, perhaps contributing to his final manic attack on Lizzie. This sequence is unfortunately marred by the fact that Tanya Ronder was clearly directed to walk towards the minibus very slowly (to allow Peter Miles to catch up with her) and by what Miles himself has referred to as 'a Disney dog,' which was interested only in licking him to death! This 'friendly dog syndrome' would also cause Pennant Roberts trouble during the recording of "Starvation".

Ronder once again briefly indulges in his interest in superstition, with an evocative piece of dialogue delivered by Lincoln suggesting that even in the short time since The Death, mythical rumours of giant rats and crows have become rife. The additional (and far more likely) possibility that lions and elephants have been sighted, having escaped from safari parks – later employed to great effect in the 1995 film *Twelve Monkeys* – is not actually confirmed on-screen until the closing sequences of "A Little Learning" in the third series.

Finding Peter remains Abby's overriding objective, and Greg perhaps echoes the sentiments of the viewer by appearing to be growing tired of her quest: 'Looking for traces of Peter in this whole wide emptiness is over the edge … He can't be alive.' Jenny too appears to be more interested in settling down: 'What I want is a house with a big fireplace and a great big kettle and I want a hot bath.' However, the trio agree to stay together for the time being on the basis that they 'need to find more people not less.' Jenny and Greg reach another significant stage in their relationship when the latter takes the lead when countering a question of Lincoln's about their status as a couple. The next time the pair are seen, they are in bed together (although they are fully clothed – this is the BBC after all!) and the comfort they derive from each other is nicely contrasted with Lincoln's affecting adoption of a foetal position. The shot in which the minibus later leaves behind a distraught Lincoln on his knees is similarly well done.

The episode's most unforgettable scene has to be the moment of realisation that Abby has brought The Death to the angels, as Nickolas Grace's Matthew is seen to perform the tell-tale action of feeling lumps under his arms. This is a crushing blow that prompts discussion of what is a truly disturbing revelation – they are all carriers of the plague. Unfortunately this carrier premise is not adhered to with any consistency as the series progresses, with those people who live in places not previously reached by the plague considered to be in no danger from those who have survived The Death (see "Over the Hills" and "Power").

Although the separate sections of "Gone to the Angels" are all accomplished, they do not quite add up to a coherent whole, perhaps because of the disparate nature of the narrative, or maybe due to the fact that it is ultimately unclear what Ronder is trying to say about religion. However, there is much to enjoy in this episode, which includes several strong guest performances and further welcome character development for the regulars. *AP*

1.6 GARLAND'S WAR

UK TRANSMISSION: 21 May 1975: 8.10pm – 9.00pm
VIEWING FIGURE: 6.51m
WRITER: Terry Nation
DIRECTOR: Terence Williams
REGULAR CAST: Carolyn Seymour (Abby Grant); Ian McCulloch (Greg Preston); Lucy Fleming (Jenny Richards); Tanya Ronder (Lizzie Willoughby); Stephen Dudley (John Millon); Ben (Ben the dog)
GUEST CAST: Richard Heffer (Jimmy Garland); Peter Jeffrey (Knox); Dennis Chinnery (John Carroll); Robert Oates (Harris); David G March (Bates); Michael Jamieson (Ken); Susanna East (Betty); Roger Elliot (Sentry); Steve Fletcher (Peter)
UNCREDITED CAST: John Cannon, Ron Musgrove, Audrey Searle, Sylvia Lane (Waterhouse Residents); Graham Chapman (Boy)
FILMING: January/February 1975
STUDIO RECORDING: 12 April 1975

LOCATIONS: Brockhampton Court, Brockhampton, Herefs; roads and fields around Brockhampton, Herefs

SYNOPSIS: Still accompanied by Greg, Jenny and the children, Abby continues the search for her son. They meet a man called Carroll who is living with a boy; Abby initially thinks the boy could be Peter, but her hopes are soon dashed. While Abby grieves alone, the boy tells the others about a nearby settlement called Waterhouse where there are some other children. Greg advises Jenny not to tell Abby for fear of raising her expectations again so soon. However, Jenny can't bring herself to keep the information from Abby, who subsequently sets off for Waterhouse alone. *En route* she rescues a man who is being hunted by a group of men armed with shotguns. He introduces himself as Jimmy Garland, the only surviving heir to the Waterhouse estate, and reveals that he is at war with its current occupants, who are led by a man named Knox. He disputes their right to stay there. Garland takes Abby to his woodland hide-out and tells her more about himself. Later that night, Garland sets out to steal a replacement car for Abby. Meanwhile, Knox locates Abby and takes her back to Waterhouse, where he tells her that Garland is at fault as he is unwilling to compromise. Garland abducts a young woman and demands that Knox release Abby in exchange. Once back with Garland, Abby persuades him to go to see Knox to negotiate a peace. It transpires that Knox actually wants rid of Garland for good. To Abby's horror, Knox begins to beat Garland. Some time later, an injured Garland agrees to lead Knox to where he has hidden his hostage. However, Abby has enlisted Greg's help in the interim, and he manages to overpower Garland's captors. Abby asks Garland to join them but he declines on the grounds that he still has a war to fight.

ANALYSIS: The Nation-scripted "Garland's War" is an effective and appealing adventure romp that contrasts sharply with the more reflective approach favoured by Jack Ronder in the preceding two episodes.

Continuity is maintained with the events of "Gone to the Angels" as Abby, clearly still affected by the tragic death of the angels, warns Carroll that they have had the plague. Although her imparting of this information is obviously adopted as a form of greeting shorthand, her statement is not actually strictly true as Jenny and Greg have previously claimed not to have suffered with the plague at all, both presumably being totally immune to its effects. Once again, when it comes to The Death, consistency does not seem to be one of the series' strengths or priorities, which is surprising given that it is a vital part of the premise.

By this point in the run, Abby's search for her son has arguably continued for far too long. As a result, her decision to call it off in favour of a new objective – 'Tomorrow we look for somewhere to settle, somewhere permanent' – comes as a relief, despite the obvious restrictions that this may place on the series' format. However, Jenny disappoints both Greg and the viewer by electing to tell Abby about their Waterhouse lead, and so the search for a place to live is temporarily postponed. Thankfully though, the Peter storyline becomes a minor sub-plot in the remainder of the episode as Abby's quest is subsumed by Jimmy Garland's war.

At first, Jimmy Garland appears to be a character in danger of becoming a caricature. As Knox states, he acts like he is 'out of some *Boy's Own* adventure story,' and it is abundantly clear from the outset that he is enjoying his existence in the post-Death world: 'I know this must be very disagreeable for you, but it is exciting isn't it?' He also initially appears to have questionable motivation for his actions, admitting to Abby that his title of Lord Waterhouse is meaningless now, but nevertheless remaining determined to dispute the right of Knox and his men to stay at his country seat. However, it is eventually revealed that unlike Knox, Jimmy does actually harbour some commendable reasons for his war, wanting Waterhouse to function as a self-supporting estate and to be of benefit to all its members. Knox's true intentions are also concealed for a prolonged period, again presumably to heighten dramatic tension. After he successfully misrepresents Garland to Abby, it is uncertain which party is in the right, at which point Abby assumes her 'one woman United Nations' guise and brings Garland to him. However, this uncertainty is short-lived, as Knox finally reveals his true colours, using survival as an excuse for his cold decision that after his hostage has been found, there will be no need to find a cellar in which to hold Garland. ('There are no Queensbury rules for survival!') Peter Jeffrey turns in a typically accomplished performance as Knox, while Richard Heffer clearly appears to be in his element. Several years later, Heffer essentially played a very similar aristocratic adventurer when he appeared as Peter Porteous in LWT's *Enemy at the Door* (1978-80).

Garland's startlingly honest response to The Death ('You can't mourn for a whole world') is unique and refreshing. Given his military training and past experiences as both explorer and adventurer, he even welcomes the new state of affairs, recognising that everything he has previously learned was geared towards such a situation: 'I couldn't have invented a better time to be alive.' Like Charles Vaughan, whom Ruth would later describe as 'a crank in the eyes of the supermarket society' ("Over the Hills"), Garland considers himself to have been a misfit in the old world. The theme of leadership is also examined through Garland and Knox, both of whom see themselves as natural leaders. As soon as Abby asks the former, 'Do you have to be leader?' she answers her own question: 'Yes, I suppose you do!' Knox is similarly inclined, and when he tells Abby that he will not allow Garland to jeopardise what they have already set up at Waterhouse, it soon emerges that what he really fears is the threat that Garland poses to his leadership. Unlike Garland, Knox does not appear to realise that 'good leadership is always in dispute.'

Richard Heffer with Terence Dudley. © Anne Christie

The action sequences are suitably suspenseful and make great use of the countryside around Brockhampton Court. The initial shotgun hunt and Garland's one-man attack on the house are particularly effective. It was originally intended that his hostage would be imprisoned in a folly or tower, perhaps to give the episode a more fairytale feel. This would have certainly been in keeping with

Garland, who is depicted as the perfect knight in shining armour, and Abby, who takes on an atypical role as a damsel in distress for the first and last time here. In contrast to the accomplished film sequences, the episode is unfortunately let down somewhat by several obviously studio-bound sequences, which bring such a strong air of unreality to the proceedings that one almost feels that the legendary BBC canteen is just out of shot.

Abby shows obvious affection for Garland, and their chat in his den somehow feels like pillow talk, although both remain fully clothed. Jimmy is an obvious contrast to the deceased David, although perhaps the latter was dashing too before he became a nine-to-five 'city man'. A bond between the pair is quickly apparent, both in Garland's brave hostage exchange and in Abby's distress at Knox's maltreatment of him as a prisoner. When they part at the episode's close, Abby is clearly surprised that Garland won't be going with them, a situation made more difficult for her by the fact that Jenny has Greg. Her sorrow at his decision to continue his war is exceptionally well portrayed by Seymour, almost matching the accomplishment of her look of utter desolation near the start of the episode. Although Terence Dudley decided that Garland was not suitable to become a regular as Nation had suggested, because the producer felt that the audience would more readily identify with more 'normal' everyday characters like Greg and Jenny, he would make a return appearance in "A Beginning". During this reunion with Abby, we learn of a surprisingly encouraging resolution to his war: Knox has died and Garland has succeeded in setting up the sort of community that he had originally outlined to Abby.

"Garland's War" is easily the most traditional piece of storytelling in the series so far, with a succession of captures, escapes and rescues that characterise Nation's many television scripts. Nevertheless this formula proves very successful here, and director Terence Williams cites it as his most accomplished contribution to the show. Although not Nation's final script for the series, from here on in he felt that *Survivors* took a direction that significantly diverged from his original conception of the show. *AP*

1.7 STARVATION

UK TRANSMISSION: 4 June 1975: 8.10pm – 9.00pm
VIEWING FIGURE: 8.48m
WRITER: Jack Ronder
DIRECTOR: Pennant Roberts
REGULAR CAST: Carolyn Seymour (Abby Grant); Ian McCulloch (Greg Preston); Lucy Fleming (Jenny Richards); Talfryn Thomas (Tom Price); Hana-Maria Pravda (Emma Cohen); Julie Neubert (Wendy); John Hallett (Barney); Tanya Ronder (Lizzie Willoughby); Stephen Dudley (John Millon); Ben (Ben the dog)
OB RECORDING: 21 - 25 April 1975
LOCATIONS: The Vauld, Marden, Herefs; Driveway, Broadfield Court Vineyard, Bodenham, Herefs; Hampton Court, Hope-under-Dinmore, Herefs

SYNOPSIS: The elderly Jewish matriarch Emma Cohen and the young and impressionable Wendy, having taken refuge at the weekend cottage of the former's son, are without food. Wendy sets off to forage for supplies one last time. Abby, Greg and Jenny tell the children that they have called off the search for Peter, and that the time has come to settle. Wendy encounters Tom Price fishing in a nearby river, and he shows off his meagre catch. Wendy senses Tom's predatory intentions and flees – stealing both of his precious fish. The school minibus passes the Cohen cottage, just as Emma is being attacked by a dog pack. While Jenny entices the dogs away, Abby leaps from the vehicle to save Emma – checking that she is uninjured, and promising to find food for them all. As she is about to set off to hunt, Abby finds herself held at gunpoint by Tom. He is keen to trade food for 'company' from Abby, and heads into the woods to hunt. Trying to evade the dogs, Jenny spots a large house in some grounds nearby, and they set off to investigate. When Tom returns, Abby and Wendy trick him and lock him up inside his own van. Greg and his new 'family' enter the large house – the Grange. In the morning they explore the house and grounds. Jenny finds leeks to make a welcome broth, and the children relax with a game of hide-and-seek. Lizzie is terrified to discover a figure lurking in the shadows – Barney, a gentle and mentally-impaired young man, has been hiding after being bitten by the dogs. They light a fire to boil water to tend to Barney's wound. The smoke attracts Abby, now driving Tom's van, and the group are reunited. With Tom disarmed, the group enjoy a 'feast' – fresh meat and tinned provisions from Tom's stocks. Surveying their new surroundings, Greg convinces Abby that they have found their new home.

ANALYSIS: Often subject to a critical battering, "Starvation" is an absorbing and thoughtful episode that secures the series' changeover from the wanderer to the settlement format, and in doing so establishes the enlarged community that will populate its new home.

"Starvation" is a transitional episode in numerous senses. In terms of the first series' plot arc, it marks a shift in the central dynamic, as the heroes cease to be the temporary guests of other settlements and instead begin to play host to visiting travellers (both welcome and unwelcome) who happen upon their community.

In production terms, the episode marks another watershed – heralding the moment at which the mix of on-location film and in-studio video comes to an end. From the opening scenes of "Starvation" to the closing moments of "A Beginning", every frame of *Survivors* is recorded by the OB unit working on location. "Starvation" also heralds a shift in the seasons. The importance of spring has already been commented upon in the events of "Corn Dolly", but here the analogy between the bursting forth of new life in nature and the birth of a new human community is more explicitly drawn. From "Starvation" onwards, the focus of the series shifts – there is far less looking back to mourn the scale of what has been lost, and far more looking forward in the hope of shaping the new future now apparently on offer. To make the most of the contrast between the hunger evident at the start of the story and the 'bounty' of the settlers' new home revealed at its conclusion, a note appended to the shooting script emphasised that: 'This episode depends upon the absence of livestock.' In turning its attention forwards, the episode also includes the final continuity references to the threat posed by Arthur Wormley's putative military government – introduced in "Genesis" and "Gone Away".

"Starvation" sees the introduction of a wave of additional characters (something extended further in the next episode, "Spoil of War"). Wendy is a bright, though perhaps somewhat immature, young woman, who frequently finds the maternal ministrations of the elderly Emma Cohen tedious, although probably more welcome than she cares to admit. As Julie

Neubert, who played Wendy, recalls: 'The point with Wendy was that she was so impractical, and was skipping around the countryside in pretty frocks and sandals, at a time when everyone else was wearing sensible trousers, heavyweight shoes and anoraks ... That gave her character an appearance of vulnerability and naivety.' When Wendy leaves on another scouting trip, Emma is keen to impress upon her that she 'couldn't cope alone.' When Wendy replies, 'I need you,' the sense of uncertainty and doubt is evident on her face, but it does not take long for the privations of the world to convince Wendy that she needs the protection of others (although, for Wendy, that protection will quickly prove illusory). Wendy even momentarily considers eating both of the fish that she steals from the lecherous Tom to satisfy her own hunger, before thinking better of it and returning to the house to share her treasure with Emma. The gentle and innocent Barney (given the name Aston in the script) is something of a less

John Hallett. © Anne Christie

complete character, though his impaired mental state and limited vocabulary mean that his 'simplicity' is actually part and parcel of his nature. There is no doubt that the lottery of survival will have seen many 'vulnerable' people emerge unscathed from The Death, and there's little doubt that Barney represents a menace-free and hard-working addition to the community. Tom relishes the encounter with Barney – their friendship gives Tom a rare and welcome power advantage, and Barney's limited comprehension serves Tom's enthusiasm for spinning tall tales well: the former being unable to challenge the latter's stories of greatness and heroism. And yet both Wendy and Barney are characters introduced to serve particular plot outcomes in episode nine. With Wendy's appearance in the series so short-lived, she is also deprived of much in the way of character development. With the return of Tom Price, the drama in which all three are involved (that culminates in the events of "Law and Order" and "The Future Hour") is set in motion.

The 'starvation' referred to throughout the episode is about more than food. It refers also to the lack of connection, the pain of isolation, and the enrichment that comes from community. Throughout the episode are indications of characters struggling to make their way on their own: Wendy and Emma are in dire straights at the Cohen cottage; Abby observes, quite correctly, to Tom that 'You're no good on your own'; and Barney is unable to fend for himself, even to the level of tending his own wound. But even for the central three characters there is recognition of the need, the imperative, to settle, and to gather around them people sufficient to sustain a new community. However reluctant any of them might appear, independence seems only a guarantee of further hunger and dispossession. Survival, this episode firmly suggests, can only be a collaborative, collective affair.

As well as the question of community, the issue of family looms large in this episode. Emma serves as surrogate mother to the innocent Wendy; Abby tricks and disarms Tom as she might manipulate a naughty child (however much he wants to perceive the encounter as sexual); but most noticeably it is the fusion of Jenny, Greg and the children as a family unit that spells this out. In an early scene in the minibus, Jenny rebukes the children for calling her 'Mummy', and in response John and Lizzie deliberately 'wind-up' the adults with their incessant repetition of 'Mummy, Mummy, Mummy ...' Lizzie observes on their arrival at the Grange that Greg is 'not Daddy, is he?' but when the children awake the next morning they call out for 'Mummy' and 'Daddy' and are not chastised for doing so, as Greg and Jenny tacitly accept their parental roles. The process is completed in the first sequences involving Barney, when the four of them appear in a tableau of mother, father and children, in the settlement's kitchen. All this is achieved on screen in a way that is far more accomplished and subtle than it sounds on the page.

Hampton Court is a startlingly good location; its labyrinth of rooms and corridors is gradually revealed through the games of the children, and the scale of its grounds is hinted at as Jenny wanders the gardens in search of food. It provided a convincing, spacious and atmospheric setting, in which the seven remaining episodes of the first series could unfold, and its geography is introduced to good effect here.

Easily the episode's low-point is the sequence in which the minibus is laid siege to by a pack of 'wild dogs'. The timid canines assembled by the animal handler are utterly unconvincing in the role, squatting subdued and sullen in the path of the road, watching for the next instruction from behind the camera. Director Roberts and actor McCulloch both do their best to invest proceedings with as much menace and danger as they can together muster, but the results are disappointing and, as such, the threat that the dogs pose is greatly diminished. It seems that an important lesson was learned from the experience, and future dog packs looked much more the part.

The shift in mood in "Starvation" is unmistakable. The dissolute and disparate community has come together in recognition that there is no alternative to the hard business of settling down to forge a future. With their bellies full, and the difficult decision to stay put made, our survivors have found themselves returned 'home', a place they had all lost sight of since The Death. There is evidence too of human resilience in the face of disaster. After the worst that could possibly have happened has happened, Emma tells Abby that she is 'not frightened any more.' Even the immature Wendy discovers sufficient guile to help Abby trap Tom in his van. Music and song are heard for the first time since The Death – as Greg strums his guitar, and Emma sings as she relishes the chance to cook once again. The uplifting final scene in which the characters are seen revelling in the excitement of their new possession as the titles roll is far and away the most optimistic moment yet seen in the series. To underscore the power of the finale, notes added to the shooting script made the plea: 'Please: Sunshine! Stream! Sheep! Sparrows!' Some reviewers, and even cast members, have complained that "Starvation" is devoid of action and incident and that the establishment of the community is insufficient to sustain fifty minutes of engaging drama. It certainly gave voice to scriptwriter Jack Ronder's interest in the 'human predicament' elements of the *Survivors* premise, and downplayed the high adventure element that dominates episodes such as "Garland's War". Yet what "Starvation" lacks in gunplay it more than makes up for in rich character exchanges and insightful reflections on the difficult choices that these survivors are now forced to confront. The series needed to settle and, if anything, it could be argued that *Survivors* had remained rootless for too long. In any case, new 'adventures' would not remain long in coming. *RC*

1.8 SPOIL OF WAR

UK TRANSMISSION: 11 June 1975: 8.10pm – 9.00pm
VIEWING FIGURE: 6.77m
WRITER: M K Jeeves (pseudonym for Clive Exton)
DIRECTOR: Gerald Blake
REGULAR CAST: Carolyn Seymour (Abby Grant); Ian McCulloch (Greg Preston); Lucy Fleming (Jenny Richards); Talfryn Thomas (Tom Price); Christopher Tranchell (Paul Pitman); Hana-Maria Pravda (Emma Cohen); Michael Gover (Arthur Russell); Julie Neubert (Wendy); John Hallett (Barney); Eileen Helsby (Charmian Wentworth); Terry Scully (Vic Thatcher); Tanya Ronder (Lizzie Willoughby); Stephen Dudley (John Millon)
OB RECORDING: 28 April - 1 May 1975
LOCATIONS: Hampton Court, Hope-under-Dinmore, Herefs; Firing Range, Midsummer Hill, Worcs; Castlemorton Common, Worcs

> SYNOPSIS: Abby and Jenny are failing in an attempt to plough the pasture just outside the Grange, when they meet a man called Paul who claims to have some farming expertise. They invite him in and he tells them rather bluntly where they are going wrong. Talk of getting a tractor going reminds Greg of the quarry in which he met Anne Tranter and Vic Thatcher several months ago. He thinks that the provisions they gathered may still be there and sends Tom and Barney off to

Introducing Paul Pitman (Chris Tranchell). © Anne Christie investigate. That evening, former businessman Arthur Russell and a woman named Charmian Wentworth, who is still acting as his secretary despite The Death, arrive at the Grange looking for shelter. Arthur's imperious manner does not go down well with the rest of the community. When Tom and Barney fail to return, Greg and Paul appropriate Arthur's Land Rover and head off for the quarry. On arrival, they observe that the Portakabin of supplies appears to be being guarded by several armed men, while Tom and Barney have abandoned their van and are trapped unarmed behind some rocks. An attempt to wave a white flag meets with further gunfire. While Paul covers him, Greg makes his way down the steep quarry side to the back of the Portakabin. Once there, he is amazed to discover that all the guns are being controlled by just one dishevelled man: Vic Thatcher. Vic assumes that they have come to steal his supplies, and when Greg reveals that he was the man who tried to fix Vic's legs, the cripple attacks him. Greg gives him his version of events and once Vic learns that Anne left him to die, he becomes intent on seeking revenge. Greg asks Vic if he will return with them to the Grange and he reluctantly agrees.

ANALYSIS: Clive Exton's first script for the series, originally titled "Promised Land", sees the introduction of several interesting new characters and the first serious treatment of the significance of agricultural expertise. The episode is comprised of two separate stories, with the title assuming relevance only in the second half when Greg remembers the supplies stored at the "Genesis" quarry. In some ways "Spoil of War" is a representation of the whole series in microcosm, in that it depicts the need for the survivors to get back to the land (Paul's advice) countered by a dependence on the irreplaceable provisions of the old world (the quarry quest), while screen time is divided between dialogue-heavy and action-centred sequences.

Christopher Tranchell's Paul is introduced well and immediately comes across as an interesting person who would have stood out from the crowd in the old world as much as he does in the new. Unfortunately, like many other new characters, he is rarely given the opportunity to be as strong again and never quite fulfils his initial promise. Here, Paul expresses a tenet that will be espoused regularly as the series progresses – 'Never depend on anything you can't replace' – and his harsh assessment of their agricultural achievements ('Unless you get yourselves organised you're wasting your time') is later echoed by Mark Carter in his judgment of the Whitecross set-up in "New Arrivals". His advice that the survivors will have to work on the assumption that the new world is never going to change, not only serves to emphasise the seriousness of their predicament and dire need to become acquainted with the land, but also highlights just how deluded is Tom Price's view that: 'Everything's gonna get back to … normal by Christmas.' Despite Paul's sound agricultural advice, there is never a feeling that the Grange community really seriously engages in a move to get back to the land; the suggestion is that the settlers are doing little more than 'playing at it.' Paul brings with him the first news of London since Jenny fled the gridlocked capital in "The Fourth Horseman". He considers himself to have been lucky to get out alive and explains that it was overrun with snipers. London is not heard of again until the two-part "Lights of London" in the second series.

Charmian Wentworth and Arthur (named Ernest in the initial drafts and in the *Radio Times* listing for this episode) Russell also debut here. Both characters are still clinging to their old world roles, namely of secretary and successful businessman, and seem unable to adapt to their new circumstances. The facts that Charmian continues to call Arthur 'Mr Russell' and that the disturbing of his sleep worries her more than encountering armed strangers, depict just how much she is denying the new reality. Arthur's plan to travel north to live with Charmian on his own island off the coast of Argyllshire seems similarly ridiculous and provokes Paul to observe: 'For a businessman you don't seem to be showing much foresight.' This is further emphasised by his assumption that alcohol is not in short supply, to which Abby pointedly responds: 'For now.' Interestingly, Charmian and Arthur are the first characters to be introduced who knew each other before The Death, confirming that at least one of Charles Vaughan's ideas regarding survival was based on supposition.

The sudden influx of new characters both here and in the preceding episode feels a little contrived and results in a rather over-populated regular cast, although to be fair this is an obvious corollary of a narrative that seeks to depict the foundation of a community. Here Wendy, Emma and the children have to take a back seat. In one of the few scenes in which Wendy appears, the script clearly demonstrates the original intention that the character would be played by a younger actress than Julie Neubert, with Emma's hold over her when she is offered an alcoholic drink seeming slightly odd.

Although Greg's fragile pride is obviously hurt by Paul's self-confessed tactless straight-talking and unique agricultural expertise, the engineer is recompensed shortly afterwards through the action sequences at the quarry, which allow him to demonstrate talents Paul does not possess. In this way, Paul's knowledge is shown to be all very well, but the message appears to be that unless it is coupled with an ability to look after himself – an attribute Greg possesses – then he may not have what it takes to survive. There is perhaps an element of chauvinism in the second half of the episode as the men take centre-stage regardless of ability. Abby has recently proved her prowess with a gun ("Starvation") and yet is relegated to waving the men off alongside Jenny. There also seems to be very little concern that Greg's and Paul's departure leaves the occupants of the Grange 'pretty depleted' and therefore in some danger.

In the affectionate characterisation of the unequal relationship between Tom and Barney, the seeds are sown for the tragic events of the next episode, "Law and Order". Despite the fact that Tom considers Barney to be a 'pal' and 'more like a pet really,' when they need a branch to construct a white flag of surrender, Tom's strong sense of self-preservation immediately prompts him to place Barney in danger in his place. That Tom and Barney are chosen for this important mission in the first place is absurd, especially given Tom's known predilection for alcohol. Clearly they are sent off only for dramatic purposes, so that Greg and Paul can subsequently rescue them. The rescue itself is well directed, if a little over-long. The climactic revelation that their sole opponent in the quarry is Vic Thatcher, still manages to be startling despite the fact that, unlike Greg, the viewer knows that he may still be alive.

The terrible life Vic has led since Anne abandoned him is disturbingly conveyed through both his appearance and his dialogue to Greg ('Do you know what real pain is?'). Vic also states that this is not the first time he's had to fight to retain his supplies. Terry Scully does use his legs a little too much during the fight sequence, but his attack – which ultimately is really about the anger he feels towards Anne but doesn't want to confront – still manages to be both pitiable and distressing. Once Vic learns that Anne was not persuaded by Greg to leave him, the scene is set for the final chapter in the Anne and Vic trilogy: 'I've got something to live for now … I'm going to devote the rest of my days looking for that nicely brought up lady.' As it turns out, Vic does not have to find Anne as fate brings her directly to him.

Tom's response to overcoming the threat posed by Vic is amusing, and characteristically inappropriate: 'Now I don't mind telling you, you put up a good fight, I'll be the first to admit that ... Well spoils of war, isn't it now.' However, as Greg states, 'There hasn't been a war' – they intended to take the supplies only if the Portakabin was unoccupied – thus rendering the title of the episode ironic.

If the pig-related banter between Greg and Paul at the episode's close is an example of the sort of 'double act' element that Tranchell was reportedly keen to see more of, perhaps viewers should be grateful that McCulloch did not really go for the idea. Here, their inconsequential dialogue serves only to detract from the dramatic denouement of the quarry sequence; a close-up on the haggard face of Vic – his ordeal over – sat in the back of the Land Rover would have proved to be a far more effective ending for the episode.

"Spoil of War" makes an important and agreeable contribution to the first series, especially in respect of the introduction of new characters and the continuation of Vic's story, but there is less here than in previous episodes to provoke deep thought. Clive Exton himself was less than happy with the changes that were made to this and the following episode's scripts and elected to use a pseudonym, M(ahatma) K(ane) Jeeves – an alias that W C Fields also employed. Some years later, Exton would remark: 'I was hot-headed in those days!' *AP*

1.9 LAW AND ORDER

UK TRANSMISSION: 18 June 1975: 8.10pm – 9.00pm
VIEWING FIGURE: 8.38m
WRITER: M K Jeeves (Clive Exton)
DIRECTOR: Pennant Roberts
REGULAR CAST: Carolyn Seymour (Abby Grant); Ian McCulloch (Greg Preston); Lucy Fleming (Jenny Richards); Talfryn Thomas (Tom Price); Christopher Tranchell (Paul Pitman); Hana-Maria Pravda (Emma Cohen); Michael Gover (Arthur Russell); Julie Neubert (Wendy); John Hallett (Barney); Eileen Helsby (Charmian Wentworth); Terry Scully (Vic Thatcher); Tanya Ronder (Lizzie Willoughby); Stephen Dudley (John Millon)
OB RECORDING: 12 - 16 May 1975
LOCATION: Hampton Court, Hope-under-Dinmore, Herefs

SYNOPSIS: Abby proposes a May Day party to revive the community's flagging spirits. The festivities are spirited and good-humoured – and Tom introduces Barney to the delights of hard liquor. Soon, Barney feels unwell and goes to lie down. When Wendy also retires, Tom follows her unnoticed. She firmly rejects his amorous advances, but he chases her upstairs into the darkness. In the morning, the children find Wendy's cold and bloodstained body – she has been the victim of a frenzied stabbing. Suspicion quickly falls on the absent Barney. Tom finds Barney first, and urges him to flee, but he is captured. The community question Barney, but his bemused answers do nothing to exonerate him. After a series of heated and emotional exchanges, they agree to reach a verdict on Barney's culpability before deciding what to do with him. Barney is judged to be guilty by a clear majority. After a subdued lunch, the adults reassemble to decide between banishing Barney and carrying out the death penalty. Emma insists that they cannot execute such a vulnerable person; Greg counters that the community must face their collective responsibilities. They vote again, and the results are tied – leaving Abby with the casting vote. Her silently sobbing figure indicates her decision. The men assemble to select the executioner and Greg draws the fateful 'short straw', to Tom's utter relief. Paul and Arthur dig twin graves, as Greg marches Barney into the grounds. At the sound of the fatal shot, Tom's resolve cracks. He shows Greg and Abby the bloodied weapon hidden beneath the floorboards. Greg launches himself at Tom, but Abby holds him back. Greg convinces Abby that the community could not withstand the shock of their complicity in Barney's death. They agree to keep the truth secret. Alone in his room, a penitent Tom pleads for forgiveness.

ANALYSIS: Without doubt one of the most celebrated and best-remembered episodes of *Survivors*' first series, "Law and Order" is as claustrophobic and unsettling as it is shocking. The drama, in which the community must shoulder awesome responsibilities in conditions in which they lack the knowledge and facilities they previously took for granted, is horribly plausible. In some respects, the character of Barney remains something of a cipher – the innocent who lacks the awareness either to defend himself effectively or to recognise the seriousness of his predicament – and the necessary contrivance that sustains the drama of the trial. Yet although Barney remains an 'instrumental' participant, John Hallett's convincing performance as the bemused and childlike accused helps to give the interrogation scenes a compelling atmosphere. The malevolence at the core of Tom Price's nature is here revealed in some of Talfryn Thomas's most finely judged work. Tom's mounting anxiety as the trial unfolds is completely believable. Thomas provides a complex, layered and acutely observed performance, which sheds an entirely new light on the comedic moments that have preceded Tom's darkest hour.

Of course what helps to give the narrative such strength is the unexpected shift that occurs after the first few minutes, when the melancholy of the party's conclusion gives way to the shock of murderous deeds, discovered in the cold light of the following morning. The party scene – one of the longest single takes in the entire first series – provides a number of revealing and acutely observed character interactions. The fact that the dancing is somewhat clumsy seems entirely in keeping with the likely reality. Tom's unintentionally witty discussion with Barney about the 'acquired taste' of hard liquor nicely serves to misdirect the viewer about the events that are to follow, and highlights again the uneven relationship between Barney and Tom. Perhaps the only questionable exchange is the one between Greg and Jenny, in which they discuss the history of May Day and blood-sacrifice (drawn from the veins of a virgin no less), as a means to ensure future fertility. It is a moment of heavy sign-posting that belies both the subtlety and sophistication of what comes after.

After the warmth and light of the party sequence, the meeting between Tom and Wendy is chillingly lit, and the exchanges between them evoke a growing sense of menace. The shot of Wendy's bloodied and lifeless body is perhaps even more shocking than the director intended, despite its brevity. Julie Neubert remembers 'being absolutely intrigued by the make-up people … particularly in preparing for the scene where Wendy was found. They made a false layer of skin over the leg … and I couldn't watch! It looked as if they were opening up my own leg to put the blood underneath. It looked so realistic.' The original intention had always been to have Jenny killed off as Tom's victim. Yet her character had proved particularly popular, and Jenny was reprieved – with the new character Wendy being drafted in to take her place. The power of the moment is reinforced still further by the writer's decision to have the children find her corpse – they come running to the adults announcing uncertainly that 'something's happened to Wendy.' The close-up of a haggard-looking Tom sitting silently in

Julie Neubert and John Hallett. © Anne Christie

his bedroom awaiting the inevitable discovery is all the more blood-chilling for its understatement. Neubert is keen to emphasise her view of one critical aspect of the storyline: 'Everybody I've spoken to about it... presumes that Wendy was raped. Yet that was never stated in any way ... She could have been killed just putting up a fight ... You never *know* what happened, at all.'

With Barney identified as the most likely suspect, a search party is sent to retrieve him from his hunting trip. The sequences in which Greg and the others sweep through the woods provide an incongruous light and airy contrast to the darkness and enclosure of the previous evening, before the drama is once again shut up indoors. Tom's inept attempt to have Barney flee suddenly makes sense – Tom is hopeful that if Barney gets away, his guilt will be assumed and that Tom will be free of suspicion. From the moment that Barney is caught, the pressure on Tom ratchets up to the point where it is unbearable. He hopes next that Barney might be sentenced only to banishment, all the time fearful that the innocent defendant may yet betray Tom's own complicity. As Barney's fate looks darker, Tom is stuck between bewilderment and dread – and as the time approaches where he might have to fire the fatal shot, he reaches breaking point. It is interesting to think what might have happened if Tom, rather than Greg, had drawn the short straw and been confronted by the executioner's lot – might that have been the moment when his cruel and cowardly façade would have collapsed?

The community's predicament is realised in some of the most emotionally and dramatically intense scenes in the whole series. As the trial gets underway, the world beyond the Grange's walls disappears from view, as the community turns inwards to scrutinise itself and the principles it is now compelled to live by. Greg's insistence that the settlement must acknowledge the horrible realities and shoulder the responsibilities that the murder demands of them – they have 'got to think and feel and act' for themselves – is one of the high points of an electrifying performance by Ian McCulloch.

Within the acutely observed drama, there are some superb secondary developments. With the memories of his abandonment at the quarry still raw, Vic cannot countenance the idea of Barney being locked up in isolation. The votes over first Barney's guilt and later his sentence reveal a sharp (though incomplete) gender split amongst the community (with the women – and Tom – voting for banishment and the rest of the men for the death penalty), although this is not commented upon, while Abby has to shoulder the responsibility of leadership to break ranks. In an understated but significant character development, Charmian here asserts her independence from Arthur – staring at him intently while she casts her own votes the other way. The interventions of the children over a tense and silent lunch-table actually serve to accentuate the sense of apprehension even further. Ironically, it is the children who are the more effective judges of Barney's true nature. Unwittingly, they unlock Barney from his confinement, and he makes no attempt to leave as they involve him in their games.

The outside world is revealed again only as preparations are made for Barney's execution, as the children play in the grounds unaware, in the care of a pensive Jenny. The fact that there is no image of Barney being led to his death, or of his actual demise, oddly adds to the horror of the moment. Viewers witness only the return of a silent and stony-faced Greg, grimly clutching his rifle. This is also an episode where the absence of incidental music is brought into sharp relief. Whether it is the cut and thrust of the debates in the library, the silence over lunch, or the reactions to the sound of the fatal gunshot that ends Barney's life, the lack of invasive and mood-setting music does nothing but add to the tension.

The end sequences offer little respite, as Tom's resolve cracks and he reveals his crimes to an appalled Abby and an incensed Greg. It is interesting to hear Greg reflect that the loss of Wendy and Barney takes the community to the brink of collapse (and therefore Tom must be spared). It is notable too that the decision is taken by the community's leaders to hide the truth from those who share a responsibility for Barney's wrongful death – but only after Greg has threatened Abby that he will challenge her for control if she shares the truth: in which case the settlement will, he predicts, 'fall apart.' Emma had asked earlier if the community was a democracy – the evidence here powerfully suggests that it is not.

Several cast members remember the excited and febrile atmosphere on set during production, where the episode's issues were intently debated – particularly the morality of the death penalty. Carolyn Seymour hated the conclusion to the episode and pressed both producer and director for an alternative in which Barney might be spared. Although her own moral sensibilities were clearly offended, it does seem an odd decision for an actor to object to being asked to deliver such mesmerising dramatic material.

With themes reminiscent of the trial scenes from the 1950s post-apocalyptic novel *Earth Abides*, "Law and Order" might be thought of above all as concerned with the loss of innocence: the community gets irrefutable confirmation of the full extent of their new 'self-reliance'; the young and naïve Wendy loses her life; Barney is unable to protect himself or act in his own interests; Abby and Greg learn the horrible contradictions and pressures that come with leadership; and the settlers are forced to acknowledge that the plague has done little to temper the darker impulses of humanity.

The final shot, a quite shocking image of Tom in tears and rocking back and forward pleading for forgiveness, provides final confirmation if any were needed that *Survivors* is a drama of adult mettle and sensibility. At this moment there is no indication that Tom's own comeuppance is but an episode away.

The claustrophobia and intensity of "Law and Order" amply demonstrate both the sophistication and the versatility of *Survivors*' first series format. Whether "Law and Order" should be celebrated as the 'best' episode of *Survivors* – as some have suggested – depends entirely on the criteria applied, but there is little doubting its superlative quality for a drama of its type. *RC*

1.10 THE FUTURE HOUR

UK TRANSMISSION: 25 June 1975: 8.10pm – 9.00pm
VIEWING FIGURE: 7.12m
WRITER: Terry Nation
DIRECTOR: Terence Williams
REGULAR CAST: Carolyn Seymour (Abby Grant); Ian McCulloch (Greg Preston); Lucy Fleming (Jenny Richards); Talfryn Thomas (Tom Price); Christopher Tranchell (Paul Pitman); Hana-Maria Pravda (Emma Cohen); Michael Gover (Arthur Russell); Eileen Helsby (Charmian Wentworth); Terry Scully (Vic Thatcher); Tanya Ronder (Lizzie Willoughby); Stephen Dudley (John Millon); Ben (Ben the dog)
GUEST CAST: Glyn Owen (Bernard Huxley); Caroline Burt (Laura Foster); Denis Lawson (Norman Reed); James Hayes (Phil)
UNCREDITED CAST: Alf Costa (Jack); Fred Clempson (Harry); John Sarbutt (Willie); Jeff Shane (Unnamed gang member)
OB RECORDING: 20 - 24 May 1975
LOCATIONS: Hampton Court, Hope-under-Dinmore, Herefs; Sallings Common, Grendon Bishop, Herefs

SYNOPSIS: Through binoculars, Greg spots a plume of smoke in an area thought to be empty of people. Investigating, Paul and Greg discover a trader convoy, complete with pantechnicons stuffed with foodstuffs, hardware and consumables. They meet Huxley, a salesman in the bartering business – swapping the goods he has amassed in return for gold, which Huxley believes to be the currency of the future. To Huxley's consternation, his pregnant partner Laura and assistant Norman have fled the camp. Norman and Laura are given temporary sanctuary at the Grange, where the settlement learns that Huxley is refusing to care for the child that Laura is expecting, as it is not his own. When Huxley arrives at the Grange, Abby leads the pretence that the community knows nothing of the pair's whereabouts, but the children unwittingly give the game away. That night, Huxley leads a raiding party into the Grange to seize Laura and Norman, but the tables are turned and his men disarmed. Norman returns the gold that he foolishly took, but Huxley still threatens to get back all that is his due. Huxley puts the Grange under armed siege. Fearful of the burden that she has imposed on the settlement, Laura leaves in secret – but Norman has to return to summon help when she goes into labour. With help from the settlement's women, she gives birth to a healthy baby girl. The community agree with Greg's plan to surprise Huxley's gang and seize their weapons. In the shoot-out that follows, Tom is badly injured, but the gunfire stops when Abby arrives with Laura (who has decided she must return to Huxley's side). Tom shoots Huxley dead, and is killed by a volley of shots from Huxley's men. Their resolve evaporates with the death of their leader. With the battle over, Laura and her baby return to the shelter of the Grange.

ANALYSIS: "The Future Hour" is a simple but effective Nation-scripted adventure story that delivers some solid action sequences and reveals a little more of the picture of developments in the outside world in the process. When compared to the intensity of the previous episode, "Law and Order", this is fairly undemanding stuff emotionally and intellectually, but there is much to enjoy along the way, and events here unfold at a satisfying narrative pace.

Glyn Owen, as the seemingly relaxed roving trader Huxley, is far and away the best of the guest cast, particularly when the character shifts unexpectedly between affable and aggressive in the early scenes at his makeshift campsite. These scenes also reveal some important differences between Paul's and Greg's views of the world. Greg is at his suspicious best, determined to size up Huxley before revealing too much about himself or his community. Paul meanwhile is open and accommodating to the point of being thoughtless: helping himself to Huxley's cigarette haul (against Greg's advice), and willing to mark the exact location of the Grange settlement on Huxley's map (until Greg intervenes). However, both share a sense of disbelief that Huxley is trading his hoard of goods for 'worthless' gold – and at his insistence that their community should prioritise the hunt for gold in any form (necklaces and rings – it is implied – as well as gold bullion or coins) with which to barter in the present, and to stockpile as the likely currency of the future. Neither Paul nor Greg are taken in by Huxley's stated motives in setting fire to the locations that his men ransack for supplies. This is not because it 'clears out disease' as Huxley claims, and is in reality driven by a concern, as Greg observes, to maintain a level of scarcity in a market that Huxley with his sense of 'vision' is keen to dominate, as the pickings around the country get thinner. It is only when Huxley learns of the disappearance of Laura and Norman, along with two

bags of his 'precious' gold coin, that the veneer of jovial conviviality slips, and Greg's caution is vindicated. Some notes from Nation on the camera script provide character details about the runaway pair and their backgrounds that are not all revealed in the episode itself. Laura Foster is described as: 'Very attractive, originally from Bristol, she lived in London for many years.' Norman Reed is introduced as a: 'Pleasant young man, a bank clerk from Huddersfield.'

It is clear that Huxley sees himself as a wily capitalist, and not a brigand robber baron, and he certainly makes use of devices other than the barrel of a gun to get his way. He has however also been involved in several shoot-outs over contested loot, and considers the death of members of his workforce a 'legitimate trading risk.' There's little doubt what would happen to the

Ian and Carolyn. © Anne Christie

'price' of Huxley's ever more valuable supply of essential goods a few winters on.

When Greg and Paul discover that the two escapees (and their stash of gold) have been given shelter at the Grange, the scene is set for an inevitable confrontation. Some might complain that the plot on offer here feels too familiar – that once again our heroes are under threat from armed outsiders – but the episode succeeds in the assured execution of what is unquestionably a straightforward linear storyline.

It is interesting to see gold make an appearance here as a possible candidate for a future currency. The Grange community consider Huxley mad to want to exchange goods with real 'use value' for what is now worthless 'precious metal', but from his present vantage point two possible futures would seem to await him – either that of the wealthy feudal tycoon, commanding both resources and power; or that of the unhinged obsessive, living abandoned and hungry in his empty warehouse, surrounded by useless stacks of gold bullion. Much has been made by this point in *Survivors* of the conflict between scavenging on the leftovers of the old world and seeking to be self-sufficient in the new one. Huxley is the archetypal scavenger, making no long-term provision for future needs beyond the (hopeful) acquisition of personal wealth: the antithesis of the efforts being made collaboratively at the Grange. Indeed, Huxley sees the pregnant Laura's baby as an 'unproductive' investment and a drain on resources, failing – as Emma observes – even to think through the question of who might care for him in later years. Abby even seeks to deflect Jenny's interest in night-lights for the children – not wanting the community to make any sort of relationship with the traders, nor to think in terms that corrode their sense of self-sufficiency.

What triggers the siege at the Grange is the decision to give sanctuary to Laura and Norman (and, less plausibly, the failure of any of the adults to fill the children in on the plan). This is preceded by some fierce clashes between Abby and Greg over Laura's fate. Greg is concerned that the community must prioritise its own best interests, and that the decision to shelter Laura will put everyone at unacceptable risk. There are strong echoes here of the events in the series finale where Greg threatens to challenge Abby for the settlement's leadership after she ignores the dangers of taking in the ill and potentially contagious Ruth. Amidst the arguments here Abby overrules two important objections. In the light of the danger of possible bloodshed and death, Arthur's suggestion that the community adopt and care for Laura's baby after its birth would seem to warrant more reflection than it is granted. Laura herself explains that this was Huxley's own ultimatum. Given the sacrifices that Laura is asking the community to make on her behalf, it might be a suggestion that she should be asked to reconsider. Although she is understandably frightened and confused, Laura's behaviour in "The Future Hour" is repeatedly self-centred and puts others in the firing line. She deserts Huxley, asks for shelter at the Grange, refuses to return to his side when he raids the settlement, leaves when she hears of Huxley's ultimatum and has to be carried back in the midst of labour; then, after the birth, she insists on being taken back to Huxley, only to ask to stay on after his demise. At the height of the siege, Huxley's threats even lead the community to consider the option of abandoning the Grange.

Many of the burdens that Laura brings fall on Greg's shoulders. He has to arrange the Grange's defence and persuade Norman to return the gold he took from Huxley (although by this point, with Huxley's ego so dented, even the return of his loot was unlikely to be enough to satisfy him). Greg also has to endure Abby's wrath for telling Laura the seriousness of Huxley's ultimatum, which precipitates her departure. (An anonymous handwritten note on one copy of the shooting script wryly observes that when Abby strikes Greg: 'There is no way of doing this without Ms Seymour killing Mr McCulloch with her gold knuckle-duster'). Greg also has to comfort Laura as she awaits her stretcher-rescue, and has later to lead the raiding party that he hopes will disarm and disable Huxley's gang. All the while, Greg's instincts are that the community should prioritise its survival ahead of dangerous acts of compassion. It can only be hoped that Laura makes clear her gratitude to Greg and the rest of the community for all their efforts to protect her in some unseen off-screen moment!

There are some notable weaknesses in the episode's execution: the performances from several of Huxley's henchmen are pretty leaden, and some of the gunplay in the siege sequences is less than convincing (as the shotguns that the Grange's defenders use would, at that distance, indiscriminately injure or kill the hostages as well as Huxley's gang members). Abby's 'shock' at the likelihood that Huxley would seek to maim or kill members of their community in his campaign to force Laura out, also seems entirely out of character. By this point, Abby is acutely aware of how brutal and vindictive those who see themselves in positions of power have frequently proven themselves to be in the months following The Death, and Greg has already revealed that the violent and unpredictable Huxley had previously killed another of Laura's partners.

In some respects, it could be thought that Tom's comeuppance at the close of the episode comes too soon after the deaths of Wendy and Barney. Greg's own guilt about Barney's death may lie behind his insistence that there be no killing in their raid on Huxley's convoy (unless in self-defence). It might have been more grating and uncomfortable for Greg and Abby for Tom to have survived and to have slid back towards his old complaining and needling ways. His despatch does, however, give a strong sense of closure, and the moment where Greg reflects on the weight of the secret he is carrying – and ponders on the nature of Tom's actions ('He did worse things') – provides an extremely strong conclusion. It is interesting to reflect on the decision to write out Tom, and the differing perspectives of both Dudley and Nation on the decision. Dudley clearly felt that the series benefited from the presence of a grumbling down-and-out figure, and although it is easy to overstate the comparison, there are clear similarities between the characters of Tom and Hubert (who is introduced, under Dudley's guidance, in series two).

As the episode finishes on the image of Emma holding the new baby, it seems clear that the infant is herself a metaphor for the inheritance that the next generation are bequeathed by their parents. Nation's script notes make clear that the young baby is 'meant to depict the future.' The moment might have had more resonance if the drama that preceded it had itself had greater emotional depth, and yet "The Future Hour" remains agreeable if unexceptional *Survivors*. The clash between the value of human life and that of material things is a theme that the series would soon revisit. *RC*

1.11 REVENGE

UK TRANSMISSION: 2 July 1975: 8.10pm – 9.00pm
VIEWING FIGURE: 7.83m
WRITER: Jack Ronder
DIRECTOR: Gerald Blake
REGULAR CAST: Carolyn Seymour (Abby Grant); Ian McCulloch (Greg Preston); Lucy Fleming (Jenny Richards); Christopher Tranchell (Paul Pitman); Hana-Maria Pravda (Emma Cohen); Michael Gover (Arthur Russell); Eileen Helsby (Charmian Wentworth); Hugh Walters (Vic Thatcher); Tanya Ronder (Lizzie Willoughby); Stephen Dudley (John Millon);

Ben (Ben the dog)
GUEST CAST: Myra Frances (Anne Tranter); Robert Tayman (Donny)
OB RECORDING: 28 May - 1 June 1975
LOCATION: Hampton Court, Hope-under-Dinmore, Herefs

SYNOPSIS: The community set off on a hay-making trip, leaving Emma and Vic behind. When Emma finds a note from Vic, she rings a bell to call the others back. After Vic makes an abortive suicide attempt, his state of mind is discussed; Greg believes that if he had really intended to kill himself, he would have succeeded. Emma is convinced that finding a proper wheelchair would help. The following day, Vic is left with the children, and he begins to tell them a story that relates to what has happened to him. Greg is certain that they can convince Vic of his importance to the community through his teaching of John and Lizzie and, together with Paul, retrieves a wheelchair for him from a nearby school. Anne Tranter turns up at the Grange with a man called Donny and a tanker full of petrol. Greg is surprised to see her again and tells her that Vic did not die and that he is living there, prompting her to retreat to an upstairs room. Vic is not convinced about his new role of teacher and instead continues to tell his story to the children. Soon after, he learns that Anne is at the Grange and begins a desperate search for her. He tries to persuade Greg that he just wants to talk to her and later asks that she join them for dinner. During the meal, he reveals to everyone what she did to him. It is agreed that Anne will leave the next morning. That night, Vic summons up all his energy and crawls upstairs to confront Anne. She is waiting for him and pleads with him for her life. At the last moment, Vic decides he cannot kill her and instead the pair spend the night talking together on her bed. The next morning, Anne leaves the Grange on her own.

ANALYSIS: "Revenge" concentrates on the dramatic resolution of the Anne and Vic trilogy and boasts mesmerising performances from both Myra Frances and the hastily-drafted Hugh Walters, who together bring Jack Ronder's emotionally-charged script to life. Despite the difficulties that beset its production – the recasting of Vic due to Terry Scully's sudden illness, and the associated script rewrites – "Revenge" is undoubtedly one of the strongest episodes of the entire series.

It is a great testament to Hugh Walters' acting talent that he is quickly accepted as a believable successor to Terry Scully, especially given the range of feelings he is required to convey here. Ronder was reportedly tempted to withdraw his name from "Revenge", primarily due to the rewrites that Dudley felt were required to cover up Vic's change of appearance. Although – as Ronder's wife Anne has commented – Vic's injuries make him look more like he has skidded off a bike, the suicide sequence does not in fact detract from the main storyline. In the original script – which was altered just prior to recording – Emma tries to draw Vic out of his reverie after the others have gone off haymaking by telling him that he has to adapt to his new existence as she has tried to: 'Vic, I was brought up Jewish. Not strict, but I kept to it. Now I feed these people as best I can. I tried, I got myself a piece of pork and went into a corner and tried to eat it but I couldn't get it down. That's just a lifetime's way of thinking, but everything else – what I'm saying is, we've all got to change, Vic. Make do, for ourselves and each other.' However, Vic seems unimpressed by her speech, especially as the role she subsequently offers him is only as nursemaid to Laura's baby. Another victim of the rewrite was a startlingly prescient discussion about Paul taking chances to find a wheelchair for Vic, by entering a town and thus risking infection.

After Vic's suicide attempt, there appears to be an overwhelming lack of sympathy for his predicament; only Charmian appears to recognise his action as a cry for help rather than as attention-seeking behaviour. She suggests that he is treated as a 'lame duck', thus prefiguring Lizzie's later poem about 'all folk who quack and everyone who knows how to swim'; in "Revenge" swimming is used as a metaphor for survival. Although Vic enjoys a strong relationship with John and Lizzie (indeed, Jenny comments that 'They only listen to Vic'), Greg's conviction that he can be made to believe that he is the most important person at the Grange because of his new teaching role is short-sighted. Greg is clearly

Myra Frances (Anne Tranter). © Anne Christie

pursuing a 'quick-fix' solution to Vic's problems, for which he has already been shown to have very little patience.

Given the dialogue at the start of the episode, both the discovery of the wheelchair and the arrival of the petrol tanker feel a little too convenient; and when Paul asks, 'Would you believe a tanker of petrol has just arrived?' the viewer does not really. However, both devices are important in dramatic terms, with the former required for this episode's storyline, and the latter for the next episode, "Something of Value". When the wheelchair is presented to Vic, his reaction betrays his state of mind: on one level he is pleased that he'll now be able to get around the place more easily; but on another level, he realises that the pressure is now on to make the effort in return, and he is not ready for this. When he attempts to start teaching the children, he quickly accepts John's and Lizzie's view that the Romans and mental arithmetic are now irrelevant. Vic's choices – perhaps deliberately – ignore the fact that a great deal could be learned from books on subjects that are critical to the survivors' future, such as plant and animal husbandry. It could be argued that, given the potential importance of Vic's teaching role, Greg should have provided him with more initial guidance. Vic's reluctance to teach John and Lizzie may be due to the feelings of inadequacy of a self-declared uneducated man, but is more likely to stem from the fact that he can't concentrate on such an endeavour while continuing to dwell on the fate that has befallen him and his related thoughts of revenge. It does seem a little surprising that Greg and the others appear content to leave the children in the company of a unstable man who is recovering from a suicide attempt, but perhaps less so when one considers that Ronder's original script saw Vic as depressed rather than suicidal.

The story that Vic uses to explain to the children what happened to him is particularly affecting due to the analogous imagery used, in which he describes himself as 'a tiger with good legs' and Anne as 'a beautiful snake.' As he begins his tale, Anne is immediately reintroduced; her unrestrained catalogue of complaints – 'I'm sick of eating out of tins and I'm tired and I want a bath and I want a drink' – and immaculate attire indicate that she has not changed since we last met her, and also that in Donny she has found another sap to wait on her. Despite her portrayal as a born survivor, there is a perceptible feeling that she may finally receive her comeuppance here. The narrative is therefore dominated not only by the theme of revenge but, just as strongly, by that of survival. Anne is visibly shaken by Greg's news that Vic is alive, and the tension builds inexorably as her inevitable reunion with the man she left to die draws closer. As Anne retreats to hide in an upstairs room, her potential fate is underscored by the sound of (grim) reaping outside.

Vic's wheelchair-bound search is particularly well-executed and has a tremendous sense of pace and desperation. Initially at least, it is due to the hurt that Anne caused him – rendering him crippled – that he is prevented from reaching and hurting her in return. The dining room scene that follows is electric, and underlines how lucky the production team were to find Walters. Vic's reassurances of false normality are sinisterly expressed through controlled conversation about burping babies and the adoption of a fake smile. Anne's entrance is worth waiting for and the sense of unease – as well as lack of eye contact – is extended for as long as possible before she slowly turns to look at him. The fact that their reunion takes place around a civilised evening meal is especially ironic given his intentions towards her. Vic's speech about Anne – which includes an emphatic 'There she is' and, as he draws to a close, its counterpoint 'Here I am' – is Ronder at his best. No punches are pulled as far as Anne is concerned; despite being confronted with what she has done, she remains brutally honest and to the point: 'If you were a horse or a dog, I'd've shot you!'

However, even darker scenes follow in an ambitiously intense denouement, which is admirably full of emotion and meaning. There are few scenes in *Survivors* as memorable as Vic's all-consuming determination to pull himself up the back stairs towards his final confrontation with Anne. His useless legs are contrasted with Anne's 'good legs' as she stands above him armed with a sickle. That it is she who is wielding this weapon neatly reverses previously raised expectations. Anne is incredulous that Vic is prepared to take his revenge ('You want to kill me … How can you kill me? … I want to live … I'm going to live!') and is determined to survive, even if it means killing him to do so. Vic's sudden, and entirely believable, revelation that he in fact wants her to put an end to his misery, leads Anne instead to take pity on him. However, Vic's desire for revenge has been underestimated and once again viewer expectation is confounded as he takes his chance to strangle her. Anne's desperate defence is honest and heartfelt: she never loved him and, more importantly, 'never loved anyone or anything but living.' For Anne, survival is all, and Vic is momentarily put in mind of Lizzie's poem, 'God protect those who know how to swim,' and realises that he cannot take her life. These scenes are captivating and unique because they depict genuine raw emotion and do not attempt to provide a simple explanation for the confused motivations and feelings of both characters. As morning arrives, the pair have reached a new understanding; and although Anne has removed herself from the pedestal Vic originally placed her on (she lies atop a pile of mattresses but is not a princess), he is clearly still in awe of her. The closing sequence is one of the most striking of the series and shows Anne confidently walking away from Vic and the Grange. She has been given the opportunity to start again and her continued survival seems more certain than ever.

"Revenge" is the only episode of *Survivors* that does not concentrate on one or more of the series' four leads, and is one of the few narratives to deal almost exclusively with the theme of the will to survive. This conclusion to the Anne and Vic trilogy is rewarding and the final ten minutes are quite unforgettable. *AP*

1.12 SOMETHING OF VALUE

UK TRANSMISSION: 9 July 1975: 8.10pm – 9.00pm
VIEWING FIGURE: 8.43m
WRITER: Terry Nation
DIRECTOR: Terence Williams
REGULAR CAST: Carolyn Seymour (Abby Grant); Ian McCulloch (Greg Preston); Lucy Fleming (Jenny Richards); Christopher Tranchell (Paul Pitman); Hana-Maria Pravda (Emma Cohen); Michael Gover (Arthur Russell); Eileen Helsby (Charmian Wentworth); Tanya Ronder (Lizzie Willoughby); Stephen Dudley (John Millon)
GUEST CAST: Matthew Long (Robert Lawson); Murray Hayne (Jim Buckmaster); Paul Chapman (Thorpe)
OB RECORDING: 5 - 9 June 1975
LOCATIONS: Hampton Court, Hope-under-Dinmore, Herefs; Hill between Bodenham and Litmarsh, Herefs; Church House Farm, Pencombe, Herefs

SYNOPSIS: While Greg teaches the children to fish, a solitary visitor approaches – the apparently sociable Lawson. He tells the Grange community of developments in the world, and of his own desire to settle. That night a terrible thunderstorm hits. Early next morning, Lawson slips quietly from his bedroom and searches the grounds – discovering the community's prized petrol tanker. He heads off to rejoin his trio of wandering scavengers, led by the cultured Buckmaster. At the Grange, the cellar housing the community's precious stores has flooded. It is agreed that Greg and Jenny will trade petrol with a nearby settlement to replenish vital supplies. Buckmaster's gang arrive to discover the tanker gone. The raiders force Abby to reveal the tanker's destination. When the tanker reaches a steep descent, Greg finds that the brakes have failed, and narrowly avoiding disaster he brings the tanker to a halt. Sheltering in a nearby barn, Greg gets to work on repairs. Sent back to the Grange to retrieve tools and spares, Jenny comes across Lawson and his gang. She is taken hostage and driven back to the farm. When Buckmaster scouts the area, Greg knocks him to the floor, and a tense exchange of hostages follows. A standoff ensues, before Greg persuades Jenny to break free to raise the alarm. Greg does his best to hold out, but he is soon overwhelmed. Elated, the gang set off aboard the tanker. Out of control, the runaway tanker races downhill and careers off the road, flinging its occupants from the vehicle. Only an injured Buckmaster survives, and enraged he lunges at Greg and opens the tanker's outlet valve, allowing petrol to pour on the roadway. Greg shoots him dead, closing the valve just before Abby arrives with help. Sickened, Greg reflects on the cheapened value of human life.

ANALYSIS: "Something of Value" is a strong action and adventure piece, that showcases the characters of Jenny and Greg, and that returns Abby to the background to await the resolution her character is afforded in the series finale. McCulloch excels in the role of Greg as action hero, and Jenny gets to flex some adventurous muscles (in a way that Fleming was to find sorely absent in series two). The three guest villains of the story are also surprisingly well-evoked through some economic character development, before the siege at the farm takes centre stage.

Greg teaches the children to fish © Anne Christie

1.12 SOMETHING OF VALUE

The apparently amiable loner Lawson, who is given the traditional hospitable welcome at the Grange on his arrival, offers some intriguing glimpses of the situation developing across the country now that the immediate panic and shock of The Death has passed. The character notes describe him as: '30 – good-looking with a great deal of charm. He is instantly likeable.' He describes: a patchwork of settlements trying to eke out a new existence; groups of wandering nomads, unwilling to commit and settle in one place; and, more unsettlingly, criminal gangs who seek to pillage and loot unwary communities. When he declares his support for the growth of 'interdependence' and the forging of 'a common aim' amongst communities, he appears to be a forward-thinking survivor.

Although Abby and Greg seem quite genuine in their offer to him to join the Grange community, Paul and Arthur are rightly suspicious of a lone traveller, who travels light and shows no signs of having been sleeping rough. When Lawson slips away early the following morning, having located the community's precious petrol tanker, those suspicions are confirmed – as Lawson is revealed as a member of Buckmaster's gang, who are scouring the countryside in their hunt for petrol. The other gang members have had no luck on their scouting trips, and have even been fired upon during their approaches. It is an unpleasant irony of the new world that the Grange community will pay the price for their generosity, while other more closed settlements escape – by treating all 'intruders' as hostile in the first place.

There is some sparkling dialogue between gang leader Buckmaster (formerly 'a successful executive in an ad agency') and his underling Thorpe, who is even now struggling to come to terms with the full ramifications of the calamity. Thorpe makes what he clearly considers is an insightful observation about the gang's likely future diet: 'I've just been thinking … I bet we'll never see another orange again as long as we live … Lots of things: oranges, lemons, pineapples, bananas, grapefruit.' Buckmaster first patronises and then berates him for his ignorance: 'There are times when you really make me wonder … You haven't actually thought about things at all, have you?' Hurt and embarrassed, Thorpe retreats from the argument, insisting: 'All right. Don't go on about it … Know-all.' These exchanges help to flesh out and give a more rounded picture of characters who could easily slip into the mould of routine 'villains of the week'. This is something evident at the end of the episode, when Buckmaster almost tenderly checks the bodies of his friends for signs of life, and is seen to be acutely distressed at their deaths rather than simply angry with Greg. There is also an effective inversion of the usual apparent class prejudices of *Survivors* – as the gang is led by the cultured, well-educated and obviously well-to-do Buckmaster. In the original script, Buckmaster had been accompanied by a fourth gang member named Stacey, but his role was judged redundant prior to recording, and the part was never cast.

After the tight focus of "Revenge", it is a welcome change of pace to have a story that ranges across the countryside and again makes such good use of the empty, rolling landscape and silent roads. The staging of the flood that ruins the community's stores is convincingly done – and in fact is extremely sophisticated given its brief screen time. Unfortunately, the ingenuity of the set dresser seems to have dried up when it came to the 'rain-drenched' garden, represented by what looks like a quick once-over of a single vegetable patch with a hosepipe.

The plot unfolds extremely well, and the sequences around the siege have a real tension and uncertainty to them, especially as we know how high the body count amongst the regular characters has already been this series: there is no reason to be confident that Jenny and Greg will escape unharmed. It is interesting to note that it is Lawson who suggests that their raid be

Paul Chapman (Thorpe) and Tanya Ronder. © Anne Christie

abandoned – so concerned is he that none of them gets hurt as a consequence: however valuable the fuel might be, their own lives are worth more. Once again, the drama of *Survivors* benefits hugely from its dependence on real-life locations. The isolated farm in which Jenny and Greg find themselves holed up helps reinforce the completeness of their plight. On so many series of the day, the barn interiors would have required a return to a stilted studio interior.

Before he is overwhelmed, Greg delivers a defiant and emotionally charged speech to Buckmaster, insisting: 'That petrol's the only trading commodity we've got … [Without it] our community is going to have to break up. Now I'm not going to let that happen. I'd set fire to the whole damn lot before I'd let you get any part of it.' Delivered with typical conviction by McCulloch, these words go to the heart of the dilemma about the changed value of things in the new world.

That the tanker's failed brakes get forgotten in the ensuing gunplay seems to be a reasonable dramatic contrivance. It does seem a shame though that Nation's instruction that Lawson's body should be seen slumped over the steering wheel crushed up against a smashed windscreen, had to be set aside (presumably for reasons of cost and time). The drama, however, does require some significant suspensions of disbelief – and there are some implausible aspects that become more apparent with repeated viewing. The first is that the tanker is so lightly defended. Greg is alert to the need to hide their convoy from sight after the near accident, and the community is acutely aware that the petrol represents effectively the last 'something of value' with which they have to trade. The very survival of the community depends upon it. And yet it is sent on its way with only Jenny as backup and second driver. It is much more likely that the community would have provided as many armed escorts as could be spared.

There are also two weaknesses involving disclosure. When Abby is forced to reveal the tanker's route, while Lizzie is held hostage, she opts to tell the truth – although there is no reason for her to do so. The same Abby who stole the jeep keys from Wormley's militia in "Gone Away" might have thought it prudent to send the tanker's would-be thieves off on a wild-goose chase in the opposite direction. Later, when Jenny has been kidnapped, she immediately reveals the location of the barn where Greg is hiding – although she knows all too well the likely consequences of doing so. She could also have sent the gang on a run-around and 'got lost', knowing now that Abby is aware of the threats and will doubtless have sent out a search and rescue party (as she has). Finally, Greg opts to shoot Buckmaster to stop the flow of petrol. It seems a brutal, if desperately necessary, act. Perhaps more jarringly, the act of

78

discharging a spark-spitting shotgun into an environment thick with petrol fumes seems positively suicidal.

Others might also complain that Greg's brutal matter-of-factness about survival and the need to do what is necessary to protect the community contrast rather sharply with his reflections here on the piteously low value of human life (especially as the script initially indicated that Greg should be 'in full tears' by the episode's end). And yet, Greg might reasonably still be seen as reeling from his killing of Barney, and he has again been forced to take a human life. This might suggest that the character is complex rather than simply contradictory – and bitterly disappointed that the siege ended in such pointless tragedy.

There are also a couple of plot discontinuities. When Lawson first arrives, Greg immediately reveals the exact size of the community to an armed stranger. Yet surely the events of "The Future Hour" would only have reinforced the self-defensive reflex apparent there not to give out such potentially revealing information? Much more noticeable is the fact that the community's one remaining 'something of value' disappears prior to the next episode. Both Lawson and Greg independently estimate that at the outset there are around 1,000 gallons in the tanker, and Abby confirms that 'a little over 150 gallons' were lost following the fatal road crash. In "A Beginning", Arthur states that Greg traded a total of 200 gallons with the Little Barton community for their entire haul of supplies. The remaining 650 gallons appear to have evaporated along with the tanker. Although given the tragedy that awaits the settlement at the start of the following series, this is probably just as well.

"Something of Value" has many of the hallmarks of a classic Nation 'adventure', and here the 'heroes in peril' motif works to great effect. It also serves as evidence once again of Nation's concern that the focus of the drama be kept in motion and remain action driven. As author Jonathan Bignell reflects, Nation was very attached to the mobile *Survivors* narrative structure he originally devised and was 'not at all keen on having the characters fixed in one location and becoming preoccupied with domestic problems.' Such thinking quickly proved to be in direct conflict with the direction in which producer Dudley was convinced that the drama now needed to move. *RC*

1.13 A BEGINNING

UK TRANSMISSION: 16 July 1975: 8.10pm – 9.00pm
VIEWING FIGURE: 7.58m
WRITER: Terry Nation
DIRECTOR: Pennant Roberts
REGULAR CAST: Carolyn Seymour (Abby Grant); Ian McCulloch (Greg Preston); Lucy Fleming (Jenny Richards); Christopher Tranchell (Paul Pitman); Hana-Maria Pravda (Emma Cohen); Michael Gover (Arthur Russell); Eileen Helsby (Charmian Wentworth); Hugh Walters (Vic Thatcher); Tanya Ronder (Lizzie Willoughby); Stephen Dudley (John Millon); Ben (Ben the dog)
GUEST CAST: Richard Heffer (Jimmy Garland); Annie Irving (Ruth); Harry Markham (Burton)
UNCREDITED CAST: Harry Oaten (Man with scythe)
OB RECORDING: 13 - 17 June 1975
LOCATIONS: Hampton Court, Hope-under-Dinmore, Herefs; Vauld House Farm, Marden, Herefs

SYNOPSIS: Greg has traded 200 gallons of petrol for supplies that include some bad seed. Abby, who is clearly tired of the pressures of command, absents herself from the ensuing argument. When further problems are brought to her attention, she has a heart-to-heart with Jenny and reveals that she is considering looking for Peter again. During their conversation, she correctly guesses that Jenny is pregnant. A group of survivors led by a man named Burton arrive on the main driveway; they have been driven from their settlement. They have a young woman with them whom they want to leave at the Grange; she is very sick and the community decides that they cannot risk taking her in. The incident prompts discussion about defence, leading Greg to mention the possibility of a federation of communities. It is agreed that a meeting should be convened at the Grange to discuss these aims and that Arthur should spread the word by cycling to various local settlements. The sick woman is discovered, abandoned, at the back of the Grange; despite Greg's protestations, Abby is adamant that she be taken inside and cared for. Abby leaves and is reunited with Jimmy Garland, who since their last encounter has taken over the Waterhouse estate. After Greg injures himself sawing wood, it transpires that the recovering sick woman is a one-time medical student named Ruth. She advises Jenny on how to dress Greg's wound. At his cottage, Jimmy offers to help Abby with her search for Peter while, back at the Grange, Ruth reveals to Jenny and Greg that she has recently met a boy called Peter Grant. Arthur's cycle trip has been a success and, as the delegates are due to arrive, Abby returns with Garland in tow. Welcoming her back, Jenny tells her that she has some good news.

ANALYSIS: Terry Nation's final script for the series focuses, rather appropriately, on his heroine Abby Grant once again, in order to re-examine her thoughts and feelings now that a significant amount of time has elapsed since the events of "The Fourth Horseman". The episode (initially titled "Directions") is also notable for its preoccupation with the idea of the possible foundation of a federation of communities, the return of Jimmy Garland, and a surprise conclusion to the first series. Although "A Beginning" is full of incident, it lacks the trademark menace and threat of Nation's earlier work for *Survivors* and therefore seems more in keeping with Ronder's and Exton's contributions.

The surprising revelation that Abby's son is alive and well does not actually appear in the episode's camera script. It is therefore all but certain that this last minute change was made by Dudley, as by June 1975 Nation had few remaining connections with the series. It is unknown whether or not Dudley sought Nation's approval for this significant addition to the script, which changes the focus of the episode's conclusion – originally relating more strongly to 'a beginning' for Greg's federation. However, all that was actually specifically dropped from Nation's script was the introduction of two non-speaking characters, Philip Hamilton and Gordon James, who would not have imparted anything of dramatic value other than the fact that they had arrived for the meeting. Although Dudley's motive for instigating this change may simply have been to end the first series on a more memorable and upbeat note, it is also possible that the new finale was added to provide a plausible explanation for Abby's absence from the second series, which had already been commissioned by this time. This latter explanation fits with Carolyn Seymour's view that Dudley had already made the decision to drop her from the show halfway through production of series one. Either way, the fact that

Carolyn Seymour and Richard Heffer. © Anne Christie

Peter is actually alive may be considered to be a little too optimistic a plotline for a series that usually prided itself on its unremitting pessimism.

As this is Abby's swansong, the episode quite rightly brings the first series full circle to resume focus on our heroine's thoughts and feelings. Above all else, the script and the direction demonstrate both how far she has come and what she has left behind. In a beautifully delivered piece of dialogue, Abby states 'I think that's the trouble really. I suddenly realised that whatever we do, however hard we work, there's no going back. What we've got is what we're going to have for the rest of our lifetimes.' She may still miss her late husband David and the life she led before 'like mad,' but it is unmistakeably a very different woman looking back at her from the bedroom mirror than the one she saw in "The Fourth Horseman". Although The Death robbed her of a great deal, it also offered her a unique opportunity to use previously untapped talents that she otherwise may never have known existed. It also, of course, brought her into contact with Jimmy Garland.

Since we last met Garland, he has won his war. This time around he is providing some much needed mental and physical solace and a sympathetic ear, rather than a daring rescue, although the introduction of Garland's horse, Jasper, ensures that a parallel can be drawn with a knight in shining armour atop his white charger. Abby and Jimmy meet on far more equal terms than before, having spent recent months leading their respective settlements. Both understand the pressures of command, although Garland is one step ahead in that he has already had the sense to set aside his cottage for those times when he needs to think or be alone. Garland appears to know an awful lot about human nature, and one suspects after a while that anyone might become irritated with his omniscient demeanour. His views that Abby should be true to herself and that there is more to life than mere survival are themes later revisited in a more spiritual sense in "By Bread Alone". There is a strong chemistry between Abby and Garland, both appearing to be very believably comfortable with each other; this was, according to Seymour, made easy because she found Richard Heffer very attractive indeed. Proximity to Garland also makes Abby noticeably less arch and more vulnerable than she would allow in anyone else's company (and therefore perhaps more interesting to watch).

Behind the scenes, the extent of Abby's proximity to Garland caused problems for director Pennant Roberts when he received a last minute instruction from Ronnie Marsh (Andrew Osborn's successor as BBC Head of Series) that on no account should a scene between Garland and Abby be shot in bed, as planned, because the couple weren't married to each other! Roberts remembers he protested to Dudley that 'the chances of Abby simultaneously finding Garland and a priest was in *Survivors* terms remote in the extreme, but to no avail.' In order to avoid a three-minute underrun, it was decided to stage the seduction scene on the sofa downstairs instead. Roberts recalls that, ultimately, Marsh's interference actually had the opposite effect to that intended, as the sequence turned out to be more erotic than it would have been otherwise!

Despite the many benefits of Abby's return to centre-stage, the initial depiction of the community's dependence on her feels like it is over-played and artificially employed to explain Abby's decision to take off, rather than a true reflection of her position at the Grange.

Annie Irving (Ruth). © Lucy Fleming

For instance: Arthur would be far more likely to ask Paul about the cattle or, as an accomplished businessman, offer a solution to the problem himself; while Lizzie would surely seek a less volatile member of the community than Abby to ask to attend the scene of devastation at the chicken run. These scenarios also don't quite ring true, because Abby has already been firmly established as only a nominal figurehead – as Jenny points out: 'You may be Queen of the Castle, but it's Greg who actually runs it.'

The experiences of Burton and the other members of the Goston community prompt Nation (through Paul) to use a fox's attack on the community's chickens as an effective analogy for the vulnerable situation of every undefended settlement in the post-Death world. When Arthur asks, 'How do we stop being chickens?' Greg's answer is, 'We all join forces into some sort of alliance or federation.' This proposal marks the first significant reference to an idea that will later dominate the series, although here, as Abby observes, the initial emphasis is upon mutual defence rather than any other benefit. However, the achievements of this first meeting of local representatives at the Grange are plainly as inconsiderable as those in "A Friend In Need". This is evidenced by the fact that, after the fire that opens the second series, Greg looks for help beyond their neighbouring settlements to Whitecross, a community that Arthur clearly did not visit during his initial cycle ride.

Although her presence here is low-key and gives no clues as to how prominent the character will become, the introduction of medical student Ruth Anderson would pay dramatic dividends in the second series, allowing thorough exploration of themes such as: the scarcity of doctors; the lack of contraception; and the ever-present threat of disease. Despite the fact that Ruth's primary function in "A Beginning" appears to be to reveal that Peter is alive, Nation's original intention was simply to use her as a catalyst for Abby's temporary departure from the Grange and to reinforce the issue of how lost the survivors are without medical expertise – a reality last discussed in "Genesis". Jenny's and Charmian's conversation relating to this issue – not to mention Greg's accident – feels somewhat contrived in the light of the subsequent revelation that Ruth was a medical student.

No doubt all three series of *Survivors* would have had a markedly different atmosphere had production begun in the second half of 1974, as was originally planned, with each series reaching its conclusion in the winter months. In the case of "A Beginning", it is certainly difficult to imagine the episode without its intensely summery feel courtesy of a late June recording date, with Pennant Roberts's direction making the most of Hampton Court's picturesque surroundings.

Fittingly, "A Beginning" sets in motion more storylines than it resolves. However, this is indeed the end of the line for series heroine Abby Grant, a handful of other characters and the iconic Hampton Court location. Nation's script makes for a suitable and – thanks to some significant last-minute additions – uplifting conclusion to the first series, leaving the viewer waiting for the next with much anticipation. *AP*

SERIES 1: REVIEW

A huge gulf separates the worlds glimpsed in the opening and closing episodes of *Survivors'* first series. Although the time that has elapsed on screen is only a matter of months — marked by the shift from the chill of an overcast winter to the warmth of a sunbathed spring — a profound dramatic transformation has taken place.

What began in "The Fourth Horseman" with the terrifying and total collapse of modern human society, concluded in the events of "A Beginning" with a surge of optimism about the opportunities this new and scarcely populated world holds. *Survivors'* opening episode was about loss, grief, fear and shock; the final episode of series one is marked by expectation, even by a sense of excitement and anticipation, about future possibilities. At the end of "The Fourth Horseman", the survivors stand bereft, isolated and full of uncertainty and dread; their old world consumed by The Death. In spite of the many challenges and tragedies visited on them in the ensuing months, by the time of "A Beginning", the series' central characters have become able to contemplate and plan for a future for themselves and for those around them (on whom they now recognise they have become mutually dependant).

Central to the success of *Survivors'* first series is the strength of the triumvirate of leading characters at its core. Terry Nation's characterisation of his three leads is perceptively judged: Abby, the privileged housewife and homemaker, who overcomes her grief and fear to rise to the challenges of leadership in the desperate conditions of the new world; Jenny, the young city woman desperate to join up with others in the days following The Death, who later finds herself far more resilient and capable than she had believed; Greg, the headstrong loner, who finds an unexpected connection with them both, and who takes on fresh responsibilities and risks to protect their shared community. The casting of each of these recognisably flawed central characters proved to be inspired, and in the hands of skilled writers and accomplished directors, Abby, Jenny and Greg secure that sense of audience identification vital to *Survivors'* success.

The series remained permeated by a sense of melancholy and an often harsh view of human temperament; nonetheless the contrast in mood and atmosphere between the opening and closing scenes of *Survivors'* first series could hardly be more starkly evoked. This change is epitomised by Jenny's pregnancy. Whether her impending motherhood was planned or unintentional, the shift in Jenny's perspective that this symbolises is enormous. In the events of "Corn Dolly", Jenny spoke of her dread about the idea of becoming a mother in this new world. 'Survival', she confided to Abby, 'can wait for a bit.' Now Jenny faces the thought of motherhood with stoicism, if still with anxiety. The change is also expressed in the arrival of a doctor for the community, in the shape of former medical student Ruth; the unexpectedly joyous resolution of Abby's search for Peter; and the arrival of delegates from other settlements for a conference on forming a defensive alliance – hopefully the first stage in a new process of federation and interdependence.

It says much about the storytelling talents of the show's scriptwriters and directors that this change in the emotional ambience of *Survivors*, although compressed, rarely feels artificial or forced. With the commissioning of a second series not guaranteed until the closing scripts were in front of the cameras, it was only prudent to provide a sense of closure for *Survivors'* principal characters and storylines. It remains clear, however, that in the unlikely event that the BBC had decided in the summer of 1975 to cancel its ratings-winning end-of-the-world drama, *Survivors* would have 'worked' as a satisfying single series drama; its future narrative left to the viewers' imagination. "A Beginning" could have quite effectively (if very disappointingly) served as *Survivors*' end.

Amongst its small-screen contemporaries, the first series of *Survivors* was also distinguished by the surprising variety of drama that it offered. Jack Ronder's four scripts were rich in thoughtful reflections on the predicaments that the survivors faced; his storylines always infused with an impressive emotional depth. Nation's own scripts tended to prioritise instead action and adventure themes, putting the clash of characters at the heart of the episodes' drama. Clive Exton's twin contributions to the series were themselves diverse. The opening segments of "Spoil of War" shares Ronder's interest in the question of the survivors' reactions to the traumas they have all endured; the armed stand-off that dominates the second half of the episode bears many of the hallmarks of a classic Nation story. Exton's electrifying "Law and Order", in contrast, has an almost theatrical ambience, as it inverts the 'whodunit' formula in an intensely claustrophobic tale of guilt and deception. What the first series made clear was that there was to be no simple *Survivors* 'formula', and that the premise could support storytelling of many different styles and approaches.

Behind the scenes, series one of *Survivors* came to be defined by the very different visions of creator Terry Nation and producer Terence Dudley. Nation had developed an incredibly strong premise, and introduced a rich ensemble of effective and engaging characters. Although Nation accepted that Dudley was an accomplished and capable producer, he became exasperated at what he saw as the latter's inability to appreciate the show's full dramatic potential. Nation enjoyed recounting the story of Dudley's visit to his home, during pre-production, to discuss the development of the series. He recalled with disbelief Dudley's apparent assertion that, even after The Death had decimated the world, the BBC would still be broadcasting. Whether apocryphal or not, the anecdote illustrated how far Nation came to feel alienated from Dudley. Yet in his work on the series itself, there are few signs of Dudley seeking to put such counter-intuitive and absurd ideas into practice, and a wealth of evidence of his astute creative judgment and appreciation of *Survivors*' real worth. Dudley was not simply, as Nation seemed keen to depict him, an overbearing technician with delusions of grandeur. He was not a manager devoid of vision, but a figure who used his pre-eminent status on the series to press home his own sense of how it should be realised on screen.

They perceived their respective roles markedly differently. Nation considered the writer's brief self-evident – to prepare the best scripts possible – and the producer's role as being to secure the translation of the writer's vision to the screen. Any revisions that a script editor might suggest should only be, in Nation's reasoning, to enhance the scriptwriter's original intent. Dudley, in contrast, considered that the producer's remit was to conceive and clarify the 'essence' of the show for which they were responsible, and to identify those elements that had to be prioritised if it was to realise its implicit potential. For Dudley, where a scriptwriter appeared to misconceive or misrepresent the imperatives of the series, it was self-evident that his work had to be redrafted.

Dudley's forceful approach helped to give the first series its clarity, edge and compelling dramatic focus. Nation was also reluctant to credit Dudley for his success in managing the production process, and for ensuring that his teams delivered their set of thirteen episodes by deadline and on budget, overcoming constraints of time and money that would have made many of his contemporaries blanch. There can be little doubt that Dudley was no diplomat, and the often-frustrating business of compromise and accommodation with others did not come naturally to him. His forthrightness and sense of self-belief led to irreconcilable conflicts with lead actress Carolyn Seymour and scriptwriter Clive Exton as well as with Nation himself. Dudley's reluctance to negotiate a way out of conflict helps to explain an apparent paradox of the production process on all three series of *Survivors*: that those with whom he did not cross swords found Dudley a congenial and supportive colleague; while many of those with whom he clashed considered him a stubborn and intractable opponent, used to getting his own way.

Had Nation and Dudley been able to resolve their differences, and found a way to work collaboratively that merged their creative approaches, *Survivors* would certainly have evolved along rather different lines. Yet circumstance made such a reconciliation unlikely. First, the lack of a script editor on the show (a situation of which Dudley himself approved) meant that there was no buffer or middle-man between the producer and Nation and his fellow scriptwriters. A resourceful script editor might have been able to prevent relationships between Dudley and his writing team from corroding so badly. Secondly, there was the distance that Nation kept (or was encouraged to keep) from the production process. Had Nation ventured from his home in Kent to press his case at production meetings in London, his ideas would potentially have carried more weight and won some useful allies. Yet Nation, reluctant to be drawn into the fray in this way, conceded that he found such battles draining. With Nation absent, the balance of power between him and Dudley remained decidedly uneven. Thirdly, there was the important issue of personality. Nation remained fond of his maxim that the scriptwriter should sign off on his episodes as he submitted them, thus avoiding the disappointment of seeing others 'tamper with' and 'ruin' his work. In truth, Nation often remained sensitive to the criticism of his scripts that inevitably still reached him. When such criticism was voiced in the direct and self-assured terms that Dudley favoured, the results were unlikely to be harmonious. In their recent book *Terry Nation* (2004), authors Jonathan Bignell and Andrew O'Day suggest that Nation chose not even to reply to Dudley's correspondence. The lack of an intermediary; Nation's detachment from the production; and a sharp clash of personalities, all conspired to push their working relationship past the point of no return.

Nation did not hold back from blaming Dudley for his departure from the show, insisting that with Dudley at the helm there was no prospect of him continuing to write for *Survivors*. Nation was less vocal, however, in outlining his own alternative vision of the series' next steps, which he could have contrasted with the clarity of Dudley's own. Although he disliked intensely the direction in which Dudley would take the series, Nation never fully explained his own counter-proposals. It is possible that the depth of Nation's alienation rendered such musings irrelevant – Nation felt there was no prospect of his ideas coming to fruition under Dudley's aegis. Nevertheless, the conflict between the two was again unevenly matched: the BBC Drama Department had to choose between the complaints and dissatisfaction of Nation, and the outlines, characters and situations drawn up by Dudley and his remaining scriptwriter Jack Ronder. The BBC could have chosen to replace Dudley with a producer that Nation felt better understood the show. Instead, a disgruntled Nation found no support for his criticisms, and thus decided to submit no further scripts to the series. The *Survivors* novel that Nation would go on to write the following year showed one possible alternative conception of where he thought the storyline might involve. Nation, though, would have harboured few illusions that his tale of the trans-European quest of a band of nomadic survivors was anything that BBC budgets could have translated to the small screen. It is also important to acknowledge that, as series two of *Survivors* entered pre-production in the autumn of 1975, Nation had effectively 'moved on' – having won a commission from the BBC for a new thirteen-episode space adventure entitled *Blake's 7*.

Nation drew one clear lesson from his experience on *Survivors*. When it came to *Blake's 7*, he decided that the only way to ensure effective series-long control over the nature of the show was to script the entire first series himself. As for *Survivors*, the BBC clearly felt that the series was strong enough to survive the departure of both its creator, two of its three scriptwriters and its lead actress. Dudley himself remained undaunted by the prospect of change, confident that the strength of the series and the clarity of his vision would more than compensate for the various departures and losses with which it had to cope.

The first thirteen episodes of the show must be recognised as a remarkable chapter in television history. Despite the high death count and the powerful sense of sadness and gloom that imbued the series, it remained concerned with the challenges of survival, not the inevitability of death. Yet *Survivors* could itself not remain in stasis. It had to put down more substantial roots and take forward the struggle to secure a future for those that had endured the aftermath of The Death. As would soon become apparent, the next series of *Survivors* would come to rely upon a markedly different set of survival instincts.

Ian and Lucy at Church House Farm. © Lucy Fleming

SERIES 2 (1976)

Series Creator
Terry Nation

Producer
Terence Dudley

Main Cast
Greg Preston: Ian McCulloch
Charles Vaughan: Denis Lill
Jenny Richards: Lucy Fleming
Ruth Anderson: Celia Gregory
Pet Simpson: Lorna Lewis
Hubert Goss: John Abineri

Writers
Jack Ronder (2.1, 2.3, 2.4, 2.6)
Don Shaw (2.2, 2.5)
Ian McCulloch (2.7)
Martin Worth (2.8, 2.12, 2.13)
Roger Parkes (2.9, 2.11)
Roger Marshall (2.10)

Directors
Eric Hills (2.1, 2.7, 2.9, 2.12)
Pennant Roberts (2.2, 2.4, 2.8, 2.11)
Terence Williams (2.3, 2.5, 2.6, 2.10, 2.13)

Title Music
Anthony Isaac

Production Assistants
Michael McDermott (2.1, 2.7, 2.9, 2.12)
Edwina Craze (2.2)
Derek Nelson (2.3, 2.5, 2.6, 2.10, 2.13)
Jeremy Owen (2.4)
Tony Virgo (2.8, 2.11)

Production Unit Managers
Michael Bartley
Landon Revitt (2.1, 2.2, 2.6)

Designers
Ian Watson (2.1, 2.2, 2.5-2.13)
Peter Kindred (2.3)
Geoffrey Winslow (2.3)
Paul Allen (2.4)

Designer's Assistants
David Wilson (2.2, 2.5, 2.7, 2.8)
Ken Ledsham (2.4)

Cameramen (VT)
Frank Hudson (2.1, 2.2, 2.5-2.8, 2.10, 2.12, 2.13)
Simon Fone (2.1, 2.2, 2.5, 2.6, 2.8, 2.10, 2.11, 2.13)
Derek Wright (2.7, 2.11, 2.12)

Sound
Ian Leiper (2.1, 2.7, 2.11)
Vic Godrich (2.2, 2.8, 2.12)
Alan Fogg (2.3, 2.4, 2.9)
Robin Luxford (2.5, 2.6, 2.10, 2.13)
Peter Bailey (2.7, 2.12)
John Nottage (2.7, 2.12)

Lighting
Clive Potter (2.1, 2.7, 2.12)
Hubert Cartwright (2.2, 2.8, 2.11)
Howard King (2.3, 2.4, 2.9)
John Wilson (2.5, 2.13)
Bill Jones (2.6, 2.10, 2.13)

Film Cameraman
Godfrey Johnson (2.3, 2.4, 2.9)

Film Editor
Bernard Ashby (2.3, 2.4, 2.9)

Senior Cameraman
Colin Reid (2.9)

Assistant Floor Managers
Michael Morris, Robert Gabriel, Tony Virgo,
Liz Mace, Michael Brayshaw, Bill Harman,
Carolyn Southwick, Maggy Campbell,
Marion Wishart

Director's Assistants
Winifred Hopkins, Adele Paul, Judy Munk

Technical Managers
Peter Greenyer, George Jakins, Brendan
Carr, John Sterling, John Wilson

Vision Mixers
John Barclay, Nick Lake, Shirley Coward,
Paul Cole, Fred Law, Sue Thorne, James
Gould

Costumes
June Hudson (2.1, 2.6, 2.8, 2.10, 2.12)
Janet Tharby (2.2-2.5, 2.7, 2.9, 2.11, 2.13)

Dressers
Liz Lintott, David Terry, Kate Osborne,
Bob Springett, Mel Freedman, Jack Duggan

Make Up
Eileen Mair

Make Up Assistant
Val Keen

Floor Assistants
Jackie Spilling, Val Birch

Graphics
Dick Bailey

Visual Effects
Peter Day, John Horton

Scene Crew Supervisors
Les Runham, Frank Lowry, Alf Bringlow

Prop Buyer
Roger Williams

Crew
18

Secretary
Sue Robinson

Armourer
Jack Wells

SERIES 2: PRODUCTION

Following Nation's departure, *Survivors'* second series saw it take a new direction based on deeper anthropological concerns and a desire to bring scientific and agricultural accuracy to its developing narrative. These changes were widely applauded by the TV critics of 1976, who found the characters and situations to be more wholly convincing than those of the first series. The British public appeared similarly impressed, as viewing figures – which were as important to programme-makers in the seventies as they are today – rose by several million.

Terence Dudley was first given the green light for a second series while the last few episodes of the first series were still being recorded at Hampton Court. By this time, work on refurbishing the property as a business centre was well-advanced (the estate having been bought before filming on *Survivors* began) and the production team had to negotiate a strict recording schedule with the developers in order that much of the building's interior could be used unchanged in the remaining episodes. However, in terms of his plans for the second series, Dudley did not consider this situation to be a problem, having already decided that an entirely new location was required in order that certain themes could be explored in more depth.

A particularly pressing concern for Dudley was the composition of the new series' regular cast. Carolyn Seymour recalls that she and Dudley did not get on 'from the get-go' and that she 'was fighting the producer all the time' over matters such as: the plight of the extras during the cold winter months; the ending of "Law and Order"; and her request for better facilities for herself and Lucy Fleming. However, as Seymour was playing the central heroine and as she

Terence Dudley observes rehearsals for the second series at the Acton Hilton. © Denis Lill

cared so much about the part of Abby, she was both surprised and upset to learn that she was not going to be contracted to return. Dudley, who had clearly had enough of the reportedly constant verbal sparring with his leading lady, had elected to bring another character into the fray instead. During production on "Corn Dolly", Dudley had enjoyed both the performance and company of Denis Lill – with whom he had previously worked on *The Regiment*, in which Lill had played the regular character Captain (later Major) Alfred Slingsby – and consequently decided to bring the charismatic Welshman Charles Vaughan back into the series. Dudley felt confident that the new series could work equally well as the first with two male leads. This decision was not popular with Ian McCulloch, who – although he had nothing against Lill personally – was unhappy to find himself sharing the limelight with another prominent male character, feeling as though he 'had built something, which was being taken away.' He also missed the chemistry that he had shared with Seymour and the cohesive triumvirate of Abby, Greg

90

and Jenny, which did so much to define the first series. Lucy Fleming was also affected by the rethink, but not only in terms of the loss of Seymour, with whom she had become close. Having enjoyed her prominent role in "Something of Value" immensely, Fleming asked Dudley to give Jenny a bit more action along the same lines. However, her request did not fit with Dudley's new formulation of the series, and Fleming instead found her character saddled with the

Stephen Tate (Alan). © Denis Lill

children even more, a situation that later prompted the actress to recognise that 'the second series wasn't great for Jenny,' as she felt that she became 'the wet one in the background.' Conversely, the dramatic potential of affording increased screen time to medical student Ruth Anderson – given the ever-present threat of disease in the world of the survivors – had not been lost on Dudley. Ruth had been briefly introduced in "A Beginning", but Dudley now felt it necessary to recast the role, dropping Annie Irving, perhaps as a reaction to continued criticism that *Survivors* was almost entirely populated by middle-class characters. Pennant Roberts, who had already counselled against losing Seymour, was now charged with the task of telling Annie Irving the bad news. For the second series, Ruth would now be played by the more bohemian and down-to-earth Celia Gregory, who up until that time had primarily worked in the theatre and was keen to gain more television experience. Her most recent television role had been in an episode of the 1975 BBC spy drama *Quiller*.

His principals in place, Dudley now set about making significant alterations to the supporting cast. Although several characters needed to be written out between series due to unavailability, others were also removed because it was felt that there was no place for them in the newly-envisaged scenario. One such casualty was Hana-Maria Pravda (Emma), whose departure caused considerable torment to Jack Ronder – now the series' principal scriptwriter – and soured his relationship with Dudley. Ronder had felt personally obliged to inform a concerned Pravda that her contract would not be renewed before the producer had spoken to her. Although Dudley had already set up a plausible explanation for Abby's absence from the new series by adding news of Peter's survival to Nation's script for "A Beginning", he still needed a credible narrative solution by which the series could lose several supporting players and relocate the action elsewhere. Together with Ronder, he came up with the idea of a terrible fire that would consume not only the Grange, but also the unwanted or unavailable characters. The tragedy would also bring some much-needed dramatic import to the opening episode of the new series, now that – in narrative terms – there was some considerable distance from the terrors of The Death itself. As a result of this scripting, the series now required a new location to double as the burnt-out Grange, and on a production recce in early June a suitable manor house with a ruined wing was found at Michaelchurch Escley near Hay-on-Wye.

Although the production of *Survivors* (both the completion of the first series and the

John Abineri in Monmouth. © Anne Christie

direction of the second) was a number one priority for Dudley at this time, he still managed concurrently to put together a treatment for a potential thirteen-part BBC series entitled *Bodyguard*. The plot concerned a private security organisation operating under the front of Eversley Insurance Brokers Ltd. The first episode, "Free Sword Hand", which Dudley had set out in some detail, featured the vetting of John Regan (35, unmarried, tough, an ex-professional soldier and cheerful cynic) for his potential as a bodyguard, and his first meetings with firm founder Geoffrey Parker and sophisticated love interest Joanna Gresham. Dudley was understandably keen to create and write (at least part of) a new series for the BBC, and was disappointed to hear in late summer 1975 that *Bodyguard* 'was not the kind of series that Controllers were looking for.'

By this time, Dudley had worked out the basic premise for an interesting new direction for *Survivors*, which was in keeping with his personal motivation to tell stories that concentrated more on the characters and rather less on those action-adventure elements that had featured heavily in Terry Nation's scripts. In essence, the survivors' natural and inevitable return to the land would provide the new context for the drama, which would crucially attempt to be more attuned to real science and to further tap into society's burgeoning interest in self-sufficiency in a much more direct way than had been attempted in the first series. One vital way in which Dudley intended to achieve these key objectives was by assembling writers for the new series who possessed relevant interests: Ronder – the only one of the original three to continue on the series – had worked in the chemical industry for many years, while Don Shaw, Martin Worth and Roger Parkes had all worked with Dudley before on the ecological thriller series *Doomwatch*, for which plots were extrapolated from current scientific fact. In line with this attempt to achieve a new level of authenticity, Ronder duly produced notes for the series' production team detailing exactly how to make soap and surgical spirit from scratch, and the other writers were encouraged to discover similar activities that would be key to the survivors' new existence, with the proviso that where possible corners should not be cut for the sake of the narrative. Martin Worth's scripts were directly influenced by John and Sally Seymour's in vogue and best-selling *Self-Sufficiency* (1973). Sections of the book were even directly referenced in his original scripts (for example, the scenes in "Over the Hills" in which Pet makes cottage cheese and Charles fashions a large fish hook were realised in line with the detailed descriptions of these processes given in the book). Worth also ensured that Greg's PROMIFR (PROtotype Muck Into Fuel

Refinery) was similarly bona fide, basing it on a methane-producing contraption ('System II') devised by a company called Bioga Plant.

Crucially, the new set of writers also shared Dudley's passion for drama centred on human interest, of which "Greater Love", "Face of the Tiger" and "By Bread Alone" stand as fine examples. Responsible for two of these episodes was Don Shaw, who was very much an up-and-coming writer at the time – much sought after because of his contributions to *The Wednesday Play* and *Play for Today*. He remembers that Dudley '... really, really appreciated writers; I think he trusted you, and he picked writers that he could trust.' Interestingly, he also recalls that the initial plot and character outlines '... were not detailed, they were more sketchy and open-ended. I met Terry and a couple of the other writers. We'd have a parley for two or three hours and then go away and do it.' Fellow scriptwriter Roger Parkes remembers that to write for the series, one required '... the scientific interest which would inspire you to find plots which were different and acceptable,' but that one also '... needed to be interested and fascinated by people and the things which brought them into conflict, passion and life.' Undoubtedly Dudley felt that with the establishment of a more obviously anthropological and sociological premise, *Survivors* had the opportunity to strike a deeper emotional chord with a loyal and hopefully larger audience. Another key characteristic of the new series' approach was a willingness to explore more complex and challenging philosophies and ideas. Don Shaw remembers that it was this aspect that made *Survivors* '... such a great series... I wrote for an intelligent audience. I wasn't writing down. I was writing at my own level... It was very cerebral in a way, because it made people think, which was what was intended.'

Another new writer on the second series was none other than *Survivors* actor Ian McCulloch. His debut script arose from a discussion with Dudley during which he asserted that he could write better episodes for the series than some of those he had worked on thus far. Dudley decided to give his leading man a chance, but pointed out that if he didn't like his script, he wouldn't buy it. McCulloch consequently set about writing a story set on a houseboat, but soon dropped that idea in favour of a suspenseful tale concerning the threat of a sniper. This script became "A Friend In Need", which alongside Parkes' "The Chosen" adhered more to Nation's writing style than Dudley's new approach. Roger Marshall's sole *Survivors* contribution, "Parasites", and Ronder's epic two-parter, "Lights of London", appear to be more of a fusion of these two polarised styles.

The idea of recording the second series at Callow Hill – an isolated hilltop farm near Monmouth – was given to Dudley by the author Ronald Higgins, who lived nearby. His interest piqued, Dudley investigated and quickly realised that it would be the perfect setting for his new series of *Survivors*. Not only was Callow ideal in terms of the technical limitations of television production – as a single location at which almost all of the series could be recorded – but also in view of the stunning visuals that it would afford. Dudley and Ronder – who first visited the hill in September 1975 with his wife Anne, at Dudley's suggestion – soon learned that the place was steeped in a fascinating history. The 19th Century ancestors of Callow's inhabitants – the large David family – had been fantastically wealthy Armenians who had come over to England from India and married into an upper-class but poor local family. The great-grandfather of the five brothers who were now living on the hill had made his money in the jute trade and London property, but by 1975 there was very little left in the family's coffers. To make matters worse, the philanthropic father of the five brothers (who had also brought a total of nine orphans to live at Callow) had died intestate ten years previously, leaving his sons to feud over the land. It was this volatile and colourful scenario that greeted

Dudley and the Ronders on their visits. In a far more dilapidated state then than today, the forty-acre estate was littered with ramshackle wooden dwellings – all of which had gone up without planning permission – and several original buildings that were crumbling, having been left to rot. At the time, a total of about thirty to forty people were living on the hill, and the sprawling grounds were a paradise for the estate's many youngsters, who were either not encouraged to go to school or irregularly taught at home. The way of life there was essentially that of a bohemian commune, with many of the residents having bought into a self-sufficient hippie lifestyle. What they found there particularly inspired the Ronders, with Anne recording in her 1975 diary: 'The place was extraordinary and we wondered what real-life explosions of social chemistry could occur when the circus caravanserai of television crew and actors arrived and mingled with the exotic and isolated inhabitants of the neglected hilltop farm.' Many of the hill's residents, particularly the children, were excited at the prospect of *Survivors* being recorded in and around their homes, having faithfully tuned in to the first series; however, it is certain that the impact that the production would have on their daily lives was severely underestimated, and the six months during which *Survivors'* cast and crew were based there was set to form a turbulent and memorable chapter in Callow Hill's history.

As soon as the second series' location had been finalised, Dudley encouraged all his scriptwriters to visit Callow Hill in order that their work could be informed and inspired by the place. Martin Worth in particular found it 'a joy to be able to write in this way' knowing that the exact gates, paths and trees that he had seen, and subsequently written about, would make it into the finished episodes.

By November 1975, Dudley had devised a set of briefing notes entitled 'Survivors II,' which were distributed to the new series' directors and writers. The document detailed: those survivors who possessed specialist skills; where the characters would live in terms of the dwellings at Callow Hill; and the key events of the first two episodes. Also included were notes on the state of play at the start of the series in terms of available supplies, in order to ensure an agreed goal of accuracy on matters such as: how much petrol the community have left; how they made fire and ironed their clothes; and their future plans for development. Jack Ronder was to write four of the first six episodes of the second series, including the decisive opening episode "Birth of a Hope", and was therefore charged with the significant responsibility of introducing the new set-up and also creating a new group of supporting characters. He based kind-hearted and affectionate Pet Simpson – the community's matriarch and Charles's common-law wife – on Cherry David, the wife of Robin David (one of the five brothers). She would be played by American actress Lorna Lewis, whose previous work was predominantly theatre-based (including a performance on Broadway alongside Albert Finney in *Luther*). Her TV roles included an appearance in *The Wild, Wild West* (1965-70) on US television, and after her arrival in the UK, a small part in an episode of Dudley's *Doomwatch* (Miss Brandon in "Deadly Dangerous Tomorrow"). She watched the first series of *Survivors* when it went out and, noticing Dudley's name on the end credits, wrote to him asking if there might be a part in it for her. After a subsequent interview she won the part. Hubert Goss, a dishevelled, trouble-making shepherd, was another Ronder creation who would initially fulfil the same narrative function as the late Tom Price, before undergoing something of a transformation in the final series. He would be played by character-actor John Abineri, who prior to *Survivors* had given an Emmy-nominated performance as Chingachgook in the 1971 BBC adaptation of *Last of the Mohicans* and guest starred in two *Doctor Who* tales: as General Carrington in "The Ambassadors of Death" (1970) and Railton in "Death to the Daleks" (1974). Other new characters included: the aptly named carpenter Jack Wood, played by Gordon Salkilld – a relative unknown who had taken up acting late in life and who is now probably best known as Holly's chess partner, Gordon, in the *Red Dwarf* episode "Better Than Life" (1988); and the reclusive herbalist Mina, played by Delia Paton. Paton remembers that she was probably offered the part because of her performance as Mme Meister in the acclaimed 1974 BBC2 series *Microbes and Men*: 'Not an awfully big part but a rather intense character, so I could see why they thought of me for Mina.' Upon reading the scripts, Paton decided to make the character Welsh – 'I thought that if I adopted a Celtic accent for the part that would also make her more intense' – and asked a Welsh friend to give her some coaching before production began. Paton, like Lewis, was already known to Dudley through a role in *Doomwatch* (Mrs Norman in "Friday's Child").

From an early stage in the planning process, Dudley recognised that the production order would necessarily have to differ from the eventual broadcast order, owing to the temporary unavailability of Lucy Fleming – who, like her character, was due to give birth in late December 1975 – and the fact that Jenny

Denis Lill at Callow Hill. © Lucy Fleming

would have to appear in the opening instalment. The solution was to record "The Witch" first, in early January, adding an explanation that Jenny was away on an expedition to the Cheshire salt pans. Don Shaw's "Greater Love" came next, which for the most part didn't require Jenny to leave her bed – and was set to include Fleming's baby Diggory, born on 20 December 1975, who it had been decided would play Jenny's baby Paul – while "Birth of a Hope", which required a more active role from Fleming, was to be recorded third. Given that the second series episodes would be broadcast in a different order to that in which they were made, overall continuity was more difficult to maintain than it had been on the first series. Dudley oversaw these complexities and would advise the writer if he needed to insert a scene or dialogue into their script connecting their storyline to the preceding or the following episode (for example, the addition to "Face of the Tiger" of the scene in which Jenny tells Greg how frightened she was when he was away during the events of "Lights of London", and Greg's ensuing plea to Jenny that she should think about going away on the next salt expedition).

In his script for "Greater Love", Don Shaw had the task of writing out Paul Pitman, played by Christopher Tranchell. The actor had become disillusioned with the direction taken by the latter half of the first series and had asked for a swift exit. It is somewhat ironic that his decision to leave was prompted by specific concerns over the absence of themes such as getting back to nature and a more thorough depiction of human relationships, given that it is

The lawn party in "Over the Hills". © Anne Christie

exactly these elements that unquestionably define the second series. Nevertheless, Tranchell regarded his tragic exit as 'rather glorious.'

Both Pennant Roberts and Terence Williams would return to direct further episodes, while Gerald Blake was replaced by Eric Hills, who had known Dudley since the latter's first day at the BBC when Hills worked as his assistant. He had previously directed episodes of both *Doomwatch* and *Out of the Unknown*. Williams and Hills gained affectionate epithets during their work on the second series. Williams became known as 'Wet-weather Williams' due to the fact that his shoots were invariably characterised by torrential rain, while Eric Hills, who could often be seen in his trademark bobble hat running backwards and forwards between the scanner van and the shooting location, was dubbed 'The Road Runner'.

Rehearsals were held in Acton for the first few episodes; however, as the production progressed, the remainder of the series would be shot 'as live' on location. As director Pennant Roberts recalls: 'Once the principal actors had travelled to Monmouth to shoot, it made little sense to call them back again to North Acton to work in a rehearsal room. The regulars had five days between episodes to prepare for the next – four rehearsal days and a day off. Apart from the travel cost and relocation hassle involved in bringing them to and fro, they would have lost a full day's rehearsal out of the five-day turnaround.' During the January recording of the first production block at Callow Hill, the cast and crew found themselves at the mercy of the elements, the windswept hilltop affording little shelter. However, they were regularly plied with tremendous amounts of food supplied from large catering vans, which were also frequented by Callow's many children – who Frances David remembers were turned away at first, but eventually secured regular meals and began to refuse their mothers' cooking! In keeping with the rest of the run, the production consisted of eleven-hour days and a pressurised four-and-a-half day shoot for each episode (eleven minutes of material being the demanding target for each day). Before recording began, the actors would be taken around the estate with their scripts – which Dudley always ensured were ready on time – by the director as the scenes were blocked. Several dwellings, especially Jenny's and Greg's house – dubbed the 'Do-It-Yourself' house – were quite run-down, and although the actors were certainly conscious of the insects ticking away in the woodwork, for the most part they were not averse to the rough and tumble conditions; indeed, the dressing rooms were located in the stable block. However, the location did cause some technical problems for the directors and their crew, including: the limitations of recording in small rooms; poor sound as a result of plastered walls; and the need to bounce light in order to hide boom shadows. Some difficulties also arose due to the fact that different David brothers owned separate parts of the hill, and permission had to be sought in each case. The hill's central tennis court was used as a parking area for all the vehicles required for the production, including the OB scanner van from which lengths of cable were laid out to the shooting location. It was also here that a monitor was rigged up so that costume and make-up personnel and Callow's many interested residents could see what was being recorded. Don Shaw believes that OB continued to liberate the series: 'You could go out and do the whole thing like film, without the quality of film, but nevertheless with the freedom of film.'

Celia Gregory. © Denis Lill

Throughout the majority of the second series, the cast and crew were put up in nearby Monmouth at the King's Head Hotel, which still overlooks the central market square. The late night drinking at the hotel bar is almost legendary, and led Stephen Tate, who played Alan, to take accommodation elsewhere because 'the drunken nights there nearly killed me.' Only those actors with the strongest constitutions managed to drink every night and still get up in time for the 7:30 am departure, with lines duly memorised ready for rehearsals on camera from 8:30 am. As the series began its broadcast on BBC1, the cast members staying at the

Lorna Lewis. © Denis Lill

hotel would gather together on Wednesday evenings to watch the episodes as a group.

Anne Ronder had chaperoned her daughter Tanya throughout the filming of the first series; an arrangement that had proved hugely disruptive to the Ronders' family life, as Tanya was one of three children. In order to alleviate this situation during production of the second series, Pennant Roberts's wife, Betsan, when not required for her role in the new Welsh language soap opera *Pobol y Cwm*, would come to Monmouth and take over as Tanya's chaperone, enabling Anne to spend more time at home with the rest of her family. As well as being an actress, Betsan was a qualified primary school teacher, and so used to dealing with children.

On the morning of Saturday 24 January, the production nearly suffered a tragic blow when a coach carrying the series' crew from Monmouth to Michaelchurch Escley crashed into a lorry. Seven members of the unit – including make-up artist Eileen Mair and costume

Roy Herrick. © Denis Lill

designer June Hudson – were taken to hospital. Hudson remembers that the crash occurred because the driver had regularly driven along this road and had previously found it to be deserted at that time in the morning. She had hit her mouth on the metal handrail in front of her and damaged half her upper teeth, but considered herself 'quite lucky' as two other people suffered hairline fractures. Those crew members that were not injured seriously soldiered on to achieve half a day's worth of recording for "Birth of a Hope" and were subsequently commended for dedication above and beyond the call of duty.

In February and March 1976, there was a temporary break from recording at Callow Hill, for the filming and studio recording of Ronder's showpiece two-parter "Lights of London" and Roger Parkes' "The Chosen". The "London" episodes were treated as two separate productions, but used many joint locations, such as Hanwell Station and stretches of the London Underground. They also marshalled the same impressive guest cast, who included: Coral Atkins, who by then had embarked on her admirable work caring for disturbed children ('When you have eleven disturbed children to look after, you'll do anything to get away – even wade through rats!') but at the time was still best known for her regular role as Sheila Ashton in ITV's *A Family at War* (1970-72); Nadim Sawalha, who would play Aziz Fekkesh in the Bond film *The Spy Who Loved Me* the following year; Roger Lloyd Pack, who would later find fame as Trigger in *Only Fools and Horses* (1981 onwards); and Wendy Williams (wife of director Hugh David), who had played the prominent guest role Vira in the *Doctor Who* story "The Ark in Space" the previous year and, like Lill, had previously worked with Dudley and Roberts on *The Regiment*. "Lights of London" marked the first return to the capital since "The Fourth Horseman". It featured the revelation that five hundred people are left alive there and a welcome opportunity for Celia Gregory's Ruth to take centre-stage. In front of the camera, these episodes were a happy affair – aside from the fact that all three principal actors had rat phobias – however, behind-the-scenes, there had already been some serious wrangling over scripting. The troubles arose out of Dudley's assessment that the second part of the London tale (originally entitled "Exodus") was below Ronder's usual standard and his decision to take it upon himself to rewrite it. As a member of the Writer's Guild Committee, an infuriated Ronder felt that he had no choice but to report the matter. This incident, coupled with their earlier disagreement over the loss of Hana-Maria Pravda, signalled the end of Ronder's association with the series. Pennant Roberts's subsequent decision to rewrite Dudley's revised "Lights of London Part 2" script in order to make it more in keeping with Ronder's style also provoked a row with the producer, which would ultimately lead the latter to decide not to invite Roberts back for *Survivors'* final series.

The second series began its broadcast run with "Birth of a Hope" on BBC1 on Wednesday 31 March 1976, two weeks after filming had completed on "The Chosen". The new series was previewed in *Radio Times* with a half-page feature written (before his departure) by Jack Ronder, which reminded the viewer of the circumstances of The Death and examined the dangers and shortages that the survivors were now facing a year on. The piece concluded with an observation that reads as wholly in keeping with Nation's original vision: 'The challenge the survivors face now is the need to acquire – and acquire fast – the skills to replace the things that they had always taken for granted. Slowly they are reverting to a medieval way of life.' This feature also provided the ages of the principal survivors for the first time. The new series was previewed in the same issue by Chris Dunkley, who wrote: 'I decided that even if the plots in these programmes were all second rate, which they're not, they would still be well worth watching for the marvellous film of the British countryside.' The episode received a substantial increase in viewing figures compared with the first series, and a largely favourable reaction from the press. Philip Purser wrote in *The Sunday Telegraph* that, 'The first series of *Survivors*, when they were trying to communicate the shock of the epidemic and immediate reactions of those who found themselves still alive, never seemed wholly convincing ... Now that a year or so has passed in story-time, though, and a kind of society is starting to function, the whole make-believe is more complete and satisfying.' Shaun Usher writing in the *Daily Mail* also felt the series was on 'stronger and more convincing ground' and welcomed not only 'the idea of a world virtually untenanted and constantly challenging' but also '... the introduction of Lorna Lewis as the fresh commune's leading lady. She offers such natural warmth and charm that one wonders where casting directors have been hiding her.' Stanley Eveling of *The Scotsman* meanwhile simply stated that it was 'good stuff' and that he was 'hooked already.' Survival expert Anthony Greenbank was also a fan of the new series. Writing in the 15-21 May 1976 issue of the *Radio Times* in a review piece entitled 'Grave New World', Greenbank, like Purser, stated that the present series was 'more convincing', although he cited the representation of the 'conflict between selfishness and selflessness' as the reason why. He felt that the series also 'holds up' because 'it gently breaks the fallacy that to those who feel that humanity is already too bombastic and life too complicated, the dream of a virtually uninhabited, and always challenging, world is Utopia.'

When scriptwriter Martin Worth paid a second visit to Callow Hill in April 1976 (after the second block of recording had commenced) to consider locations for "Over the Hills" and "New World", he was reportedly alarmed at the changes he found there; essentially that the community had shut themselves away in caravans, having moved out of their homes, which were being used for the production. In an interview in 1994, he would go so far as to blame *Survivors* for 'destroying' the community. Although the David family had clearly not realised how disruptive the recording of *Survivors* would be, and have since acknowledged that the 'BBC invasion' opened up their horizons to a world beyond their inward-

Stephen and Tanya at Callow Hill. © Anne Christie

looking existence, the fact is, as Robin David's son, historian Saul, related to *The Sunday Times* in October 2004: 'Everybody fell out ultimately, as my father and his siblings scrabbled over the last bones of a once immense fortune.' Furthermore, many of the cast and crew still talk fondly today of how integrated they became with the colourful and occasionally bizarre inhabitants, with some also recalling how the way of life there really got under their skin: both Denis Lill and John Abineri left their hotel accommodation to go and live on the farm, with the former even turning his hand to restoring a tractor and ploughing a field. Stephen Dudley remembers that: 'The people who lived at Callow Hill were wonderful, and I retain that romantic ideal that stuffy people do of those with the courage to be unconventional. I was lucky enough to see a lamb being born there, and that is a very happy memory.' June Hudson recalls that: 'The actors had a ball and got really involved with the commune members, who were all very friendly – we really got into the spirit of the place.' She adds that: 'It was like a sort of Shangri-La really. You were cut off from ordinary life and ordinary living and we went off to this place where there was that lovely feeling of freedom and doing what you wanted to do.' The integration with the community also extended to the regular use of Callow Hill-ites (as they were often called in the original scripts), particularly the children, as handy extras who were paid a small sum for their involvement. But perhaps the clearest indication of how intertwined the cast and crew had become with the people of the hill can be found in the fact that Ian McCulloch composed a risqué calypso especially for their new friends, and that the end-of-shoot party took the form of a huge joint barn dance.

The second production block at Callow boasted some strong guest appearances by the likes of John Line ("Face of the Tiger"), Kevin McNally and Patrick Troughton (both in "Parasites"). "By Bread Alone" introduced Roy Herrick – another regular (Lt/Capt Jeffrey Sissons) from Dudley's *The Regiment* – as cleric Lewis Fearns, and Stephen Tate playing Alan. Tate began his career in West End musicals, appearing – aged nineteen – as the original Judas in *Jesus Chris Superstar*, before taking his first television roles in *Z Cars* and *The Onedin Line*.

Crew prepare for action during "Over the Hills". © Anne Christie

From "New Arrivals" on, the regular cast was also swelled by some more new – and notably younger – faces, including: Heather Wright, who had already appeared in two feature films, family favourite *The Belstone Fox* (1973) and *Shout at the Devil* (1976) with Roger Moore; June Page, who would later appear in *Doctor Who* (Keara in "Full Circle" (1980)); and, in the smaller role of Dave, a young Peter Duncan, who was still some years off his debut as a *Blue Peter* presenter. As director of "By Bread Alone" and "New Arrivals", Roberts was responsible for casting these new characters, some of whom were deliberately scripted as rather more working class than the original Whitecross survivors. This move was once again an effort to combat the ongoing criticism of the likes of Patrick Stoddart, who had written a review of the new series in the 13 April edition of *The Evening News* entitled 'It's the Poor Wot Gets the Plague!' In it, Stoddart asked: 'Why is it that the working classes always cop the plagues and

Ian McCulloch. © Denis Lill

pestilences of the world? … The survivors are all good-looking middle management tennis club types, all awfully well spoken and very much the right sort. There's the odd yokel of course, just to do the menial work, but the poor old *hoi-polloi* seem to have gone forever.' Writing a month later, Shaun Usher mused as to what the series would have been like had it been 'done by the Americans,' imagining that in non-BBC hands 'invaders from Mars or impossibly groomed sexpots would have made their appearance long ere now.'

As production of the second series reached the halfway mark, Pennant Roberts remembers that Dudley appeared to be becoming disenchanted with his role on location: 'To be fair, there really was little he could actually contribute, because his directors and their teams were running around to get everything in the can in time, and there was little opportunity for him to sit comfortably in the scanner. He became an increasingly lonely figure on the periphery of things, with his family labrador as his only companion.' Dudley's wife, Hilde, was much less in evidence on location during the second series. While waiting around at Callow Hill, Roberts's wife, Betsan, would find herself trying to coax a conversation out of a disconsolate Dudley: 'He was invariably out of sorts and would extol the virtues of his labrador – "Dogs are much more affectionate than humans," he would say.' Stephen Dudley recalls: 'It is quite possible that Terry was miserable because, burdened with his wife, son and dog on location, he was precluded from the fun and frolics necessary to relieve the tension after packed and stressful days, but I don't think so. Away from location, I can remember him leaving home in the small hours to gain extra time at the editing suite. I can remember how passionate he was about his art and how difficult he was to please. Perhaps he only really achieved happiness when his work was broadcast and he saw that it was good.'

Although Ian McCulloch's request to have his episode recorded in a wooded location away from Callow Hill was refused, for the later episodes in the second series the production would descend on nearby Skenfrith (where they had previously taped several short sequences for "The Witch") for the shooting of a considerable amount of footage. The chief location used here was the old mill that nestles beside Skenfrith Castle (tight shots ensured that the castle was barely seen on screen) and opposite the famous Bell Inn. For the purposes of the narrative, the mill would become the lodgings of Whitecross's younger splinter group.

Despite his new-found role as a scriptwriter, at an early stage in the production of the second series, Ian McCulloch had informed Dudley that he wanted out of the series due to what he considered to be poor scripts. He was also somewhat unhappy with the fact that Greg now had to share the limelight with Charles, but claims that there was no bad feeling between himself and Lill as has previously been reported (particularly in Kevin Marshall's 1994 book *The Making of Terry Nation's Survivors*). Pennant Roberts asserts that the two actors simply had different temperaments and approaches to filming: 'Denis was one of the Callow Hill crowd, enjoying the life of Riley and living life to the hilt twenty hours a day. Ian had taken a cottage to the south of Monmouth for the summer and so didn't see much of Denis of an evening, and prepared for his work much more studiously and seriously.' However, writer Martin Worth – who was keen to keep *Survivors* at the Whitecross setting, for fear that moving on would 'kill the series' – recalls that it was the 'conflict' between McCulloch and Lill that actually made him give in to Dudley's wish that they should leave Callow Hill behind at the end of the second series. Therefore, in the final episode of the second series ("New World"), Worth dreamt up a way in which Greg could temporarily leave the narrative by introducing a hot-air balloon to whisk the engineer – and whoever else Dudley wanted to 'lose' – away to Norway.

"New World" was broadcast on 23 June 1976, receiving a below-average-for-the-series 7.98 million viewers. Ratings had remained high throughout the second series, reaching a peak of 10.66 million for "By Bread Alone" (although this figure was no doubt helped by the transmission of the UEFA Cup Final between Liverpool and FC Bruges, which followed it, and the glowing review by Anthony Greenbank in that week's *Radio Times*, referred to above). The BBC's Audience Research Reports – the BBC's main means of gauging reaction to their output – gave an average audience reaction index of 64 (marginally down on the first series' figure of 67). Negative comments contained in these reports included the view that the survivors' costumes were 'too clean, tidy and fashionable' and, conversely, that due to its realism,

Survivors made the audience feel 'apprehensive about the future.' Others stated that it was easy to forget the apocalyptic premise of the series now that some time had elapsed since The Death. In addition, John and Lizzie were considered 'irritating' by some viewers, and a small number felt the series to be little more than a 'run-of-the-mill melodrama.' Positive comments, however, were far more plentiful. It was widely agreed that the cast should be used 'en bloc' again and that the series boasted a high standard of natural and convincing acting. The subject matter was judged to be 'intriguing and thought-provoking,' while the scenery was described as 'ideal and beautiful.' John and Lizzie were once again singled out, although this time to be 'especially commended,' while the comment that would no doubt have pleased Dudley the most was that *Survivors* was a 'good human drama.'

Kevin McNally and Brian Grellis rehearsing on the barge in "Parasites". © Denis Lill

102

2.1 BIRTH OF A HOPE

UK TRANSMISSION: 31 March 1976: 8.10pm – 9.00pm
VIEWING FIGURE: 9.34m
WRITER: Jack Ronder
DIRECTOR: Eric Hills
REGULAR CAST: Ian McCulloch (Greg Preston); Denis Lill (Charles Vaughan); Lucy Fleming (Jenny Richards); Celia Gregory (Ruth Anderson); Lorna Lewis (Pet Simpson); John Abineri (Hubert Goss); Christopher Tranchell (Paul Pitman); Michael Gover (Arthur Russell); Tanya Ronder (Lizzie Willoughby); Stephen Dudley (John Millon)
UNCREDITED CAST: Terry Denton (Vic Thatcher)
OB RECORDING: 20 - 25 January 1976
LOCATIONS: Callow Hill Farm, Monmouth, Mons; Michaelchurch Court, Michaelchurch Escley, Herefs

SYNOPSIS: Greg arrives at the Whitecross settlement looking for Charles Vaughan and meets the latter's ebullient new partner Pet Simpson. Reunited with Charles, Greg brings news from the Grange and explains that he needs to locate Ruth soon as Jenny is almost due to give birth. Charles informs him that after the delivery of Isla's and Lorraine's babies, Ruth left to minister elsewhere. While Greg stays at Whitecross overnight, a fire starts at the Grange and spreads rapidly. Jenny, Paul, Arthur and the children escape, but the others are not so fortunate. Greg returns to find the survivors of the blaze, cold and hungry, sheltering in one of the barns. After exploring the devastated building with Paul, Greg tells John and Lizzie that Emma and the others have died. Greg decides that they should go to Whitecross for help. Jenny is scared for their unborn child, but Greg reassures her that all will be well. When the weary travellers arrive at Whitecross, they are warmly welcomed and installed in one of the makeshift houses there. However, Charles knows that Greg will not be content to follow him and is soon brooding about their arrival. Greg too has concerns and tells Charles that there is not room for them both at Whitecross, but the Welshman elects to persuade him otherwise. Jenny is becoming increasingly concerned about Ruth's absence and, when her contractions begin, Greg decides to speak to Charles about finding Ruth. Charles goes off in search of her on his motorbike, using the remainder of their petrol. While he is away, Greg shares his misgivings about Charles with Pet, but she remains convinced that the future is bright for them all at Whitecross. Against all odds, Charles returns with Ruth and she begins to tend to Jenny. Charles outlines his vision for the development of Whitecross.

ANALYSIS: "Birth of a Hope" is a brave new beginning for *Survivors*. Terence Dudley's and Jack Ronder's re-working of the show's format sets up an appealing premise, which will take the series in many interesting new directions. The phenomenally difficult task of transplanting the remaining cast to an unfamiliar but believable setting populated by new characters, all within the space of one episode, is successfully achieved. However, the loss of Carolyn Seymour's Abby as well as several supporting characters and the departure from the Grange is disconcerting to regular viewers to say the least.

The cruel tragedy of the fire once more presents an opportunity to examine the human condition in terms of the will to survive. The indomitable children soon bounce back from the terrible news that Mrs Cohen and the others have all died, but Arthur despondently admits that he 'can't take it,' observing the irony that, 'You don't really want to live and yet you still crave warmth and shelter.' Jenny is also very distressed, although this perhaps has more to do with her worries over the fate of her unborn child and Greg's and Ruth's continued absence, than her grief for the victims of the fire; Fleming's moving performance during the scene in which Greg returns is wholly believable. During the sensitively realised night-time scene amongst the hay, Greg (in a change to the original script) sensibly shields Jenny from the truth regarding the stillborn baby at Whitecross, but in truth the prospects for her child do not look good. In this subplot and elsewhere in the episode, the 'hope' of the title is barely evident. The distressing content of Ronder's tale therefore contrasts sharply with the upbeat conclusion of "A Beginning", as the optimism of summer makes way for the cold, harsh reality of winter.

Central to the new series is the return of visionary leader Charles Vaughan, who now runs the settlement at Whitecross. Ronder has clearly elected to tone down his creation since his previous appearance in "Corn Dolly", so that Greg is reunited with an apparently monogamous and less fanatical character altogether. The presence of new character Pet, introduced as Charles's partner, implies that his sexual exploits in the name of the human race appear to be a thing of the past. This has the immediate effect of making the former architect a far more viable character, enabling the audience to identify with him on a level that they could not before. Given Pet's shocked discovery in "Over the Hills" later in the series that Charles has previously fathered children, it must be assumed that when Greg speaks to him in this episode about his babies, she understands him to just mean the babies at Maredell and not actually his own flesh and blood.

The competition between 'alpha males' Charles and Greg is the main focus of the episode, with the decisions each makes about future living arrangements being heavily signposted as promising to have a lasting impact on the continuing storyline. Early on in the episode, both men are depicted as self-styled 'feudal barons' who are keen to impart their achievements to each other (Greg cites his dynamo, Charles his windpump), although their sharing of expertise does involve a discernible degree of one-upmanship. During his initial visit, Greg makes a point of telling Charles that he did not care for the tension between himself and Abby, realising that he needs to be in charge: 'It's easy with just the one boss.' However, the fire and Greg's subsequent return to Whitecross means that the same tension – albeit with a different natural leader – is set to plague him again. Charles's brooding over Greg's return – first in the kitchen and then by the side of his house – is particularly well played and directed. In the following scene, in which Charles looks out over his land and opts to persuade the engineer to stay on (presumably for the reason that Charles needs his engineering expertise, as much as on compassionate grounds), Greg is quick to make the point that, 'There just isn't room for the two of us here.' Charles's assurance to the contrary that 'With this sort of set-up there's room for both of us, each to his own kingdom' is generous but unconvincing, principally because he and Greg both know that they are entirely incapable of stopping themselves from demonstrating their respective abilities. This is immediately – and amusingly – demonstrated by Greg asking Charles whether he minds if he improves on the design of the tinder box, swiftly followed by Charles's decision to choose that very day to begin immediate and noisy repairs to the new arrivals' roof, before descending the ladder to Greg in an unforgivably

Tanya Ronder and Ian McCulloch rehearse at the Acton Hilton. © Denis Lill

showy style! The fact that Greg is initially ungrateful for Charles's assistance in finding the missing Ruth, given that Jenny's and the baby's lives are in more danger if she is not found, shows just how much of a problem for him that Charles's supposed 'pouring out of superiority' actually is. As a result, Pet's assertion that 'We're going to have a lovely time here together' seems to be said more in hope than in expectation.

Greg is shown to have come a long way since his no-strings introduction in "Genesis", in which he was depicted as unwilling to commit himself to anyone. By "Birth of a Hope", he is carrying a heavier burden than any other character in the series. Not only is he the husband to a pregnant wife, but he is also a father to two adopted children and – following Abby's departure – a leader responsible for the welfare of the survivors of the fire.

Lorna Lewis is an undoubted asset to the new series, with the scene in which Pet explains to Jenny why she is a natural optimist being particularly notable. Ronder's script notes describe her as 'continually smiling with amazed delight at her own happiness.' Her presence adds a reassuringly cheerful warmth to the proceedings, which is perhaps just as well, given the tragic air and feeling of uncertainty that otherwise characterise this episode. John Abineri's comic turn as Hubert is similarly rewarding, especially in the scene in which he fails to recognise the distress he is causing Jenny as he briefly regales her with his experiences of delivering lambs. Hubert is unmistakeably cast from the same mould as the troublesome Tom Price and promises to fulfil a similar role as a thorn in the community's side.

It is a great shame that the scenes of the Grange on fire could not be staged at Hampton Court; the building used is so obviously different – with its Tudor style and smaller rooms – and certainly adds to the general feeling of discontinuity with the first series. In the episode's closing stages, Ruth – who surprisingly makes no on-screen reference to the victims of the fire

– turns out to have been re-cast between series. On the evidence of this episode, it is difficult to tell how Celia Gregory's Ruth will compare to Annie Irving's brief portrayal, except perhaps for the observation that she seems more approachable and a little less well-spoken.

What is perhaps most striking about the content of this episode is the degree of emotional tenderness on display. This is evident throughout, but particularly notable in: Jenny's declaration of love for John and Lizzie; Pet's warm exchanges with Greg and Jenny and her tactile relationship with Charles; and Greg's loving reassurance of Jenny. This scripting was entirely in keeping with both Dudley's and Ronder's interest in *Survivors* in human terms; how the individual characters would react to situations and each other in the new world. This rich emotional core to proceedings has the much-needed effect of offsetting the more tragic and desolate elements of the piece.

The exposed hilltop setting of Callow Hill farm, which doubles for the Whitecross community, could not contrast any more strongly with that of the Grange, and more than any other element defines the second series. It is obvious that Ronder and the production team put a great deal of thought and work into the Whitecross set-up, as the second series begins as it means to go on: examining the detailed day-to-day realities of survival in the post-Death world. To this end, we discover that the Grange community has learnt the art of curing skins, that making charcoal is just one of the specialities of the Whitecross settlement, while both groups use mutton fat in their oil lamps. At the episode's conclusion, Charles also outlines those skills – including the making of lime and soap – that he hopes they will be able to master in the future. Although this information is by no means vital to the plot, it does provide an admirably accurate scientific foundation to the series which, in turn, lends a stronger sense of reality to the survivors' existence. It should of course be noted that, given their original 1976 context, some of these elements would have also been deeply fashionable due to a growing fascination with self-sufficiency – Charles's home-brew now cannot help but nostalgically put us in mind of Boots' best-selling wine and beer kits and Tom Good's pea-pod Burgundy.

By the time the credits roll, "Birth of a Hope" has delivered a high quota of deaths, and the significant change of location and mood inevitably make the episode feel unsettling. However, thanks to the introduction of solid new characters, the return of Charles Vaughan and the striking Callow Hill visuals, the episode is certainly a promising starting point for the second series. *AP*

2.2 GREATER LOVE

UK TRANSMISSION: 7 April 1976: 8.10pm – 9.00pm
VIEWING FIGURE: 8.53m
WRITER: Don Shaw
DIRECTOR: Pennant Roberts
REGULAR CAST: Ian McCulloch (Greg Preston); Denis Lill (Charles Vaughan); Lucy Fleming (Jenny Richards); Celia Gregory (Ruth Anderson); Lorna Lewis (Pet Simpson); John Abineri (Hubert Goss); Christopher Tranchell (Paul Pitman); Michael Gover (Arthur Russell); Gordon Salkilld (Jack Wood); Tanya Ronder (Lizzie Willoughby); Stephen Dudley (John Millon)
OB RECORDING: 11 - 16 January 1976
LOCATIONS: Callow Hill Farm, Monmouth, Mons; Welsh Newton Common, Herefs

SYNOPSIS: Relief at the safe delivery of Jenny's baby turns to dread when she falls seriously ill. Ruth diagnoses complications from the birth that require surgical intervention – yet she lacks the equipment necessary to perform the urgent life-saving operation. Greg volunteers to travel into the ruins of Birmingham to collect the necessary medical supplies from an abandoned hospital, but Paul pre-empts him and sets off in his place. Paul returns, bringing with him all the materials Ruth requires, but complains of feeling unwell. While Paul is put into impromptu quarantine in a disused barn, Ruth carries out the vital surgery on Jenny. While Jenny convalesces, Paul's condition worsens, despite Ruth's efforts to get him to self-medicate. The community learn that Paul may have contracted a mutation of bubonic plague – a contagion that threatens the settlement as a whole. Charles, Greg and the others row when they try to agree what should be done to comfort Paul and minimise his distress. They also discuss what might happen to Whitecross if an outbreak of the infection develops. When a child stumbles into the isolation barn, the risks to everyone are all too plain. Ruth treats those exposed with DDT. Greg improvises a homemade protection suit, which Ruth uses to go to Paul's side. While John celebrates his birthday, Ruth and Paul confess their love for one another, before Ruth gives Paul the fatal injection that will end his suffering. Setting fire to the barn to ensure the end of the disease, Ruth flees into the woods to confront her grief and sense of hopelessness, before she is found and comforted by Greg. The community agree to establish a quarantine house for visitors, and Jenny and Greg announce that their new child will be named after Paul, in recognition of his sacrifice.

ANALYSIS: After the shock of the new series' opening episode, in which the catastrophic fire at the Grange takes the lives of so many of the first series' ensemble cast, viewers hopeful of some temporary emotional respite are to be sorely disappointed. Instead, "Greater Love" (originally commissioned as "A Very Gallant Gentleman") keeps up the pressure by confronting the viewer with the additional loss of one of the series' more colourful characters. The death of Paul, however, is not the result of a tragic accident, but is presented here as one of courage and of self-sacrifice, bringing a new dimension and depth to his character at the very moment of his departure. The story also establishes Ruth as a key member of the Whitecross community – she is in constant demand throughout, continually 'on call' and forced to respond to medical challenges that stretch her capabilities to the limit. Though at one point she suggests that she feels 'totally inadequate,' Ruth in fact deals admirably with everything thrown at her.

By the close of series one, the character of Paul had already begun to soften somewhat. The cocksure hippie who revels in his lack of tact, mocks the Grange's first efforts at farming, and thinks Vic should 'snap out' of his self-pity, becomes an enthusiastic and hardworking member of the settlement, committed to its collective success. At the start of series two, Paul is a less certain and more subdued figure, unsure if he will find love, and so shocked by the tragedy of the fire that it takes Greg's return for him to 'snap out' of his own inertia. His mission in "Greater Love" allows him to reconfirm his commitment to the community and demonstrate his belief in the capabilities of his new love Ruth.

The dilemma at the heart of the plot is horribly plausible. In "Corn Dolly", Charles had raided a village chemist for supplies of morphine that could ease the passing of those in his community who had fallen victim to an accidental poisoning for which there was no known treatment. Here the community are forced to recognise that Jenny will die unless one of their number ventures into the disease and danger of Birmingham to retrieve vital medical supplies, sufficient for Ruth to carry out the necessary rudimentary surgery that might yet save Jenny's life. It is natural enough that the gruffly heroic Greg volunteers to make the journey for his partner's sake, but it feels entirely genuine and in keeping with the atmosphere at the new settlement that both Arthur and Paul ask to go in his place, and then that Paul avoids a conflict with Greg by pre-empting his departure. In an earlier version of the script, the settlers debate the best mode of transport for the trip, and conclude that, after Charles's mercy mission to collect Ruth (in "Birth of a Hope"): 'We're out of petrol, it's got to be horseback.'

As Paul sets off on his journey (promising Ruth, in the original script, that he would 'find some bottles of stout for you, love') he rides past an abandoned and tyre-less ice-cream van. This single short scene leaves little doubt that Paul's escapades on the streets of Birmingham will be left to the viewers' imagination. It would certainly have been beyond the budget of the programme to depict inner-city landscapes on the scale that the storyline demands, but here *Survivors* is almost toying with the expectations of its audience. Viewers are invited to think that they'll never again see the inside of a post-Death city, because the series simply cannot afford to render such images on screen. The unexpected twist comes with the following two episodes, when the series returns to the streets of London – a place Paul reminds them is full of 'packs of wild dogs [and] rats.'

Events from 'real world' history do intrude on the events of "Greater Love", in the guise of the story of the plague at Eyam – a small village in Derbyshire devastated by an outbreak of the Black Death in 1665-1666, unwittingly imported from London by a local tradesman. Writer Don Shaw had been planning to write a play for television based on the Eyam plague, but had been beaten to the screen by writer-director Don Taylor's celebrated 1973 drama *The Roses of Eyam*, which was broadcast on BBC2 on 12 June, and repeated in January 1974 and again in June 1975. Shaw readily acknowledges: 'It was a very, very good play indeed. It did inspire me – and not just his play, but the whole history of the Eyam plague.' As Ruth recounts, the villagers of Eyam agreed to quarantine themselves to prevent the spread of the infection. In recognition of their sacrifice, and to make their isolation possible, villagers from surrounding farms and hamlets left food and other supplies at the edge of the cordon. Most histories of the outbreak suggest that the villagers were sustained and persuaded by the religious strictures of local rector Mompesson, who reminded them that 'Greater love hath no man than this, that he lay down his life for a friend.' There is an obvious echo of the Eyam story evident in the title of Shaw's episode. Ruth suggests that the Eyam villagers (unaware of the cause of the contagion) should have burned down their homes and farms, and fled to save themselves; and it adds to the drama hugely that this option is the least tenable for the Whitecross community. Not only is Jenny too unwell to be moved, but also the survivors – a large and rootless itinerant group – would have nowhere to go, and would find no easy welcome elsewhere. Unlike the Eyam villagers, the Whitecross survivors lack even the semblance of a choice.

The children from Callow Hill appear on camera, as Charles explains to the community's youngsters that they must all stay away from the ailing Paul because, 'He might have a germ, and we don't want to catch it.' In a line cut from the final script, John, thinking of ways to warn others to keep their distance, had asked: 'Why don't you put a bell around his neck?' Given that there are several other instances in the episode where the community's children misread the seriousness of the situation, this cut appears a prudent one.

Shaw evokes some unsettling dramatic moments, without becoming either mawkish or melodramatic. In an early scene, Ruth comforts John, who is distressed that one of the community's horses has had to be put down after suffering a broken leg. She tries to convince John that putting the animal out of its misery was the only compassionate thing they could do. The obvious ramifications of this exchange become apparent only later. The innocence of the children is communicated through the playfulness of an I-spy game at a birthday party, which suddenly develops an unexpectedly dark tone as the children spot the 'bonfire' that is Paul's funeral pyre. It is suggested too in Lizzie's conviction that Ruth, in her improvised biohazard suit, must be preparing for a fancy-dress party. The confidence of the direction here ensures that what might have been an unintentionally ludicrous setup – a suit made of lashed together plastic sheeting, topped with a motorcycle helmet and scarf – is so powerfully otherwise. Like the forced trip into Birmingham, it serves to emphasise the chasm that will forever separate the new world from the old.

The episode requires Celia Gregory to deliver a challenging emotional range, fully establishing her character in the series. Although Ruth's return in "Birth of a Hope" had been central to that episode's dramatic finale, it is "Greater Love" that brings Gregory's portrayal of Ruth convincingly to life. What makes the drama work so well is that in their scenes together both she and Tranchell skilfully resist the temptation to stray towards the melodramatic – an inherent danger with such highly-charged dramatic material. Director Roberts deserves particular praise for helping the actors to judge the tone of the piece so astutely.

Amidst the main drama, there are some interesting character developments. Jenny persuades Greg to commit to staying at Whitecross – to Charles's evident satisfaction. Emerging from his grief over the Grange fire, Arthur finds renewed purpose in compiling a 'skills register' for the community – just the type of census that Charles was working on at the time of "Corn Dolly", and is pleased to see revived. As the community waits for news of both their patients, there are some reflective exchanges between Charles and Greg over the degree of suffering that people can endure. As they wait for 'a bigger world, better days,' Charles wonders if they will become brutalised or scarred; while Greg describes the resilience of a Dutch survivor of the Belsen concentration camp who seemed able to blot out the horrors he endured, after the war. Lastly, as the pressures mount, Ruth expresses her wish that Abby Grant was still among them. Shaw and Roberts succeed in incorporating these additional elements without detracting attention from the central plot.

The scene in which Ruth administers the fatal sedative to Paul, declaring her love for him as she does so – releasing him from his pain, and protecting the community at the same time – is touchingly handled, and with the necessary restraint. The exchanges between Paul and Ruth are one of the emotional highlights of the entire series. The only thing that intrudes on the drama of the moment is that the connection between the Paul and Ruth has been such a recent phenomenon. In "Birth of a Hope", Paul confesses his loneliness to Jenny, who reassures him of Ruth's interest in him, and early on in "Greater Love" viewers witness the first playful intimacy between them. The situation is unavoidable, given the constraints that dictated the episode's place in the run, and the necessity of maximising the emotional power of Paul's departure, but it remains noticeable nonetheless.

The finale is wrenching, as Ruth flees from the burning barn and hides from the community to confront her grief alone. When Greg locates her the following morning, it seems clear that his view of the survivors' predicament, and of human nature, has evolved. When Ruth tries to shock him by revealing that she had considered suicide, he recognises that this is an empty threat – because Ruth has so strong a sense of life's worth and her obligations to others. Greg tries to convince her to see Paul's sacrifice as an illustration of the best that humans are capable of, and as a vindication of the importance of what they are all striving to achieve. The final scene shows Ruth returned from collecting Paul's horse from the field where he left it to graze after it had gone lame. The script directions indicate that she is 'in silent communion' with the animal and that 'her eyes and hands say "welcome home."' As she and Jack lead the horses off to the stables, Ruth's quiet resilience is plain to see.

The decision to construct a quarantine house, to test the health of settlement visitors – a key plot device subsequently – seems an eminently sensible and practical response to the tragedy. It is interesting to observe how the different characters respond to the question of whether cities are now permanently out of bounds. Charles insists that the dangers are too great, and recommends a blanket ban. Ruth, who has suffered the most from Paul's death, is commendably more realistic, insisting that they must leave open the option of making future scavenging trips if conditions demand. In many respects her insistence could be seen to validate Paul's sacrifice – demonstrating that his action was not unrepeatably foolhardy, but rather a calculated risk made for the best of altruistic motives. Little do any of the characters know how much their resolve about the dangers of urban travel will be immediately put to the test in the next episode.

"Greater Love" provides Paul with a superb finale and exit, and a fitting epitaph that enriches and enhances his character. Jenny's recovery and the previous episode's birth of her baby provide a counterbalance to the series' mounting death count, but the balance of the mood at the episode's end is decidedly melancholic and downbeat. Even a year after The Death, the costs of survival remain painfully high. *RC*

2.3 LIGHTS OF LONDON PART 1

UK TRANSMISSION: 14 April 1976: 8.10pm – 9.00pm
VIEWING FIGURE: 10.40m
WRITER: Jack Ronder
DIRECTOR: Terence Williams
REGULAR CAST: Ian McCulloch (Greg Preston); Denis Lill (Charles Vaughan); Lucy Fleming (Jenny Richards); Celia Gregory (Ruth Anderson)
GUEST CAST: Nadim Sawalha (Amul); Coral Atkins (Penny); Sydney Tafler (Manny); Patrick Holt (Doctor); Lennox Milne (Nessie); Wendy Williams (Barbara); David Troughton (Stan); Roger Lloyd Pack (Wally); Lloyd McGuire (George); Paula Williams (Maisie)
UNCREDITED CAST: David Pike (Mac); James Haswell (Male Orderly); Judy Rodger (Female Orderly); Maisie Merry, Jill Goldston, Jean Channon, Bill Lodge, Bob Raymond, Eddie Leroy, Stenson Falke (Patients); Lennox St. Louis (Boy)
FILMING: February 1976
STUDIO RECORDING: 25 February 1976
LOCATIONS: Hanwell Station, Hanwell, London; Deep Level Shelter, Camden Town, London; Bank Station – London Underground; The Oval, Kennington, London

SYNOPSIS: Two visitors arrive on a horse-cart at Whitecross, bringing greetings from Abby Grant. The travellers, Amul and Penny, ask if Ruth will visit their settlement to help treat a number of sick people – Abby included. Although the risks are great, Ruth agrees to go. Charles and Greg remain suspicious, and ask the visitors for a route to their destination, Denning Farm. When Ruth arrives at the farm, she learns that she has been tricked, and that Abby is in London, where a serious illness is devastating a large community. Penny and Amul force Ruth to travel to London, this time by police car. Crossing underground tunnels on foot, and avoiding the rats, Ruth eventually arrives at the Oval, where she meets Manny, the leader of the London community. She learns that Abby is no longer there, but that the doctor and nurse Nessie are in desperate need of her help to combat the debilitating 'London sickness'. This malaise has whittled down the London community from a thousand to just over five hundred – the figure below which, Ruth is assured, the human race cannot survive or reproduce effectively. Although resentful at the deception, Ruth enjoys the welcome luxuries of electric light, hot water, make-up and plentiful medicines that the London community offers, and agrees to help out on the ward. There she learns of the 'Big Move' – an audacious plan to relocate the community to the Isle of Wight – and of her unwitting part in it. There is clearly no intention of allowing Ruth to return to her settlement. Back at Whitecross, Charles and Greg belatedly decide to make the trip to Denning Farm. When they learn of Ruth's final destination, they set off for London. As they make their way along the rail network, they are set upon by rats …

ANALYSIS: This first instalment of *Survivors'* only two-part adventure offers a range of unexpected surprises and plot twists, as the series returns to the capital for the first time since the events of "The Fourth Horseman". A previously unknown London community enjoys an existence of relative privilege, by scavenging resources from warehouses and docksides, but the increasing threat of an infectious malady known as the 'London sickness' is leading them to take desperate measures to protect their way of life.

The script directions make clear that the opening close-up of the masked doctor's face was intended to replicate directly the image of the scientist from the title sequence – who was the cause, and the first victim, of The Death. Unfortunately the execution is not quite sufficient for the intended comparison to be completely transparent. As the camera pulls back to reveal the hospital surroundings, however, some very deliberate uncertainty is introduced. Is this some kind of flashback to a time before the plague? If not, how can this level of technology exist? This ambiguity is extended into the next scene, as the camera follows a police van winding its way around country lanes towards a farm. It is only when the focus changes to the fields around Whitecross that the viewer can be certain that the drama has remained in the present all along. In some ways it seems a shame that the efforts of the writer and director to inject a sense of mystery into these opening sequences are somewhat undermined by the giveaway episode title: there is little doubt about the drama's destination. That said, Amul's and Penny's off-screen switch from their patrol car to the horse and cart does help to misdirect the viewer about their connections with the unexplained hospital physician.

The two directors involved in the "Lights of London" episodes had to strike a deal about the way the narrative, the characters and the location work would be handled. Although each production was largely self-sufficient, agreements were made for the reciprocal shooting of some key location scenes – with Terence Williams providing the closing shot of the second episode, and Pennant Roberts taking responsibility for the whole of the cliffhanger segment, which was cut in as the finale to this first instalment.

The first few minutes of "Lights of London Part 1" also confirm that the series' production method has, at least temporarily, reverted to that used for *Survivors'* first six episodes – film footage for the location work and videotape for all the main studio-set interiors. Shot in the weak daylight of January 1976, the early film sequences are richly atmospheric. They also give the impression of being some of the coldest location work yet endured on the programme.

Is there any excuse at all for the deception practised by Penny ('In her thirties, thin, articulate Cockney') and Amul ('35, ex-postman, punctilious') in kidnapping Ruth? There's certainly no doubt that the London community are in dire straits. There's also little question that the London doctor ('About 50, well-built, tall, with a humorous face') is 'now extremely tired' and in need of relief. Even so, the only possible justification for the seizure of Ruth would be if the 'Big Move' to the Isle of Wight was a real and imminent prospect. Ruth could then have been given the option to help the settlement relocate, before being allowed to return to Whitecross. What makes Manny's actions criminal, in all senses of the word, is his prevarication over the evacuation: he insists that everyone accept how important the London community is to the fate of the human race, and to recognise how desperate the situation in the capital is becoming, yet he finds every reason possible to postpone the 'Big Move'. In reality, Ruth's abduction from Whitecross is just another of Manny's delaying tactics – which is what ultimately renders it indefensible by any standard.

The London community provides a series of effective and incongruous juxtapositions. Sat amidst the ruins of London is a settlement that prides itself on its reclamation of electric power, hot and cold running water, a fully equipped medical facility and a wealth of other resources and luxuries. Yet it becomes clear that these are sustained at the corrosive cost of the debilitating 'London sickness' and that the settlers will have to forgo many of them if they flee the capital. Although not commented on, it is a cruel irony that the realities of London life should be revealed so soon after Paul's fatal journey into Birmingham in "Greater Love". Paul would certainly have stood a better chance, and Jenny's surgery have been far less risky, had the survivors known of the London community at the time.

The producer's decision regarding the character of Abby Grant reveals some perhaps surprising choices. It was inevitable that Abby would be name-checked and her departure from the Grange be explained (to Charles by Greg) in the early scenes of "Birth of a Hope". Given that Abby was the lead character in the first series, such a 'resolution' was unavoidable. Yet in "Lights of London Part 1", Abby 'returns' unseen to fulfil a vital role in the storyline. It is Abby who – after leaving the Grange settlement – unwittingly sets the kidnapping plan in motion, by revealing Ruth's existence to the avaricious Manny. It is her supposed presence at Denning Farm that is the lure to draw Ruth away from Whitecross, and a key reason for Greg and Charles to later follow in her footsteps. When Stan reveals that Abby has never been at the farm, the script calls for a close-up on Greg 'looking fiercer even than usual.' Her appearance is even discussed as Greg attempts to double-check the credibility of the visitors. Jenny is also delighted to be told by Amul that Abby has at last been reunited with her son Peter. She sees this as an important endorsement of her essentially optimistic temperament, and reminds Greg that they should 'never give up' on hope. Yet it later transpires that Jenny's relief is based on a fraud, and that the lone Abby (who Manny thought was 'a bit bossy') was last heard of as she disappeared into the wastelands of north London – never, it is suggested, to reappear. Given that there was no chance whatsoever of Carolyn Seymour's character making a return appearance on screen, such repeated references to her serve more than anything else to emphasise her absence from the proceedings. This leaves unanswered the question of whether or not there was an agreed position behind the scenes on the 'truth' about Abby's ultimate fate.

The episode provides some of the widest perspectives about the true state of the world that our heroes have yet been able to access. It is clear that the situation in London has altered significantly since Jenny fled from the looters in "The Fourth Horseman". In "Gone Away", Tom Price had spoken of his own abortive visit to the capital: 'Terrible ... The stench. It was like a brick wall, man. Like a wall. I got out of there double-quick, I can tell you.' After his arrival at the Grange in "Spoil of War", Paul Pitman had described London as a death trap where marauding gangs and lone snipers were waiting to pick off 'anything they see moving for a gold filling or a packet of fags.' For these reasons the capital had long been considered off-limits, and the evolution of a new community in London had occurred unseen. The episode also gives us the first reliable international glimpses since Greg's return in "Genesis", with its depressing revelations of a tiny and now unreachable group of survivors in Cairo. As pictured from London, the fate of humanity hangs in the balance.

The suggestion that five hundred persons is the lowest limit to ensure the survival of a credible human tribe is a fascinating one. The key issue here is not whether the theory is entirely plausible but that the characters wrestling with the dilemmas it raises believe it to be so. Indeed, without the appropriate statistical specialists, the survivors' calculations about such things would have had to remain educated guesses at best. In comparison, Charles's own earlier estimates of a 1-in-5000 survival rate from The Death, which he outlines in "Corn Dolly", are premised on rough-and-ready extrapolations of some basic known facts.

There are some fascinating subtexts to the episode. It is striking that the London community's leadership has essentially written off the rest of the country, seeing Ruth as a resource to harvest, and basically discounting the survival role of those outside the capital . This might be seen as a thinly disguised dig at the urban-obsessed, sitting amongst the rats and ruins while they succumb to the Sickness, typhoid and dysentery – even though their numbers have been cleaved in half. A fatal combination of arrogance, complacency and stupidity appears to be in evidence. Also, given the belief in their own importance to the world's future, it seems a shame that so many Londoners are such enthusiastic smokers!

Another one of the messages in evidence here is that 'power corrupts'. It seems likely that Manny ('45, a Cockney Sparrow, ex-fruit and veg man') was a self-important chancer, obsessed with his own self-interest, long before The Death, who now finds himself wielding power on a scale he could never have imagined. But the nature of his rule is having a profoundly corrupting effect on his inner circle – Amul and Penny are prepared to lie, bribe and threaten violence in their kidnap bid. The idea that they might, in an honest and open way, try to convince the Whitecross settlement of the importance of coming to London's aid, never crosses their minds. Even Nessie ('55, small and plumpish ... a very quick assessor of people and situations'), supports the plan to seize Ruth – before she reconsiders her own responsibility to her community. (And in the next episode George is unmoved by Manny's attempts to kill Wally). Only Barbara, lost in a whirl of statistics and logistics, seems unable to recognise the extent to which the Manny cabal rules by deception and ruthlessness.

The plotting here is robust – a good strong adventure story – and the different elements are locked into place only slowly and in stages, so connections between scenes become apparent later. The glimpses of London seen in the episode are appropriately chilling. Outside the protection of the Oval settlement, the capital is a rat-filled nightmare – dark, scary, strewn with detritus, and rife with danger. On their way to the Oval, Amul warns Ruth that single rats, who have become separated from the roaming packs because 'they're dying' are no less dangerous. Moments later, a mysterious solitary figure emerges from the darkness to watch their progress, muttering to himself: 'You won't get rid of me … I'll get back.' The parallel being suggested here – of the diseased and dangerous loner – is hard to miss. When this character later confronts Manny and George, he is sent scurrying back into the empty tunnels alone. A true picture of Wally's nature will not be revealed until the next episode.

The two special effects on show here are of entirely different calibres – the image of the Oval cricket ground turned over to cultivation (realised through a painted glass overlay) is of acceptable, if transparently fake, quality. A note on the script observes that: 'There's no question of tampering with a square in the ground.' The image of the distant flames of piles of spontaneously-combusting corpses is so poorly executed, and so obviously shot in miniature, that the power of what could be a stomach-turning moment evaporates completely. It would have been better to rely on the firelight dancing across the faces of those reacting to the horrific vista than to attempt to depict it on screen at such meagre expense. Yet this dent in credibility is made up for by some excellent dusk and night-time location work, and by the sequences of the journey taken by Amul, Penny and Ruth along the tube network.

The cliffhanger ending comes as a real surprise, and although there are many obviously stuffed and sewn-on rats on show amidst the frenzied pack that attack Greg and Charles, there are sufficient live rodents to sustain the drama of the moment. A note on the camera script reminded the production team: 'Special Effects made rats for this purpose when we did "Day of the Rat" *Doomwatch*. They were stitched to Robert Powell who did the rest.' In the *Doomwatch* story (actually entitled "Tomorrow, the Rat") there were no live rats whatsoever on the studio set where the attack took place, so the 'realism' of the moment depended entirely on the spirited performance of Powell and his fellow actors (who included Eileen Helsby – Charmian from the first series of *Survivors*). In "Lights of London", McCulloch and Lill had to do battle on location with a mix of real-life and simulated rats – although the involvement of live animals proved to be a headache for both cast and crew. John Holmes – the same animal handler who had worked on "Tomorrow, the Rat" – was disappointed when his supplier delivered a large quantity of (entirely unsuitable) domestic white rats. The Visual Effects teams devised a way of dying their fur brown, better to resemble the wild sewer rats required, but the process turned out to be toxic, and all the rats perished. A second consignment of brown rats was acquired, who looked much more the part, but once filming was underway it was difficult to corral the rodents (given the need for them to have free range in front of the on-location cameras) and many of them either escaped or refused to perform. Despite the difficulties, the finished sequence works extremely well, and as our heroes are plunged into darkness and the credits roll, their fate remains in the balance. Given the relentless slaughter of characters that has been evident thus far in the series, Greg's and Charles's survival is by no means assured. *RC*

2.4 LIGHTS OF LONDON PART 2

UK TRANSMISSION: 21 April 1976: 8.10pm – 9.00pm
VIEWING FIGURE: 6.67m
WRITER: Jack Ronder

DIRECTOR: Pennant Roberts
REGULAR CAST: Ian McCulloch (Greg Preston); Denis Lill (Charles Vaughan); Celia Gregory (Ruth Anderson)
GUEST CAST: Sydney Tafler (Manny); Nadim Sawalha (Amul); Coral Atkins (Penny); Patrick Holt (Doctor); Lennox Milne (Nessie); Wendy Williams (Barbara); Roger Lloyd Pack (Wally); Lloyd McGuire (George)
FILMING: February 1976
STUDIO RECORDING: 6 March 1976
LOCATIONS: Hanwell Station, Hanwell, London; Deep Level Shelter, Camden Town, London; Bank Station – London Underground; The Oval, Kennington, London; Docklands, London

SYNOPSIS: Greg and Charles are rescued from the rats by Wally, who was exiled from the London settlement for speaking out against Manny's regime. They are brought to the Oval, where they meet Manny and demand to see Ruth. Ruth is pleased to see them, but feels she cannot return with them as she is needed to help the Londoners with their 'Big Move' to the Isle of Wight. Manny promises Wally that his exile will be lifted if he travels to Whitecross to let them know of Greg's and Charles's safe arrival. Although they suspect that Manny is stalling operations, Greg and Charles agree to help him out by checking routes out of the city. Their suspicions are confirmed when the old doctor dies and Manny decides to put back the 'Big Move'. Manny is surprised when Wally returns and, the following day, shoots him down on some waste ground near the Thames. Charles overhears Nessie telling Manny that she knows he never intends to leave London and decides that it is now definitely time to go. He and Greg try to persuade Ruth, but she still does not think she can leave, until Nessie provides her with a bag full of medical supplies and convinces her that she will cope perfectly well without her. Penny has been instructed that Greg and Charles may go, but not Ruth, and helps them on their way. However, the pair pick up Ruth *en route* to the London Underground. An enraged Manny discovers Ruth's absence and, armed with a gun, follows them into the tunnels. After a stand-off at the station platform, Greg, Charles and Ruth escape. Manny catches up with them, but is shot by Wally, who did not die after all. They start the long journey home.

ANALYSIS: Jack Ronder's "Lights of London Part 2", originally entitled "Exodus", is an accomplished and fitting conclusion to the story so far. Given that both "London" episodes were treated as entirely separate productions and that this second part stands as the most rewritten script in the series' entire history, this outcome seems all the more remarkable.

The surprising trappings of superficial comfort and luxury, epitomised here by the brandy quaffing scene in Ruth's apartment (played out to the strains of Elgar's Cello Concerto), are revealed to be, as the viewer first suspected in the preceding episode, unsustainable in the long-term. The reasons for this are two-fold: the inexorable rise in the number of cases of 'London sickness' (depicted by a rather silly graph); and Manny's increasingly obvious and self-serving determination to remain as a 'big frog in a wee pond,' an approach that promises to seal the fate of the lives of 'the five hundred'.

"Lights of London Part 2" is dominated by the theme of perceived dictatorship, personified by Manny, and its antithesis, democracy, embodied by Wally and the arrivals from Whitecross. In the case of the latter, we learn that a vote was taken as to whether or not Greg and Charles should attempt to rescue Ruth, thus demonstrating the existence of a truly democratic system at the countryside settlement. Although Manny also claims to lead a democratic regime, exiled idealist Wally insists that the community is run along fascist lines, and refuses to live under such tyranny. However, Wally is presenting an overly simplistic view of the situation. In point of fact, Manny is no dictator, but rather an elected bureaucrat who, unlike Wally, has a flair for manipulating and abusing the democratic system to his own ends. Although Manny readily retreats behind the defence of 'one person, one vote' when Wally speaks out against him, there is no question that the democracy at work in the settlement and the future of 'the five hundred' are severely compromised by their leader's ambitions. When Greg questions Amul about the undue cruelty of putting Wally 'out to cool,' Amul at first responds, 'We've decided,' but when pressed adds, 'It's not my decision.' Amul, like Penny, has been chosen by Manny for his unquestioning and short-sighted loyalty. The good-natured doctor and preoccupied planner Barbara also fail to see through him. In fact, Wally aside, only Nessie has never underestimated her leader's self-serving intentions, but her undoubted worth to the London settlement as a nurse has protected her from a fate similar to Wally's.

It takes Manny's obvious stalling of the 'Big Move' to finally give the game away to Charles and Greg. The latter's observation that 'For a so-called democratic man, you're really wedded to your own opinions,' coupled with Wally's sarcastic interjection relating to his controlling nature, rattles the leader so much that he feels the need to state defensively that there is one chain of command and that he is 'at the top.' From here on in, Manny's true colours are revealed: he is a deeply unpleasant and dangerous person who will seek to maintain his authority whatever the cost to human life. His callous nature is shown by the glib reference to his intended murder of Wally as a mere 'jaunt.' Manny's gradual descent into a state of near mania, believably played by Sydney Tafler, brings a startling level of danger to the closing sequences. These brilliantly shot scenes seem all the more remarkable considering the constraints of filming in the Underground (which led to an additional day's filming – principally caused by time-consuming lighting set-up). Ruth's shock as she suddenly comes face to face with Manny, and Charles's terrified flinches to the shots Manny fires in order to prove he has enough ammunition left, are particularly convincing. However, given the magnificent build-up, it does seem a missed dramatic opportunity that there is no question that the victim of the final gunshot is Manny. Wally's reappearance is a genuine surprise, and as the prospective new leader of the London settlement, it feels appropriate that he is executing his predecessor. However, one has to doubt how readily his idealistic principles will be accepted by Manny's surviving cronies, especially as, with the exception of Nessie, they appeared curiously content with their previous leader despite his faults.

Although Ruth has less to do than in the previous episode, we nevertheless learn more about her principles here. She is clearly pleased that Charles and Greg have come back for her, but finds their views on her prior responsibility to her friends at Whitecross untenable. She responds to Greg's view that because the patients at the London settlement are unknown to her she should therefore consider them to be less important, by replying that this fact makes no difference to her. She explains that it is this attitude that makes her a doctor, 'not the qualifications.' Given the later direction of the series, it is also interesting to note that Greg clearly states in this episode that his personal motivation does not currently extend beyond a simple tenet: 'I'm not interested in saving the human species, all I want to save are my family and my friends.' As we reach the end of the final series, we learn that despite appearances to the contrary, he has never lost sight of this principle: Agnes observes (in "Long Live the King") that he could have achieved so much more if Jenny and the children had not been more important to him than his work to restore the nation.

The location sequences depicting devastated London are well realised. The vehicle-strewn street through which Amul and Greg ride their motorbikes deserves particular mention, given the obvious disparity between the set-up time that must have been involved and the sequence's eventual screen-time. Similarly effective is the scene shot on Thames-side waste ground in front of the iconic Tower Bridge, a location which at that time perfectly suited the production team's needs, but has since been transformed beyond all recognition.

Eleventh hour casualties of the episode's overlong script were several scenes involving Greg's and Amul's discovery of an old woman, originally named Mrs Roberts and later Mrs Pollard, living alone. These were intended to follow on from the scene in which Amul talks to Penny by radio. The script describes Mrs Pollard as dressed in many layers of cardigans and several pairs of baggy trousers, while the dialogue would have revealed that she had been burning furniture to keep warm and even tried eating dog-food when she ran out of provisions. After she has been persuaded to go with Greg and Amul to 'the Centre', the scene was to have finished with a rat emerging from a hole in the skirting board. The subsequent sequence was to take place in the surgery and involve Mrs Pollard refusing an injection from the doctor, followed by Penny coming to take her away while promising her some 'smart gear' to wear. The doctor's reference to Mrs Pollard's immunity to disease as 'rude health' and heartfelt comment, 'I wish she'd spread her immunity round a bit,' leads directly on to the broadcast scene that starts with his question to Ruth: 'If only we knew when it's all going to end.' Vivienne Burgess was contracted to play Mrs Pollard, but would later be compensated for her loss of work by appearing as Mrs McGregor in "A Friend In Need" instead. Although these scenes sound interesting – albeit to a large degree dependent on the performance that Burgess would have given – Roberts felt that their removal would not damage the episode's central narrative, and in order to bring the episode in under the allotted fifty minutes decided to drop them from the recording schedule.

Both "London" episodes make for a brave and interesting break from the Whitecross environs and bring a very welcome action-adventure element to the gentler-paced second series. *AP*

2.5 FACE OF THE TIGER

UK TRANSMISSION: 28 April 1976: 8.10pm – 9.00pm
VIEWING FIGURE: 9.04m
WRITER: Don Shaw
DIRECTOR: Terence Williams
REGULAR CAST: Ian McCulloch (Greg Preston); Denis Lill (Charles Vaughan); Lucy Fleming (Jenny Richards); Celia Gregory (Ruth Anderson); Lorna Lewis (Pet Simpson); John Abineri (Hubert Goss); Michael Gover (Arthur Russell); Gordon Salkilld (Jack Wood); Tanya Ronder (Lizzie Willoughby); Stephen Dudley (John Millon)
OB RECORDING: 6 - 11 April 1976
GUEST CAST: John Line (Alistair McFadden)

LOCATION: Callow Hill Farm, Monmouth, Mons

SYNOPSIS: Playing on the edge of the settlement, the children encounter the lone wanderer Alistair McFadden. This genial and articulate visitor settles into quarantine, occupying himself with the nature poetry of Wordsworth. Alistair's knowledge of herbal remedies is welcomed, but he joins the community at a time when petty squabbles and conflicts are growing, amongst which he feels ill at ease. Hubert meanwhile is outraged that McFadden should enjoy preferential treatment. Hubert searches Alistair's discarded jacket, and takes his findings – an old press cutting – to Charles. It reveals that Alistair is a convicted child killer, a fact that Hubert is willing to 'keep secret' if his own living conditions are improved. Alistair complains about the theft and, admitting the truth of the story, describes to the community his experience of illness and incarceration. He reveals how, in the quiet and isolation of countryside after The Death, he discovered solace, and insight into his condition. Later, Hubert cautions the children not to trust Alistair, warning John that – like a tiger – behind his smiling face lurks the menace of a predator. Later, Alistair innocently surprises John while the children are playing in the woods. John freezes, and then flees. Angry that a child is once again frightened of him and deciding that he cannot remain in the company of others, Alistair prepares to leave – but when John's disappearance is noticed, he is held captive and questioned. In the early hours of the morning, Greg, who is still carrying the guilt of Barney's wrongful death, decides to release Alistair unharmed. Passing the quarantine house, they spot John – who, with a child's literal logic, has isolated himself after leaving the settlement, just as the community's rules dictate. Despite the reprieve, Alistair decides he cannot stay, and – abandoning his poetry and herbal-cure books – he leaves Whitecross, alone.

ANALYSIS: "Face of the Tiger" is the kind of reflective and thoughtful character-driven episode around which opinions neatly divide. Those eager for action and adventure will certainly find its pace and preoccupations frustrating. In place of gunplay or high drama, the episode offers some acute observations on the relationship between the individual, the community and the natural environment, and it questions the relationship between trust and rehabilitation in the post-Death world for those guilty of past crimes.

What prevents such heavyweight themes from becoming tiresome or alienating is the combination of a superbly judged guest performance from John Line, in the role of the 'rehabilitated' child killer Alistair McFadden, and the subtleties of Don Shaw's most lyrical script for the series. For Shaw, "Face of the Tiger" 'was one of the most satisfying things I've ever done.' The episode (originally entitled "Child in Danger") certainly serves as a further rebuttal to the myth that *Survivors'* second series is simply a treatise on the new agrarianism. The character of McFadden, cerebral, literate and cultured (while hiding some dark and distressing secrets), is richly drawn and given the necessary screen time and space to develop. The character notes suggest: 'Alistair is 45, slim, bearded and although sensitive he is calm looking. He carries a battered briefcase.' A sequence excised from the camera script that would have changed significantly the viewer's perception of Alistair's arrival at Whitecross, featured him watching from a hiding place while a wild Alsatian devoured a lamb. Had it been recorded, this would have formed the opening scene of the episode, and could have been intended either as a metaphor for McFadden's past, or to reflect the danger to an innocent (a child rather than a lamb) that was potentially to come.

The nature poetry that McFadden recites to Charles (from Wordsworth's 'The Old Cumberland Beggar') is not only evocative in itself, but integrates well with the setting in which it is spoken – as Whitecross emerges from its own dark winter into the warmth and rebirth of spring. The moment is here unforced, as the words both reflect and describe the scenery all around – with its sunlight and birdsong evident on screen. McFadden reflects on the recuperative power of nature and the rural landscape, and contrasts their beauty and purity with the corruption and soulless misery of overcrowded urban existence. Charles needs little convincing of the wonder of the rolling hills of his new estate, but while he wants to band with others to work the land and harvest its fruits, McFadden seeks simply to wander through its peaks and valleys in pursuit of spiritual contentment.

With Shaw once again delivering dialogue of the sharpest and most convincing flavour, there are numerous richly evoked character moments. The speech around Pet's kitchen table, where McFadden reflects with real insight on his condition, the nature of human existence, and the processes of self-healing, is a standout moment. In it, he depicts his own psychosis as a reaction to the crushing clamour of modern life and the unbearable pressures that it exerted on his psyche. He killed a child because the boy saw in him something to be fearful of. While psychiatrists had looked for explanations and suitable treatment, McFadden found in the silence and solitude of The Death the means to overcome his dysfunction. The scene was delivered in a single take, and greeted with spontaneous applause from the assembled cast and crew after director Terence Williams had called 'cut'; such moments demonstrate the sophistication and adult themes that help to distinguish *Survivors* from so many of its contemporaries. For Shaw it was one of the highlights of the piece: 'It was wonderful to be able to do that. Today, you couldn't get away with it. They wouldn't allow you.' Indeed, one of the more surprising things about the nature of the episode is the darkness that permeates it – psychotic mental illness, a child killer on the loose,

Lucy Fleming. © Denis Lill

the apparent murder of one of the settlement's own youngsters, and all the complex character issues around it – which was quite remarkable for a pre-watershed slot. Despite the disturbing subject matter, Shaw was not asked to tone down the material in any way. He recalls: 'No, there was no pressure. I just wrote it as I felt.' It seems unlikely that comparable material would break that broadcast threshold today.

There are some strong elements of plot continuity in evidence here, as the writer takes care to integrate his story into the wider narrative. There are references to the trials of the London excursion, from where the fence wire was collected, and about which Hubert is reminded that the events were 'no picnic.' Arthur uses the predicament of the five hundred Londoners to try to convince Alistair of the seriousness of humanity's shared predicament. It is also from the London adventure that Ruth concludes that the making of soap, and the priority given to cleanliness in the community, is so important – however tedious and unpleasant the actual production process remains. In addition, Alistair describes his recent encounter with Jimmy Garland, who was following a lead on the whereabouts of Abby and Peter Grant. It is notable that Ruth is willing to acknowledge and respect Alistair's expertise as a herbalist, reassuring him that she sees his medical capabilities as complementary, rather than antagonistic to her own. In future episodes, the tension between 'traditional' and 'modern' skills and technologies will not be so easily reconciled.

That the community have begun to snipe at each other, and petty rivalries have surfaced, is just the kind of realistic development that some shows would simply have steered away from. In *Survivors*, similar frictions amongst the Grange settlers are depicted in the series one episodes "Law and Order" and "A Beginning", but here their impact on the struggling community is amplified. As Ruth reflectively observes: 'A year ago we were just happy to be alive.' Yet it is in the nature of the human predicament that, as the pain and horror of The Death recedes, the more trivial and prosaic realities of life intrude once again. As Charles attempts to rekindle the spirit of the kibbutz, and Jenny mocks his assertion that 'We each do what we do best,' the quiet distress on McFadden's face – that this is the inevitable cost of living amongst others – is plain to see. Yet McFadden's expectations of perfect harmony amongst a struggling and overworked settlement are unreasonable, and the release of tension and irritation is clearly a necessary part of any sort of communal living arrangement. Alistair expresses his disappointment that not everyone was transformed by The Death, as he has been. Yet unless McFadden can come to accept imperfections in human relationships, he seems destined to live the life of the hermit, with all the material and psychological restrictions that implies.

Jenny is presented as being in a particularly weak and vulnerable state throughout the episode. She snaps at Ruth and Charles, complains defensively that others are criticising her work, pleads unsuccessfully with Greg that he promise never again to leave her, and sobs in distress while clutching baby Paul in her arms when John goes missing. For the most part, she is depicted performing housework and chores. Lucy Fleming came to find such conceptions of the character acutely restricting, and pushed for a more active role.

Aside from the naked racism he espouses in series three's "The Peacemaker", this is arguably Hubert's own darkest hour. His rifling of McFadden's pockets, and his clumsy attempts to blackmail Charles to keep the truth of Alistair's past a secret (when it is clear he would betray such a confidence the next time that he felt cornered), are simply unpleasant. Hubert is prepared to hide a child killer in the community's midst if he can profit from the deception. As he fumes and grumbles about his lot, he remains his own worst enemy – getting insensibly drunk and rebuffing offers of help. And yet, despite his malodorous appearance and anti-social tendencies, Hubert does have something of a case. While Arthur and the others enjoy comfortable, warm and congenial dwellings, Hubert's leaking outhouse seems a dank and miserable place. Although the justifications are clear, Hubert is correct when he complains of favouritism and discrimination, as McFadden is welcomed as a houseguest into homes where he has been refused access.

There are some well-rendered sequences in which Alistair attempts to find connections within the community and struggles to integrate himself. Unwittingly, Jack dismisses him as impractical, rejecting his offers of help with the building work, and asking him instead to rustle up a refreshing drink. At a crucial turning point, John flees from him when he attempts to entertain him in a woodland game. The script had suggested a slightly longer reaction shot from Alistair than appears in the final edit; it was originally envisaged that his expression would change 'from bewilderment and despair to resolution and determination' before he ran out of shot 'after John?' On the page, the implication is made more forcefully that Alistair's intentions may have again become murderous. The moment where Hubert warns John of the dangers that lurk behind 'the smile on the face of a tiger' is beautifully played, with Stephen Dudley delivering a nicely judged sense of disbelief and incredulity – replying, 'But that's Alistair.' An earlier excised section of the script had shown Hubert entertaining John with a tale of how he stopped a wild pack of dogs from attacking him when he 'looked 'em right in the eye.' This would have helped to set up John's later question about Jack's tale of how best to look into the face of a tiger.

The less palatable aspects of the settlement's democracy are revealed in the decision as to how the truth of Alistair's past will be handled, as Charles, Greg and Ruth agree to manage the distribution of information, and Ruth takes it upon herself to convince others of Alistair's reformed nature. This raises some interesting questions about the location of authority within the settlement. It seems entirely in character when McFadden complies with his captors without fuss – reflecting on how little has changed in the desire of others to look after his best interests. Alistair's possible guilt is genuinely open to question here. Before John is discovered alive and well, Greg has already decided that there will be no capital punishment in the event of Alistair's guilt. Ruth, who had yet to arrive at the Grange settlement at the time of the events of "Law and Order", suggests that punishment for Alistair would have to be either incarceration or banishment. Greg, determined that the tragedy of Barney's death will never be repeated, tells her that he will circumvent Charles and let Alistair go in any case. Given the catalogue of death that is haunting the series throughout, there is no absolute certainty that John has not in fact been killed. And yet, it could be argued that John and Lizzie are perhaps the two characters with the best chances of survival. The death of a regular child character in the series might have seemed unacceptable even by *Survivors'* own harsh standards. John's self-imposed quarantine, in line with the community's rules, seems entirely plausible, and an excellent plot twist.

Ruth could, however, be seen as too ready to accept Alistair's claim of self-rehabilitation. Can his mental health be entirely trusted? It is certainly notable that Alistair does not reveal the truth of his past until Hubert's theft forces his hand. If he found a brief row around the dinner table onerous and wearing, can the community be sure how he might react in conditions of stress or when the petty gripes and grumbles of others finally grind him down to breaking point? Once his innocence had been proven, McFadden would have made an interesting and challenging addition to the Whitecross mix had he opted to stay on – and yet the risks that this could still involve seem more threatening than Ruth is prepared to concede.

There are a couple of isolated aspects of the production that are not up to the usual standards. In an otherwise solid performance, Gordon Salkilld's delivery of the lines about dredging the nearby canal with a weighted line ('so it *sinks*') seems unnecessarily overdone. Additionally, Ruth's judgment that Alistair can leave quarantine because he has not been in contact with others (although necessary from the point of view of the story) seems bizarre from a medical perspective: he might be carrying any number of infections not acquired from contact with other humans.

Yet the episode remains an exemplary instance of a strong, character-driven drama. "Face of the Tiger" also confirms that the rollercoaster ride of the early episodes of the second series has, at least temporarily, come to an end, and that *Survivors* has taken on a more settled timbre as the spring sunshine emerges to envelop Whitecross. In McFadden, viewers encounter for the first time a survivor who seeks solitude and the contentment of isolation, and for whom comradeship and communal living are burdens and intrusions to be avoided. McFadden's perspective is the opposite of that proposed in series one's "Starvation" – that people need connection and engagement with others for both material and spiritual well-being. For McFadden, convinced that he has recovered from his mental nightmares, 'Hell is other people'. *RC*

2.6 THE WITCH

UK TRANSMISSION: 5 May 1976: 10.05pm – 10.55pm
VIEWING FIGURE: 7.83m
WRITER: Jack Ronder
DIRECTOR: Terence Williams
REGULAR CAST: Ian McCulloch (Greg Preston); Denis Lill (Charles Vaughan); Celia Gregory (Ruth Anderson); Lorna Lewis (Pet Simpson); John Abineri (Hubert Goss); Gordon Salkilld (Jack Wood); Tanya Ronder (Lizzie Willoughby); Stephen Dudley (John Millon)
GUEST CAST: Delia Paton (Mina); Catherine Finn (Peggy)
OB RECORDING: 2 - 6 January 1976
LOCATIONS: Callow Hill Farm, Monmouth, Mons; The Mill, Skenfrith, Mons

> SYNOPSIS: Pet discovers that the cows' milk has dried up. Meanwhile, Charles and Greg temporarily succeed in getting a water mill working again. Hubert is eagerly pursuing Mina, an eccentric herbalist who lives at Whitecross with her baby, but she is having none of it. While Mina is out, Hubert tells the children that she bakes children in her oven and that they shouldn't come up there again. When Mina returns, she rejects Hubert's advances once more. That night, Hubert visits Mina again; she refuses to let him in and throws a dirty nappy in his face to get rid of him, causing him to sprain his ankle. The next day, Mina collects mud to make marbles and a joke 'Hubert figure' and bakes them. The children visit Mina and at first think that she really has baked Hubert. When Mina accidentally breaks one of the figure's legs off, the children run away and upon seeing Hubert with his injured leg become convinced that she is a witch. Ruth tries to reason with them, while Peggy and Hubert go to see Pet to discuss the possibility further. Pet decides to visits Mina and

discovers that she is sculpting a clay head which resembles Charles, which the herbalist destroys in front of her. Peggy takes Mina's baby away and when she arrives to reclaim him holds her at bay with a crucifix. An angry Charles intervenes and returns the baby to Mina. Charles tries to make Pet see reason and Ruth explains that the cows were dry due to Hubert's negligence. Charles tries to convince a distraught Mina to stay on, but Hubert scares her and she runs away. That night they all look for her and she is eventually found by Hubert at the mill. Fearing for her life, Mina attacks him, before Greg arrives to comfort her. Hubert is put on grinding detail.

ANALYSIS: "The Witch" draws on Jack Ronder's keen interest in superstition and its inevitable emergence in the less sophisticated post-Death world; an idea explored in some detail in George R Stewart's classic work *Earth Abides*. Unfortunately the episode does not live up to the undoubted potential of this theme and often slips into melodrama; the subject matter appearing to encourage some uncharacteristically over-the-top performances from the series regulars.

Although sixth in broadcast order, "The Witch" was actually the first episode of the second series to go in front of the cameras, in January 1976. The consequent prevalence of fur coats, balaclavas and cold wintry weather, is out of keeping with the brighter episodes that precede and follow it. Some of the dialogue also fails to reflect this later position in the run; for example, Greg advises Charles that they should start on the mill in the spring and work on it through the summer, implying that it is still winter, even though in "Face of the Tiger", spring has already sprung. However, these seasonal problems are minor compared with the overall feel of the episode.

John Abineri. © Denis Lill

Although there is merit and interest in Ronder's idea that superstitions would start to be taken more seriously due to the absence of 'newspapers, and radio and television and doctors, psychiatrists and priests to explain it all,' its presentation here is not nearly enough to sustain the episode's fifty minutes. This seems odd given Ronder's previous multi-layered scripts for the series and suggests that several other factors may have contributed to the unsatisfactory end result. Lorna Lewis (Pet) clearly remembers 'falling about' with laughter when "The Witch" was first broadcast and thinking that the finished episode was 'bad'. She believes that the problems were partly attributable to the fact that as this was the first episode to be recorded, several actors, including herself, were still trying to find their way in their roles; asserting that the script gave her no real clues about their characters. Denis Lill (Charles) has described the episode as 'cobbled together,' despite the fact that "The Witch" was one of only a handful in the second series to receive rehearsal time in London. Whatever the truth of the matter, the episode quite obviously required firmer direction than the usually reliable Terrence Williams provided.

The Mina storyline aside, the episode contains only one subplot. This relates to Charles's and Greg's attempts to get an old water mill up and running again. These scenes, recorded in the village of Skenfrith, are interesting in that Charles is portrayed as the excited idealist while, in counterpoint, Greg is seen as the experienced and dour realist. The debilitating absence of power is briefly picked up later when Charles bemoans, 'Oh, for power, man is in bondage again,' but the theme is not given the opportunity to develop sufficiently. This is another problem with the plot: it is simply too linear to be engaging.

The broadcast of "The Witch" immediately after "Face of the Tiger" is inopportune in terms of the repetitive nature of Hubert's role in the story. Once again, he is responsible for the spreading of a vicious rumour and is lucky not to be ejected from the community for his antisocial behaviour. Indeed, Greg orders him to go and apologise to Mina or 'get the hell out of this settlement and go and contaminate somewhere else.' (In the original script, he goes so far as to describe him as 'a turd'!) It is ironic that the genesis of the rumour is actually fairly innocent: Hubert's initial tale-telling is employed simply to ensure that the children don't disturb his subsequent attempts to win Mina round, rather than to blacken her name. It is only after Mina has firmly rebuffed him that he selfishly embellishes the rumour he has started – although it has to be said that he is aided by a major plot contrivance that sees Mina break the leg of her clay Hubert, just before the children see him with his injury.

Given Mina's extremely poor 'clay Hubert', her sudden progression to a sculpture of a life-size head that actually resembles Charles is less than believable – but not quite so much as the scene that accompanies the head's destruction. The sequence in question couples oddly emphasised delivery from Paton and Lewis with incomprehensible dialogue such as, 'The man Hubert has broken his leg,' 'What are you meaning?' and then suddenly, out of nowhere, 'What about your baby?' That the baby is taken away by Peggy concurrently to Pet's and Mina's exchange is also strange, as Pet had only just left Peggy and Hubert, saying, 'We must be sensible, keep our heads.' The melodramatic crucifix sequence that follows is also a little overdone, but presumably Ronder wanted to emphasise the lunatic actions that anyone is prone to when they let their imagination run away with them. That said, it is perhaps unsurprising that the character of Peggy does not return in later episodes.

Although many scenes in "The Witch" feel overplayed and awkward, it should be noted that those of the exterior night time 'witch hunt' are well-realised and truly elemental. Given that Mina has recently stated her fear that the community may end up wanting to kill and burn her, the flame-torch holding search party are portrayed as particularly insensitive, but the sequence does seem like an appropriate narrative development and adds some much needed atmosphere to the piece. However, it does seem a little predictable that it is Hubert who eventually locates Mina. Her subsequent attack on him is quite welcome considering the trouble he has caused, but his prescribed punishment (grinding the community's corn by hand) is, as Ruth implies at the episode's close, getting off lightly.

As Hubert has thus far in the second series fulfilled a function similar to that of Tom Price, the nasty feeling that Mina may possibly pay for her rejection as Wendy did is initially pointed up. However, as the episode progresses, Hubert's actions when wooing Mina suggest that he actually possesses few of the more sinister aspects of Tom: the bringing of his mother's ring to Mina's hut implies that his intentions towards her may be more than just carnal; and although he is shown to have little or no social skills in this scene, we do catch a rare glimpse of his vulnerability as he stands outside holding the ring hopefully. John Abineri appears to enjoy himself enormously in the role and is totally believable as this cantankerous old reprobate.

Pet's behaviour in this episode seems entirely out-of-character, as indeed does her accent, which sounds different here. It seems that those elements of her character that were deemed not to be working here were subsequently toned down or removed, so that by the time "Birth of a Hope" was recorded (third in production order) we have the warm and maternal Pet we are familiar with, rather than this neurotic and easily-led initial version.

The children continue to be important in dramatic terms, and both Tanya Ronder and Stephen Dudley come across as more endearing than irritating. Good examples include: Lizzie asking Ruth if she is able to cure witches; and John precociously, but amusingly, stating, 'Don't tell me it's bedtime already!'

As Mina, Delia Paton has to shoulder the most scenes in the episode. Her introduction, alongside the sudden presence of Peggy, is jarring given that we have never seen her before. Both come from what Dudley and Ronder termed 'a standby pool of characters,' agreed upon during the formulation of the Whitecross setup – i.e. a pool that could be dipped into from time to time as appropriate. Paton is solid enough, but the histrionics required of her character do not always make for comfortable viewing, especially when she is running about the place shouting for her baby 'Matthew!' Her scenes with Charles are the most accomplished – Denis Lill's performance rising above pretty much everyone else's here – with the charismatic leader showing genuine affection for the herbalist. During his visits to Mina, Charles almost adopts the persona of a charitable country squire paying a visit to a poor tenant. Given his preoccupation with the importance of repopulation, it is probably fair to judge that during such visits, Charles is not only looking out for Mina's welfare, but also for the health of her baby, especially as, with the exception of Jenny's Paul, there seem to be no others at Whitecross at this time.

Unfortunately the exaggerated tenor of proceedings and the prevalence of misunderstandings in the episode are far more reminiscent of soap opera than they are of *Survivors*, the narrative lacking the maturity of the rest of the second series' scripts. Although "The Witch" deals with a valid subject, the way in which it is examined lacks substance, and the content on offer is often poorly realised. *AP*

2.7 A FRIEND IN NEED

UK TRANSMISSION: 12 May 1976: 8.10pm – 9.00pm
VIEWING FIGURE: 8.28m
WRITER: Ian McCulloch
DIRECTOR: Eric Hills
REGULAR CAST: Ian McCulloch (Greg Preston); Denis Lill (Charles Vaughan); Lucy Fleming (Jenny Richards); Lorna Lewis (Pet Simpson); John Abineri (Hubert Goss); Michael Gover (Arthur Russell); Gigi Gatti (Daniella); Tanya Ronder (Lizzie Willoughby); Stephen Dudley (John Millon)

GUEST CAST: William Wilde (Boult); Vivienne Burgess (Mrs McGregor); Emrys Leyshon (Roberts); Paul Grist (Morris); Andrew Bradford (Sniper)
UNCREDITED CAST: Amanda Humby (Girl)
OB RECORDING: 24 - 29 April 1976
LOCATION: Callow Hill Farm, Monmouth, Mons

SYNOPSIS: A meeting of settlement delegates at Whitecross is – somewhat reluctantly – discussing plans for co-operation. Earlier, at the home of delegate Roberts, a hooded sniper takes aim on a young woman, and fires. Jenny interrupts the meeting with news of the murder, and Greg and Charles learn of a spate of similar killings. The pair accompany Roberts to his home, and study the murder scene. From the available clues, Greg deduces that the killer is crippled, and that he executes his victims – all young women – with a high-velocity rifle. Charles and Greg realise that Whitecross is in the killer's path. The community set traps and begin patrols to catch signs of the sniper's arrival. An alarm is raised when a prowler is spotted, but it turns out to be a willing settlement recruit named Daniella. Discussing the killer's possible identity, Jenny and Pet agree to act as bait to lure the sniper into the open. The ploy works, and the killer's presence is confirmed. A hunt is organised to flush out the assassin, with the help of a team from a nearby settlement. While his camp is discovered, the killer slips through the net. The men keep watch by the only water supply available. After a tense wait, the sniper fires first, and while Charles keeps him pinned down, Greg circles behind him. Unknown to Greg, his rifle has been accidentally broken by John, and when he fires, it jams. As the sniper flits between targets – with John, Lizzie, Jenny and Charles all in his sights – Greg lunges at him. As the two men fight, a shot is heard. The killer plunges from the wood but collapses dead on the ground. Greg emerges from the trees unharmed, and as the party gather around the corpse, the killer is revealed to be female.

ANALYSIS: This murder-mystery adventure story is an impressive first outing for Ian McCulloch as a scriptwriter. "A Friend in Need" (originally titled "Sniper") is a practical demonstration of the basis of McCulloch's unhappiness with the direction that *Survivors* had taken in its second series, providing an effective on-screen riposte to the type of drama he felt was hampering the show's evolution. In McCulloch's action-rich, fast-moving drama, there are some strong echoes of Terry Nation's style of plotting, and in contrast to some of the more static and dialogue-driven series two episodes, there is a strong sense of movement and dynamism evident throughout. McCulloch was the only *Survivors* actor to write scripts for the series, yet the complications of being an actor-author meant that the experience proved to be as frustrating as it was rewarding, especially given the degree of creative control that Dudley and director Hills exercised.

What is notable about the creative decisions that McCulloch makes is that he is both true to the prickly and irascible nature of Greg's character, and that the heroics and principal focus of the episode are shared with Denis Lill's Charles, rather than focused on Greg alone. The script makes use of the 'salt detail' device to construct a story in which Ruth, Jack and several others are away from the settlement on a foraging trip.

McCulloch's script does not dwell solely on the serial sniper story. As well as introducing (at Dudley's request) the new character Daniella, whose joy at being found overwhelms the community's quarantine regulations, McCulloch is interested both in the organisation and politics of the situation as well as the drama of the story (although in the case of the former, continuity is weak). The delegates from nearby communities who assemble at Whitecross at the start of the episode appear to be unaware of the earlier attempts at co-operation instigated at the Grange (seen in "A Beginning") and cut short by the devastating fire. It is frustrating that Greg makes no reference to these earlier efforts at cross-settlement co-operation, however limited these proved to be. At the very least, the revelation that they are not being asked to sign up to something entirely without precedent might help to persuade some of the

Ian McCulloch. © Denis Lill

more reluctant representatives about the viability of the Whitecross settlement's plans. That said, it is good to see explored the tensions between settlements, such as Boult's, that seek to be 'tightly knit, undisturbed [*and*] separate' and those, typified by Whitecross itself, that aim to maximise interdependence and transparency. The existence of such a contrast in the world-views of different communities seems wholly plausible.

Several scenes cut from the camera script reveal some interesting and colourful character moments that McCulloch originally intended to include. In particular, there was a lengthy exchange between John, Lizzie, Pet and Jenny outside the conference – as the children playfully try to attract the attention of Greg, who eventually waves them away with a scowl. This sequence led in to the intended on-screen arrival of a horseback messenger from Roberts's settlement, who brings news of his wife's murder. In another cut sequence, which would have appeared during the scenes of Charles's and Greg's patrols of the settlement, Hubert gently explains to the children about the work of the shepherd when a lamb has lost its mother: 'You both lost your mums and dads, didn't you? Well, so did that little feller.' The scene ends with Greg arriving to ask if Hubert thinks he could make a shepherd out of John.

Elsewhere, McCulloch explores some interesting aspects of the series' continuity – with uneven results. Jenny's conviction that the hunter could be the crippled and revenge-seeking Vic seems something of an odd dramatic choice, as this reaches back to a character not referred to since the last series and only glimpsed in the blaze in "Birth of a Hope". The suggestion does allow McCulloch to make reference to the events of "Spoil of War" and "Revenge", but little is done to make Vic a convincing suspect. One parallel that the characters may be unaware of in relation to Vic is the symbolism of the tiger. In "Revenge", Vic improvises a story for John and Lizzie in which he depicts himself as a powerful tiger, who unwisely falls in love with an evil serpent after all the other animals in the jungle die. Before his pursuit of Anne takes over, Vic is developing the story towards the point where the tiger is left for dead by the duplicitous snake after becoming crippled. In "A Friend in Need", Arthur draws an analogy between a wounded tiger, and people whose disability or weakness renders them resentful outcasts. Not having heard the children's story, neither Greg nor Arthur would be aware of the connection between the two metaphors. What stands out even more notably is the revelation that the awful truth of the events of "Law and Order" (where the community convict and execute the wrong man for a murder committed by another of their number) is now the common knowledge of all. Given Greg's reluctance to disclose the information at the time for fear of the corrosive consequences, it seems implausible that he would have reconsidered his view since – particularly given the compound losses and miseries that the community has endured in the months since the trial. This is also a rare instance where Greg and Hubert see eye to eye: neither have any interest in exploring the killer's motivations, and both think the sniper must be hunted down and shot.

In cast and character terms, the episode is outward looking rather than Whitecross introspective, introducing delegates and representatives from other settlements (including Vivienne Burgess, as Mrs McGregor, whose earlier scheduled appearance as Mrs Pollard in "Lights of London Part 2" had to be cut when the episode overran) and several relatively heavily populated sequences in the woodlands around Whitecross. Director Eric Hills makes great efforts to keep the story on the move, setting up short scenes in the fields and hillsides around Callow Hill, and to utilise what were for *Survivors* some under-used techniques – voice overs; the sniper's line-of-sight shots; hand-held point-of-view shots as the sniper crashes through the woods. McCulloch's hope had been for the drama to be recorded away from Callow Hill in another setting entirely, but here the restrictions of time and budget do little to hamper the delivery of the drama.

The delegate Boult is an interesting and well-drawn character, butting up against what he sees as Greg's bullying and invasive tone at the meeting, and mocking what he sees as his pretensions to order others around. In a line cut from the script, Boult had sneered at Charles's interest in accompanying Roberts to the crime scene, asking: 'Judge and jury now, are you?' When, against expectation, Boult turns up to help with the hunting party, his behaviour might be more in character than first appears. Boult may just as easily consider 'a policy of containment' to be the best way to secure the safety of his own settlement than be drawn to Whitecross for purely altruistic reasons. One comment that does seem entirely out of character is Pet's suggestion, 'Sometimes I think that [Charles] wouldn't miss me much anyway,' if she were to fall victim to the sniper. At this point, Pet certainly has no need to express such a poor sense of self-esteem, and there's no evidence that her feelings are well-founded.

Using Jenny as bait to lure out the killer seems an incredible risk – especially considering all the efforts that Greg has made to keep her safe, and that her 'safety' is premised upon the assassin being Vic. There are some good, tense exchanges as the community watches for the gunman to make his move – and here Arthur is allowed a rare emotional outburst as his resolve cracks before Greg's. There was one additional scene that was removed from the final script. While Greg and Charles are on armed vigil, Jenny and Pet hear what they think are the sounds of the sniper approaching. As they grab a knife and an axe to defend themselves, it is Hubert who bursts through the door, carrying a hedgehog. Spotting their weapons, he teases: 'Oh, you won't need them, this little feller won't hurt you.' Although likely to have been cut for reasons of length, the sequence would have helped to ratchet up the tension in the episode's endgame still further. The closing sequences, in which characters flit in and out of the sniper's gun sight as she tries to select a target, are both well conceived by McCulloch and executed by director Hills. Understandably, at the climax McCulloch allows Greg to play the avenging hero, wrestling the assassin to her death, while Charles is left looking on helplessly without ammunition.

What weakens the drama most significantly is something that was outside McCulloch's control – the decision to employ a male stunt man, Andrew Bradford, to play the female assassin. The director's decision over this appears hard to fathom. The plain truth that the killer is male is shown in the first close-up of his hands preparing the rifle for his next hit. The build, gait, movement, heavy breathing and guttural noises made by the killer in the scenes that follow all repeatedly confirm this fact. On first viewing, the twist at the end when the killer is revealed to be female is simply bewildering – as viewers immediately reflect 'No, he's not,' and wait for a close-up of the assassin's face that never comes. Given that the 'stunts' required of the killer in the course of the episode amount to little more than some rough and tumble scrambling around the woodland, the 'necessity' for a male stunt man seems far from self-evident. It feels simply incongruous that, as the cast gather around the prone body of Bradford, John queries why the 'poor lady' had to meet such a fate. Many years later, director Hills acknowledged: 'I think I really should have had a [stunt]woman, but it was slightly before feminist times.' What also seems to be confirmed again here is the series' often regressive perceptions about disability in the new world. The killer in "A Friend in Need" – whose coat bears the androgynous name-tag 'George Oliver' – is a 'cripple' for little reason other than to emphasise her 'otherness', and to make her more the disfigured villain. There is no explanation as to why her physical impairments – a marked limp and (judging by the wheezing) an asthmatic chest – might have rendered her a bitter and amoral outcast and a ruthless assassin. Nothing is known of the events that set in motion her murderous campaign, and there is no explanation as to why her targets are young, attractive, able-bodied women – but the likely subtext is not a difficult one to discern: she is taking revenge on those she envies, and has no hope of emulating.

Although it is frustrating, the lack of any account of the killer's motives also remains oddly appropriate – it reflects the realities of the survivors' lives in the post-Death world. There are now no social or legal mechanisms through which the truth of the killer's back-story might be revealed or her motivations unpicked: who was this serial murderer?; why and how did she become an animalistic sociopath? Viewers are left to share the incredulity of the Whitecross community over the killing spree. These uncertainties aside, McCulloch's first script is an effective adventure drama with a strong sense of narrative drive and some intelligent action pieces. *RC*

2.8 BY BREAD ALONE

UK TRANSMISSION: 19 May 1976: 8.10pm – 9.00pm
VIEWING FIGURE: 10.66m
WRITER: Martin Worth
DIRECTOR: Pennant Roberts
REGULAR CAST: Ian McCulloch (Greg Preston); Denis Lill (Charles Vaughan); Lucy Fleming (Jenny Richards); Celia Gregory (Ruth Anderson); Lorna Lewis (Pet Simpson); John Abineri (Hubert Goss); Michael Gover (Arthur Russell); Gordon Salkilld (Jack Wood); Gigi Gatti (Daniella); Stephen Tate (Alan); Tanya Ronder (Lizzie Willoughby); Stephen Dudley (John Millon)
GUEST CAST: Roy Herrick (Lewis Fearns); Julie Peasgood (Judy); Martin Neil (Philip)
UNCREDITED CAST: Harry Oaten, Mike Britton-Jones, Marie-Claire (Whitecross

residents)
OB RECORDING: 15 - 20 April 1976
LOCATION: Callow Hill Farm, Monmouth, Mons

SYNOPSIS: Lewis Fearns, one of the community's less practical members, is feeling troubled. While working with Alan on a drainage ditch, he spots a flower in some nearby rubble and goes off to think. Meanwhile, new arrivals Judy and Philip are being shown around the settlement by Ruth. Lewis returns and asks Greg to help him put his shirt on back to front, having decided to reveal that he used to be a curate before The Death. While Daniella is thrilled, thinking she will now be able to take confession, Charles, Pet and Ruth are less enthusiastic. Jack and Hubert ask Lewis whether he will be leading services, while Jenny – who has post-natal depression – is angered by the news of his decision to wear his dog collar again. A concerned Greg asks Lewis to visit her, but when he does, she gives him short shrift, unable to understand his faith in the face of The Death. When Daniella makes a clerical shirt for Lewis, and Jack spends time away from repairing the plough to restore a prayer desk, Greg becomes frustrated by Charles's philosophy, whereby everyone is free to do their own thing. When Alan, Jack and Hubert abandon their work to fetch hymn books for a possible church service and the ditch floods as a result, Charles finally loses his temper. His outburst prompts Judy and Philip to decide to leave; they believe that there is a 'boss class' at Whitecross which is more interested in production than in spiritual welfare. Jenny, who has snapped out of her depression, speaks to Lewis – who has again removed his collar – about his faith and is impressed by his honesty. On the basis that he cannot let his fellow residents down, Charles persuades Lewis to lead a service of thanksgiving, which he and Greg choose not to attend.

ANALYSIS: Martin Worth's first script for the series is a well-constructed philosophical examination of the linked themes of spiritual nourishment and leadership. Interestingly, the episode was initially written by Worth with his father in mind – a priest who he believed had lost his faith. Although the episode features no threat other than a fluctuation in commitment to the ongoing work of survival – which will disappoint devotees of action-orientated *Survivors* – "By Bread Alone" provides a fascinating insight into daily life at Whitecross and what exactly makes the main characters tick.

Roy Herrick gives a sensitive and credible performance as Lewis Fearns, who decides to physically demonstrate that he has found his faith again by returning to the cloth, underestimating the effect that this action will have on the members of the community. The scene is thus set for the airing of a thought-provoking range of attitudes that commendably go beyond a straightforward discussion of religion and the existence of God. While Pet, Ruth and several others appear bemused by his decision, Jenny – who has until now stayed very much in the background in the second series – is furious that Lewis has 'the nerve' to put his clerical collar back on, and during his inopportune visit to her house, he takes the flack for Jenny's post-natal depression (a state of mind first suggested in "Face of the Tiger"). In a beautifully written and delivered speech, Jenny reveals that she is not just angry with his faith in God ('Where was God in the plague?') but is, on a more practical level, frustrated and fearful at the absence of those things that a mother could take for granted in the old world: 'I want nappies that come in crisp, hygienic packets and safety pins and chemists. I want a doctor to call in once a week to say he's doing fine, and a hospital on hand if he's not.' Jenny's sarcastic parting comment to the clergyman – 'Thank you for calling vicar, I'm sorry I couldn't offer you a cup of tea,' – tells Lewis all he needs to know about what she thinks of his position; namely, that religion is no longer relevant to their lives and that the genteel 'more tea, vicar' era is well and truly over.

As the only overtly religious survivor, Daniella makes demands on Lewis that the curate is seen to find equally as frustrating as Alan's assertion that they don't need 'all that superstitious claptrap anyway.' Lewis, unlike Daniella, is realistic enough to see that he depends upon Charles and Greg in particular for his survival ('If it wasn't for them … I would have starved to death long ago'), but at the same time is keen to find a deeper meaning to his existence. This is a view that has a strong influence on new arrivals Judy and Philip, who share his vision of a world that offers 'beauty, truth, love, goodness' and the understanding that: 'It's the quality of life that matters, how we live – not how long.' However, through such compelling words, Lewis unwittingly provokes a situation whereby the settlement's morale and commitment is suddenly at stake.

This new scenario prompts Greg's practicality to temporarily win out over Charles's philosophy (who has until now always stood by his belief, 'If a square peg won't fit into a round hole you can't just throw them out'). Charles initially argues that people must be able to find commitment to their work in their own way and that 'maybe Lewis can help them do that,' but comes round to Greg's convincing argument that people need authority, want to be told what to do and therefore 'freed from responsibility.' The negative reaction of Judy and Philip to Charles's sudden barking of orders – in accordance with an adoption of Greg's ideas of authority – proves to be a 'startling' attack on the Whitecross set-up. Philip's well-chosen words stun Charles into silence for the simple reason that they have a distinct ring of truth. The 'boss class' that Philip describes have only just finished a meeting during which they have determined what is best for the workers in respect of Lewis's influence; he rightly surmises that they resent 'the threat from Lewis', relating the situation to the communist USSR ('And in Russia they didn't like people to believe in God either, in case it took their minds off their work for the state'). The young couple decide to leave Whitecross rather than help to build a world they feel far too closely resembles the old one. Their decision proves to Charles that he was better off sticking with his own idealistic views rather than conforming to methods born of Greg's more unilateral way of thinking. In this way, Charles proves to be Whitecross's 'good shepherd' leader for valid reasons: as he says himself, his views 'may not make for efficiency,' but at least they sustain 'a human society' and 'not just an economic unit.' This is not to say, however, that the distracting activities in which the community have become engaged aren't frustrating and – in this instance – the wrong priorities, but rather that more of a balance needs to be struck between these type of 'pie in the sky' activities and the 'bread on earth' survivalist agenda, than Greg would advocate were he the sole leader.

Roberts's direction once again takes time to focus on the nature and beauty that surround the survivors. Lewis's return to faith is effectively realised, first through a simple flower and then out among the trees to the sound of birdsong. In a similar vein, the opening shots take in lambs, daffodils and trees – these, in retrospect, are intended to represent examples of God's creation in a world where God has long remained dead and unmentioned. The scene in which Lewis overhears the effects his words have had on Judy and Philip while alone in the workshop is also notable: as Philip repeats the curate's words pretty much verbatim, Lewis is seen to be standing by Jack's prayer desk – a symbol of his influence on events; and while Judy questions the need for soap, he observes the soap pans continuing to simmer away in front of him.

That it is Jenny in whom he eventually confides about his fears is an interesting counterpoint to their earlier conversation: only to her does he admit that he threw away his Bible after The Death and that he does not feel worthy of being the community's pastor. Although a closing sequence featuring the long-trailed service led by Lewis was perhaps inevitable, it does seem like a strange finale to the episode, primarily because the activity feels anachronistic and inappropriate given the world in which the survivors are living. However, Worth's original script notes indicate that the sequence is actually intended to come over as a bit of a sham, like some people's annual novelty of attending Christmas Midnight Mass, rather than the culmination of a community's shared purpose to 'nourish their souls'. It is explicitly stated in the script that: Alan 'does not take it seriously', Jenny is 'singing rather woodenly', Ruth's presence is intended to be 'a surprise', while Daniella (who, as Lewis has just stated, only wants him to believe for her) is 'looking happily at Lewis or at least at the surplice she has made for him!' That neither Charles nor Greg attends seems fitting – both being depicted as far too attuned to the realities of survival. As this proves to be the first and last service that we witness at Whitecross, this is either a telling message as to what Lewis may actually have achieved or in keeping with Lewis's personal belief that formal worship is not 'all that important.' Of course, in a wider sense, there is the simple fact that each *Survivors* episode has been intent on examining a different theme, and as religious faith and spirituality have been explored at length here, so future episodes inevitably take the series elsewhere.

The existence of God is not debated at length in "By Bread Alone"; instead, the narrative is careful to focus on the far more dramatically interesting issue of the spiritual nourishment that may have been overlooked in the difficult fight for physical survival, and the related politics that appear to be endemic to this way of life. The foundations of Lewis's beliefs are similarly ignored in favour of an examination of the relevance of faith. These ideas are exquisitely delivered by Worth and are arrived at through levels of debate and reasoning that make this episode of *Survivors* a sophisticated drama indeed. *AP*

2.9 THE CHOSEN

UK TRANSMISSION: 26 May 1976: 8.10pm – 9.00pm
VIEWING FIGURE: 9.14m
WRITER: Roger Parkes
DIRECTOR: Eric Hills
REGULAR CAST: Denis Lill (Charles Vaughan); Lorna Lewis (Pet Simpson)
GUEST CAST: Philip Madoc (Max Kershaw); Clare Kelly (Joy Dunn); David Sibley (Kim); James Cosmo (Lenny Carter); David Neilson (Mike); David Goodland (Sammy Walters); Elizabeth Cassidy (Susan); Vanessa Millard (Nancy)
UNCREDITED CAST: Jean Channon, Martin Holand, Elison Kemp, Charles Anthony, Peter Dukes, Sally Avory, Elaine Legrand, Judy Blakstad, Wendy Marples, Wendy Marsh, Petrina Derrington, Julian Hudson, Keith Bacal, David Wilde, John Repsch, Derek Hunt, Laurie Goode, Andrew McRob (Community Residents)
FILMING: March 1976
STUDIO RECORDING: 17 March 1976

LOCATION: Army camp near Salisbury Plain, Dorset

SYNOPSIS: Charles and Pet are returning from 'salt detail' when one of their horses is taken lame. Sheltering for the night in an abandoned barn, they find their rest interrupted by two young and somewhat disturbed travellers. Pet offers them some rabbit meat, which they add to grain they have brought with them to make a rich stew. In the night, both youngsters are taken violently ill. Charles sees no choice but to take them to the nearest settlement in the hope of help. When they arrive at the camp, an armed guard named Lenny refuses them access, unmoved at the fate of two such 'termies'. When Pet offers to pay for their treatment with salt, admittance is granted, and the patients are given beds in the 'isolation

Lorna Lewis. © Lorna Lewis

hut'. It is discovered that they were poisoned by wheat that they stole from the settlement: a seed crop that had been dosed with fungicide. One of them dies; Charles and Pet leave the other in quarantine, with an assurance that Lenny will 'look after' him. When they are introduced to the settlement's head, Max Kershaw, Charles and Pet learn that the community is governed by a strict programme of selective breeding – eugenics – and a culture that prizes discipline and health-and-fitness. Charles is keen to confront the heartless and insular nature of the regime, but Pet becomes increasingly anxious to leave. Charles eventually wins the right to address an assembly of the whole community. As the meeting starts, Charles finds his survival ethos on trial, but – unexpectedly – Kershaw's deputy Joy Dunn turns the tables and, in a carefully planned bid to usurp him, exposes the multiple deceptions on which the regime is founded. Kershaw is deposed, and Joy appointed in his place. Aware that they were unwitting pawns in a power struggle, Charles and Pet are happy to leave the settlement behind, for the more hospitable and tolerant atmosphere of Whitecross.

ANALYSIS: "The Chosen" is a complex, and at times confusing, tale of political intrigue, in which Pet and Charles become unwittingly involved. In many respects, the episode is a precursor of the wandering 'community of the week' story type that recurs in *Survivors*' third series. For the first time since the adventures of "Lights of London", the story isolates some regular characters in an alien and inhospitable environment. In "The Chosen" the 'salt detail' plot device is inverted – and all attention is focused on the pair of Whitecross residents who are returning home after completing their mission at the brine pools. (Whether scriptwriter Roger Parkes was conscious of this or not, Whitecross's method of collecting salt appears to have changed since "Birth of a Hope" – in which Charles explains to Hubert that the community's salt is harvested by the laborious business of boiling seawater.)

Although the episode suffers at times from a dense (and occasionally impenetrable) storyline and an overly theatrical execution, its focus on the pairing of Pet and Charles is a clear strength. The scenes that the couple enjoy together demonstrate how effective this pairing of characters is and highlight how little attention is devoted to their relationship elsewhere in the series. Lorna Lewis relished the chance to have Pet escape from the confines of the Whitecross kitchen, and she responds well to the opportunities it affords her character.

The scarred and disturbed young travellers who bed down for the night at the fireside of Charles and Pet are provided with an alarming history and a short and painful future. These youngsters have abandoned their stores of supplies and fled into the countryside when their Birmingham home was overrun by a marauding gang. The young girl has been traumatised, and in all likelihood irretrievably damaged, by witnessing her young baby being eaten alive by city rats. The picture that this evokes of life in Britain's 'second city' is grim – and emphasises how little Paul reveals about the horrors of his own trip into Birmingham in "Greater Love". Both youngsters suffer horrific poisoning from the grain they stole from the settlement that threw them out, and they are condemned to agonising deaths. After the young girl dies, it is pointedly suggested that Kershaw's crew accelerated her partner's demise – the story that he fell victim to 'the dogs' whilst trying to flee on horseback is immediately transparent. All this death and suffering is hardline *Survivors* stuff; there is no let-up in the picture of life expectancy in the post-Death world beyond Whitecross in evidence here. It seems entirely true to the nature of the characters that Pet and Charles would take it upon themselves to seek out help for these strangers in distress, though it is almost inevitable that this act of compassion will come at a price.

On arrival at the Kershaw camp, the pace of the drama slows considerably and the narrative becomes increasingly dialogue-driven, as Parkes unpicks the politics by which this community is governed. This is an authoritarian and doctrine-driven settlement of a type not seen in the series before. In "Lights of London", the dissident Wally bemoans the tyranny of Manny's 'fascist' rule – but for all the brutality, greed and corruption of the Oval settlement, it is the community depicted in "The Chosen" that more readily fits that description (Charles's efforts to reverse the comparison notwithstanding). Kershaw runs a community that denounces the weak, the infirm and the feeble as 'degenerate' (the subhuman 'termies' whose fate has already been sealed), and that celebrates the prowess, health and vitality of its population. Favouring genetic selection, controlled breeding and a strict utilitarian moral code, the community thrives on its sense of superiority, and is reinforced in its position by the horror stories it receives of the corruption and decline evident in the world outside.

Some further scenes in which Parkes introduced different aspects of the community's life were cut from the initial script – in these, Charles and Pet learn that the settlement's fish-drying plant is nearly ready; that senior herdsman John Harper has rid the camp's cows of mastitis; and that the group's collective crèche is run with scrupulous attention to hygiene. Also dropped from the shooting script was an exchange between Charles and Pet in which he draws a light-hearted comparison between their bargaining tool in the forthcoming assembly and the nuclear disarmament talks the USSR and USA had been engaged in at the time when the plague struck:

Charles: First thing tomorrow ... at what they call Assembly ... we start the first

post-Death round of SALT talks
Pet: Salt?
Charles: Nice paradox eh? Only this time it's not the Strategic Arms Limitation
Treaty. It's the real stuff ... salt.

The script notes: 'Pet is exasperated by this talk.'

Behind the images of contented hard work, the reality of the camp's life is somewhat different. Kershaw is willing to deceive – in effect, to construct propaganda – to misrepresent the state of the world beyond the settlement's wire fences. His second in command is all the while plotting to overthrow him, and the loyalty of his inner-circle proves to be entirely conditional. Kershaw is in fact far less secure than he realises. The community's ideology retains one important distinction from the fascist canon – they have no aggressive territorial claims against their neighbours. Their ambition is not to extend their influence or increase their *lebensraum* (the Nazi term for the Reich's expansion), but to protect their way of life from 'foreign' contamination. They are isolationists rather than imperialists, and shun connection with the outside world. As a result, Charles's ideas on inter-settlement collaboration are repellent.

It is hard to criticise as fanciful Parkes's conception of the settlement's politics, because so much of it is – unfortunately – based on published pseudo-science, and in particular on Terence Rattray's controversial and discredited treatise on eugenics and reproduction: *The Biological Timebomb*. It is however easier to pass judgment on Parkes's presentation of the group's extremist sentiments: the storyline certainly ticks off a large number of themes, but the plot is so crammed with ideas and political scheming that there is little space to explore things in any depth. Charles's meeting with the leadership inner circle and the trial scene are stuffed full of the clash of ideologies, with Kershaw denouncing Charles's own convictions as crude 'communism', but the exchanges rarely get beyond the trading of slogans and soundbites. Director Eric Hills did revise one of Parkes's initial character outlines. In the original script, Kershaw was conceived as camp and effete, with a deliberate ambiguity left around his sexual orientation. Hills judged that Kershaw needed greater strength and gravitas if the power struggle at the settlement was to appear convincing. There is one moment where Kershaw briefly lets his defences down: confiding to Charles and Pet his lack of preparedness for leadership, and his sense of obligation to those who have chosen him for that role.

One element of the ideological framework that Parkes introduces appears contradictory. One member of Kershaw's inner council suggests that The Death was engineered and deliberately released by Soviet Russia, presumably – in their minds – as an act of genocide against its 'enemies'. Yet Joy, Kershaw and Susan all make reference to the 'cleansing' of the human race as the conscious 'will of God' – a challenge to which the survivors of the catastrophe are compelled to respond, and in so doing rise above 'ignorance, lust, sloth and corruption.' Unless Parkes is making a veiled comment against the glaring inconsistency of the settlement's extremist world view, it is problematic to have them conceive of the plague both as a criminal act of human aggression and as the intentional outcome of 'divine intervention'. To add to the uncertainty, Kershaw also insists that The Death was the 'inevitable' result of genetic degeneration in the 'old world'.

It is, however, a neat piece of plotting, and one entirely true to the nature of the characters, that while Pet is instantly repulsed by the settlement and the dictates that control it, and impatiently urges that they leave immediately, Charles – the politician and negotiator – is drawn into a critique with its leaders, attempting to win over converts of his own. It is even better that Charles's position is complicated by the fact that he is a would-be 'baby farmer' too, and convinced by the need to prioritise reproduction above all else (even though his evangelism does not fully resurface until the events of "Over the Hills").

"The Chosen" has a larger cast of extras than any other series two episode, and there are a number of well-populated scenes, although the staging of these sequences is quite static and stage-bound. There are also several long, single-take scenes, including the trial itself, which involve a great deal of unnatural looking movement on the part of the characters, as the director struggles to inject some dynamism into very talk-heavy interactions. For this episode, Hills was required to revert to the earlier *Survivors* mixture of on-location film and studio-bound video (a combination last seen in "Lights of London"). The film segments generally work well, although a missing shot (that was either never recorded, or left out of the original edit) results in a glaring jump and the loss of four snippets of dialogue in the opening scene on the roadway. There is also a noticeable difference in the physical demeanour of the actors as they shift back and forth from the chill of the wintry locations to the warmth of the studio sets at Television Centre.

Both Philip Madoc (Kershaw) and Clare Kelly (Joy) give creditable guest performances, even though the amount of exposition that the script demands of their characters leaves little room for creative manoeuvre. Kelly has the hardest job here, particularly in making sense of Joy's complex and duplicitous bid for power, the motivations for which are not always entirely clear. That neither Charles nor Kershaw recognises the coup that Joy is engineering until it is too late is one of Parkes's better twists: and it is a genuine surprise to see Charles hoodwinked by a more skilled and ambitious political manipulator than himself. The original title of the episode, "Kangaroo Court", had signposted the trial conclusion too heavily.

Back in "Gone Away", Abby Grant had spoken of her forlorn hope that political conflict would be a relic of the old world, and that common collaborative effort would now overrule dogma and disagreement. Abby was quickly disabused of such notions, and "The Chosen" demonstrates above all else that, even in the post-Death world, 'politics' is alive and well. *RC*

2.10 PARASITES

UK TRANSMISSION: 2 June 1976: 8.10pm – 9.00pm
VIEWING FIGURE: 9.29m
WRITER: Roger Marshall
DIRECTOR: Terence Williams
REGULAR CAST: Ian McCulloch (Greg Preston); Denis Lill (Charles Vaughan); Celia Gregory (Ruth Anderson); Lorna Lewis (Pet Simpson); Tanya Ronder (Lizzie Willoughby); Stephen Dudley (John Millon)
GUEST CAST: Delia Paton (Mina); Roy Herrick (Lewis Fearns); Patrick Troughton (John Millen); Kevin McNally (Jeth Kane); Brian Grellis (Les Grice)
OB RECORDING: 3 - 8 May 1976
LOCATIONS: Brecon and Monmouthshire Canal, Pen-groes-oped, Mons; Callow Hill Farm, Monmouth, Mons

SYNOPSIS: On a foraging trip along a canal towpath, Mina falls into conversation with the amiable barge owner John Millen, whom she persuades to call at Whitecross to discuss the trade of some of his stock of Wellington boots. The pair find themselves at ease in each other's company, and an immediate mutual attraction is apparent. Millen readily accepts Mina's offer of a home-cooked dinner, and she returns to Whitecross in an upbeat mood. Yet when the barge arrives the following day, it is in the care of the uncouth and abrasive Kane and the ill at ease Grice, and there is no sign of Millen. They seem ignorant of Millen's plans, and fend off Mina's questions. Greg and Charles are keen to make a deal, but Kane shows no hurry to leave. The truth is that Kane is a convicted killer, and Grice a warder from his former prison. Kane has plans to steal all the 'easy pickings' he can amass from Whitecross. Pet suddenly remembers where she recognises Kane from – as the convicted defendant in a robbery-murder trial on which her father had served as a juror. Fearing foul play, Mina scours the canal for any clues to Millen's fate. Horrified, she discovers his corpse floating in the water, a knife protruding from his back. Mina confronts the pair, threatening to kill them. Grice and Kane hole themselves up in the quarantine house, take John and Lizzie hostage, and begin to drink some wood alcohol that they have found, unaware of its lethal toxic effects. When Lewis attempts to negotiate, Kane shoots him dead. Escaping to the barge, Kane and Grice drink more of the wood alcohol and begin to suffer the devastating effects. As their eyesight fails and they are taken ill, John and Lizzie slip away and rejoin Greg and Charles. With Kane and Grice still aboard, the wood alcohol ignites and the barge explodes in a fireball, killing them both. Later, a grieving Mina describes to the children of Whitecross the meaning of the word 'parasite'.

ANALYSIS: In "Parasites", Whitecross is once again menaced by unwelcome visitors who bring death and destruction in their wake. But unlike the mysterious sniper from "A Friend in Need", who threatens the community from without, these villains disguise themselves as legitimate traders and enjoy the hospitality of the settlement until their real identities are uncovered. For an incoming writer immediately to grasp the potential of the series' format and deliver so effective and inventive an episode suggests that it was *Survivors*' loss that Roger Marshall (perhaps best known as co-creator and lead writer of the long-running ABC/Thames series *Public Eye*) contributed no further scripts to *Survivors*.

Patrick Troughton puts in an apparently effortless guest appearance in the role of the barge owner John Millen. His performance is textured and believable, wringing every shade possible from an excellent script, and finding immediate warmth and chemistry in his exchanges with Delia Paton's Mina. Paton remembers: 'It was absolute bliss working with him.' Troughton's screen time is all too brief, yet in a way that adds to the poignancy of his character's disappearance. Again the series plays with audience expectations: the viewer is reluctant to believe that a performer of Troughton's calibre will not make a reappearance later (although his voice is the last heard in the episode, as a mournful Mina recalls their meeting just before the closing titles roll). This is made all the more credible by the fact that Millen's encounter with Grice and Kane occurs off-screen, and that the viewer is not certain of his fate until Mina's shocking discovery of the body in the water. Paton also puts in her most finely judged performance here, restraining the temptation seen in other episodes to 'over-play' in a way more suited to the stage than the small screen. This is an episode in which Mina gets to be more than the 'misunderstood eccentric' of the community, and her character is given some room to develop.

The first meeting between Mina and John is playful and flirtatious, managing at the same time to feel both respectful and restrained, as the two characters gently acknowledge their mutual attraction and arrange their first dinner date. How different a suitor is the gentlemanly John from the rascally Hubert.

As Greg and the children fish from the canal bridge and the barge approaches the rendezvous point, the narrative suddenly switches direction and tempo as the barge's new owners are revealed. After the quiet introspection of "By Bread Alone", with its affable if footloose young visitors, the arrival of Grice and Kane provides a first-rate contrast. Kane (whose first name is given in the script as Jeth – presumably short for Jethro) is unkempt, surly, aggressive and cocksure, while in his shadow Grice appears nervy and unpredictable. Charles in particular is taken aback by his new guests and unsure how to respond. Kevin McNally is superb as the contemptuous and malevolent villain, spitting out his indignation and sense of injustice with his lot in life, and burning with a desire for retribution. He loathes the 'privileged' survivors of Whitecross and their 'Duke of Edinburgh Award' efforts at self-sufficiency, contrasting their smug contentment with the thrill and satisfaction of the robber's life. Brian Grellis also delivers a creditable performance as his put-upon former prison guard Grice, transformed by The Death into Kane's willing (if unhappy) partner in crime. It is interesting to see how little the former gaoler is able to control his former charge, yet it is hard to forgive Grice, or see him as a victim or 'prisoner' of circumstance. Whatever objections he raises to Kane's murderous schemes, he makes no effort to break away, or to warn the community of the danger in their midst. It is also Grice who, in the episode's finale, shoots at the backs of the fleeing children he has helped to kidnap.

Kane and Grice. © Denis Lill

As they first tour the Whitecross estate, taking a mental inventory of potential loot, Kane can hardly believe his good fortune. He overrules Grice's appeal for caution and makes it clear that he intends to satisfy his rapacious appetite at the settlement's expense. While Charles tries to discuss the deal over Wellington boots that Mina first raised with John Millen, Kane is more interested in refilling his glass with Whitecross homebrew. Even as their story unravels and Greg and Charles begin to doubt the visitors' good intentions, Charles in particular seems unable to work out how to respond to the mocking disrespect of Kane calling him

'Uncle', or to the growing undercurrent of menace that accompanies their visit. Mina's determination to uncover the truth, and the explosive confrontation that erupts in the kitchen after her discovery of John's dead body afloat in the canal, help to give a real edge to proceedings.

One scene that was cut from the original script offered an entirely different perspective on both Charles's and Pet's interest in the world beyond Whitecross than had previously been apparent. Set in their kitchen before the arrival of Kane and Grice, the sequence begins with Charles reading an old copy of the *Daily Telegraph*, and joking: 'The damned paper-boy's always late.' Scanning the paper, he and Pet discuss the prospects of a trip across to continental Europe:

> Charles: How many marinas are dotted around the coasts of England? Yachts, cabin-cruisers, catamarans. No! *Steak au poivre* at a French farmhouse within ... what ... the next two years – how about that for a goal?
> Pet: No *poivre*.
> Charles: Why not?
> Pet: No pepper.
> Charles: (mock heroic) The French will find a way!

Although the exchange hints at ideas explored in Terry Nation's *Survivors* novel (published the same year as the second series was broadcast), the most striking aspect of their discussion is Charles's and Pet's mutual enthusiasm for the idea of European travel. It is not known whether Marshall had been encouraged to include such dialogue in the discussions with Dudley and others that would have preceded his draft, or whether he devised the sequence at his own inspiration. The scene may have been dropped because it pre-empted the key revelation of the series' finale "New World" – that the horizons of the survivors were about to be dramatically expanded – or because it suggested that two key residents of Whitecross were already inspired by the idea of roaming beyond British shores. It may also have been cut because it undermined the forthcoming conflict between Charles and Pet about the future viability of Whitecross. There still remains the possibility that Marshall was signposting a possible future direction for the series that the producer had reconsidered after his script had been commissioned.

As a one-off scriptwriter, Marshall here delivers an interesting reading of the character of Greg. This episode features some of Greg's warmest and most generous interactions – from his good-natured teasing of the children during their fishing vigil, to his gentle rebukes to Charles for his excessive abrasiveness and over-demanding nature regarding the next generation. When Greg warns Charles not to adopt too off-putting a manner, it is in some ways hard to reconcile this with the character we more readily expect – the critical, short-tempered and often intolerant Greg of old. Greg's criticisms also seem somewhat unfair, given that more of the weight of the Whitecross leadership rests on Charles's shoulders than on his own. Unusually for *Survivors*, Marshall also repeatedly places the children at the heart of the action, rather than simply relying on their characters for light relief: John has a near-fatal accident with a shotgun; both are taken hostage at gunpoint; they have to escape from captivity on the barge; and they are close at hand when the wood alcohol detonates.

With the evil intentions of Grice and Kane increasingly apparent, it seems inevitable that their visit will end in bloodshed. What comes as a jolt is that it is Whitecross's own man of the cloth who is shot dead as he attempts to negotiate for John's and Lizzie's release. Earlier in the episode, Pet had gently teased Lewis – who had been hard at work planting cabbages on an exposed hilltop – with the Biblical edict: 'Whatsoever a man soweth so also shall he reap'. Grice and Kane may ultimately get their comeuppance for their own murderous ways, but Lewis is also 'rewarded' for his compassion and openness by violent death. Lewis pays the 'ultimate price' for his own attempts to act morally. It is not simply the murder of Lewis that is shocking, but its manner. Kane blasts him with a shotgun without any emotion and barely a flicker of reaction. As Lewis's body crashes to the floor (with actor Roy Herrick yanked backwards by a Kirby-wire), Kane takes a final slug of alcohol, and then flings the empty bottle towards his victim. It is interesting too to see Dudley and the BBC take the decision that Lewis's religious storyline had reached its conclusion. Rather than have Lewis slip off into the background ensemble of characters never to be seen again, they decide to end his presence in violent death. After the demise of Lewis, *Survivors* never again focuses on the religious conviction of a major character.

This episode contains some nasty and close-to-the-knuckle stuff, including a total of four deaths – a stabbing and drowning, a close quarter shooting and a deadly explosion that takes the lives of two others. It seems extremely unlikely that material of a similar nature would be transmitted in the same timeslot today. Indeed, satellite station UK Gold considered the sequence in which Lewis is killed too disturbing for the early Sunday morning transmission slot in which it broadcast repeats of the series in the 1990s, and cut the scene almost entirely.

In many ways reminiscent of the gang from "Something of Value", Grice and Kane represent the selfish and acquisitive smash-and-grab strand of survivors, probably not seen again in such stark relief until the events of "The Last Laugh" in series three. In living off the efforts of others and seizing what they will, they contribute nothing and care for no-one but themselves. In post-Death conditions their villainy has wider social repercussions – there is no surplus against which the damage inflicted by such 'parasites' might be written off. All are obliged to contribute – even back in "Birth of a Hope", Charles had – perhaps over-bluntly – told Greg that he would be required to work if his people agreed to settle at Whitecross. It is entirely fitting that it is the recklessness and lack of understanding of Grice and Kane that leads them to their doom – they do not understand the workings of the barge that they have killed to steal and, like their ignorance about the effects of drinking wood alcohol (it will render them blind before killing them), such stupidity seals their fate.

It is great to see canal waterways featuring in the *Survivors* world – an entirely appropriate throwback to an earlier age, convincingly evoked on screen. Marshall, who was actually no great enthusiast for the series, recalled in an interview in *Action TV* in 2005 that his work on "Parasites" allowed him to write about one of his own interests: 'It was a messy production, but memorable for me in that I got to write about barges for the first time; a theme I returned to in [the 1984 Granada TV fugitive drama] *Travelling Man*.' Marshall remembers researching the mechanics of canal travel at the Stoke Bruerne Barge Museum near Towcester. There is real confidence and assuredness evident in the scripting throughout, and the sense of foreboding that grows after Grice's and Kane's arrival is well paced. The visual effects team were clearly keen to expand on the script's outline of the barge's destruction. Marshall had written: 'Suddenly there is a dull muffled explosion in the distance. Small mushroom cloud of smoke – Hiroshima Junior.' Yet it seems that the fireball that the crew designed in preference detonated at a far larger size than even they had intended (and Stephen Dudley is the slowest to flinch in response). Its scale gives the moment all the more impact as a result – even if the inability to display much in the way of the sunken wreck in the aftermath again highlights the restraints of budget and time against which the series always had to struggle.

The final scene, in which Mina is teaching the Whitecross children about plants and herbs, allows Marshall to make his 'parasite' metaphor unambiguous. Mina reflects to herself on the analogy between the nature of parasitic plants and the actions of their human counterparts. Yet, given the rich quality of the drama that has preceded this moment, it feels like something of an unnecessary add-on, spelling out an implication that the audience has already absorbed.

"Parasites" offers believable guest characters, engaging dialogue, picturesque canal locations and an explosive finale, to dispel once again the myth that series two is a study of pig manure and soap production. *RC*

2.11 NEW ARRIVALS

UK TRANSMISSION: 9 June 1976: 8.10pm – 9.00pm
VIEWING FIGURE: 7.02m
WRITER: Roger Parkes
DIRECTOR: Pennant Roberts
REGULAR CAST: Ian McCulloch (Greg Preston); Denis Lill (Charles Vaughan); Lucy Fleming (Jenny Richards); Celia Gregory (Ruth Anderson); Lorna Lewis (Pet Simpson); John Abineri (Hubert Goss); Michael Gover (Arthur Russell); Gordon Salkilld (Jack Wood); Stephen Tate (Alan); Heather Wright (Melanie); June Page (Sally); Peter Duncan (Dave); Roger Monk (Pete); Tanya Ronder (Lizzie Willoughby); Stephen Dudley (John Millon)
GUEST CAST: Ian Hastings (Mark Carter)
UNCREDITED CAST: Harry Oaten, Michael Britten-Jones, Doreen Purchase, Pat Montrose, Wilfred Limbrick, Robert Wilson, Carole Carvin-Jones (Whitecross Residents)
OB RECORDING: 12 - 17 May 1976
LOCATIONS: Callow Hill Farm, Monmouth, Mons; The Mill, Skenfrith, Mons

SYNOPSIS: One of a new group of arrivals to Whitecross, Mark Carter, appears to be butchering the settlement's heifers. However, when Charles arrives on the scene, he finds that Carter is merely curing a condition called 'clover bloat.' Carter styles himself as something of an agronomist guru and believes that Charles has a lot to learn in agricultural terms. The new arrivals are from a failed settlement at which Ruth has been tending the sick; she brought them to Whitecross to join the community and suggests that they live in the old mill. Carter is quick to pass on his advice and criticism to Charles, Pet and Greg and is keen to sort out Whitecross's agricultural problems. Unfortunately, Arthur seems to have contracted the same illness as the older members of Carter's old community. Although he finds Carter abrasive, Charles recognises the value of his expertise and agrees to his proposal to draw up a five-year plan based around crop rotation and livestock management. Another of the new arrivals, Melanie, recruits Alan to come and live at the mill, which prompts Charles to become worried about the development of a potentially damaging generation gap. Melanie is convinced that Carter's plan is about his feelings of inadequacy in relation to Charles and Greg. Pet too has grave doubts about Carter's ability and motivation. As Arthur's condition worsens, Mina and Jack also become ill. Carter suggests calling a meeting to vote on his five-year plan, which relies on the success of Greg's PROMIFR (PROtotype Muck-Into-Fuel-Refinery) contraption to make methane to power a tractor. When Arthur dies, Ruth reveals that she believes that the illness relates to post-Death depression and low morale – what used to be called 'broken heart syndrome.' At the vote meeting, Carter sets out his priorities, but Greg questions him on his views on morale – which the agronomist does not consider to be as important as farming efficiency. Although Carter's leadership is rejected, his plan is not. He leaves alone, while Melanie and the others decide to stay on at Whitecross.

ANALYSIS: Like Martin Worth's "By Bread Alone", Roger Parkes's second script for the series, originally titled "The Newcomers", concerns priorities at Whitecross and concludes once again that it is a more subjective non-survivalist agenda that is the most appropriate for the settlement's morale and future. The episode is also significant for its introduction of a group of youngsters who are set to shake up Whitecross during its final days.

Although well-plotted, "New Arrivals" suffers from the prevalence in the dialogue of some fairly off-putting agricultural terminology (presumably due to Parkes's farming background), which often makes the episode feel like a crash course in agronomy. We learn that 'clover bloat' is chronic flatulence caused by allowing cattle to eat fresh clover after a cold night; that 'vernalisation' is the frosting of a crop in the ground after it has been sown; and that it is an enzyme affecting starch that is causing the loaves of bread to collapse. We can all too easily empathise with Pet, who holds up her hands as if to say 'enough is enough' when Jenny – who is a surprising convert to the Carter school – reveals this last fact. The inclusion of these agricultural elements may seem a little dull, but at least they base the episode in scientific fact and see the series follow Carter's directive: 'Stop playing at it and start farming.' For the first time, the realities of what the survivors need to do in actual farming terms with manpower alone are given an honest and insightful treatment. As commendable as this may be in terms of authenticity, the overriding question is of course whether or not it makes for good television – a recurrent debate associated with the second series of *Survivors*.

The principal guest character, Mark Carter, is played to condescending and disrespectful perfection by Ian Hastings. Although the character is initially depicted as being motivated merely by the desire to sort out the settlement's many agricultural problems, fellow new arrival Melanie keenly observes that there is more to his five-year plan than that: 'Make you feel small, don't they, Greg and that Charles Vaughan? ... You want to knock them down, show them up.' Melanie also refers to Carter's well-kept secret, which not only proves to be the key to his eventual downfall, but also provides an explanation for the fatalities both at their old settlement and at Whitecross. The episode is plotted in such a way that this secret is not fully revealed until it can achieve its maximum impact: at the crucial meeting that forms the narrative's climax. It transpires that although Carter may have the requisite skills to be an excellent farmer, he has no interest in morale, and that at his old settlement, he was the cause not only of a state of 'aggro-culture,' but also desertions ('Useless dropouts') and suicides ('They just couldn't cope'), due to his intolerance and 'contempt for age and inefficiency.' Ruth, who has a rare opportunity to make a professional assessment of the recent deaths among the older members of both communities, believes that they are the result of low morale and tally with 'broken heart syndrome.' Greg's statement that 'a settlement's morale reflects the worth of its leadership' would seem to indicate that Carter was indirectly responsible for these deaths as well. That it is Greg who sees off Carter's threat to how Whitecross is run by endorsing Charles's leadership is an intriguing turn of events given the pair's previous rivalry. It is also interesting that Carter, with his strong sense of mission and unwillingness to take people's feelings into account, is not all that unlike Charles as he was originally depicted in "Corn Dolly" with his single-minded approach and cold, hard logic.

"New Arrivals" deals chiefly with the question of conflicting priorities; in fact, the latter word is used frequently in the episode. Carter's priorities are depicted as too rigid and lacking in compassion and understanding, while Whitecross's priorities may superficially appear to amount to 'little more than shepherding,' but at least they ensure that morale and well-being are taken into account. Given the fatal human cost of Carter's approach, it is no surprise that ultimately the Whitecross residents unanimously choose the priority of Charles's compassionate leadership over Carter's cold efficiency, even though, as he outlines, this may mean they don't have enough grub to see them through the winter. As he says in his opening scene in the mill, Charles may indeed be 'a farmer in temperament but not in practice' but, as Pet reassures him: 'Surely more important is your concern for us as people?'

The generation gap, a problem that will dominate the next episode, "Over the Hills", even more strongly, becomes an issue for the first time here as the young arrivals add a new dynamic to the series. Interestingly it is Greg, not Charles, who has a better understanding of how to deal with the problem. Charles fears the development of a splinter group at the mill, provoked by Alan's decision to join the new arrivals there, believing that it will prevent the community from operating as a team. Greg, however, sees that Charles's adoption of 'the old heavy parent act' will not help him to achieve his long-held dream of 'responsibility, roots and children' and wisely advises that if he chooses to 'face them with social obligations, they'll just scarper.' Although Charles is, as Greg surmises, powerless to intervene, the arm of the community at the mill will indeed engender future problems.

Carter aside, Heather Wright's flirtatious and sarcastic Melanie is clearly presented as the most interesting of the new arrivals and is significantly the only one to integrate with the established Whitecross regulars. She is smart enough to recognise Carter's game ('Their place, that's what – not yours, theirs') and to openly flatter Greg ('If we'd had someone like *you* ...'). Her strong desire for independence is woefully underestimated by Carter who, right up until the last minute, honestly believes she will be happy leaving Whitecross and trudging around the country with him; this misjudgement leaves him completely defeated and with no choice but to leave alone. Of the other three arrivals, June Page's Sally stands out as perceptive and gutsy ('Use this meeting to get you in as boss – no thanks') and far less of a cipher than the two-dimensional Dave and Pete.

Of the Whitecross residents, Pet is presented here as a strong protector of Charles's interests and as possessing admirable instincts. She is the only character who has the insight and faith to appraise positively the set-up they already enjoy and therefore question Carter's new directives. Her views on the importance of good leadership over farming efficiency also prove to be spot on.

Jack finally receives an interesting subplot, although the interpolation of an overlong piece of footage from a football match in the form of a daydream sequence – the only instance of a flashback to the pre-Death world in the entire series – does seem a little bizarre. Pennant Roberts recalls that the purpose of the scene was to convey the idea that Jack had more of a will to live than Arthur, hence the fantasising that he was back at Upton Park and that England star Emlyn Hughes was playing for his home team, West Ham: 'We wanted to illustrate the intenseness of Jack's vision. It may have been a clumsy device, but we had to make do as best we could with what was available.'

While Jack pulls through courtesy of the Hammers, Arthur Russell is less lucky and is hastily ushered out of the series here. Roberts remembers: 'Criticisms that the series was altogether too middle-class were really starting to bite by this time, and a further reshuffle was overdue ... Michael (Gover) had been mightily chuffed at landing the role of a regular in a popular series – one that might provide him with some degree of financial comfort in his latter years. It is not surprising therefore that he was not best pleased at being sacrificed for the sake of bringing in new faces.' Given that Arthur was one of the few original 'Grange survivors' it does feel like something of a shame that he is written out here without even the courtesy of an on-screen death.

In spite of the climactic vote to go with Carter's new farming system based around Greg's methane-from-manure PROMIFR, the agronomist's parting shot is that the settlement is unlikely to be tractor-powered by the autumn – as Charles has suggested – and that with their priorities they will instead 'be sitting back eating grass, playing bingo.' Greg's future failure to progress the PROMIFR scheme any further at Whitecross would seem to support Carter's sardonic assessment. However, by the third series episode "Bridgehead", Greg has succeeded in engineering a methane-powered car.

Despite its reliance on agricultural jargon and the specifics of Carter's five-year plan, which make the episode a little heavy-going in places, "New Arrivals" boasts a solid plot and performances and benefits from the influx of a younger generation of characters. *AP*

2.12 OVER THE HILLS

UK TRANSMISSION: 16 June 1976: 8.10pm – 9.00pm
VIEWING FIGURE: 8.84m
WRITER: Martin Worth
DIRECTOR: Eric Hills
REGULAR CAST: Ian McCulloch (Greg Preston); Denis Lill (Charles Vaughan); Lucy Fleming (Jenny Richards); Celia Gregory (Ruth Anderson); Lorna Lewis (Pet Simpson); John Abineri (Hubert Goss); Gigi Gatti (Daniella); Stephen Tate (Alan); Heather Wright (Melanie); June Page (Sally); Peter Duncan (Dave); Roger Monk (Pete); Tanya Ronder (Lizzie Willoughby); Stephen Dudley (John Millon)
GUEST CAST: Linda Robson (Barbara); Nula Conwell (Ann)
UNCREDITED CAST: Yara David (Yara)
OB RECORDING: 21 - 26 May 1976
LOCATIONS: Callow Hill Farm, Monmouth, Mons; The Mill, Skenfrith, Mons

SYNOPSIS: At the mill, Melanie, Alan and the other younger members of the community are playing a dangerous rope-climbing game. On the farm, Greg and Charles discuss the prospects for methane-based tractor power. While enjoying some time off work in the countryside, Melanie resists Alan's attentions, given the risk that she may conceive. Meanwhile, Sally is concerned that she may already be pregnant. When Ruth confirms this, Charles is delighted. Sally reveals that Alan is the baby's father and says she wants to live with him as if they were husband and

Midsummer Party. © Anne Christie

wife. While Greg works on getting a motorbike engine going, Melanie muses about the world beyond Whitecross. Pet suggests that they throw a Midsummer party to celebrate Sally's baby, and Charles thinks that such an event may give everyone a renewed sense of commitment. However, he is incensed when he discovers that Ruth has been trying to invent an effective form of contraception. She believes that one of the worst effects of The Death is that women are in danger of becoming just child-bearers again. She also argues that Charles must consider the fact that people like Melanie miss the life they led in the old world. At Sally's party, Charles talks about their collective responsibility for her baby and for the future of the settlement. After the meal, Melanie tells Charles that she does not find the new world exciting; he responds that she should be acting more responsibly because of her influence on others. Meanwhile Pet, who has yet to conceive, propositions an inebriated Greg, but he turns her down. She is surprised to learn that it is she who must be infertile, as Charles has fathered children before. Soon after Greg leaves, Charles returns and makes up with Pet. At the mill, the party has continued through the night. After insisting on playing the rope game, Sally miscarries. When he learns of this, Charles is furious. To Mel's and Alan's excitement, Greg manages to get the motorbike engine going.

ANALYSIS: Martin Worth's second script for the series marks the beginning of the end of the Whitecross community and focuses on the interrelated themes of the emancipation of women, procreation and fulfilment. "Over the Hills" departs from the second series' standard template in that its issues are explored by having Whitecross look in on itself rather than react to yet another new arrival. Such a backdrop allows significant and rewarding character development for virtually all the regulars, many of whom rise to the occasion to give their very best performances.

The episode title refers to Melanie's and Alan's stated belief that there is always something better to be had over the next hill, which explains their unwillingness to put down roots at Whitecross. Conversely, Charles is seen to be preoccupied with encouraging the birth of a new generation that would give them just such roots: 'Unless we commit ourselves here, we're always going to be squatters, wherever we go' (which in itself is an interesting assertion given the wanderer narrative of the final series). The issues arising from this conflict of interest are explored through a central plot that sees Sally discover that she is pregnant by Alan.

As in "Corn Dolly", Charles appears to be incapable of sustaining a sense of proportion when it comes to the issue of reproduction and is seen to adopt the same unnerving fervency of manner and dominance over proceedings. He is characteristically overjoyed that Sally is pregnant, insisting that this is the best thing that has happened at Whitecross, and is shocked when others, such as Ruth, are less enthusiastic; he appears to have conveniently forgotten about the complications that surrounded the birth of baby Paul. Convinced that all will be well, Charles is altogether more interested in the opportunity Sally's baby will give him to engender a sense of commitment in the community by impressing a collective responsibility upon them, not only for Sally's baby, but also for the future. He chooses a Midsummer party in Sally's honour as the platform for a pivotal speech in which he attempts to employ all his political skill and natural charisma: 'This is our land … It's capable of infinite prosperity … We have a stake in the future, and Sally's baby … will have no bitter memories of the old world to mar the excitement of the new one.' Unfortunately, Charles seems unable to comprehend the alternative point of view advocated by Ruth and Melanie. Despite the fact that glasses are subsequently raised by all in a toast to the future, he has crucially failed to take on board the fact that the new world is not deemed to be 'exciting' by everyone present and that most have better memories of the old one. He makes this error despite the fact that Ruth has only just argued that The Death has brought fulfilment to only a select few, making her 'the only known doctor' and transforming Charles from 'a crank in the eyes of the supermarket society' into a 'king.' She sagely presents Melanie as the antithesis of their experience: 'Living with her film director boyfriend in St Germaine de Près … Movies and parties, shops and clothes. A world you despised, but she revelled in.' Charles is presented as effectively offering Melanie an existence that could not be more of a contrast to her old life, which is uninvitingly, but accurately, summed up by Ruth as: 'Harvest supper once a year and motherhood.' Celia Gregory is in top form here, as Ruth's views are powerfully aired through some compelling and memorable dialogue.

The rope game devised by Melanie and the others (the rope replaces a chain specified in the original script) is symptomatic of Whitecross's younger set's boredom with the new world, providing them with the excitement – such as it is – that they crave. Melanie presides over the game, maximising its danger and accentuating her position as the leader of the splinter group. Charles is all too aware of the threat that Melanie poses in this role ('You need to be more responsible – you're an influence here, so make it a good one') but he underestimates just how coldly determined she is to defend her own and Sally's freedom of choice. It is to this end that she ultimately uses the rope game to take a pro-choice stance, knowing exactly what is at stake, as Sally starts her ascent; this is powerfully illustrated by her statement: 'Everyone has the right to play.' Melanie is depicted as a surprisingly formidable opponent to Charles, and as a more self-serving character than is perhaps first suggested in "New Arrivals". As this episode was in fact written first – Martin Worth having created Melanie – Roger Parkes must have chosen to soften the character somewhat for her debut episode.

Ruth also poses a threat to Charles's plans for the future, as it transpires that she has tried to invent an efficient contraceptive for fear of women losing the freedom and rights they had only so recently gained before The Death. Charles is depicted as uninterested in these rights, interpreting the woman's right to choose as 'freedom to let the world die out' and instead seeing the matter as a question of female responsibility. However, when it comes to male responsibility, an entirely different picture is presented. The idea of Sally marrying Alan is presented as 'very unfair on the other girls' on the basis that, with a view to the next generation, Alan must be allowed to take as many sexual partners as he desires. Charles attempts to make this sound more acceptable by rationalising that there are '... more girls under twenty-five than there are boys. We can't deny them children just because there's no-one to live with them permanently.' Worth is keen to emphasise this double standard, as well as the fact that Charles's 'progressive' take on the situation ('We need to establish a completely new set of mores if we're going to have a future') is not widely shared by either the young or the old. Daniella and Hubert both naturally espouse old world values: the former hears what she wants to hear about Sally's party, believing that Charles is talking about a traditional wedding breakfast; while the latter unhelpfully comments that Alan should be 'gelded' and describes Sally as a 'little slut.' As for the younger generation's views, which Charles admits worry him more, there are further signs that his ideals will not be adopted: Melanie and Alan have a progressive attitude only in old world terms, as they seek no-strings promiscuity; while Sally seeks the security that the now defunct state of marriage would have offered her. Interestingly, Greg's assertion to Melanie that he would have married Jenny (and Charles, Pet) by now 'if it didn't create a moral precedent that we can't afford for the present time' doesn't recognise the fact that the simple existence of their monogamous relationships sets a precedent that is just as influential; Sally tells Pet that she doesn't seek literal marriage in the new world but 'living together properly like you and Charles.' As Sally eventually loses her baby, Worth ensures continuity with her predicament here by writing in a sensitive scene in "New World" in which she offers to help Jenny with baby Paul while Greg is away.

The childless relationship between Charles and Pet underpins the narrative and is used to great effect by Worth to explain not only Charles's sudden fervour ('It's not Sally's baby he's so anxious to see born, it's his own'), but also Pet's startlingly open suggestions that Charles should pursue relationships with both Ruth and Melanie, as well as Pet's own willingness to give herself to another man. The scene in which Pet attempts to seduce Greg and learns that she herself is infertile rather than Charles, is beautifully played by Lewis and McCulloch and one of the highlights of the piece. Similarly moving is the subsequent kitchen scene in which Charles redeems many of his earlier outbursts and distasteful theorising by unconditionally declaring his love for Pet 'even though anything,' providing the comfort she sorely needs. Despite his ambitions for a new generation at Whitecross, Charles commits to Pet and therefore proves that he is a different man from the one we first met in "Corn Dolly". Nevertheless, his protestation to Ruth that 'If you don't believe in having children, there won't be a world' lingers effectively as the episode draws to a close. Melanie's assessment of Greg's motorbike engine as 'the best thing that's ever happened here' is a direct and calculated counterpoint to Charles's earlier view on Sally's pregnancy, neatly illustrating the opposing points of view. Despite the legitimacy of each perspective, it is difficult not to have sympathy with Charles as he rides off on his horse in utter frustration, his ambitions thwarted.

There is a fairly serious continuity error early on in "Over the Hills". This relates to the PROMIFR and unfortunately directly contradicts the action of "New Arrivals". When Greg states that he intends to use the methane it produces for a tractor and not for heat and light, Charles is visibly and vocally surprised. However, a methane-powered tractor was central to Mark Carter's dung stock-piling farming plan, which was unanimously voted as the way forward by the community. It appears that either Worth was not briefed on the intended content of "New Arrivals" – which was written after "Over the Hills", although it would be recorded first – or that the production team decided that more piles of dung were not what the series needed!

Through the colourful lawn party, Midsummer is once again presented in *Survivors* as a time of hope and expectation, just as it was in "A Beginning". However, producer Terence Dudley was by now gearing up once again to rip apart another content community – which in these scenes may have come over as a little too settled and comfortable for his liking. The lawn party is also notable as the point at which the boundaries between the fictional Whitecross and the real-life Callow Hill location seem the most blurred: not only are Callow children such as Yara referred to by name, but the party – which although staged was actually enjoyed for real – is attended by previously unseen Callow folk too.

"Over the Hills" is a great example of how 'on form' *Survivors* can explore all sides of a theme in a dramatic and interesting way. Worth's strong script is backed up by memorable and affecting performances from the principal players. *AP*

2.13 NEW WORLD

UK TRANSMISSION: 23 June 1976: 8.10pm – 9.00pm
VIEWING FIGURE: 7.98m
WRITER: Martin Worth
DIRECTOR: Terence Williams
REGULAR CAST: Ian McCulloch (Greg Preston); Denis Lill (Charles Vaughan); Lucy Fleming (Jenny Richards); Celia Gregory (Ruth Anderson); Lorna Lewis (Pet Simpson); John Abineri (Hubert Goss); Gordon Salkilld (Jack Wood); Stephen Tate (Alan); Heather Wright (Melanie); June Page (Sally); Peter Duncan (Dave); Roger Monk (Pete); Tanya Ronder (Lizzie Willoughby); Stephen Dudley (John Millon)
GUEST CAST: Sally Osborn (Agnes Carlsson); Dan Meaden (Seth)
OB RECORDING: 30 May - 4 June 1976
LOCATION: Callow Hill Farm, Monmouth, Mons

Lucy and Ian learn their lines at Callow Hill. © Anne Christie

SYNOPSIS: Whitecross is filled with excitement as a hot-air balloon is spotted floating towards the settlement. Alan, Melanie and others all rush off in its direction, but it disappears from view. Returning, disappointed, they spot the downed balloon, which has crash-landed in trees – killing its solitary pilot. There are some surprises amongst his belongings – including a camera loaded with film and a notebook filled with jottings in a foreign language. Melanie deduces, from a set of aerial postcards, that the pilot originated from Chipping Camden, and she and Alan set off to investigate. There they discover Seth, who explains that the balloonist came from Norway, and that his daughter Agnes was travelling with him. When John finds the balloonist's map, Dave, Ruth, Jenny, Charles and Greg together work out that this Norwegian was carrying out a survey of settlements in the south of Britain. Agnes meanwhile is making her way towards Whitecross on foot. Meeting Hubert, she learns that her father has been killed – which only strengthens her resolve to see his plan through. She explains that the Norwegian survivors are desperate to restart their industries, but that their experts are preoccupied with hunting for food. If settlements in England can provide foodstuffs and manpower, then Norway can provide engines and other machinery in exchange. This will require communities in Britain to specialise and to trade their surpluses. Greg and Charles are enthused by the plan, but both Pet and Jenny are appalled at the thought of Whitecross being pulled apart. Despite her sense of dread, Jenny acknowledges that Greg is duty-bound to travel to Norway and do what he can to help. After an emotional farewell, Greg and Jack join Agnes in the hot-air balloon and set off for the coast, beginning the long journey to Norway.

ANALYSIS: "New World" proves to be another critical turning point in the *Survivors* narrative – and things are never, ever the same again after its conclusion. Whether the drama of "New World" can be said to introduce overdue or unwanted developments, depends almost entirely on how positive a view is taken of *Survivors*' sojourn at Whitecross. It is a reflection of Worth's considerable skills that he is able to deliver some unsettling dramatic upheavals and still produce a story that is, for the most part, emotionally and dramatically convincing.

This is certainly the last time that *Survivors* would exude a sense of 'warmth' – in all senses of the word. Never again would the sun shine so brightly, or the surroundings look so attractive and welcoming. When the series returned in 1977, the remaining survivors would discover a darker, dirtier and more unstable world than the one they were becoming accustomed to. As with the first series finale "A Beginning", "New World" is also the last time that large numbers of the existing cast are seen.

It is the arrival of the hot-air balloon (which the script had specified should be red in colour – presumably to stand out against the green of the countryside) that turns the Whitecross world upside-down. "New World" is distinguished as the last *Survivors* story to feature film sequences, with all the shots of the balloon in flight being captured on a mobile film camera. This produces an unfortunate mismatch in the opening sequence of the episode, in which the Whitecross regulars (being recorded by the Outside Broadcast video unit) are seen reacting to the 'appearance' of the balloon (clearly a film insert). Yet it is hard to see that director Terence Williams had any other option than to use a film-video split. It was certainly beyond the capabilities of the production team to have engineered repeated fly-bys by a largely unsteerable hot-air balloon for multiple reaction shots, even if the necessary recording time had been available. As Peter Duncan, who played Dave, rightly suggests: 'The video cameras were quite chunky in those days ... They were big things to lug around – and they used to have the umbilical cords. Whereas the little film cameras – you can take a little 8mm thing anywhere ... to get the image of something that you couldn't get a big camera close enough to shoot.'

Even as the balloon disappears from sight, its impact on the Whitecross community is immediately divisive. It is not only the youngsters from the mill who are thrilled by the sight of it, but Jack and even Hubert as well. Charles is disappointed that the community seems so eager to 'be rescued' from their predicament and that their commitment to Whitecross seems so transient. It is only when the balloon, its dead pilot (originally named Dagmar in the script) and his belongings are discovered, that Charles and Greg also become caught up in the excitement.

Worth allows the truth about the mysterious balloonist to be revealed gradually, as more pieces of the puzzle are retrieved and made sense of. As his notes are translated and his survey analysed, Whitecross's field of vision of the world around them expands beyond recognition. What this demonstrates very well is how narrow the survivors' field of perception has been until now. Even the existence of chestnut-flavoured honey ('a speciality of the Cotswolds,' as Jenny observes) comes as a complete surprise to them. Lars Carlsson's notes reveal a country, and a situation elsewhere in Europe, about which they are almost entirely ignorant. Agnes later reveals, for example, that there are 3,000 survivors living and working between Hereford and Grimsby. This also exposes again how misconceived the struggling London community's own sense of self-importance ("Lights of London") really is.

Melanie feels vindicated by the discovery of the hot-air balloon, helium canister, and film camera – evidence, she is sure, of the persistence of civilisation elsewhere. Charles is still keen to downplay her expectations of the significance of these finds, as she and Alan head off to discover the balloon's origins. From their meeting with Seth, the blacksmith living on the far side of Ross-on-Wye, Melanie and Alan learn that Denmark is now virtually empty of people, and that less than 100 malnourished survivors remain alive in Norway. So keen are Charles and Greg to hear of their news on their return to Whitecross that the ten-day quarantine rule is simply forgotten.

Sally Osborn (daughter of Andrew Osborn, the BBC Head of Series who first commissioned *Survivors*) is quite superb as the febrile and determined young Agnes – whose atheism and sense of mission afford her little opportunity to mourn the passing of her father. She skilfully communicates the combination of urgency and energy that help to make a compelling case for the Norwegian mission. British survivors must, she insists, provide the food, supplies and expertise to get the machine tool plants near Bergen going again and begin the process of specialisation and expansion.

As the consequences of the plan become clear, deep divisions in the Whitecross community are revealed – with Pet and Jenny anxious at the serious implications for the settlement, and Greg and Charles increasingly enthused by the possibilities Agnes outlines. Pet may complain to Charles that he's 'breaking the place up,' yet of course this is precisely producer Dudley's intention.

There are precious few signs of any sort of democratic decision being taken within the settlement. In "New Arrivals", Mark Carter's five-year plan had been put to a full meeting of the community for debate and vote. Here, despite the protestations of their partners, Greg and Charles simply assume by default that this plan – which will completely transform life at Whitecross – is to be enacted, and with it the necessary forced relocation of labour. Rather than heading off to adventures in Norway, Jack might have dusted off his shop steward's badge (last mentioned in "Greater Love") and mused that the old days of bosses and workers now seemed to be making a comeback. Melanie would likewise doubtless have jumped at the chance for a space in the balloon if that had been offered – rather than the drudgery and monotony of a weaver's life that she is instructed to accept instead.

The element of "New World" that it is most difficult to accept is the speed and ease with which Whitecross's place in the scheme of things is surrendered. This feels unnatural, in part because of the about-turn in Charles's vision of the importance of the community and of the self-sufficiency it requires. He has previously been an advocate for wind-power, water mills and replaceable, sustainable low-level technology. In "Over the Hills", he could barely contain his frustration at Alan's and Melanie's enthusiasm for Greg's new methane engine, seeing it as a distraction from the real business of long-term survival. Yet here he is willing to ransom all their futures to an untested plan to restart the kinds of industrial machinery that Charles would have previously dismissed as the relics of an earlier age. Perhaps more importantly, after all the effort that Charles has put in to nurturing and expanding the Whitecross settlement, he seems willing to have its residents scatter, and the community unravel, with alarmingly little thought. The reason that this feels somewhat forced is, of course, that it is. Worth is required to hit his dramatic targets within the confines of a

Gordon Salkilld (Jack Wood). © Denis Lill

single episode, which means that some aspects of the storytelling inevitably get compressed. The different themes suggested by the original episode title "Flight" might have highlighted the abandoning of Whitecross more directly.

The one point where Worth appears to take this process too far is in Jenny's observation to Greg that all the Whitecross residents want to 'be free to run … if the worst happened.' She goes on to state that: 'This place is just a refuge, and everybody knows it. You and I felt it in our bones when we got here.' Even given Jenny's agitated state, the suggestion that there is no real commitment to the community amongst its members seems badly out of character, as well as wholly unfounded. Moreover, this remark risks devaluing the importance of all the Whitecross adventures that have delivered the series to this point – in suggesting that the characters involved simply saw themselves as 'in transit', marking time while they waited for something better to come along. This feels acutely misjudged.

Elsewhere, Lucy Fleming does get to show her more adventurous side, after many episodes in which she appeared only as washer-woman, nanny and soap skivvy. She proves herself to be an accomplished horsewoman, galloping across the fields around Whitecross with considerable skill. It was a talent that Fleming would be allowed to make more extensive use of in the following series. The outdoors sequences, shot in the lush green fields and woodlands around Callow Hill, demonstrate once again how much the OB cameras brightened and enriched the images they captured. Even the rain that lashes down while Carlsson's corpse is lowered from the balloon basket is barely visible on screen (as cast and crew press on through inclement weather to finish the scene on time).

As it becomes increasingly likely that Greg will join Agnes on the return trip, Jenny recalls the anxiety she felt while he was away during the events of "Lights of London". The later scene in which Jenny finally reconciles herself to Greg's inevitable departure to Norway is played with great skill by both Fleming and McCulloch. The setting and composition of this sequence, in subdued indoor light and without distracting background noise, with the characters sat motionless facing one another, enhances the feeling of intimacy. The understated playing, and the physical distance between the two characters, actually helps to heighten the emotional power of the moment. What gives it still greater retrospective impact is the knowledge that this is the last time that these two characters will ever be together, and that Greg will not make good on his promise to return. At the start of series two, Greg had accepted the constraints and commitments of becoming a 'family man'. As it concludes, he takes on a wider set of social responsibilities that see him leave his familial obligations behind.

In "New World", characters predict future developments with varying degrees of accuracy. Charles will find his insistence that the rail network is now 'obsolete' is premature. Although Pet's comments are meant sarcastically, her suggestions that 'government' and even 'money' are now set to return will prove to be prescient. Meanwhile, Greg's assurance to Charles that he realises that good communications are 'essential' to the success of the Norwegian plan will not be borne out in practice.

The final shots of the community gathered together to watch the balloon lift off provide a fitting and suitably dramatic end to the series, as the vessel takes to the air and the closing theme soars. The script notes that the reaction to Jack's joke about his impending air-sickness should be greeted by: 'Loud laughter from everyone, overdone – covering up the tension and anxiety and loss' with which everyone is struggling. The moment is only slightly marred by the obvious tether line still attached to the basket as the balloon takes flight with the actors aboard. As with the conclusion of "A Beginning" in series one, there is a sense both of closure and of renewed opportunity suggested by this finale – which would have given the programme a workable farewell had its renewal not been assured.

Despite the strong melancholic undertones, and the feeling that everything is now in a state of flux, "New World" is an effective and affecting send-off for the second series – though not all of the changes that it heralds will prove to be welcome. *RC*

SERIES 2: REVIEW

The second series of *Survivors* is primarily concerned with the practical mechanics of survival and the demands of communal living. Both are themes that, given their somewhat under-developed treatment in the first series, were arguably deserving of more screen time. However, the extent of their exploration through this second set of thirteen episodes has always firmly divided the critics, particularly in the years since its first broadcast.

Crucially, however, with Terry Nation now estranged from his creation, Terence Dudley's new approach involved not merely a thematic change but, more significantly, a considerable revision of narrative style. With the aid of Jack Ronder – the only surviving first series scriptwriter – Dudley developed a bravely introspective and largely dialogue-based new format for the series. More often than not, the new episodes were in keeping with his passion for issue-led human drama, examining the emotional and physical demands of survival without recourse to lengthy action sequences or perilous situations. Dudley was confident that the unique predicament in which the survivors now found themselves was interesting enough in itself to connect with the viewing public. Although, as has already been mentioned, healthy viewing figures and a considerably more positive press reaction bore his assertion out at the time, it is nevertheless this new version of *Survivors* that has since been dubbed 'ersatz *Emmerdale*'.

Appropriately enough, the new style is nowhere more clearly portrayed than in the series' opener, "Birth of a Hope", in which the way of life at Whitecross, the characters that populate the settlement, and the emotional well-being of the survivors of the fire at the Grange, take narrative precedence. The fire is short on screen-time and essentially a means to a new beginning, whereas the only other action element – Charles's motorcycle mercy dash to find Ruth – is used as the opening chapter in a series-long power-play between Greg and the charismatic Welshman. (This settlement, it is being suggested, ain't big enough for the both of 'em.) Action for action's sake appears to have no place here. However, this is not to say that the second series is devoid of action. Reflection on its key moments immediately brings to mind the dramatic stand-off in the Underground ("Lights of London Part 2"), Greg's tussle with the sniper ("A Friend in Need"), and the barge explosion ("Parasites"); but the difference is that such action does not characterise this series in the same way as it does the first. Equally memorable and far more prevalent here are outpourings of emotion (such as Ruth's grief over Paul), soul-baring (Alistair McFadden's monologue) and impassioned speeches (Jenny to Lewis, and Charles to anyone within earshot!)

One aspect of the new run that might be considered off-putting is the inclusion of a significant amount of exposition detailing the various self-sufficiency processes attempted or at least considered by the survivors, such as the extraction of methane from manure and the method by which charcoal is made. While this detail may inject a strong sense of scientific realism into the series, making the activities of the Whitecross community infinitely more believable than the endeavours briefly depicted at the Grange settlement (e.g. the deeply unrealistic hay-making in "Revenge"), this is nevertheless achieved at the calculated expense of pace and excitement.

The core debate of *Survivors* – whether they should choose to depend on the industry of the old world or learn to be more self-reliant – is principally developed in series two by the opposing views of Charles and Greg. In "Over the Hills", Charles has cause to remind Greg that the Whitecross 'way' has always been not to depend on anything that they cannot replace themselves; however, Greg is anxious to put his engineering talents to good use and succeeds in convincing Melanie and her young friends that his working motorbike engine is the best thing that has ever happened there. Although it is easy to find sympathy with Charles's view that, on the contrary, Sally's pregnancy is far more important than Greg's engine, his unwillingness to embrace any of man's considerable technological achievements does seem unnecessarily limiting and short-sighted. However, this apparent myopia is immediately addressed in the next episode ("New World") as – for the sake of narrative progress – Charles is portrayed as suddenly enthusiastic about the promise of rebuilding the old world. This change of heart, prompted by news from Norway and around Britain, paves the way for Charles's role as industrial evangelist in the final series.

Well-drawn characters are perhaps the greatest asset of the second series. Principals Greg and Jenny are joined by Charles and a whole host of supporting players, of which community doctor Ruth, Charles's common-law wife Pet and shepherd Hubert are the most accomplished. In marked contrast to the first series, which sees the central trio of characters in the foreground pretty much throughout, this wider cast of characters step in and out of the limelight. Ruth is a good example of this – taking centre-stage in "Greater Love" and "Lights of London", before merging into the background until "New Arrivals" and "Over the Hills". Possibly it is this 'characters of the week' approach that has contributed to earning the second series its soap opera tag. There are some ostensible further grounds for this label: the static setting; a place where everyone meets (Pet's kitchen); and the large cast of characters who move in and out of the action. The crucial difference is the post-Death context. This unique backdrop means that the challenges the characters face, the answers to their problems, and the reasoning behind the decisions they make, are arrived at through an altogether different connection with the world than is to be found in a rural soap opera. Sociologically and anthropologically speaking, this is a fascinating premise that perhaps explains the series' enduring popularity with fans of other character-driven dramas, such as *Tenko* and *Secret Army*, which also seek to ask fundamental questions about the nature of existence, faith, hope and love in conditions of extreme adversity.

One aspect that is shared with both the preceding and following series is the journey from a cold and unremitting winter beginning to a bright and summery, if uncertain, conclusion. The seasons appear to have an inextricable relationship with the narrative's emotional lows (the devastation of the Grange and the dangers facing pregnant Jenny) and optimistic highs (the luxury of leisure time and the promise of a wider world beyond Whitecross). This correlation, perhaps more intentional here than in the rescheduled first series, is entirely fitting given the survivors' new-found dependence on the laws of nature and the land. Interestingly, despite the fact that it is only the last few episodes that actually feature blue skies and bright sunshine, somehow the overriding impression left with the viewer is that Whitecross is a comfortable rural idyll, and that the second series is considerably less dark than its predecessor.

The handful of episodes that leave the Whitecross community behind also serve to enhance its haven-like feel, especially when it is contrasted with the bleak London community ("Lights of London") and an army camp run by fanatics ("The Chosen"). Both these episodes change the pace of the series and seem to hark back to Nation's vision of *Survivors* rather than Dudley's. However, they both deliver strong socio-political themes as well as an action-adventure quotient. Despite its staging back at Whitecross, the pace of Ian McCulloch's "A Friend in Need" also causes it to stand out. The key difference is that its writer was primarily motivated by a desire to see the series return to its roots, and to situations he believed to be more interesting than those explored in the episodes on which he had recently been working.

It has to be said that McCulloch largely succeeds, but one episode does not a series make, and the following episode, "By Bread Alone", immediately returns to the tenets of Dudley's *Survivors*. Unhappily for McCulloch, this episode also introduced Greg's experiments with a methane-gas converter, the PROMIFR, an ongoing sub-plot that he actively disliked.

Once again, the second series would see somewhat clouded departures from *Survivors* both in front of and behind the camera. Disappointed by what he considered to be poor scripts and a rough deal for his character, McCulloch advised his producer early on that he wanted out of the series. Jack Ronder and Pennant Roberts on the other hand ended their contributions to the series because of their clashes with Dudley over the script for "Lights of London Part 2"; a great shame given that both would have been keen to continue their association with a series that they, like McCulloch, had been very much responsible for shaping.

Although the change of format and content for the second series was vindicated by both healthy viewing figures and reasonable audience appreciation findings, Dudley decided that the time had come to broaden *Survivors'* scope. Looking to the world beyond Whitecross and its parochial day-to-day difficulties, the final run would, in sharp contrast, seek to dramatise the difficult rebirth of a nation …

Ian and Tanya. © Denis Lill

SERIES 3 (1977)

Series Creator
Terry Nation

Producer
Terence Dudley

Main Cast
Charles Vaughan: Denis Lill
Jenny Richards: Lucy Fleming
Hubert Goss: John Abineri
Greg Preston: Ian McCulloch
Agnes Carlsson: Anna Pitt

Writers
Terence Dudley (3.1)
Ian McCulloch (3.2, 3.10)
Martin Worth (3.3, 3.5, 3.11, 3.12)
Don Shaw (3.4, 3.6)
Roger Parkes (3.7-3.9)

Directors
Peter Jefferies (3.1, 3.3, 3.9, 3.10)
George Spenton-Foster (3.2, 3.5, 3.7, 3.12)
Tristan de Vere Cole (3.4, 3.8, 3.11)
Terence Dudley (3.6)

Title Music
Anthony Isaac

Production Assistants
Maggy Campbell (3.1, 3.3, 3.9, 3.10)
Christina McMillan (3.2, 3.5, 3.7, 3.12)
Gordon Elsbury (3.4)
Jean Esslemont (3.4, 3.6, 3.8, 3.11)

Production Unit Manager
Michael Bartley

Designer
Geoff Powell

Designer's Assistant
Les McCallum

Cameramen
Frank Hudson (3.1, 3.4, 3.6, 3.8-3.11)
Alan Hayward (3.1, 3.7, 3.9, 3.10, 3.12)
Simon Fone (3.4, 3.6, 3.7, 3.8, 3.11, 3.12)
Roger Prior (3.4)

Sound
Robin Luxford (3.1, 3.3, 3.10)
Vic Godrich (3.2, 3.5, 3.7, 3.12)
Ian Leiper (3.4, 3.6, 3.8, 3.9, 3.11)

Lighting
Clive Potter (3.1, 3.3, 3.9, 3.10)
John Wilson (3.2, 3.5, 3.7, 3.12)
Hubert Cartwright (3.4, 3.6, 3.8, 3.11)

Assistant Floor Managers
Robert Gabriel, Alan Wareing,
Robert Ashburn, Kate Osborne

Director's Assistants
Diana Baldwin, Judy Munk, Patricia Preece,
Janet Ogilvy, Beryl Watts, Pam Butcher

Technical Managers
Peter Greenyer, John King, George Jakins

VT Engineers
Alan Throup, Ian Rutter, Pete Belcher

Vision Mixers
Fred Law, David Hanks, Graham Giles,
Paul Cole, John Barclay, Jim Stephens

Boom Operators
John Cox, Peter Bailey, John Caulfield,
Doug Whittaker, Ian Furness, John Nottage

Costumes
Andrew Rose (3.1, 3.2, 3.4)
Richard Winter (3.3, 3.5, 3.7, 3.8, 3.10-3.12)
Christine Rawlins (3.4, 3.6, 3.9)
Janet Tharby (3.12)

Dressers
Andre Salat, Kay Woodley, Arthur Funge,
Sue Edwards, Gay Heath, Mervyn Bezar,
Kevin Rowland

Make Up
Susan/Lisa Westcott
Suzanne Broad (3.2)

Make Up Assistant
Jill Thomas

Scene Crew Supervisors
Frederick Flay, Cliff Richardson,
Alf Bringlow, Mike Jennings,
Freddie Nye, Arthur Hendy

Prop Buyer
Roger Williams

Dog Handler
Sam Perrie

Horses
Ben Ford

Armourers
Alf Trustrum, Jack Wells, Des Stewart

SERIES 3: PRODUCTION

Innovation and reinvention were recurring features of *Survivors*. When the series returned in the spring of 1977 for its third and final run, viewers had once again to absorb some significant on-screen changes. The show was uprooted from its settled Whitecross home and its characters forced out into the wider world, opening up its vista and giving it a viewpoint and sense of scale it had never enjoyed before. Denis Lill recalls: '[In series two] we were "locked-off" in Whitecross. You had this static location, and all the troubles and all the drama and all the adventures came in from the outside, and were dealt with one way or another by the regular cast. In series three ... we found ourselves travelling a great deal more. It was a bit like being on tour, and fetching up in a different theatre every week.'

At the start of the second series, viewers had had to become accustomed to the loss of leading character Abby Grant, and the return of guest character Charles Vaughan, who was to take up a co-starring role alongside Greg Preston. In series three, viewers were to discover that Greg would appear in only two episodes and that a revised triumvirate of leading characters – Charles, Jenny Richards and Hubert Goss – would take centre stage.

Scriptwriter Martin Worth believed that the decision to break up the Whitecross settlement was premature. He remained convinced that the dramatic potential of a settlement struggling to establish itself and prosper had not yet been fully explored. Fellow scriptwriter Don Shaw thought that both routes had potential: 'There was still dramatic mileage there, we could have stayed in the Whitecross community and we could have moved on: there was a choice. It was a good idea to reinvent the format, but it was also a good idea to have stayed behind. But I didn't have that kind of strategic thinking in mind. I had three weeks in which to write an episode!' Yet Terence Dudley had been adamant that a shake-up was required, and that

Crew members at Lochay. © Denis Lill

through the storylines of the second series, *Survivors* had become both too settled and too introspective. He was convinced that the series' heroes needed to be exposed to the predations of the feral world beyond Whitecross, and that viewers would become frustrated if the survivors appeared to become too reconciled to their primitive new way of life. Dudley believed that for *Survivors* to continue to engage its audience, it had to demonstrate that progress towards the rebuilding of society and civilisation was well underway. A key source of evidence on which Dudley based his considerations were the BBC Audience Research Reports. Alongside a widespread view that the series remained 'exciting and thought-provoking viewing,' there were several recurring themes in the opinions expressed in the reports that Dudley took seriously. In particular, he homed in on comments about the series two finale "New World", which welcomed the idea of 'turning towards the reconstruction of society rather than back to the fields,' and which felt 'that "change must be sustained" in order that any further programmes would avoid a rut.' Dudley clearly felt that there was an audience mandate for a significant overhaul of the series.

The second factor that shaped Dudley's thinking was his desire to secure Ian McCulloch's continued involvement. McCulloch had signalled to Dudley his lack of interest in participating in any third outing that retained the same format. Recognising that he needed to separate the characters of Charles and Greg, and that McCulloch sought a 'closure' for the Greg storyline, Dudley agreed to reduce Greg's appearances in the third series to just two episodes, which McCulloch was also contracted to write. Furthermore, he agreed that McCulloch would script Greg's exit from the series in the second of these. Denis Lill recalls: 'I still have the letter somewhere from Terry Dudley saying that they are in the process of commissioning series three; that Greg is to be written out; and that he would very much like Charles to lead; and would I be prepared in principle to give my agreement to that – which, of course, I was delighted to do, thinking "Well, at last, perhaps here is a chance to actually take over as a leading man."'

For a short time, Dudley considered the possibility of basing the third series on a triangle of trade and communications that would connect stories based in England, Norway and Sweden, with a recommissioned ferry shuttling the series' heroes back and forth across the North Sea. (Coincidentally, Dudley would later direct episodes of the BBC's soap *Triangle* (1981-83), which was conceived along similar lines, although of course without the post-apocalypse premise!) The idea was quickly rejected on grounds of both cost and practicality. Instead, two central themes would together provide the dramatic momentum for *Survivors'* final series. The hunt for Greg, now returned from Norway and roving the country as an ambassador for the Norwegian plan, would provide the plot dynamic for the first two thirds of the series. Charles's own efforts to encourage the development of a federation of trading communities would serve to support and supplement Greg's work, as he too tours the country following in his tracks. But in the closing episodes of the series, Charles would set aside the hunt for Greg to pursue a new objective of his own – the revival of the hydroelectric power plants in the Scottish Highlands, a quest that he hopes could be the catalyst for a new age of industry and civilisation.

The creative and production teams behind *Survivors* were once again overhauled. Dudley's enthusiasm for a high turnover of talent certainly helped to maintain the series' energy, but at no little cost to its overall coherence.

Over specific plot developments and themes the series could retain a high level of continuity: for example, the pethidine manufactured at the settlement in "Manhunt"

Keith Varnier (Owen Walter) shows his strength! © Denis Lill

resurfaces in the plots of "Sparks" and "Reunion"; while the fate of the Walters' farm is a recurrent feature of the storylines of "Law of the Jungle", "Mad Dog" and "Bridgehead". However, over more significant elements, *Survivors'* third series at times proved both inconsistent and forgetful. Perhaps the central paradox of the final series is that its roving storylines and sharp sense of narrative purpose produce some of the best – but also some of the weakest – episodes of the entire run. There was, Lill suggests, '... some wonderful stuff ... but it was so fragmented.' The mix of high adventure and 'community of the week' episodes that became the series' hallmarks, illustrated both the potential and the limitations of the changed format, and left unexplored the many possible counterfactuals of *Survivors'* final run.

Although the direction in which Dudley took *Survivors* in its third series has always remained contentious (amongst cast and crew, reviewers, fans and the viewing public), it seems that there were fewer clashes amongst the cast and crew than had been the case previously. In part, this was because Dudley's earlier conflicts with actors, writers and directors (and with Terry Nation himself) had ended with Dudley securing the final say. Many of those dissenting voices were no longer involved with the series, and in 1977 (as opposed to in 1975-76) fewer members of the cast and crew were eager to take issue with Dudley's approach. Yet there were other factors involved ...

During the first series of *Survivors*, Dudley had kept a close personal eye on the work of his teams, and had been present while his directors shot their episodes. This had begun to change during the making of series two, however, and was now to become even more pronounced. In the third series, rather than having a central static base, the story (and the crew) travelled to locations as far afield as Dorset, Derbyshire and the Scottish Highlands, to depict the diverse types of settlements (and solutions to the question of survival) that had sprung up across the country. The fact that the Outside Broadcast unit was now being despatched further away than ever before, increased the autonomy of the individual directors and their production staff. With the film unit working at locations hundreds of miles away from the London production office, it was no longer straightforward for Dudley to be a frequent visitor – a fact that director Tristan de Vere Cole remembers clearly: 'Terry Dudley seldom came on the shoot, and he never came and sat behind me in the van with the monitors and said "Oh, don't you think you ought to do a close-up *here*," or "Don't you think we ought to emphasise *this* a bit more." None of that at all. I had total – as far as I could see – total creative freedom.' However, logistics seem to have been only part of the explanation for Dudley's withdrawal. Dudley appears to have become less motivated to intervene directly in the mechanics of the production process, content to remain an 'enabler' rather than a 'chaperone'. In assuming, effectively, the position of 'executive producer', it seems likely that in early 1977 Dudley was looking beyond *Survivors* to his next television project. Indeed, perhaps the key reason for the continuity problems that crop up in the final series is Dudley's apparent loss of interest in monitoring the progress of the series as closely as he had done previously: having set the general terms of reference for series three, Dudley allowed, if not encouraged, his teams to make the most of their independence.

As with the transition from the first to the second series, significant numbers of supporting cast members were lost. The departure of many of those characters is once again acutely felt. The absence of the group of energetic youngsters from the Whitecross watermill robs the series of some well-drawn and engaging characters – not least, the vivacious Melanie and the spirited Alan – and removes some interesting generational conflicts from the drama. The series also suffers from the departure of physician Ruth and the sidelining of carpenter Jack. Perhaps the most notable change is the reduction in Pet's status to that of a peripheral character, often glimpsed only briefly on the end of a telephone line. The effective marginalisation of Pet was certainly not a development that Lorna Lewis had anticipated as a consequence of the series two finale. Had she recognised the implications of the series' new direction she would, she concedes, 'have protested' at the time, urging Dudley to retain the Whitecross settlement as the fixture around which the new, more mobile adventures he was planning could revolve.

The corollary of the reduction in the core *Survivors* cast was the introduction of a large and often overlapping group of guest characters – mostly residents of the assorted communities encountered on the journeys of Charles's wandering troupe. Notable appearances included those by Brian Blessed (Brod), Barbara Lott (Edith Walter), Morris Perry (Richard Fenton), John Bennett (Queenie) and Iain Cuthbertson (The Laird). The size of the supporting cast dwarfed anything seen on

Edward Underdown (Frank Garner) during "The Peacemaker". © Denis Lill

the previous two series of the show, and was another factor that reinforced the final series' distinctiveness. As well as the development having its attractions for the series' stars (not least in that it made *Survivors* a more varied show), it also had some major drawbacks – most obviously that the episode's guest characters often enjoyed more screen-time and plot significance than the regulars. Denis Lill suggests: 'We found ourselves acting more as foils or ciphers to a series of colourful guest-leads than we had done before … [which meant] … having to stand back a bit and play second fiddle to a lot of other people – which is rather ironic for me to say, since I was a colourful guest-lead in the first series!'

Of the second series characters who remained, two (in name at least) stayed the same, while the actor who played them changed. The recasting of regular characters had become a relatively frequent occurrence on *Survivors*, although in most instances change was forced by circumstance. The recasting of Lizzie, a character who was now to have only brief appearances on screen, was the unavoidable consequence of scriptwriter Jack Ronder's departure from the show at the close of the second series. The role that had been played for two series by Tanya Ronder was now taken on by Angie Stevens. Stevens was given little dialogue, and few attempts were made to disguise the fact that the young actress bore little physical resemblance to Tanya Ronder. Both girls were pupils at Drayton Manor High School in West London, and Stevens recalls: 'I did feel worried that people might compare me with her, and I was also worried that Tanya wouldn't like me as I was taking over her part. I didn't get to talk to Tanya much at school, I think there may have been a bit of rivalry, but we were both always in the school plays.'

The young and feisty Norwegian, Agnes, whose arrival had been the trigger for the break-up of the Whitecross settlement in the closing episode of series two, was to play a significant role in the events of the final series. In "New World", the role of Agnes had been played to great effect by Sally Osborn, but with Osborn unavailable to reprise the role in series three, Dudley opted not only to recast the part but also to reconceive the character. Osborn's Agnes had been self-possessed, passionate and persuasive. Dudley hired Anna Pitt to take on the role of a much less excitable and much more emotionally reserved Agnes. Although both portrayals invest Agnes with a similar sense of drive and determination, the discontinuities between the two conceptions of the character are striking, and never properly accounted for.

Series three also saw the one and only example in *Survivors* of an actor returning in a new role. Robert Gillespie had previously appeared in "Gone Away", the third episode of series one, as the put-upon militia man John Milner. He was recast in the new role of former heroin addict Sam Mead to reappear in three episodes of the third series – "The Enemy", "Long Live the King" and "Power". Mead was to function as the unknown 'enemy within', determined to wreck Charles Vaughan's plans for reconstruction.

Alongside the significant cast changes, there were some important elements of character development for both Jenny Richards and Hubert Goss. Lucy Fleming had become concerned during *Survivors'* second series that the previous balance in Jenny's character – between the self-sufficient and the vulnerable sides of her nature – had been lost, with her becoming too emotionally needy, excessively dependent on Greg and often far from the on-screen action. Without doubt, series three reinstated Jenny's former equilibrium. Although she remained an anxious mother, and a partner distressed by Greg's continued absence, Jenny also found a new strength of character – joining Charles's roving group, demonstrating her equestrian skills and rediscovering her bravery when conditions proved threatening. Jenny proves willing to challenge what she sees as Charles's pomposity and sense of self-importance, and to travel

Lucy fishes in the Tay. © Denis Lill

alone and unaided through uncharted terrain when the situation demands. By the series finale, Jenny appears reconciled to Greg's loss, and feels sufficiently at ease to decline Alec's offer of an emotionally secure future for her and the children. If Jenny's behaviour remains sometimes erratic, her character is once again more plausible and rounded, and she frequently finds herself back in the centre of the storyline.

It is Hubert, however, who undergoes the most significant set of changes in the course of the third series. Throughout series two, John Abineri had gone to great pains to ensure that the character did not slide into either parody or repetition, and that the rogue's more likeable sides remained evident alongside the more unsavoury aspects. A central figure in Charles's band of travellers in series three, Hubert retains his grumbling and prejudiced qualities, but in episodes such as "Law of the Jungle" is allowed to display altruistic and even heroic traits. Yet Abineri was to discover that not all the scriptwriters would follow through consistently on this early evolution. Although Hubert is still shown as able to overcome his baser instincts for the greater good, he finds his status as an equal member of Charles's group repeatedly put in question in subsequent storylines – and by the events of "Power", his renewed demotion appears complete. It is not clear if the inconsistent handling of Hubert was simply the consequence of the individual judgments of different scriptwriters, or if a decision to follow through on the evolution in his personality was later rescinded. In either case, the situation seems to be a further indication of a lack of editorial clarity amongst the creative team in the course of series three.

Denis Lill was understandably delighted to be offered what was effectively top billing on the series' final run, something that was to bring an end to the alleged frictions between himself and Ian McCulloch that had been an irritant for both actors during the making of series two. Yet he became frustrated that Greg remained a constant reference point in numerous storylines: 'I found myself in the series constantly saying: "Where is Greg? Why is Greg not here? If only we had Greg!" That sort of thing. So Charles was constantly, once again, under the shadow of Greg the whole time!' Despite this, Lill was certainly given ample opportunity to depict the fiery and driven aspects of Charles's character, as he remained the locus of the series' roving narrative, and was rewarded with a 'showcase' episode in the guise of the classic and distinctive "Mad Dog".

Neither Pennant Roberts nor Terence Williams was invited to rejoin the team to direct episodes for the third series. Dudley chose to rebuild his directing team from scratch – hiring three seasoned television professionals: Peter Jefferies, Tristan de Vere Cole and George Spenton-Foster.

Peter Jefferies had recently worked on Brian Clemens' *Thriller* series for ITV, directing three episodes in 1973 and a further instalment the following year. In 1974, he also directed episodes of the detective series *Father Brown*. After *Survivors*, Jefferies would go on to work on the wartime aerial drama *Wings* (1977-78), *Empire Road* (1978-79) and the popular 1980 television adaptation of *To Serve Them All My Days*.

Between 1966 and 1967, George Spenton-Foster had served as an associate producer on the classic supernatural TV anthology show *Out of the Unknown*, and directed several episodes. He had also worked as a producer on TV shows *Boy Meets Girl* and *The Link Men* (1970), and as a director on *Paul Temple* (1969), *Sutherland's Law* (1973) – on which Pennant Roberts also worked – and *The Perils of Pendragon* (1974). After *Survivors*, Spenton-Foster would, like Roberts, join the directing team on Nation's science-fiction drama *Blake's 7*.

Prior to *Survivors*, Tristan de Vere Cole had worked on numerous television series, including *Z Cars* (from 1967), *Take Three Girls* (in 1969), *Warship* (in 1974), *Trinity Tales* (1975), the nursing drama *Angels* (in 1976), and – notably – the 1968 *Doctor Who* story "The Wheel in Space". In subsequent years, de Vere Cole would work on the final, 1979 series of *Secret Army*, *Buccaneer* (1980), *Kessler* (1981) and several episodes of *Bergerac* between 1988

On the Severn Valley Railway for "Law of the Jungle". © Denis Lill

and 1991. In 1989, he would direct the Anglo-Norwegian big-screen film *Dykket* (*The Dive*), a deep-sea thriller.

Such a significant retooling of the behind-the-camera team certainly helped to prevent *Survivors* from developing an overly familiar dramatic texture, but also had the downside of weakening the coherence of the series as a whole.

There was far greater continuity in the area of scriptwriting. Dudley had retained the services of Don Shaw, Martin Worth, Roger Parkes and Ian McCulloch from the second series. Although he parted company with just two of his six writing staff, both losses were significant – Roger Marshall had proved himself an inventive and engaging writer in his single contribution to the series ("Parasites"), but a much greater wrench was signalled by the departure of Jack Ronder, whose scripts for series one and two had been richly evocative and emotionally sophisticated. The first third series scripts to be commissioned in August 1976 were Parkes's "The Kingmaker" (which became "The Peacemaker") and "Sparks". These were followed in October 1976 by Worth's "Law of the Jungle" and Shaw's "Mad Dog" and "Reunion".

There are some strong indications that, in general, Dudley made far fewer interventions in the scripting process this time around than during the previous two series. Shaw remembers: 'I happened to look at the *Radio Times* and saw that one of my episodes from series three (I can't remember if it was "Mad Dog" or "Reunion") was billed to go out that week – and I hadn't even been to the read-through. I hadn't been asked to change a word … They'd actually made it as I'd written it.' Dudley did however contribute, for the first time, a script of his own: that for the third series' scene-setting opener, "Manhunt". His contract to do so was not finalised until 11 January 1977, just over four weeks before recording on the episode was due to commence. This would have been a tight deadline, even if Dudley had not had the supervisory responsibilities that came with being the series' producer. It may therefore indicate that he was filling in an unexpected gap in the writing assignments – in much the same way as, that same year, producer Graham Williams (along with script editor Anthony Read) came to write the *Doctor Who* series finale "The Invasion of Time" as a replacement for a script that fell through. An alternative possibility is that it was intended all along that Dudley would script "Manhunt" himself, and there was simply a delay in the completion of the official paperwork – a not uncommon occurrence at the BBC at that time, particularly where scripts were effectively 'in house' commissions. The truth of the matter is not known, but in either case, scripting "Manhunt" enabled Dudley to establish the series' new motifs and direction and set in motion the subsequent drama. He gave the task of scripting the series' last two episodes to Worth, and the preceding block of three to Roger Parkes. The decision to assign Parkes a 'trilogy' of stories was unprecedented – only Nation himself had previously penned three consecutive *Survivors* episodes (the opening instalments of the first series), and the move was to impact significantly on the mood and pace of the series' closing stories.

Dudley was convinced that several features of the series' atmosphere needed to be changed – to heighten the 'desolate' ambience he now saw it necessary to reinstate. There had been numerous profoundly dark and melancholic themes in *Survivors'* second series, but many of the later Whitecross episodes had been shot against the backdrop of a famously warm and bright English summer. The video cameras that the production used had further enhanced the colour-palette of the light-dappled countryside around Callow Hill. Dudley had come to view the setting as overly comfortable, not to say idyllic.

As pre-production on the third series got underway, conscious efforts were made to give it a more 'gritty' on-screen appearance, to match its new dramatic mood. The Costume and Make-up Departments were encouraged to 'dirty things up', and give the main characters a more ragged and grubby look. In a 1977 press interview, Lucy Fleming commented: 'We are not made up and are supposed to look as ratty as possible. We are not allowed to have our hair washed before any filming, and our clothes are not exactly the latest from Paris.' Angie Stevens remembers that her wardrobe '… was very drab: wellies, trousers, jumper and anorak.' Additionally, technical adjustments were made to the OB cameras to give the recordings a starker and less colourful hue. What heightened the effect of these changes was that the early episodes were once again recorded in the chill and subdued light of early January. As a result, the difference in tone between the sunbathed denouement of "New World" and the bleak and breathless opening sequences of "Manhunt" was dramatic.

The move away from the previous series' settled Whitecross base required numerous new locations to be sourced. Lill recalls that the excitement of filming '… wasn't just that we were shooting this extraordinary story, but the fact that we were fetching up in a different town every time – moving in like a great circus and taking over vast areas of the place – which was quite amazing in itself.' Stevens remembers '… going to Ipswich to film one episode. We stayed in a lovely hotel for a couple of nights. We filmed another episode in Cardiff. We were always filming in farmhouses or barns, not very glamorous.' Speaking in 1977, Fleming suggested that series three filming was itself proving '… something of a survival exercise. There is no studio work and everything is filmed out of doors. Even the interior shots are done in cold, empty houses. I have spent days [during the recording of "A Little Learning"] trudging around on a horse.' Lill more fondly remembers that director Peter Jefferies in particular was keen to make the production process as pleasurable as possible – identifying places that cast and crew could enjoy after the day's shoot: 'Peter would sort out locations armed with *The Real Ale Guide* under one arm and *The Good Food Guide* under the other!'

Mavis and Edith. © Denis Lill

As had happened on both previous series, episodes were frequently recorded out of sequence – partly to make best use of particular locations, but also to accommodate Ian McCulloch's involvement by recording the two episodes in which he appeared (the second and tenth) in close succession. The first episode to go before the cameras was the Martin Worth-scripted "Law of the Jungle", the third episode in the broadcast run. Recording began at locations near Bridgnorth and Bewdley on 15 January 1977, under the direction of Peter Jefferies. As they shared several locations on the Severn Valley steam railway line, the episodes "Mad Dog" and "Bridgehead" (four and five respectively) were recorded next, with a five-day schedule for "Mad Dog" continuing at locations further north in Monsal Dale and close to Ilam in

Derbyshire on 28 January. Coincidently, the Hampton Loade train station used to stage the closing sequences of "Mad Dog" had been used as a filming location five years earlier on the BBC *Drama Playhouse* production *The Incredible Robert Baldick* – written by *Survivors'* creator Terry Nation. The Monsal Dale locations that were to feature throughout "Mad Dog" had also been utilised in the Granada TV production of "The Watercress Girl" (part of the BAFTA award-winning series *Country Matters* (1972-73)), starring Gareth Thomas (*Blake's 7*), filmed the same year as *The Incredible Robert Baldick*. There were real challenges posed by the deep-winter start for the production – not least the need to 'thaw out' the camera equipment each morning before recording could get underway. Although the mist,

Eric Deacon (Steve Walter). © Denis Lill

sleet, snow and ice visible on screen all became integral components of the drama, they once again made the production process something of a gruelling exercise for all involved.

Ian McCulloch's two episodes were taped in sequence in early spring, as the weather began to improve and the recording day lengthened. The five-day shoot for "A Little Learning" began, at Lodge Gate House and other locations around Kidderminster, in mid-March 1977. After the production unit returned to London, to allow a changeover of crew and a brief cast rehearsal, the recording of McCulloch's final episode, "The Last Laugh", commenced at locations around the Brecon area on 23 March.

On the series two episode "Lights of London Part 2", an additional Sunday filming session on the London Underground had had to be added to the schedule, when the original shoot overran its allotted time slot. A further reshoot was required on a series three episode, "Mad Dog", when director Tristan de Vere Cole had to return to Monsal Dale on 12 and 13 March for an additional two days of recording to shoot a significant number of scenes that bad weather had prevented his team from completing back in January. The original footage that de Vere Cole had been able to shoot on his initial outing had also had to be trimmed at the instruction of the BBC's Head of Series – who was concerned that the sequences in which the character Richard Fenton became deranged with rabies were too graphic for pre-watershed transmission, and would need to be re-edited and cut back. The excising of part of the rabies footage made the remount on "Mad Dog" all the more necessary, to ensure that the episode was not underlength.

With *Survivors* reliant on the services of a single OB unit, and with a single episode scheduled to be shot in a maximum of seven days, the "Mad Dog" reshoot inevitably had a significant knock-on effect on production. As series one and two director Pennant Roberts recalls: 'Series were always thirteen episodes in length. Because there was only one OB unit, if it was committed elsewhere, you just didn't have it. And if you had overrun by several days on an earlier shoot – well, tough.' The extra two days of "Mad Dog" recording is clearly an

Cast and crew of "Law of the Jungle". © Denis Lill

important factor in explaining why *Survivors'* final series is one episode shorter than its predecessors. Work on a fourth Roger Parkes script, which had been commissioned back in November 1976 and had the confirmed title "Black Start", was scrapped as a consequence.

The final two episodes of *Survivors* were recorded in May 1977, at locations hundreds of miles apart. Shooting on "Long Live the King", which took place between 6 and 11 May, centred on locations in southern England, including Piddlehinton Army Camp in Dorset. Cast and crew then reassembled in Perthshire, in the Scottish Highlands, to shoot the very last episode, "Power", between 26 and 28 May, at locations including the Lochay Hydroelectric Power Station and Stronuich Reservoir near Killin, and Taymouth Castle at Kenmore.

The post-production deadlines on *Survivors'* final series were some of the tightest in the three-year run. After the reshoot on "Mad Dog", there was no more 'slack' left in the production cycle, meaning there was only a ten-day gap between the end of the recording of "Power" and its transmission on 8 June. Under enormous time pressure, all the editing and dubbing had to be completed, the soundtrack enhanced and the episode credits merged in.

Across series three, *Survivors'* audience figures were down noticeably on the levels enjoyed previously. "A Little Learning" registered the series' lowest ever tally of 4.55m viewers (having been transmitted – like the lowest-rated second series episode, "Lights of London Part 2" – opposite a one-off special of the popular *Benny Hill Show* in ITV regions), less than half the series' highest rating, closely followed by "The Peacemaker" with 5.10m (opposite *This is Your Life*). The BBC's Audience Research Report for "Power" also registered a significant reduction of interest in the show. Although this final episode was widely reported as 'among the best of the present series,' there were other comments that overall *Survivors* 'had lost a lot of its original energy and freshness.' Among the specific views were complaints that 'some of the plots … had been too far-fetched,' that 'there had been too little action and too much political discussion' and that 'its focus had been blurred by introducing too many new characters,' with several viewers commenting that the series had been 'considerably weakened by the loss of Greg.' Such criticisms were somewhat offset by the observations that 'the acting was good,' that 'the production consistently created an authentic atmosphere' and that 'the camera work in the countryside scenes was particularly good.' Yet if the report was to be considered representative, it did suggest that an imbalance had developed between a continued enthusiasm amongst viewers for the premise and on-screen realisation of *Survivors*, on the one hand, and a growing unhappiness with the direction of the scripts and storylines, on the other.

Scriptwriter Martin Worth was certainly not alone in thinking that Dudley had brought the reconstruction theme to a dramatic climax too quickly – and that in depicting the winning of the battle for electric light, he had effectively lost the show its future. Watching from a distance, Nation was acutely disappointed (if not much surprised) that his original premise – of the irretrievable loss of civilisation – had been successfully reversed under Dudley's direction. In an interview in 1992, Nation recalled that he reached the point 'where I didn't watch too many [episodes],' but that he was profoundly dismayed by the events of the third series' finale and the decision to 'throw the switch on a giant hydroelectric plant,' so that viewers could see 'the dynamos start to roll and see things sparking.' In his view, it reflected series producer Dudley's – wholly inappropriate – determination to end the series with the message: 'Everything's going to be lovely now, folks!'

Although it is tempting to think that a different dramatic journey across series three could have won *Survivors* a renewal, director Pennant Roberts remains convinced that a change of leadership in the BBC Drama Department had already sealed the series' fate regardless: 'Andy Osborn commissioned *Survivors* in the first place. Ronnie Marsh came in to take over and was uncomfortable with it. I think he felt that *Survivors* wasn't his project.' Lill concurs that Marsh was no fan of the series: 'He was never wildly enthusiastic about it. I think he thought it rather depressing.' In a letter dated 15 September 1977, Marsh replied to a inquiry from a *Survivors* fan about the possible renewal of the show, suggesting that the costs of the series had become disproportionate: 'Because of the amount of location work involved in making *Survivors*, it is a more expensive programme to produce and on this occasion, after three successful series, the decision has been taken not to have a further run next year but to replace it with something different.' When Marsh announced the BBC drama schedule for 1978, *Survivors* was absent.

Brian Blessed (Brod) on location. © Denis Lill

3.1 MANHUNT

UK TRANSMISSION: 16 March 1977: 8.10pm – 9.00pm
VIEWING FIGURE: 7.42m
WRITER: Terence Dudley
DIRECTOR: Peter Jefferies
REGULAR CAST: Denis Lill (Charles Vaughan); Lucy Fleming (Jenny Richards); John Abineri (Hubert Goss); Lorna Lewis (Pet Simpson); Gordon Salkilld (Jack Wood); Angie Stevens (Lizzie Willoughby); Stephen Dudley (John Millon)
GUEST CAST: Michael Hawkins (Colonel Clifford); Anthony Jacobs (Miedel); Dan Meaden (Seth); June Brown (Susan); John Rolfe (Summers); David Freedman (Roberts)
OB RECORDING: 17 - 23 February 1977
LOCATION: Woodbridge, Nr. Ipswich, Suffolk

SYNOPSIS: Six months after Greg, Agnes and Jack left Whitecross, Jack is back in England travelling alone, clutching letters from Greg for Charles and Jenny. He is found in a delirious state by Seth the blacksmith, who subsequently makes a phone call to Challenor, where Charles is now living with Pet, Jenny, Hubert and the children. Charles and Jenny set off for Seth's home. There, they learn that Greg and Agnes have also returned and are at Wellingham in Suffolk. Greg plans to talk to as many people as he can about the plight of the Norwegians on his way back to Jenny and Charles. Jenny is unsettled by the news, especially when Jack starts to shout out about Greg having a broken arm. After Charles and Jenny head off to find Greg, Jack's further ravings about 'killing' prompt Seth to contact Pet, who in turn sends Hubert off after them. As they near Wellingham, Jenny and Charles find a man staked out on the ground whom they suspect to be a junkie; they release him. They are taken captive and brought before a man called Colonel Clifford at a nearby settlement. He tells them that Agnes and Greg left a week ago and explains that they make drugs there. They are introduced to an elderly scientist called Miedel who is attempting to synthesise a substitute for pethidine, which is itself a substitute for morphine. Suspicious of the setup there, Jenny and Charles begin to explore, but are soon confronted by a guard. Jenny escapes while Charles is taken to Clifford, who tells him about recent attacks from groups who want to steal their drugs. Jenny is reunited with Hubert and goes back to Wellingham alone to rescue Charles, but accidentally knocks him unconscious with a rifle butt in the process. Some time later, misunderstandings forgotten, Miedel and Clifford wish Charles, Jenny and Hubert luck as they set off after Greg.

ANALYSIS: The third series opener, Dudley's only script for the series, marks a distinct departure in style for *Survivors*. In line with Dudley's conviction that the dramatic potential of the idyllic Whitecross scenario had been exhausted and that the series should be characterised by a grittier and darker representation of day-to-day survival, "Manhunt" exhibits a very different look and feel to its predecessors. The episode is also significant for the start of a quest by Charles and Jenny to locate Greg, taking the series back to its wanderer roots.

Aside from the adoption of an edgier style, distance from the cosier second series is also

170

achieved through the unexplained relocation from Whitecross to Challenor and an unsettling reduction in the series' regular cast. Several Whitecross characters – including the previously indispensable Ruth – are rarely, if ever, mentioned again; the younger set is not represented at all, which seems a waste given the positive impact of characters such as Melanie and Alan on the second series. It is also disappointing to see Lizzie re-cast (Tanya Ronder being a casualty of the deterioration of Dudley's relationship with her father). However, the most crucial missing regular is of course Greg, the hunted man of the episode's title. The decision to concentrate so much of the third series on the search for Greg only serves to highlight the fact that, for the most part, McCulloch had declined to be involved. This is less of a problem in "Manhunt", given that this is the first time he fails to put in an appearance, but his absence still makes the episode feel palpably incomplete.

"Manhunt" has the unfortunate tendency of consistently promising more than it intends to deliver. From the outset, Jack's delirious fever – which incorporates ravings about a broken arm and, as Susan puts it, 'talk of killing' – strongly indicates that Charles and Jenny are going to be in danger at Wellingham. On their arrival there, Miedel's mad Transylvanian scientist act ('I absolutely insist that you stay overnight'; 'Be sure that we will make you most comfortable') also suggests undisguised menace. The cited disparity between Greg's description of the settlement and Charles's take on the setup ('Why should Greg write praising this place, if it's obvious to anyone with even half an eye that there's something very wrong here?') not only promotes the exciting possibility that Greg and Agnes may still be incarcerated there, but also that Charles and Jenny may have to fight for their lives to escape. And finally, after Jenny runs away and Charles is overpowered, it seems as though the scene is set for a disturbing revelation. However, what we get instead is almost ten minutes of exposition from Colonel Clifford, which deflates any promise of an exciting denouement and instead reveals the anticlimactic truth that nothing sinister is going on at Wellingham at all! The message of the episode, as articulated through Clifford's monologue, is discovered to be merely the idea that Charles and Greg may jeopardise their chance of federating the survivors if they are to behave in as frightened and suspicious a way as the people they hope to get through to. This is a deeply unsatisfying return for the audience's attention; having stayed with a plot that has consistently alluded to a more exciting development just around the corner, it is now clear that this will not materialise. The fact that Clifford's viewpoint is untenable doesn't help either: if there is one thing that Charles and Greg *have* learnt in the post-Death world, it is that they absolutely have to be suspicious in order to survive. Clifford's own open suspicion of Charles and Jenny, when faced with the latter's rescue attempt – he is heard to instruct 'Lock them up' – also rather stamps on his argument.

There are several other missed opportunities in "Manhunt", which could have elevated the drama from its pedestrian pace. Given the significance of the junkie raids on the settlement, to represent their threat merely through Miedel's broken arm and a brief encounter with Roberts is short-sighted and cheap. It is also baffling that one of the episode's most iconic elements – a human skeleton staked out on the ground – is robbed of its dramatic potential by being shown only after Clifford's explanation that it is a fake. Jenny's brave attempt to rescue Charles provides some much-needed action, but is unfortunately over far too quickly (and the shot in which Charles is hit by Jenny's gun is clumsily executed).

Where the episode does succeed is in its injection of realism, aided by director Peter Jefferies' discovery, while on location, of a camera technique that could make settings appear colder and more miserable than they actually were. The wild dogs that open the episode –

Lucy Fleming. © Denis Lill

which are thankfully fiercer than the cuddly canines seen in "Starvation" – and the beautifully shot bleak countryside of a British winter also add considerably to the coldly realistic atmosphere of the piece.

Another positive is the increased prominence of Charles and Jenny, now unquestionably the series' leads; this not only provides an opportunity for Lill and Fleming to demonstrate their considerable horse-riding skills, but also allows for a greater depth of emotion and motivation in their characters. Jenny is seen to behave hysterically for the last time here, as her extended separation from Greg begins to toughen her up and, as the series progresses, makes a true survivor out of her. Charles, meanwhile, is seen to have lost some of his buoyant idealism, and even greets Miedel's citing of his own long-held 'from each according to his ability' communist maxim with cynicism.

As for the other remaining members of the regular cast, while "Manhunt", and indeed the rest of series three, relegates Pet, Jack and the children to reduced supporting roles, Hubert is promoted to a new level of importance. His contribution here is restricted to light relief, but in later episodes will explore a previously untapped practicality, which will prove invaluable, if unrewarded.

As befits a series opener, the episode includes several elements and themes that will re-occur or be examined in greater depth later. Charles's belief that Jenny is more important to Greg 'than getting his blessed machinery going' will be stretched to the absolute limit before it is finally confirmed in "Long Live the King", alongside Jenny's long-held suspicion, first aired here, that Agnes may pose a threat to her relationship with Greg. Clifford mentions that Greg 'is making his way back to you as fast as that Norwegian girl will let him,' but suggests it is her impatience to save her fellow countrymen that will cause her to stall him. Later, however, we learn that it is perhaps more to do with her love for Greg and a deliberate attempt to keep him from Jenny. The recurrent debate over the enforcement of law and order, which will also reach its conclusion in "Long Live the King", is raised here through Clifford's conviction that he has to be tough and protect what they stand for, demonstrated through his implementation of an effective deterrent against the attacking junkies. Miedel's pethidine – which later becomes an instrumental part of Alec Campbell's recovery in "Sparks" – marks the beginning of the final series' interest in medicinal substitutes and alternative remedies, which is continued in "Bridgehead" and "Reunion". Drugs are described by Clifford to be more precious than gold ever was, although it is petrol that is referred to as the new gold in "Long Live the King". Clifford's related views about the pre-Death liberal treatment of drug addicts ('If we'd been tougher in the old days we might have stamped it out, as it was we gave them prescriptions') are as good as repeated by former addict Sam Mead in "The Enemy". However, the most significant question that arises from "Manhunt" is not only whether there are still enough 'decent and reasonable people left' for Charles and Greg to federate, but also whether either is finally going to be successful in such an endeavour; as Charles states: 'That's what we've got to find out, isn't it?'

Although the cast do their best, "Manhunt" lacks enough pace or incident to be engaging. The uninspiring revelation that there is really no mystery at the Wellingham settlement after all, despite all the pointers otherwise, is very disappointing. This is a jarring and uneven start to the third series, but the adoption of a new wanderer format – and the freedom it promises to provide – does suggest that better things are to come. *AP*

3.2 A LITTLE LEARNING

UK TRANSMISSION: 23 March 1977: 8.10pm – 9.00pm
VIEWING FIGURE: 4.55m
WRITER: Ian McCulloch
DIRECTOR: George Spenton-Foster
REGULAR CAST: Ian McCulloch (Greg Preston); Anna Pitt (Agnes Carlsson); Lucy Fleming (Jenny Richards)
GUEST CAST: Sylvia Coleridge (Mrs Butterworth); Joseph McKenna (Eagle); Sean Caffrey (Millar); Prentis Hancock (McIntosh); John Barrard (Mr Oliver); Richard Beaumont (Cliff); Christopher Huxtable (Philip); Keith Collins (Bernie); Johanna Sheffield (Libbie); Nicola Glickman (Annie)
UNCREDITED CAST: Gary Rich (Tommy); Joy Ashford, Anthony Beswick, Debbie Bird, Carol Dunseith, Ivor Fletcher, John Hardy, Robert Guinivan, Mark Ingleby, Carol Laniosh, Philip Mountford, Kerry Palmer, Beverley Poulton, Fiona Spence, Julie Trott, Paul Westwood, (Children)
OB RECORDING: 12 - 17 March 1977
LOCATIONS: Wolverley Court, Wolverley, Kidderminster, Worcs; Lodge Gate House, Kidderminster, Worcs; Half Penny Green Airport, Wolverhampton, Wolves; West Midland Safari Park, Kidderminster, Worcs

SYNOPSIS: Jenny is searching for Greg on her own. He and Agnes, who are close by, meet an eccentric old woman named Mrs Butterworth, who tells Greg that she was recently raided by 'Red Indians'. The Red Indians turn out to be a community of independent children who are living at an old school and are led by a boy called Eagle. One of the children, Libbie, is suffering terribly from an unknown disease, but Eagle insists that they tell no-one, fearing adult interference with their hard-won freedom. Meanwhile, Jenny is further frustrated in her search for Greg by two roguish traders named Millar and McIntosh. On finding the school, Greg is captured by the children, who are now armed and hunt him through the grounds. The hunt stops when Greg encounters a boy who is showing signs of the disease. Eagle shows Greg the other sick children. Mrs Butterworth suspects that Libbie has gangrene, and later that night, Greg puts the girl out of her misery. Eagle then reveals that Libbie was his sister. He tells Greg that they have had dealings with the traders and that Libbie made bread from the rye they provided. Greg realises that the children have ergotism – otherwise known as 'St Anthony's Fire' – caused by a fungal growth on the rye. He makes the sick children march about the school playing musical instruments in an attempt to soothe the effects of the disease. While seeking out Millar and McIntosh, Greg once again just misses Jenny. He returns to the school to find that Eagle and the children have gone off to a nearby civil defence centre for guns and food. Learning from the traders that the centre is mined, Greg rides off to warn them, but luckily they are unharmed. Greg instructs Agnes to go back to Whitecross and promises to follow on. The children discover an elephant in a nearby field and Greg spots a familiar figure in the distance, not realising it is Jenny.

ANALYSIS: Ian McCulloch's second script for the series, which reunites the viewer with Greg and Agnes, recently returned from Norway, is an interesting diversion from the broader concerns of the third series. McCulloch has often stated that the episode suffered under the direction of George Spenton-Foster, writing it off as 'a disaster.' But this is far too strong a criticism of an episode that, given that it takes the risk of incorporating both children and animals, actually works rather well.

The episode's success relies chiefly on the talent of principal guest artist Joseph McKenna as Eagle, a tough Glaswegian kid who has taken on the responsibility of leading a whole community of children. Thankfully, McKenna is a great actor who is entirely capable of dealing with the demands of the part. His compassion for his 'team', as he calls them, is sensitively played, while his bullying alter ego is equally believable. In an unexpected twist on the obvious *Lord of the Flies* scenario, rather than depicting this large group of children to have degenerated into primitivism and violence, McCulloch chooses to portray Eagle and his team as being capable of looking after themselves and living by their own rules. Eagle is also shown to be a leader who is just as aware of the importance of morale as that of physical sustenance: the 'Red Indian' raids and the hunting of Greg are discovered to be merely distractions, devised to help his charges to forget the terrible illness that has begun to afflict them.

The title of the episode – the beginning of the well-known saying that concludes '… is a dangerous thing' – would seem to suggest that the situation at the settlement has been caused by the children's lack of experience due to their age. However, this is later belied by Greg's stated intention to check if the other settlements that have traded with Millar and McIntosh have been similarly affected by the contaminated rye. The traders themselves do not know that the rye will induce ergotism (the symptoms of which include vomiting, diarrhoea, hallucinations and, in serious cases, gangrene), and it is unlikely that purchasers of their goods from these more typical settlements would have any more idea of the dangers than the children; it would be more accurate to conclude from the episode that though a little knowledge may be a dangerous thing in the post-Death world, ignorance is reliably fatal.

Through "A Little Learning", McCulloch was clearly keen to show what might have happened to those children who had survived The Death but who were far less lucky than John and Lizzie. In this context, freedom becomes a central theme; this is particularly highlighted by Eagle's startling account of his immediate post-Death experiences: 'I ran away four times … I got beaten, chained up, locked in a cellar for two weeks.' That Eagle refuses to consider Philip's suggestion that they should accept assistance from 'grown-ups' – even stating that he'd 'rather die here' first – is not only another indication of the torment he has already suffered, but also of the great store he puts by their new-found freedom. This last point is further demonstrated by his impassioned cry to Greg, with his arms outstretched: 'We found the right settlement. It's here. It's ours. We're free!' The uncomfortable conclusion that all the members of his team must have been victims of neglect or slavery in bad settlements before finding a safe haven at this unusual community is difficult to ignore and provides another bleak vista of the social landscape of the post-Death world. The elephant that makes a surprising appearance at the episode's close is also used to drive home the point further, as Eagle observes that they shouldn't keep the animal chained up as a pet with 'nae freedom,' as they 'wouldn't want to be cooped up again' either.

Libbie's gangrene and the children's unaided endurance of her pain is a terrible prospect. Her screams are perhaps more haunting because drama rarely depicts such horror visited on a young child. Greg's decision to carry out the one thing that Mrs Butterworth suggests he *can* do for the girl is a disturbing scene, made all the more moving by Greg's obvious affection for children; during the previous series, he was seen to be closer to John and Lizzie than any other character, appearing to have a complete understanding of their wavelength and needs. The shot of Greg, numb with grief, sat in the darkened room by the dead girl's bed and clutching the pillow he used to suffocate her, lingers in the mind long after the end credits roll. Even by the standards of the final series, McCulloch paints an unremittingly dark picture of the uncompromising world the survivors now inhabit.

Although the central themes of "A Little Learning" are engrossing and well played out, the episode does have a few less successful elements – the first of these being the inclusion of Jenny, who is entirely superfluous to the episode's action and whose presence only serves to engender further viewer frustration with the 'search for Greg' plot. A curious delight is taken in implementing a contrived 'ships in the night' theme throughout, with Jenny consistently arriving at places just after Greg has left. Hardest to bear is the final sequence, in which Greg actually sees Jenny riding in the distance and thinks she looks like someone he knows. The Jenny subplot serves to distract from the main action, which arguably contains more than enough potential for fifty minutes. Presenting the search for Greg to appear as hopeless is a dangerous game to play, given that it is this very premise that has been chosen as the backbone of the third series.

A less important flaw is the sudden and unexplained relocation of the episode to 'The Outpost' for the closing minutes. McCulloch had in fact scripted several extensive sequences for this location that were not recorded, and included: the children making their way through the minefield; Eagle digging up a mine and inventing a dangerous game – 'There's a prize for the first one who hits it'; and a tense scene in which little Annie sits on a mine, unaware of the danger she is in. Also dropped prior to recording was a scene from earlier in the episode in which Greg, while being hunted, escapes from an attacker called Bernie by pulling the child's trousers down so that he can't run after him. Bernie's ensuing humiliation at the hands of his peers later prompts him to run off and warn Millar and McIntosh that they know about the rye.

"A Little Learning" is particularly significant for its introduction of Agnes Mark II. Anna Pitt is a very different actress from Sally Osborn, and her Agnes lacks a certain persuasive charm and girlish vulnerability. Pitt's Agnes appears more mature and confident and – judging by the scene in which Greg is asking about legends – more easily irritated and aggressive. However, Norwegian speakers will know that the new Agnes also has a sense of humour as her response to Mrs Butterworth, after she is left behind by Greg, translates as 'I don't know whether I prefer you with your teeth in or out!'

It is a shame, given that Agnes and Greg are now centre-stage, that we learn nothing more about their Norwegian sojourn or their future plans. What we do learn is that Agnes strongly resents Millar's implication that Greg is her 'bloke.' While this would seem to conflict with later revelations, it is perhaps more indicative of both the character's independence and her related unwillingness to let the engineer know her true feelings.

Sylvia Coleridge's performance as Mrs Butterworth is worthy of note. The character is one whose gait and gruff manner bears a stunning resemblance to *The Dark Crystal*'s Ogra, and who is described in the original script as: 'A woman who in the middle ages would have spent much of her time being stuck on the scold's chair and ducked in a pond.' The character's glorious eccentricity is thankfully underlined by an intense practicality when it really matters. McCulloch recalls that her casting was one of the few suggestions of his that the director actually took on board. Spenton-Foster was clearly impressed with Coleridge, and would use her soon afterwards as the bizarre Croupier in the *Blake's 7* episode "Gambit".

McCulloch has asserted that "A Little Learning" is thoroughly spoilt by direction that gives the game away; he cites the early inclusion of the 'School' and 'Sick Bay' signs, which he feels ruin the surprises of, respectively, the community of children and Libbie's screams being due to sickness rather than torture. However, this does a disservice to an interesting episode that has far more to recommend it than plot twists. That the viewer has to wait until "The Last Laugh" both for another McCulloch script and for another appearance by Greg is a tremendous shame. *AP*

3.3 LAW OF THE JUNGLE

UK TRANSMISSION: 30 March 1977: 8.10pm – 9.00pm
VIEWING FIGURE: 6.72m
WRITER: Martin Worth
DIRECTOR: Peter Jefferies
REGULAR CAST: Denis Lill (Charles Vaughan); Lucy Fleming (Jenny Richards); John Abineri (Hubert Goss); Anna Pitt (Agnes Carlsson)
GUEST CAST: Brian Blessed (Brod); Barbara Lott (Edith Walter); Eric Deacon (Steve Walter); Keith Varnier (Owen Walter); Cheryl Hall (Mavis)
OB RECORDING: 15 - 21 January 1977
LOCATION: Bridgnorth to Kidderminster Severn Valley Railway, Shrops

SYNOPSIS: Pursued by packs of wild dogs, Jenny and Charles finally meet up with Agnes and – joined by a grumbling Hubert – set off for the thriving Walters' farm, which Agnes and Greg recently visited. They find the farm populated only by rats, and when Jenny and Charles go hunting in the woods they are detained by two men toting crossbows, who insist they meet with their settlement leader Brod. Arriving at the railway sidings where Brod has set up his camp, an exhausted Jenny is put to bed, while Charles meets up with Edith Walter. The two men turn out to be her youngest sons. Edith explains that Brod raided nearby settlements, and set up this hunting community where he operates as lord and baron. Excited by the life of the brigand, her sons are reluctant to return to their farming labours. In the morning, Charles and Jenny meet the bullying and aggressive Brod, who dismisses Charles's plans for reconstruction, and insists that hunters – and not farmers – will be the rulers of the new world. Brod is determined to humble and humiliate his 'guests'. Demanding that they pay for their room and board, he sets them to work – suggesting that Jenny can settle her debt in his bedroom. Charles refuses Brod's repugnant terms. Brod forces the visitors to leave empty-handed, and when they are driven back by dogs, he tries again to rid himself of the troublesome Charles. Desperate to re-establish the Walters' community, Charles tries to persuade Brod's followers to abandon him, without success. Jenny tries to use Brod's impotence to undermine him, while Hubert suggests doing away with him. Charles rejects both their plans, but when Hubert gets the opportunity, he fatally wounds Brod with a crossbow, claiming that it was an accident. With Brod dead, his followers pack up their belongings and head back to the Walters' farm in horse-drawn convoy.

ANALYSIS: After the setup work of "Manhunt" and the intriguing distractions of the first Greg story in "A Little Learning", "Law of the Jungle" darkens the mood of series three still further as the Whitecross refugees find themselves trapped in a settlement of hunters and outlaws lorded over by the bullying and unpredictable Brod. The episode amply demonstrates both the potential and the drawback of *Survivors'* new mobile format: one that helps to keep the drama fresh and inventive, but requires audiences to establish an immediate connection with a series of broadly-drawn one-off characters and situations.

The outstanding success of "Law of the Jungle" is to confound audience expectations about the shape of the new world. The contrast between the warm Whitecross summer afternoons and the atmosphere and setting of "Law of the Jungle" could hardly be starker. Here the landscape is defined by cold and decay, and by the predators who maraud the countryside outside Brod's stockade. Amidst the mist and mud, wild dogs fight and rats multiply. The howls of the hungry dog pack are audible throughout the episode. The full sequence of the trapped pig being despatched by Steve's crossbow at the beginning of the episode was considered too gruesome for *Survivors'* UK Gold repeat transmission. As Charles's group find what they hope is sanctuary as Brod's guests, they are exhausted, fearful and hungry.

If Whitecross represents the settler-farmer solution to the question of survival, Brod's is the hunter-gatherer alternative, in which his community live as scavengers – taking their pick of the wild animals and the fruits of the land around them. Brod sees this as the only realistic and honest response to the catastrophe that has befallen the world. He is convinced that: 'There's nothing a farmer can grow that you can't get by hunting.' Charles is appalled by what he sees as a descent into barbarism, and by Brod's rejection of any possibility of an improvement in the survivors' lot.

There are some effective contrasts to be drawn between the brute authority of Brod (actor Brian Blessed gives a committed and powerful performance that is appropriately intimidating) and that exercised by other authoritarian leaders seen in the series. Both Wormley ("Genesis") and Manny ("Lights of London") see themselves as leaders who are best placed to protect the traditions of the old world: Wormley through paramilitary might and political expediency; Manny through democratic subterfuge, bribery and deception. Kershaw ("The Chosen"), meanwhile, rules by ideology: presenting himself as the 'keeper of the faith' who can best defend his people from the contamination of corrupt ideas. In contrast to Manny or Wormley, he claims that his enlightened ideas are an improvement on those that dominated the old world. Brod, meanwhile, has nothing but contempt for 'fancy ideas' and abstract principles of any kind. His credo is that of the nihilist: convinced that the world is destined to endure forever more the chaos of the jungle, and that only the strength of the hunter can guarantee survival. Brod is a leader in the tradition of the philosopher Hobbes, who was convinced that, outside the restraints of an ordered society, life would be 'brutish, nasty and short.' In the next episode, Charles will encounter a nihilist of an entirely different calibre, in the shape of the erudite and educated Dr Richard Fenton.

Throughout *Survivors'* third series, Charles repeatedly meets those who are determined to thwart his plans for reconstruction and federation. Here the threat is not uncertainty, indifference or even cynicism – but the presence of another alpha-male who wants Charles to submit to his dominance of the pack, and who is prepared to feed Charles to the dogs in the process. Perhaps the strongest moment in the episode is where Charles attempts to lead his group back out into the wilderness, spurning the deal that Brod is forcing upon them. As the dogs close in on them, the group's resolve breaks and they all flee back up the hill – and the triumphant Brod, gloating in his victory, pulls them back up into the safety of the carriage. Charles may hope to win the intellectual argument (although his efforts to convince the settlement to abandon Brod fail) but Brod is convinced that conditions of 'life itself' demonstrate that his way is right – something he is determined that Charles should accept, or die resisting.

The notion of the 'hollow' big man, whose bluster disguises insecurities of all kinds, is not a new one, but Worth explores the theme through some interesting interplays between characters. The person who might be said to have the most leverage over Brod is his current 'chambermaid' Mavis, who knows the crushing humiliation that Brod clearly feels over his sexual impotence, and who mocks him behind his back. Brod is keen to exact his price for feeding and sheltering Charles's group, insisting that Jenny will act as his new concubine, while the others perform chores at his command. The strategy that Jenny chooses to adopt when confronted by the lustful Brod is extremely brave, if a little foolhardy. She recognises what is being demanded of her, and the sacrifice she is being asked to make to save herself and her friends. Jenny does not flee, however, but challenges Brod directly and manipulates him into revealing his frustration about his unhappy marriage and the failure of his physical relationship. She then urges him to see how his crude bravado and machismo might make him repellent to women, and insists that if he were to embrace the gentler and more tender side of his personality he might yet find love. Given the seething instability of Brod, this seems a fairly dangerous approach to take – but even though Brod dismisses her ideas out of hand, her efforts effectively save her from his unwanted advances. The notion of enforced prostitution is, of course, entirely repugnant – but it is interesting to realise that in the events of "The Enemy", Charles suggests something not entirely dissimilar: seeking to manipulate Jenny into offering sexual favours to Alec, the better to secure his co-operation with Charles's reconstruction plans.

"Law of the Jungle" also offers the first evidence of Agnes's intention to withhold information from Jenny about Greg's movements. In sharp contrast to their meeting in "Long Live the King", Jenny's and Agnes's first reunion here is warm and emotional. But although Agnes becomes aware of Jenny's earlier proximity to Greg in "A Little Learning" when Hubert tells the Norwegian that Jenny 'saw an elephant,' she keeps the information to herself.

The plot thread that ties together the events of "Law of the Jungle" with the next two episodes is the fate of the Walters' farm. What had previously been a thriving homestead had been overrun by a raiding party of Brod's. By the time that Brod had taken everything of worth from them, the Walters had no choice but to abandon their farm and join up with him.

Charles is determined that the farm be re-established as a living example for others to emulate. It is his conviction to see this through that sends him north to the Derbyshire Peak District in "Mad Dog", in search of the missing eldest son Tom Walter, and which brings him back south to set up the market at the railway station in "Bridgehead". Although it is possible to see the Walters' settlement as a symbol-in-microcosm of Charles's wider ambitions, the question remains as to whether or not the family actually deserve the attention that Charles affords them and the amount of screen time that they occupy. Steve and Owen seem happy to settle for the easy life of huntsmen-at-large, while their mother Edith (in the script notes: 'a good-looking woman of about 45') frets and complains about their dislike of hard work. In neither case do they come across as immediately sympathetic or deeply interesting. Although it goes unremarked, the Walters are at least noteworthy for being a family in which four close blood relatives have survived The Death – something Charles would scarcely have believed possible at the time of "Corn Dolly". There is, however, still something of a mismatch of scale in the work that Charles and the ever-active Greg are involved with. While Greg, unseen, is putting together the new national infrastructure that will be revealed in "Long Live the King", Charles is here preoccupied with the affairs of a single farmstead. In many respects, it feels like Charles should be looking instead at the 'bigger picture'. That said, it is at least Charles's persistence and determination that lead to the re-establishment of the Walters' settlement: until Brod's demise, even Edith is convinced that the task is too great and that instead they should all flee to the comparative safety of the isolated Sheridan farm (which Charles and Jenny subsequently visit in "Bridgehead").

The setting for "Law of the Jungle" is suitably spartan and devoid of comforts. The freezing-cold train carriages – like the churches and other dwellings seen elsewhere in the third series – make for an effective juxtaposition of the new world with the old. The whole settlement is well-realised on screen – with its jumble of tents, lashed together buildings and wood-burning braziers. The scenes played out by the riverside are also extremely evocative. In a comparative rarity for *Survivors*, the episode is well-populated by a pool of grubby and frozen extras who together help to reinforce the realism of the crowd scenes (although the shortage of young children amongst their number is notable, and probably a direct consequence of the freezing conditions).

It is Hubert who, convinced that the group is trapped and facing annihilation, decides that Brod must be killed. Taking on the role of the hunter, Hubert despatches Brod with a crossbow bolt. Although the moral picture is far from clear-cut, Hubert's perception that he has 'done right' is reinforced when Brod's death signals the end of the community and the return to the Walters' settlement that Charles has wanted all along. Charles fears that in killing Brod they have conceded his vision of the world (something that Brod himself suggests with his dying breath) and struggles

Brian Blessed. © Denis Lill

to accept the idea that Hubert was heroic. 'Hold on to Hubert,' Brod insists. 'It's hunters you need.' However, there is no hint of Steve or Owen exacting revenge on Jenny in the way that Brod had threatened were he to be slain: without Brod, their belligerence fades, and Edith's maternal authority over them appears to revive. In an earlier version of the script, as Brod lies dying, Hubert is 'blooded' by him to indicate that the shepherd is now a hunter – much to Charles's and Jenny's distaste. Hubert also takes Brod's horse, helping himself to the spoils of his conquest. Emboldened by his action, Hubert even takes the lead in urging the group to leave: 'Sun's up and if we're going to make a start on that farm today, we'd better shift.' Hubert's new-found confidence suggests that his character has begun to evolve in an interesting direction. Yet later storylines in the series will partly reverse the developments set in motion by "Law of the Jungle".

Nonetheless, as the group leave Brod's camp, it is Charles's perception of the world that has taken the hardest knock. His desire to encourage the growth of agriculture and the expansion of trade has come up against a rival worldview that sees such developments as fanciful and outmoded. All his political acumen has proved insufficient either to topple the tyrant or to incite his followers to rebel. However uncomfortable he is at the implication, as he sets out once more to bring order to 'the jungle', Charles appears to be in Hubert's debt. *RC*

3.4 MAD DOG

UK TRANSMISSION: 6 April 1977: 8.10pm – 9.00pm
VIEWING FIGURE: 7.42m
WRITER: Don Shaw
DIRECTOR: Tristan de Vere Cole
REGULAR CAST: Denis Lill (Charles Vaughan)
GUEST CAST: Morris Perry (Richard Fenton); Bernard Kay (Sanders); Ralph Arliss (Jim); Max Faulkner (Phil); Stephen Bill (Ron); Heather Canning (Ellen); Eric Francis (Engine Driver); Robert Pugh (Fireman); Jane Shaw (Young Girl)
UNCREDITED CAST: Alfreda Atkinson (Alfreda); Kenneth Reynolds, Stanley Welch (Farmers); Martin Grace (Charles's double)
OB RECORDING: 27 - 31 January 1977; (remount) 12 - 13 March 1977
LOCATIONS: Monsal Dale, Derbys; Air Cottage, Nr. Ilam, Derbys; Hampton Loade station, Bridgnorth to Kidderminster Severn Valley Railway, Shrops

SYNOPSIS: On a solo mission to track down Tom Walter in the Derbyshire Peak District, Charles is set upon by wild dogs. Rescued by the articulate and intelligent Fenton, Charles soon finds his cynicism profoundly uncomfortable. To Fenton, Charles's plans for reconstruction are absurd delusions that deny the horrible realities of the world. To Charles's horror, Fenton reveals the existence of rabies amongst the dog packs in the district, suggesting that Charles might have contracted the infection. Charles prepares to leave, until Fenton tells him of a visit by Greg Preston. Keen to read the notes that Fenton has kept on all those he has encountered since The Death, Charles accompanies him to his halfway house. In the night, Fenton falls ill with a fever. The symptoms suggest that Fenton has himself contracted rabies during an earlier attack. Determined to find Fenton's notebooks,

Charles sets out to find others who might know the location of his house, or be able to provide medical help. When he returns with locals Sanders and Jim, Fenton's condition has worsened, and – foaming at the mouth – he attacks all three of them. Realising the true horror of Fenton's illness, Sanders and Jim shoot him dead. Suspicion then falls on Charles – who Sanders fears might also be a rabies carrier. Under sentence of death, Charles flees. After an exhausting chase, he collapses in the snow, before being rescued by the simple Ron and kindly Ellen. As he prepares to leave, he is betrayed by Ron and the chase begins again. Charles's horse throws him, and he crawls away with his last reserves of energy. He stumbles across a working steam train, taking on coal by the trackside, and sneaks aboard. Nursed back to health at the station, Charles urges the crew to expand the rail network. He learns that a similar plan was espoused by an earlier visitor – Greg Preston.

ANALYSIS: "Mad Dog" is a satisfying fusion of the visceral and the intellectual – it offers an exciting and inventive adventure story, but manages to combine some striking action sequences with compelling character conflicts about the likely fate of humanity in the post-Death world. The episode also brings to the screen some of the most memorable and evocative locations seen anywhere in the series. The threat posed by rabies in the post-Death world, referred to as early as in the series one episode "Starvation", here returns in graphic form.

In this third series, Dudley had encouraged writers and directors to open up the *Survivors* canvas and to experiment with the series' format. Here scriptwriter Don Shaw and director Tristan de Vere Cole seize the opportunity with relish, producing a *Survivors* episode like no other.

Plans for a 'special' episode of the series – which would separate a single regular character from the others and place him or her in jeopardy in unfamiliar and dangerous territory – had first being raised during the production of series two. That series had included two precedents for just this kind of dramatic conceit: the "Lights of London" two-parter had, in the main, focused on the trio of Greg, Charles and Ruth, while "The Chosen" had focused on the adventures of Charles and Pet. It was Shaw's idea to take that process one stage further and place the spotlight on Charles alone.

Denis Lill had long been promised a showcase episode: '[I recall] Terry Dudley turning to me and saying, "Now you've got your Western," which really made my day, because it was one thing that I'd always wanted to do, and it had taken several years to realise that ambition!' This ambition was one he would memorably fulfil again, years later, when filming the cowboy-themed *Red Dwarf* episode "Gunmen of the Apocalypse". It has often been suggested that Dudley's decision to offer "Mad Dog" to Lill, rather than to Ian McCulloch, was a decisive factor in McCulloch's choice to reduce his involvement in series three to just two episodes. There is little question that Dudley's decision settled beyond any doubt who was now to be identified as the series' lead. It brought to a conclusion a remarkable evolution for the character of Charles, from his modest origins as a one-off first series guest star.

"Mad Dog" was certainly a bold experiment: dispensing so completely with the series' familiar environment and format might easily have ended in failure, producing something that seemed wholly disconnected from the rest of the series. Shaw was well aware that he'd 'produced something very different from a normal *Survivors* script.' As Lill remembers: 'It actually stands out as a one-off episode. Because it really does fall outside the rest of the [*Survivors*] genre, as it were.' Instead, "Mad Dog" is rightly celebrated as one of the highlights of the series' final run. De Vere Cole, who had seen very few episodes of the series prior to beginning work on *Survivors*, was certainly not intimidated by the story's distinctiveness. He recalls that having only one familiar character '... certainly did not make it harder. For all I knew, there had been other episodes in the first two series where there was just one main regular. So it wasn't particularly significant to me.'

Shaw sets up the principal conflict in "Mad Dog" as the clash between the optimism and self-belief of Charles and the corrosive defeatism of Fenton, and then overturns audience expectation by switching the drama in an entirely new direction, as a rabid Fenton is shot dead and Charles is forced to flee for his life.

In his role as the world-weary misanthrope Fenton, Morris Perry heads up the impressive and uniformly strong supporting cast. Fenton is one of the best drawn guest characters in the entire series, and Perry's portrayal of the mischievous cynic who relishes the opportunity to goad and needle Charles is as confident as it is well-judged. After rescuing Charles from the pack of wild dogs, and learning of his world-changing ambitions, Fenton sets out to demolish what he sees as Charles's delusional sense of self-importance and his denial of the realities of humanity's predicament: 'After all, what have we had? The reverse of one thousand years of social, political and economic progress, and people like you ... come along and talk as though we've just had an air-raid.' When Charles urges Fenton to take his ideas about the world's revival seriously, Fenton mockingly refers to the 'little men with big ideas' from whom he's heard it all before. Charles is appalled by Fenton's determination to sit back and watch humanity's last gasp. He finally, bitterly, concedes, 'I wish I'd never met you,' before Fenton falls ill.

Bernard Kay is instantly believable as the straight-talking, unsentimental Sanders, whose determination to track down the potential rabies carrier in his community's midst is as strong as Charles's own determination to survive. For Sanders and his neighbours, survival is

premised on mutual self-interest: 'Round here, it's your own and nobody else's. That's the way we go.' Heather Canning's portrayal of Ellen (in the script notes: '35, with a slight South African accent') is similarly convincing, with her warm-hearted and generous nature doing nothing to cloud her own pragmatic and realistic assessment of the rabies threat.

The story unfolds in the bleak wintry surroundings of Monsal Dale and Ilam, in the 'White Peak' area of the Derbyshire Dales. Although it seems hard to believe, "Mad Dog" was not written with its perfectly-suited locations in mind. Shaw recalls: 'I wanted it set in Derbyshire, in the Peak District. That was my suggestion. But not the exact locations.' The inclement weather was also not a feature present in Shaw's script. As he recalls: 'We couldn't predict that. It just so happened it was like that. It wasn't written into it ... Episodes

Morris Perry (Richard Fenton). © Denis Lill

have their slots, and they have to go out and

shoot on certain days, and you get the weather that you've got. We were just fortunate.' It was de Vere Cole who made use of the bitterly inclement weather and the rolling empty landscape to infuse the story with such a richly melancholic atmosphere. Having inherited these conditions, he determined to make the most of them: 'There was no question of waiting ... You went out, and if it was raining, you shot. And if it was snowing, you shot.' Despite de Vere Cole's persistence and resolve, it proved impossible to complete the shoot in the time available, and a later remount at Monsal Dale was necessary to complete a number of outstanding scenes. When Charles stumbles across the frozen ruts of a muddy field, or plunges into the icy waters of a fast-flowing river, the harshness and loneliness of the surroundings are brought vividly to life. Perhaps the single moment that captures the sense of bone-chilling cold and desperate isolation more than any other is the shot of the horseback pursuit in which Charles flees along the edge of the valley ridge. Shot at a great distance, and with only the sound of the wind for its soundtrack, this brief sequence is extraordinarily effective. Not since the chilling post-Death sequences of "The Fourth Horseman" has the world seemed so unpopulated, so inhospitable and so unforgiving.

In the confidently-handled chase sequences that follow Charles's flight from certain death at the hands of Sanders, the drama is kept relentlessly on the move as the fugitive attempts his escape. Charles's fiery determination and sense of conviction combine to keep him going as the hunters keep up the pressure. When, exhausted and injured, Charles finally collapses in the snow, it seems as though Fenton's earlier insistence that 'you'll lie down too, when the time comes' has been horribly confirmed – until Charles is discovered by the hapless Ron and rescued. Indeed, Shaw's script had suggested that Fenton's prediction be used here as a voice-over, but de Vere Cole judged that such a literal reinforcement was unnecessary.

Fenton's voice does return to revisit Charles when he finally locates his home, retrieves his vital notes, and reads aloud Fenton's account of his meeting with Greg. Although the theft is unacknowledged, the acerbic Fenton has appropriated the darkly gloomy *Ballad of Sir Patrick Spens* to mock the ambitions of Greg Preston. The original, anonymously-authored ballad describes a doomed sea voyage from Norway to Scotland that ends in the death by drowning of a royal Scots wedding party. Fenton's parody of the work signals his own conviction that Greg's plans for an Anglo-Norwegian alliance are the delusions of a 'messianic dreamer,' just as certain to end in tragedy and failure. Shaw can have had few expectations that many viewers would immediately grasp the full significance of Fenton's poetic allusion, but it remains an entirely fitting moment. Fenton is clearly seen to enjoy the other literary references with which he attempts to provoke Charles. He first suggests that his own diaries might yet evolve into a new *Canterbury Tales* – offering a self-mocking comparison to Geoffrey Chaucer's world-renowned 14th Century collection of the fictional stories with which a group of travellers entertain each other on their wanderings. Charles, of course, insists that what to Fenton are idle musings are in fact vital raw data for his reconstruction plans. When the pair repulse a second dog attack, in a volley of gunfire, Fenton draws a wry parallel with the doomed heroism recounted in *The Charge of the Light Brigade*. He paraphrases Tennyson's celebrated poem: 'Cannons to the front, cannons behind.' Although in this exchange it is the dogs that fall victim to the firepower of their rifles, it is clear that Fenton sees humanity as just as inexorably headed 'into the valley of Death.' Fenton later insists to Charles's disgust that T S Eliot's 1925 poem *The Hollow Men* got it right, and that, as the last vestiges of human life are extinguished (along with the last matches), the world will indeed end 'not with a bang but a whimper.' Charles finds Fenton's passivity intolerable.

There are some intriguing insights into Charles's character revealed through all this. Charles's own dogged belief in the reconstruction plan leads him to take huge risks – above all, it is his desire to see Fenton's notes that encourages him to seek help (and so learn the location of Fenton's home). Charles is also somewhat reckless in escaping, even as his survival instincts take over. Sanders' insistence that Charles must die reflects his hard-nosed assessment that the risk that he poses is simply too great. There is nothing sadistic or gleeful in his decision – and it can indeed be argued that it is Charles's own foolhardiness that has put his life in jeopardy. Charles's calculations are, however, true to his character: while others might have considered it wise to slip quietly away from the district after Fenton succumbs to rabies, Charles is incapable of abandoning the records of 'half a nation' that Fenton has compiled. Driven on by his 'sense of mission', Charles is also willing to deceive and manipulate those he encounters on his travels, and has to be repeatedly rescued by the kind interventions of strangers – Fenton, Ron, Ellen and then the railway community. This is an indication of Charles's renewed determination to engineer situations and trick those he encounters the better to attains his ends, which becomes more pronounced as the final series unfolds – particularly in the events of "Sparks" and "The Enemy".

One short speech that was cut from the script would have provided a strong sign-off for the characters Ellen and Ron. After Ron has given away Charles's hiding place, and Charles flees on horseback as the riders pursue him, an anxious Ellen turns to Ron to ask him: 'Do you remember the man who said you were too silly? Too silly to live? He wanted to shoot you. When your mother and father died. I said you'd survived them. You were a survivor. It made you special. [*She turns to look after the disappearing horsemen*] He's a survivor, Ron ... God help him... [*An afterthought, even quieter*] God help us ...'

The appearance of the steam train – which emerges through a cloud of haze and mist to provide his ultimate means of escape – comes as just as big a surprise to the audience as it does to the intrepid Charles. The images of the locomotive rushing down the track carrying the unconscious form of an exhausted stowaway in its rear truck provide an effective and visually-arresting final twist to the adventure. Nursed back to health, Charles is carried out of the district and back towards the relative safety of the Walters' farmstead. Having arrived on horseback and now departing by mechanised horsepower, Charles muses that: 'Steam saved me. Steam for survival!' He clearly hopes that enthusiasm for mechanisation will itself prove infectious.

There are inevitably one or two weaknesses in an otherwise first-rate execution. It does seem difficult to accept that Fenton's chronicles of the comings and goings of 'half a nation' should be contained within the pages of the single small notebook that Charles finally discovers at his home. Charles's escape from the clutches of Sanders and Jim at Fenton's halfway house is not entirely convincingly staged. Moreover, it is very noticeable that even in an episode that Charles alone dominates, it is the earlier exploits of the tireless Greg Preston that haunt the drama at every turn. However, even taken together, the impact of these flaws on the strength of the on-screen drama is minimal.

Easily one of the strongest episodes in the entire series, "Mad Dog" bears comparison not just with other *Survivors* stories but also with the best of the BBC's drama output in the 1970s. For the director, of his three *Survivors* episodes: 'It was my favourite. I've done hundreds of programmes, and it would be in my Top Ten of those that I enjoyed doing.' A triumph of both vision and execution, and a demonstration of how effective the series' format could be despite the tight constraints of time and budget, it was perhaps the last time in *Survivors* when an episode was not restricted by the demands of the series' wider story arc. From this point on, the drive towards reconstruction and economic and social revival comes to preoccupy not only the minds of the main characters but also the drama that unfolds on screen. *RC*

3.5 BRIDGEHEAD

UK TRANSMISSION: 13 April 1977: 8.10pm – 9.00pm
VIEWING FIGURE: 8.23m
WRITER: Martin Worth
DIRECTOR: George Spenton-Foster
REGULAR CAST: Denis Lill (Charles Vaughan); Lucy Fleming (Jenny Richards); John Abineri (Hubert Goss); Anna Pitt (Agnes Carlsson)
GUEST CAST: Barbara Lott (Edith Walter); John Ronane (Bill Sheridan); Hazel McBride (Alice); Eric Deacon (Steve Walter); Keith Varnier (Owen Walter); Cheryl Hall (Mavis); Harry Jones (Elphick); Rosalind Elliot (Susan); John Ruddock (Bagley)
UNCREDITED CAST: Eileen Matthews (Woman with chickens); Kelly Varney (Tom Walter); Tina Morris, Val Penny (Girls); Tony Herrick (Farmhand); Adam Lloyd (Child)
OB RECORDING: 7 - 12 February 1977
LOCATIONS: Highley station, Bridgnorth to Kidderminster Severn Valley Railway, Shrops; Staffs and Worcs Canal between Wolverley and Cookley, Worcs

SYNOPSIS: Edith Walter chides her sons for wanting to leave their farm to look for Charles. Meanwhile, Jenny is keen to get on after Greg and argues with Agnes over whether or not looking for Tom Walter is their responsibility. Hubert fears that one of the cows may be infected with brucellosis. Charles returns and tells Edith that he has no news of Tom. Later that evening, Hubert burns the cow's aborted calf and isolates the animal. Charles shares news of Greg and his recent adventures. The following morning, while Owen and Steve are sent after a missing bull, Jenny and Charles set off to find Bill Sheridan – an expert in homeopathy who will be able to provide treatment for the cows. They meet Bill on the river and return to his home, where they are introduced to his partner Alice. While Bill and Charles head back to the Walter farm, Jenny offers to stay behind with Alice. Charles suggests to Bill that he should organise the people in the area to meet him at Highley train station, on the pretext that he is leaving the area and wants payment – in the form of goods – in return for sharing his skills before he departs; the real intention being to get them to meet each other there to trade. Charles and Agnes set off on horseback to track down Owen and Steve, who have not yet returned. Later, Charles and Bill return to Jenny and Alice; Bill and Jenny subsequently head off after Greg. 'Market day' arrives and Charles is reunited with Edith and Hubert at Highley station. As more people turn up with their goods, Bill and Jenny arrive in a car with the news that Greg has moved on again. Charles explains to those gathered that they have been brought together to trade and they all discuss the advances that can be made there. A train pulls up bringing Tom, Owen and Steve Walter home.

ANALYSIS: Martin Worth's "Bridgehead" is commendable for its attempt to draw together the disparate feel and themes of the third series' preceding four episodes. In this respect, it serves as a bridgehead in narrative as well as plot terms. However, the episode's subject matter, which mainly concerns attempts to restore the Walter farm to working order and, more interestingly, to found a trading centre, largely fails to be involving enough.

Several elements contradict previously established ideas – especially the effort that is made to sustain an independent farm when, since "New World", it has been known that there are much larger specialist centres in existence. In the same vein, it seems inconsistent that this episode – like "Mad Dog" before it – features so many people living in near isolation, given that the general trend depicted elsewhere in this final series seems to be towards joining up to form larger communities. However, the chief problem with "Bridgehead" is that both the concerns of Edith Walter and those of the ragbag of people at Highley station are simply far too small-scale to warrant the screen time that is afforded them. The troubles that befall Betty the cow and her calves cannot help but seem trivial when directly plotted against Greg's cited investigations into open-cast mining; the crucial breakthrough of a methane-powered car; and an ever-expanding rail network – yet these important elements are presented as mere subplots, as the melodramatically overplayed brucellosis outbreak ('Hubert's lit another fire') and the equally parochial 'market day' take centre-stage.

It increasingly seems that Greg is capable of achieving just about anything he turns his hand to when off-screen and not saddled with the company of Agnes or his former Whitecross colleagues: as a result, the extent of his achievements is beginning to sound a little implausible. In the second series, it took Greg three episodes just to produce some methane in a plastic bag – without even the provision of a valve to draw the gas off – and yet the viewer is now expected to believe that he has managed to find the time to engineer a methane-powered car, as well as concurrently re-routing an entire railway line!

"Bridgehead" is densely packed with intra-series continuity. References to Worth's own "Law of the Jungle" abound: Jenny talks of 'Brod's jungle'; Charles notes that the railway carriages are further down the track; while the brucellosis problem is said to have been first encountered at Brod's encampment. Charles's experiences in "Mad Dog" dictate that he cannot return to Dovedale, meaning that Jenny and Bill have to go in his place. Fenton's notebook also makes a reappearance, and we learn more about Sanders, the man who led the hunt for Charles. Although this depth of continuity does help to alleviate the disjointed feel of the third series' narrative so far, and certainly rewards the loyal viewer, back in 1977 it may well have been alienating to those tuning in only occasionally; tellingly, the series' audience never again reached eight million viewers after "Bridgehead". A possible reason for this episode's unusually high viewing figure may have been the fact that ITV regions had, the previous week, finished broadcasting runs of popular series including *The New Avengers*, *Dan August* and *The Streets of San Francisco* (which had been *Survivors'* principal competition), and so "Bridgehead" gained those viewers who didn't stay with ITV for a one-off Bruce Forsyth special entitled *Bruce and More Girls*.

In comparison with earlier episodes, Charles is seen to develop a slightly different approach in terms of achieving his goal of federation. Here, he is heard to espouse the view: 'Distrust and suspicion – it'll get them nowhere'; and after he outlines to Bill his plan to fool the vet's clients, he is told that he 'sound[s] like a politician.' Both instances contrast with Colonel Clifford's criticisms of the Welshman in "Manhunt"; he believed that Charles didn't have the skills of 'diplomacy, politics, [and] the art of devious manoeuvre' and that his suspicion would negate his attempts to unify the survivors. The change in Charles's outlook since then may be intended to imply that the Colonel's observations have hit home (especially as these two episodes were made back-to-back), but this does not quite fit with the fact that the Charles of Whitecross days was already versed in these arts.

Hubert is once again depicted as possessing new-found qualities and depths; here, he selflessly puts himself at risk by single-handedly dealing with the brucellosis outbreak. That anyone would later describe the Hubert of the second series as a 'considerate' man who 'thinks of others' is inconceivable, but this development is nevertheless progressed and treated believably; even Charles admits to having been hard on him over his killing of Brod, and apologises.

"Bridgehead" also sheds some interesting light on Agnes's motivation and thoughts. We learn the unsurprising fact that she 'never found it easy to make friends' when she was back in Norway; while her

Eric Deacon (Steve Walter). © Denis Lill

statement to Edith, 'It's best to travel light, isn't it? I think so. I couldn't bear to be Jenny' can be interpreted as an attempt to find some comfort for herself in her obvious loneliness. However, the later revelation of her love for Greg retrospectively suggests that she is actually jealous of Jenny's 'baggage' and would prefer not to be 'travelling light' herself. Agnes's sudden absence from the action near the episode's close, and the quick explanation that she has contracted brucellosis (despite the fact that she spends as little time as Edith or Mavis in Betty's cowshed) feels like a late interpolation of Worth's that will later prove useful – if not entirely convincing – when it comes to explaining the Norwegian's ability to nurse Greg without catching his 'smallpox' (the idea being that Agnes is somehow immune because of her previous infection). References to the pre-Death world litter the script in a way that highlights the absence of leisure time and fun from the survivors' new existence and has the effect of reinforcing the dull, medieval reality of the demands of day-to-day survival. Alice warmly recalls: 'Saturday nights in the pub. Never see those days again will we?'; while Owen and Steve – who are obviously frustrated by the lack of excitement and freedom in their post-Brod existence – mockingly refer to a world in which they would have been free of their current constraints: 'Pick up a couple of birds at the local caff. Drop in the pub. Pint of Export please. What's on at the cinema? *Sex and the Single Girl*?' Interestingly, Charles openly recognises such concerns when attempting to establish a bridgehead at Highley, realising that catching up on gossip and having a few beers is just as important an element of 'market day' as the forging of trading links. Worth's treatment of this subject once again demonstrates his strong interest in sociological concerns, which always add texture to his episodes.

Barbara Lott's Edith is the archetypal suffocating mother, who fulfils an important narrative function as an oppressive force and, in terms of the continuing quest to find Greg, an obstructive one too. It is Edith's demands that sent Charles to Dovedale in "Mad Dog" to look for Tom – locking Jenny and Agnes into temporary life at her farm. In this episode, it is she who prompts Charles's and Jenny's journey to Bill Sheridan's place and, later, Charles and Agnes to search for the departed Owen and Steve. As a result of her negativity and constant scolding of those around her, Edith is a character with whom it is particularly difficult to feel any sympathy; it is little wonder that both remaining Walter sons are depicted as desperate to escape her apron strings. Barbara Lott would go on to play a similarly overbearing mother to Ronnie Corbett's Timothy Lumsden in the BBC television sitcom *Sorry!* (1981-88).

Of the guest characters, Bill and Alice are particularly well-drawn, and are sensitively played by John Ronane and Hazel McBride. (Based on this performance, Dudley would later cast McBride as Kessler's mistress, Madeleine Duclos, in *Secret Army*.) McBride recalls '… how cold it was on location at the time. And in case we didn't all look cold and rugged enough, the Make-up Department had a very good way of replicating this look by applying cream blusher with a damp natural sponge!' In the original script, Alice was to have had two children and been pregnant – 'One of his, one of mine and – on the way – one of ours!' – and it was intended that they should all be living on a converted boat. McBride remembers thinking at the time that the little girl who played Alice's only child was 'rather too old to be spoon fed.' The 'market day' characters are also interesting, if a little odd; Harry Jones's Elphick is the strongest, making the most of a small role.

"Bridgehead" contains a brief but gloriously iconic *Survivors* moment: a shot of Charles and Agnes riding on horseback over the railway line at Highley Station. Further atmospherically directed scenes take place on a mist-shrouded river between Highley and Bill Sheridan's place. Given the grim reality that has pervaded not only this episode but much of the third series thus far, the first river scene – in which Charles accidentally drops the boat's oars, prompting a rare moment of relaxed laughter – comes as a breath of fresh air. His subsequent airing of an optimistic view that, as survivors, they are 'the lucky ones' is also a refreshing take on their predicament. Charles expounds the promise of the world with a renewed poetic vigour: 'Rivers that aren't polluted anymore, fish, timber, coal, all the fruits of the Earth, just waiting, waiting for us.' However, his idealism is nicely countered by Jenny's timely fishing of a glob of dirt out of the water – rather than a fish for their supper – as if to say that the new world is not quite as bountiful, and they are not quite as 'damned lucky', as Charles suggests. This last touch was a late addition suggested during the recording of the scene.

The events of this episode take place over a greater period of time than any other. This not only serves to illustrate how much time it takes the survivors to travel long distances on foot – their considerable excitement over new mechanised transport therefore needing little explanation – but also enables Worth to cover an awful lot of ground in plot terms. However, the constant to-ing and fro-ing and the abrupt passing of whole days and nights at a time proves to be confusing and difficult to follow, with the effect that the episode occasionally feels poorly edited.

Despite this confusion and an unfortunate focus on several inconsequential plotlines, strong characterisation, superior location recording and an on-form Denis Lill and Lucy Fleming make "Bridgehead" a welcome if unremarkable entry in the *Survivors* canon. *AP*

3.6 REUNION

UK TRANSMISSION: 20 April 1977: 8.10pm – 9.00pm
VIEWING FIGURE: 6.92m
WRITER: Don Shaw
DIRECTOR: Terence Dudley
REGULAR CAST: Denis Lill (Charles Vaughan); Lucy Fleming (Jenny Richards); John Abineri (Hubert Goss); Lorna Lewis (Pet Simpson); Gordon Salkilld (Jack Wood); Angie Stevens (Lizzie Willoughby); Stephen Dudley (John Millon)
GUEST CAST: Jean Gilpin (Janet Millon); John Lee (Philip Hurst); George Waring (Walter)
OB RECORDING: 3 - 8 April 1977
LOCATIONS: Ffrwdgrech House and grounds, Ffrwdgrech, Brecon, Powys; Abergavenny, Mons

SYNOPSIS: Charles, Jenny and Hubert come to the aid of a shepherd called Walter who has hurt his leg. He tells them about a vet who lives at a place called Sloton Spencer. Charles successfully seeks out the vet, who is named Janet; she operates on Walter's leg. Some time later, Charles and Jenny tell Janet and her partner Philip about their recent experiences. Listening to Charles's views on federation, Janet and Philip can't help but smile at how much he sounds like Greg – who has only just passed through. After agreeing to stay the night there, Charles reassures Jenny over Greg's continued absence. While Charles learns about Greg's recent visit from Philip, Jenny looks through Janet's photo album and makes the incredible discovery that the vet is John's mother. Both Janet and Jenny are amazed and overjoyed. Jenny is keen to return to Challenor with Janet at once; however, Charles thinks that they should go after Greg first. Although initially persuaded otherwise, Philip's inadvertent mention of Agnes leads Jenny to decide to leave with Janet in the morning. *En route*, she finds herself in danger from a wild dog, but is rescued by Hubert. Charles makes a rendezvous with them as planned and brings the news that Greg has moved on yet again. On nearing Challenor, Jenny telephones through to Jack and asks that he and Pet prepare John for the shock of seeing his mother again; they also agree to meet up half-way. Pet is concerned when John seems uninterested in her news and, when the two parties meet up, the reunion between Janet and John is decidedly uneasy. They all agree to continue on to Sloton Spencer. Philip tries to explain to John about a foot-and-mouth outbreak before The Death. Janet realises that the problem lies in the fact that John does not realise that the reason she did not send for him to come home was that she wanted him to avoid seeing the slaughter of his favourite animals – and not, as he thinks, that she did not want him. Charles manages to talk John round, and he and Janet are reconciled. Charles comforts Jenny, promising her that he will find Greg.

ANALYSIS: Don Shaw's "Reunion" is a refreshingly heart-warming episode that, for once, sidelines the wider concerns of federation and trade and therefore provides a welcome shift of dramatic focus. The largely character-led storyline is based around the surprising and joyful revelation (spoiled for *Radio Times* readers of 1977 by a preview feature accompanying the listing for "Manhunt") that John's mother is alive and well, and the attendant emotions that cloud their reunion. Terence Dudley takes up directorial duties for the only time on the series, perhaps with a view to encouraging a suitable performance out of his son Stephen; as with Terence's work on the second series of *Secret Army* the following year, he does a great job.

Jean Gilpin – who plays Janet Millon – was reportedly nervous about playing mother to the director's son, but nevertheless manages a sensitive portrayal. The underrated Stephen Dudley also acquits himself well, and his bewildered state in his separate encounters with Pet, Philip and Charles is both touching and believable. Looking back on the episode today, Stephen recalls: 'I do remember thinking how harrowing it would be to suddenly discover, having finished grieving, that the mother you thought was dead is alive, and that the displacement and sense of betrayal would be devastating.' "Reunion" is notable for its long overdue return to Challenor to catch up with Pet, Jack and the children. Effortlessly relaxed performances from Lorna Lewis and Gordon Salkilld remind us that their regular absence from proceedings – due to the third series' wanderer format – is a great loss to the show. It is good to hear finally that the old community at Whitecross is still a viable concern, although we are not told why Charles and the others moved on to Challenor in the first place. Bizarrely, once everyone has been reunited and they all decide to continue on to Sloton Spencer – cited as a new settlement for everyone – Charles suggests that Seth can pass word back to Challenor; just who exactly is left there to receive this message is a total mystery!

It is interesting that Janet's and Philip's assessment of Greg as a 'big husky commissar' who is going to 'round everyone up and force them to be lectured' seems more in keeping with the diplomatically challenged Greg that we are familiar with (see the conference in "A Friend In Need"), than with more recent reports of his continuing off-screen successes, which conversely suggest that he has all the requisite skills to regenerate the nation single-handedly. As Philip says: 'Why must you find this Greg chap anyway? ... He's got some good ideas, but he's not going to change the world over night.' Philip's point also underlines the futility of Jenny's and Charles's search for the engineer. Although Jenny's motivation to be reunited with her husband is clear, what Charles expects to gain from hooking up with his old sparring partner is not sufficiently explained. He argues that he needs to find Greg, but fails to answer Jenny when she questions his motives for doing so and sarcastically asks if he is 'doing it for everybody, for humanity?' Perhaps he merely wants to catch up with Greg before he can achieve too much, as his final words in "Bridgehead" suggest: 'Before he sets up the capital.'

As a mother, Jenny is seen to share a common bond with Janet. This is powerfully depicted in the brilliantly acted (and last to be recorded for the episode) scene in which she discovers that John is the vet's son. The scenario is made all the more emotionally charged by the fact that she is breaking this news as John's surrogate mother. Their union in motherhood also causes the search for Greg to be put on hold, although – following some guilt-tripping from Charles – it is unlikely that Jenny would have elected to return to Paul the very next day (rather than continuing the search for a few days first) had it not been for Philip's inadvertent mention of Greg's reference to a 'Swedish girl'! The ongoing uncertainty surrounding her husband's relationship with Agnes prompts Jenny angrily to exclaim the subtext-laden line, '*She* is Norwegian!', before immediately announcing to Janet that they will go to Challenor in the morning. Although they don't always see eye-to-eye here, there is no doubting the obvious affection that Charles now feels for Jenny. He makes considerable efforts to allay her concerns over Greg throughout the episode and, in the closing scene, comforts her lovingly as she quite understandably breaks down in tears. Despite the fact that Charles is taken aback by Jenny's pleasing appearance after her bath, any kind of sexual attraction between the pair is underplayed.

Hubert takes several more steps down the road to rehabilitation in this episode. He gains a previously unseen friend in injured shepherd Walter (who in the original script he had gone on ahead to visit and regards as 'the best feller I've met since all this started'), even going so far as to considerately check up on him after his operation; more importantly, he also saves Jenny from a wild dog. Although Janet is clearly playing up to him when she tells him that he is very brave, there is no denying that he is actually up to the task of defending them, despite Charles's earlier misgivings that he is not very motivated or reliable. Charles's and Jenny's very first scene in Shaw's script did not make it to the final edit, presumably as it involved the singing of Hubert's praises ('Hubert's a changed man. Getting to be reliable. He risked brucellosis saving that herd and he went on when Agnes went down with it') and would have therefore contradicted Charles's later dialogue. "Reunion" also sees Hubert used once again as the series' resident comic turn: he tells a tall story about rescuing a sheep from a quarry and receives a slapstick bloodied nose when a door is opened in his face. However, far more interesting is Hubert's brief soliloquy (in front of a bedroom mirror) on the persistence of a class system: 'Some people can do everything, can't they, even now behaving as if they had money, as if they were our betters.' This dialogue is underscored by deliberately erudite classical piano playing and bravely seems to acknowledge the widely criticised fact that the series is populated by numerous middle-class characters. When Hubert later complains that they will 'always have bosses,' Shaw uses Charles's affirmative response to make the claim that when the priority is survival, such a social order is inevitable and necessary. In the post-Death world, natural ability (in Charles's case, exceptional leadership and organisational skills) must – according to Shaw's script – take precedence over questions of social democracy and equality.

The episode is once again overloaded with continuity. Alongside references to their German friend (Miedel) and his synthesis of pethidine ("Manhunt") and Bill Sheridan's homeopathic expertise ("Bridgehead"), Shaw ensures that the viewer is particularly reminded of several of his own previous contributions: Jenny refers to Paul's death ("Greater Love"), while Charles reminds John of Alistair McFadden ("Face of the Tiger") in order to talk him round. There is, however, a surprisingly off-beam continuity blunder in this episode, as Janet cheerfully explains that she protected herself from exposure to the plague by using disinfectant at all the entrances to her house. While this might have kept foot-and-mouth at bay, it would have certainly been no match for The Death! Even if by some miracle such actions had protected her initially, as soon as Janet came into contact with other survivors, like episode five's 'angels', she too would have succumbed to the virus.

Although the narrative suggests that 'sticking together' – a phrase used several times – is the most important lesson that the regular characters have learned, this is ironically the last time that we will see Charles united with Pet, Jenny with Paul and Janet with John. Although the tenet makes sense in the uncertain world that they live in, it does not fit with the final series' quest narrative, or with the large-scale task of industrial regeneration; these are themes which will once again see Charles and Jenny departed from their loved ones in the very next episode.

With "Reunion", Don Shaw once again proves himself to be one of the show's finest scriptwriters. The episode is well-constructed and executed and therefore something of a rarity in the third series. Although it is by no means the most memorable episode of *Survivors*, and its content is relatively unchallenging, only the hardest heart could find the fireside photo album scene or the final reconciliation of John and his mother to be anything less than uplifting. *AP*

3.7 THE PEACEMAKER

UK TRANSMISSION: 27 April 1977: 8.10pm – 9.00pm
VIEWING FIGURE: 5.10m
WRITER: Roger Parkes
DIRECTOR: George Spenton-Foster
REGULAR CAST: Denis Lill (Charles Vaughan); Lucy Fleming (Jenny Richards); John Abineri (Hubert Goss); Edward Underdown (Frank Garner); Lorna Lewis (Pet Simpson)
GUEST CAST: Alan Halley (Henry); Paul Seed (Grant); Nicolette Roeg (Blossom); Heather Emmanuel (Rutna); Norman Robbins (Bentley); Brian Conley (Michael); John Grieve (McLain); Derek Martin (Cyril)
UNCREDITED CAST: Harry H Fielder (Larry); Leslie Bates, Alf Mangan, Clinton Morris (Carters); Penny Dixon, Jo Hall, Richard King, Jimmy Mack (Community members)
OB RECORDING: 14 - 18 April 1977
LOCATIONS: Pakenham Windmill, Pakenham, Suffolk; Hitcham Forest, Hitcham, Suffolk

SYNOPSIS: Following a lead on Greg's whereabouts, Charles, Hubert and Jenny arrive at an isolated settlement – dominated by its impressive windmill. Their hosts dress in white robes, greet them 'in peace' and ask to take their weapons for the duration of their stay. The group learn than the community is governed by the Hindu principles of vegetarianism and non-violence, and by a belief that humanity has been 'reincarnated' after The Death. Frank Garner has acted as the leader of the settlement's spiritual conversion, but the catalyst and inspiration for the change has been the young Asian woman Rutna. Henry, the day-to-day manager of the settlement, is dismissive of Charles's plans for federation and is worried that he wants to lure Frank away. Charles's efforts to connect the community to his growing telephone network prove ineffectual. Frank is keen to encourage the settlement to become more independent, and is anxious to join Charles in his quest. Jenny is furious that Charles – and, by implication, Greg – is neglecting his domestic and family commitments in favour of 'playing' at their reconstruction games. When two groups of traders become involved in a shoot-out, Henry is able to demonstrate his leadership skills by resolving the conflict peacefully. Initially unhappy to be stuck at the settlement, Hubert forgets his complaints when the passionate Blossom seduces him. Frank reveals to Jenny and Charles that he is fitted with a heart 'pacemaker', the batteries for which are already failing. He announces to the community that he is leaving and that Henry and Rutna will carry on the community's good work. Henry finds the confidence to take charge. Jenny is angered once more that Charles has decided to delay the search for Greg to look for an electrical engineer at a nearby community. Rutna is upset at the news of Frank's departure, but by the time Charles's group leaves the settlement, its sense of tranquillity has been restored.

ANALYSIS: "The Peacemaker" is the first of an uneven trilogy of episodes written by a single scriptwriter, Roger Parkes. Given that all three episodes also share a similar narrative format, these stories begin to feel increasingly familiar. In each case, the travellers arrive at a new settlement; learn about its solutions to the questions of organisation and survival; and depart with a new recruit for their continuing mission. At no point in between is Charles's group threatened or put at any real risk by their hosts, who all remain welcoming to their guests. The final recurring element is that at some point in each of the stories, one or more of the series' regulars speaks or acts completely out of character. If Martin Worth, Don Shaw or another writer had been brought in to draft the middle episode of the three, the repetitive and uncertain feel of this section of the series might have been significantly dissipated.

Unfortunately, on its own merits, "The Peacemaker" (originally commissioned as "The Kingmaker") is probably *Survivors'* least successful fifty minutes. This is partly because of the shortcomings of the sometimes-confusing plot and awkward script. The mill settlers are depicted as having converted to the spiritual principles of Hinduism, but not necessarily to its religious doctrines. They believe that The Death has brought about the 'reincarnation' of humanity. The community's religious figurehead is a young Asian woman, but its secular leader is an elderly former recruitment officer, who has used the Hindu faith as a means to establish the unity and sense of purpose of the fledgling settlement. The settlement's manager is a gruff speaking Yorkshireman who wants Charles's group to leave as soon as possible; the 'head hunter' is equally keen to leave with the visitors when they depart. One of the settlers is so keen for the travellers to stay as to poison the feedbags of their horses; while Rutna warns Jenny of hidden 'danger' if they remain. The community had 'capitalist' roots, but has evolved into a productive commune that has dispensed with managers, and that views Charles's enthusiasm for a new industrial revolution with great suspicion. There are simply too many overstretched ideas fighting for attention here, and not enough effort is made to make the different characters' motivations understandable. There is great dramatic potential in the unexpected juxtapositions that Parkes introduces – particularly in this white and largely working-class community's embrace of Hindu teaching – but with insufficient effort made to bring such developments to life, they appear as largely unconvincing.

One short sequence cut from the camera script did touch on one of these themes more directly. In this exchange, Charles challenges Henry to deny that the settlement's philosophy consists of: 'The nihilistic fatalism of the East? Zen and flower people? All the old pot-headed clichés of the hippie culture?' Such notions, Charles insists, are excuses for 'opting out,' distractions from the priority to rebuild the foundations of '… order and security. So that we can live without guns, yes, Henry – but everywhere and not just here.' Henry remains unconvinced by Charles's own flowery rhetoric, certain that the settlement's beliefs are both ethical and practical. Although some elements of the clash of their world-views remain in the finished episode, affording their conflict more screen time would have helped to reinforce the philosophical clash at the centre of this story.

More problematic than questions of plotting is that the episode includes a pretty unpalatable and patronising treatment of the issues of race and racial difference. This is not to suggest that Parkes, Dudley or episode director George Spenton-Foster had any discriminatory intentions in mind, but rather that the episode reveals a level of condescension towards its principal Asian character that reflected all too common social and cultural attitudes of the day. These are the elements of the story that not only serve to date this episode of *Survivors*, but also make for some uncomfortable retrospective viewing.

The crash of incidental music that greets Rutna's first screen appearance – intended to emphasise her 'otherness' – is not only jarring, but also wholly inappropriate. The music returns as the unwelcome soundtrack to Frank's farewell. That director Spenton-Foster was allowed to use a one-off technique not permitted anywhere else in the entire three series, appears as further evidence of the loosening of Dudley's grip on the production process. Rutna

Nicolette Roeg (Blossom). © Denis Lill

then remains a painfully underdeveloped background character, 'mysterious' and 'spiritual' in nature, but requiring the elderly, white patriarch Frank Garner to keep the community running. In the camera script, Rutna was the mother of a child in the settlement called Prakash, but even this aspect of her character was excised from the finished version. When Frank agrees to leave, there is not even the suggestion that Rutna might take over leadership of the community, as Henry (a somewhat unlikely spiritual figurehead) steps in to assume command. As Frank departs, Rutna is left prostrate on the floor before the feet of the 'Master G' as he sweeps away without a word. When Charles's group leaves, Rutna is once again revived as the little-understood eastern mystic whose real-world powers appear few.

Yet if all this is profoundly misconceived and patronising, Hubert's blatant, vocal racism is another matter entirely. Although arguably true to the nature of the character, it is still shocking to hear Hubert use crude racist epithets – vocabulary that would not easily be cleared for transmission today. It is also extremely notable that none of the other main characters is given the opportunity to challenge Hubert's language or views. To be fair, Parkes does have Blossom make direct reference to the racist abuse that Rutna suffered in the weeks following The Death – as some survivors sought revenge on her for the plague's 'eastern' origins (although, as Blossom explains, Rutna grew up in the Indian Punjab and not the far east).

Other aspects of the plot remain unsatisfying. Although the shoot-out between traders provides some solid action sequences, with Hubert once again in 'heroic' form, the recourse to gunfire seems implausible and disproportionate, as does the bloodless resolution of the standoff. Jenny's outburst at Charles and Frank (the first of several confrontations to come) is also somewhat strangely presented. Her allegations are serious: that the drive to reconstruction is nothing more than 'playing at pilgrimages' – a game through which Charles (and Greg) seek to avoid unwanted domestic responsibilities. It is not an argument that Charles attempts to rebut, and the accusation is left hanging. And yet, if Jenny is right, one of the central themes of the series is built on the self-deception of Greg and Charles, and the drive to rebuild the world is a sham. It is, at the least, inelegant to set up such a premise but hold back from resolving or developing it further, when its dramatic implications are so important. "The Peacemaker" also confirms Pet's marginal status in the third series: even though this is one of the few episodes in which she appears, her contribution is reduced to a single perfunctory scene, played out under a plastic awning on an inaudible phone line.

There are some features of "The Peacemaker" that at least redeem the episode in part. The windmill setting works well, and dovetails nicely with the series' other explorations of early and alternative forms of industrial technology – including that of the remaining canal network (as seen in "Parasites" and referred to in "New World"); the water wheel (as attempted in "The Witch"); and methane and wind power (which feature in the latter stories of series two). There are some efficiently handled 'procedural' scenes, in which Henry takes Charles through the mechanics of the milling process (a motif next seen as Alec takes Sam on a tour of the dormant hydroelectric station in "Power"). From this point on, the series seems to all but disregard such low-level technologies. Even though they are not very effectively presented, the ethics of the community – its pacifism, vegetarianism and strict moral principles – are both interesting and fresh, and (although none of the characters mentions the fact) stand as the direct opposite of Brod's brutal brigand code ("Law of the Jungle"). It is also interesting to watch Charles's frustration with the quiet fatalism of the community grow, culminating in his dismissal of Henry's refusal to confront the armed traders, with the words, 'To hell with peace!' Although, again, Jenny's outburst is not very perceptively handled, the attempt to provide some character development in the relationships of the lead players is welcome, particularly given Charles's harsh reaction to her challenge, in which he accuses her of being frightened, uncertain and possessive. The introduction of 'head hunter' Frank Garner provides an unexpected new perspective on the survivors' predicament, and Edward Underdown brings a quietly understated but effective reading of the role. The storyline also delivers some unexpected twists – the 'disarming' hospitality of the settlement in its signature white robes; the introduction of a surprise love-interest for Hubert; and the revelation of the ticking time-bomb of Frank's failing heart pacemaker. It is also heartening to hear rare news of others from the Whitecross community, who are reported here to have arrived at Sloton Spencer.

One particularly interesting element of character development that was cut from the script prior to recording concerned Hubert's bid to stay on at the settlement, in the welcome company of his new partner. Charles is instantly dismissive of Hubert's claim: 'Fact of it is, squire, they *needs* me yer.' He responds, wryly: 'Sudden promotion for a low-caste untouchable …?' Charles changes tack when he realises that Hubert feels himself to be an undervalued member of his group. Hubert may think that they're all just 'chasin' off after young Greg,' but Charles insists that there's 'far more' to it than that: 'Trade to organise, technicians to recruit. And you're just as vital to it as any of us, Hubert.' As the script directions indicate, once Hubert 'assimilates this gratifying concept' – that his contribution to their collective efforts is acknowledged and valued – he tentatively agrees to leave the settlement and Blossom behind. Hubert rarely hears such words of encouragement, and this exchange would have provided him with some overdue endorsement of recent changes in his outlook and character. Perhaps if he had opted to stay on at the windmill, Blossom and Rutna might together have smoothed the edges off at least some of Hubert's prejudices. Frank, meanwhile, will never make good on his pledge to return.

This episode provides the last major turning point in the story arc of *Survivors'* final series. It is the events at the end of "The Peacemaker" that change the priorities of Charles's wandering travellers for good. From this moment on, the drive to restore electric power takes precedence over the search for Greg, as the group set off to find electrical engineer Alec Campbell. Despite the unusual setting, and this important shift in the storyline, there is a sense as the episode reaches its conclusion that the horizons of the *Survivors* narrative are once again being closed back down to serve instrumental plot needs. The journey north towards the Scottish Highlands will now begin in earnest. *RC*

3.8 SPARKS

UK TRANSMISSION: 4 May 1977: 8.10pm – 9.00pm
VIEWING FIGURE: 7.22m
WRITER: Roger Parkes
DIRECTOR: Tristan de Vere Cole
REGULAR CAST: Denis Lill (Charles Vaughan); Lucy Fleming (Jenny Richards); John Abineri (Hubert Goss); Edward Underdown (Frank Garner); William Dysart (Alec Campbell)
GUEST CAST: Gabrielle Hamilton (Letty); John Bennett (Jim 'Queenie'); Linda Polan (Bet); John White (Vic)
UNCREDITED CAST: Leila Hoffman, Mair Coleman, Corinne McCounie, Nancy Adams (Community Members); Reg Dent (Alec's Double)
OB RECORDING: 1 - 6 March 1977
LOCATIONS: Imber, Salisbury Plain, Wilts; Industrial Estate, Salisbury, Wilts; Woods around West and East Tytherley, Hants

SYNOPSIS: Picking his way through rain-soaked woodland in search of former electrical engineer Alec Campbell, Hubert comes across a lone and brooding figure. He declines to answer Hubert's questions, and lashes out at him – unseating him from his horse. Charles, Jenny and Frank find the injured Hubert being tended to by the elderly Letty. They accompany her to her settlement, based around an abandoned church, and while Hubert is tended to, Charles and Frank learn that Hubert's attacker was Alec himself. The community's leader Queenie explains that Alec is a solitary figure, who shuns companionship and responsibility. It becomes clear that Alec is locked in a state of grief over the death of his wife, Rita. Although Jenny is outraged by the plan, Frank decides to use a supply of pethidine to force Alec to confront his feelings. Tricked into taking the medication, Alec becomes delirious and Frank begins to question him about his wife's death. In his delirium, Alec mistakes Jenny for Rita, and Frank and Charles force her to act out the role. They learn that Alec blames himself for not returning home to his wife as The Death spread. She was left to die alone and without him. Their work done, Alec slips into unconsciousness. The next morning, Alec climbs to the top of the church tower, wanting to throw himself to his death. While Frank and Jenny try to keep him talking, Charles sneaks up the crumbling tower steps and drags him back from the edge. Alec remains in a state of distress until Frank resorts to shock therapy – pretending to him that they are leaving. Frank's tactic works and Alec, seemingly cured, suggests to Charles that he should forget the power stations in Norway and instead travel up to his native Scotland to bring the hydroelectric power plants there back on line.

ANALYSIS: The second of Roger Parkes's sequence of three episodes is a substantial improvement on the first. The story's setting is richly atmospheric: events unfold in the rain and mud of a misty forest and the cavernous, candle-lit surroundings of a crumbling church. These desolate and isolated locations help to reinforce the strongly 'medieval' ambience of the drama. Shooting on location in the abandoned village of Imber, in the middle of Salisbury Plain, director Tristan de Vere Cole makes effective use of the desolate surroundings to keep what could be an overly static narrative on the move as far as possible. Here, the sense of isolation evoked by the surroundings helps to increase the introspective tension of the episode, as Charles's group focus in upon themselves and their desire to win over their newest – and irreplaceably valuable – recruit.

Despite the fact that the community have chosen the church as a sanctuary from the cold and rain, there is no spiritual dimension to their decision – it has been occupied as the most practical dwelling to house them all. The fact that the occupants of the building pay little heed to its religious past helps to emphasise the pragmatic and practical preoccupations of those living in its shelter. There are, however, a number of theological references throughout the episode. In the early scenes in the wood, Frank praises Charles for his 'presence, charisma' and his 'natural' abilities to motivate and inspire those he meets. Charles demurs, protesting that he can hardly arrive at settlements as though it is 'Palm Sunday … preaching salvation.' Jenny, rather bitingly, dismisses Charles's efforts at self-deprecation, pointing out: 'I've never seen any halo.' When the travellers arrive at the church, Jenny takes the process still further, singling Charles out to make the confidential comment: 'And Jesus came unto the temple.' It would be easy to exaggerate the parallel that Parkes is attempting to draw here. It is not that Parkes wanted to portray Charles as a nascent 'Christ figure', but rather as an evangelical missionary whose talents and magnetism will become the inspiration for the community to better its lot.

The central themes of "Sparks" are grief, guilt and redemption. Alec has been effectively 'closed down' since The Death, immobilised by his sense of remorse for not being at his wife's side as the plague took her. Rather than flee home, he had struggled in his job as an electrical engineer to keep power supplies going, only setting off for home when it was too late – as the traffic chaos made the journey impossible (although the plot seems slightly confused on whether it was the state of the roads or Alec's concern to look after his mother that caused the fateful delay). The script explains that Alec '… although only 36 has been severely aged by the traumas of The Death plague. He is withdrawn in manner, very scruffy attire, coarse-bearded, often scratches at fleas.' Unable to vocalise or express his feelings of shame and self-loathing, he has become locked in a guilt-ridden stasis – one in which he shuns companionship and intimacy, and settles for a solitary and sour existence. To Charles's disbelief, Alec appears to embrace the new 'dark age', insisting that human kind will be better off without civilisation. It is clear that it will not be easy to win the confidence of 'God's gift to the industrial renaissance.'

"Sparks" makes grief a focal point of the drama for the first time since the series one episode "Gone to the Angels". In that earlier episode, Abby had allowed herself to weep inconsolably in acknowledgement of the pain of losing her son. But for the most part, characters in *Survivors* are stoic and self-contained in their management of grief. Even after the catastrophe of the Grange fire, it is only Jenny who sheds brief tears in "Birth of a Hope" for their collective loss. In "Sparks", Parkes allows a character to confront his long-suppressed pain and heartache directly and at length. It is an interesting dramatic decision, all the more so in allowing a character to have endured this debilitating private burden for so long. Those viewers frustrated by the episode's narrow focus might wish that Alec would just 'snap out of it' and join the rest of the community in making the best of things. But it is true to the nature of the clinical depression from which he is suffering that Alec is unable to 'move on', and with the tolerance of the community he contributes just enough to be accepted.

Although the theme is not properly revisited in the events of "Power", it is interesting to see

197

how closely Alec's initial critique of Charles's reconstruction plans matches the one viewers later hear espoused by Sam Mead. Provoked by Charles, Alec condemns what he sees as a distorted desire to bring back 'pensions, mortgages, taxes, rush hours – the whole crazy contrick all over again.' However, the differences between the two world views are actually quite marked: while Sam blames 'the system' for his personal downfall and insists that the old world must never be revived, Alec views his career commitments as the cause of his failure to prioritise his relationship with his wife and family. It is only when Alec has recovered that he is able to see Charles's ambitions in a new light.

As he seeks to release Alec from his emotional imprisonment, the true extent of Frank's manipulative and mischievous nature is revealed. In "The Peacemaker" he showed himself willing to use Rutna's spiritual magnetism for his own organisational ends. Here, with the complicity of Charles, he is willing to trick Alec into directly confronting the causes of his anguish (with the help of the pethidine that Hubert stole from Miedel in "Manhunt"). This is partly to aid Alec's own redemption, but in the main it is to rehabilitate him as a recruit to 'the cause' that Frank now believes in as wholeheartedly as Charles.

Some very well-handled scenes follow as Alec slips into delirium and begins to confront his demons. William Dysart gives a brave and vulnerable performance as Alec, and with director de Vere Cole shooting his redemptive scenes in intense close-up, these are powerful and emotionally wrenching moments. Fleming, on excellent form as Jenny, is at first appalled by what she sees as Frank's and Charles's callousness, but is then drawn in to guiding Alec through his hallucinations, even acting as a surrogate for his dead wife. The tender exchanges between Jenny and Alec hint at the intimacy that will be revisited – perhaps somewhat inconsistently – in "The Enemy", "Long Live the King" and "Power".

It could be objected that, even allowing for the drama on top of the church tower that follows Frank's drug intervention – during which Alec describes his recurring nightmare in which his wife is killed because of his own obsession with work – he emerges from the cathartic experience too quickly and too completely once Frank applies the final 'shock therapy'. However, this compression of the process must easily qualify as an acceptable use of dramatic licence: viewers do not need to sit through more scenes of Alec being counselled or helped through an extended and overwrought recovery. Interestingly, one outcome of the drugging of Alec is that viewers learn, for the first time, something about Charles's own relationship with his wife and the last words that he spoke to her: 'I think I said I was sorry … [for] surviving, I suppose.' Charles rarely allows himself such backwards glances.

There are some quite interesting guest characters populating the fringe of the drama, although the ruddy-cheeked, buxom Bet, and the guileless, if accommodating, Vic are not amongst the finest or most subtle of *Survivors'* characterisations. Queenie the beekeeper is a more honestly realised figure, and – a comparative rarity for *Survivors* – is notable for being a community leader who is unsure of his abilities, and eager for guidance and encouragement. Letty, the senile anticommunist, is the latest in what is probably an overlong list of *Survivors'* eccentrics, but is played with measured conviction by Gabrielle Hamilton. A character note in the script observes that, prior to The Death, Letty lived in 'a home for aging gentle-folk' but 'is now rallying with vigour if confusion to the challenge of survival.' The fact that Jenny is forced to surrender her waterproof boots to Letty serves to emphasise how basic and 'make-do' the current lifestyle of Queenie's community is.

Once again, the character of Greg haunts the drama unseen. Alec explains contemptuously to Charles and the others that he has heard all their empty words before, when Greg visited the settlement urging him to join in the effort to rebuild the world. More unusually, the episode offers a rare indication of Greg's fallibility – as Charles describes his disastrous and near-fatal efforts to get a Norwegian power plant back on line, an attempt that ends in complete failure. It is not often in series three that viewers hear of any shortcomings in Greg's organisational or technical skills.

In this episode and the next, the question of technology becomes much more prominent. Lill has a fine speech in the abandoned factory (shot on an industrial estate close to Salisbury train station), as he rails against Alec's indifference and apathy, hoping to inspire him to care as much as the technician who died attempting to 'mothball' his machine (although given Alec's guilt over his own misjudgement in staying on at work, Charles's argument may not exert much leverage). It is a nice touch that Charles's efforts to revive the community's water pump come to nought – a neat demonstration that seized-up machinery may yet thwart his ambitions. Charles does, however, get some clear evidence of his skills as an orator and organiser, as the community come to him to ask for his help in kick-starting their efforts to trade and to federate: the missionary has indeed won over new converts.

The 'sparks' motif of the title seems intended to convey a number of different meanings. Most obviously, 'sparks' is a reference to Alec's skills as an electrical engineer (and the reason behind the community's somewhat sarcastic nickname for him), but there are other 'embers' in evidence in the episode's storyline: the pethidine therapy might be seen as the spark that triggers Alec's rebirth; while Alec's recovery could be seen as the catalyst that ignites the quest

Edward Underdown (Frank Garner). © Denis Lill

for electrical power. Potentially, Charles's efforts to connect the settlement in a trading alliance with their Greenham neighbours might be seen as another 'beacon' in his reconstruction plans.

In one respect, the central flaw with "Sparks" is its familiarity – its dramatic format is too much like those of the immediately preceding and following episodes. In addition, Parkes does not find space for any interesting subplots that might complement or contrast with the main storyline. Yet the weaknesses of "Sparks" are products not simply of structure, but also of execution. In terms of mood and emotion, there are things to recommend here – but this is also an episode devoid of action, and held together by lengthy exchanges of sometimes-stilted dialogue about the most sombre of personal themes. This raises the immediate question whether or not one man's battle against deeply-entrenched depression is sufficient to sustain fifty minutes of drama. It also highlights the wider issue of *Survivors'* narrative journey across series three. There is a clear mismatch between, on the one hand, the quest for social and economic reconstruction – the theme that has come to dominate the latter part of the third series – and, on the other, an individual's private battle against psychosis. With only a handful of episodes now left in which to explore the survivors' efforts to forge a new civilisation, it feels perverse to spend so much screen time recruiting a single convert to the cause – however skilled an electrical engineer he may prove to be. Perhaps Greg Preston, who would never have been so indulgent or sympathetic a counsellor, was right in deciding to leave Alec to wallow in his own misery. *RC*

3.9 THE ENEMY

UK TRANSMISSION: 11 May 1977: 8.10pm – 9.00pm
VIEWING FIGURE: 6.31m
WRITER: Roger Parkes
DIRECTOR: Peter Jefferies
REGULAR CAST: Denis Lill (Charles Vaughan); Lucy Fleming (Jenny Richards); John Abineri (Hubert Goss); Edward Underdown (Frank Garner); William Dysart (Alec Campbell); Robert Gillespie (Sam Mead)
GUEST CAST: Bryan Pringle (Leonard Woollen); Frances Tomelty (Mary-Jean Mead); Peggy Ann Wood (Mrs Jay); Terence Davies (Harper); Martin Whitby (Grant)
OB RECORDING: 24 - 30 April 1977
LOCATIONS: Penoyre House, Cradoc, Nr. Brecon, Powys; Coal mine, Nr. Pontypool, Torfaen

SYNOPSIS: Now accompanied by a recovered Alec, Charles, Jenny, Hubert and Frank decide to spend the night at a stately home situated close to a coal mine. The home – which has been renamed the 'Toll Bar' by its inhabitants – is run like a working men's club by a man called Len Woollen. Life there revolves around a lively bar, and the travellers are soon drawn into an evening of drinking, during which they are introduced to a former drug addict called Sam who believes that The Death saved him. Charles is concerned about Frank's health and is keen to find a valid excuse for them to stay on while he recovers. Len suggests that Alec could get the mine generator going, but Charles thinks that Alec may not want to help. Frank advises Charles to enlist Jenny's help in persuading the engineer, believing the pair to have formed an attachment; however, Jenny is offended by Charles's suggestions regarding Alec, especially as she is feeling anxious about Greg's relationship with Agnes. Charles tells Alec that Jenny recently passed up an opportunity for a reunion with Greg and has half-accepted that there is something wrong with their relationship. When Alec speaks to Jenny about this, she realises that Charles has been talking to him and, enraged, goes to confront him. Alec overhears their heated exchange and starts work on the generator the next morning. Frank is fading fast, and Charles orders Hubert to fetch Janet from Sloton Spencer to treat him. Frank is harassed in secret by Sam about Charles's restoration plans for the nation's industry, and learns that the former junkie has deliberately sabotaged the generator. A little later, Frank passes away. Alec manages to restart the generator and Charles asks Sam to join them. As the pit becomes operational again, Hubert returns with news of a possible rendezvous with Greg.

ANALYSIS: "The Enemy" (which had the working title "Power Urge") is the third and final part of Roger Parkes's series three trilogy, and is perhaps the most convoluted and difficult-to-follow episode in the entire series. As with "The Peacemaker", it suffers from uncharacteristic outbursts from the regulars and stodgy, dialogue-heavy scenes. However, it does also seek to develop an interesting counter-argument to the new industrial revolution, in the form of the unstable Sam Mead.

On paper, the idea of an episode depicting a working-class community that is totally self-regulating and has tried to hang on to what it knows best by setting up a working men's club is certainly new and legitimate. Although the idea is a little unusual, it did have the potential to address the accusation of class bias in the series. However, heavy-handed and crass execution thwarts any such laudable intentions. The Toll Bar (originally scripted as 'The Jug and Bottle') is populated by a group of former miners who are heavy-drinking, dart-playing, working-class stereotypes, whose presence only serves to reinforce criticism of the series' middle-class pretensions; one man even says, 'I'll go to the foot of our stairs.' Just in case the viewer hasn't got the message clearly enough, director Peter Jefferies hammers it home by shooting the travellers' arrival at the Toll Bar through a crate of racing pigeons. The only missing cliché is a whippet!

The Death appears to have left the North-South divide intact, as there is much talk of untrustworthy Southerners. Undisguised prejudice and discrimination abound, and see Alec nicknamed 'MacSporran' and a member of 'the Tartan Army' (and, in the original script, 'Rob Roy on the way to his braeside Mecca'!), while Charles is termed a typical foreigner just because he is Welsh. Later in the episode, Jenny actually calls him a 'Welsh bastard'; although quite amusing, this does seem out of character and was a line much debated during production. Charles's response that she should be sharing Alec's bed is equally uncharacteristic. Although it can be argued that such anomalous behaviour is explainable – and excusable – in the context of Charles's and Jenny's consumption of alcohol, ultimately neither outburst quite rings true.

Given the unusually large number of people at the Toll Bar, Charles cannot resist politicising with his well-developed missionary zeal; Len, a working-class miner writ large, rightly calls him out as a 'tubthumper'. Although Charles can always be relied upon to evangelise wherever he goes, his fellow survivors' lack of interest in his arguments now appears to have become deeply frustrating for him – a feeling perhaps exacerbated by the news of Greg's relative success elsewhere: 'It's been three years now, surely that's time enough to start thinking about social organisation, mutual defence, co-operation?' Fortunately, Charles has little time to brood on these issues as the opportunity arises to get the nearby mine up and running again, providing a timely excuse for them to stay on and so give the ailing Frank a rest. Alec's assistance is presented as vital to this operation, and it is at this point that the episode falls down. Instead of asking Alec directly for his help with the mine, Charles engages in various peculiar exchanges with Frank, Alec and Jenny – all quite unfathomable, given that the Scotsman now appears to be fully cured of the depression that afflicted him in "Sparks". The complicated thread that binds these seemingly pointless conversations together is perilously easy to lose, but they do allow for some interesting character development, including: the level to which Charles will apparently stoop in order to get his way; Jenny's growing concern over the relationship between Agnes and Greg; and Alec's feelings for Jenny.

The connection forged between Jenny and Alec in the previous episode through his dead wife Rita is an interesting one that deserves the further attention it receives here. Although Frank interprets what Charles sees as their 'cat and dog stuff' as 'cock and hen stuff,' Jenny's deep-seated fears about Agnes's influence and 'her pathetic Vikings' (yet another out-of-character prejudicial interpolation) suggest that she is not only jealous of the Norwegian woman, but wholly unprepared to give up on Greg just yet. That said, Jenny is certainly affectionate towards the Scot who, in turn, is very interested in a possible relationship with her.

Hubert appears to be in his element at the Toll Bar and also receives some interesting character development, telling Sam that both The Death and 'Squire Vaughan' have been responsible for his deliverance. Later in the episode, he is dispatched in customarily rude fashion by Charles to fetch Janet Millon back from Sloton Spencer.

Bryan Pringle (Leonard Woollen). © Denis Lill

Of the guest characters, former junkie Sam Mead is played with fanatical energy by Robert Gillespie in his second *Survivors* role; he had previously appeared as John Milner in "Gone Away". Sam is portrayed as a confirmed Luddite obsessed with the idea of letting the next generation, or 'pioneers' as he calls them, become 'hard, independent, self-disciplined [and] resourceful'; he doesn't want them to make the same mistakes as he thinks were made prior to The Death. His passion arises from an interesting assessment of his own treatment when he was suffering from drug addiction; he believes that the proffered handouts and other 'soft options' were responsible for his continued inability to recover and look after himself. However,

Frank interprets Sam's strongly held beliefs to symbolically represent his subconscious intent to wipe out his own past, rather than a simple interest in destroying Britain's remaining industrial machinery. Whatever the truth of the matter, Sam is shown to be a dangerous opponent whose manic harassment of Frank accelerates the former head-hunter's death.

Sam's partner Mary-Jean, who appears to share his ideals just as fervently, is played by young actress Frances Tomelty. At the time, she was married to singer Sting, and it is their child Joe Sumner who appears here. Sting recalls in his 2003 autobiography *Broken Music* that the role put some much-needed money into their 'dwindling bank account'.

The episode appears to be one of the most under-rehearsed of the entire series. Several obvious line-fluffs make it through to the final edit, with the strange bar billiard table sequence featuring Lill and Fleming being the worst offender. Their inability to play bar billiards aside, the usually word perfect Fleming has a particularly difficult time with the script, to the extent that it feels like the scene has been improvised or even adlibbed at the last minute.

An interesting omission from the episode is the discovery that the coal mine has been overrun by rats. In Parkes's original script, when the mine shaft cage is brought up it is found to contain 'two dozen rats'. The idea may have been abandoned due to memories of the immense difficulty of working with rats in the open at Hanwell Station during filming of "Lights of London".

The best scene in "The Enemy" is undoubtedly the brief exchange between Charles and Len that directly relates to the title of the episode. According to Len – who thankfully is eventually afforded brains as well as his thick Yorkshire brogue – the real enemy is boredom. He is referring to a state that he thinks will occur once the immediate threats of the post-Death world are overcome: 'It's all right when the dangers are for real – dog packs, scavengers, hunger – but what happens when they're gone?' Len's rather profound consideration of this dilemma inevitably leads to a broader question about the future of *Survivors* itself, as this very same problem was shared by the series' production team, who must have realised by this point that the series would shortly have nowhere left to go.

Although "The Enemy" contains some interesting elements, such as the aforesaid insight into the nature of the *true* enemy, it largely remains unsatisfying due to its uneven plotting, cod regionalism and odd characterisation. It is something of a relief to come out at the other end of Parkes's trilogy, as *Survivors* gears up to a conclusion with scripts from Ian McCulloch and Martin Worth that see the series on far more convincing ground. *AP*

3.10 THE LAST LAUGH

UK TRANSMISSION: 18 May 1977: 8.10pm – 9.00pm
VIEWING FIGURE: 6.31m
WRITER: Ian McCulloch
DIRECTOR: Peter Jefferies
REGULAR CAST: Ian McCulloch (Greg Preston); Anna Pitt (Agnes Carlsson); Lorna Lewis (Pet Simpson); Gordon Salkilld (Jack Wood); Angie Stevens (Lizzie Willoughby); Stephen Dudley (John Millon)
GUEST CAST: Clifton Jones (Dr Adams); George Mallaby (Mason); Roy Boyd (Tilley); Jon Glover (Dave); Richard Cornish (Chris); Paul Humpoletz (Powell); David Cook (Irvine)
OB RECORDING: 23 - 28 March 1977

LOCATION: Brecon area, Powys

SYNOPSIS: Making his way to a rendezvous with Agnes, Greg is distracted by the sight of smoke in nearby woodland. He discovers the apparently affable and good-natured Mason, the head of a small band of nomadic tradesmen. Greg describes his reconstruction plans, and Mason seems interested in learning more. But when Greg goes to fetch his notes, he is set upon and stabbed, and his apparently lifeless body dumped in the river. A disappointed Agnes returns to Sloton Spencer alone. This band of brigands wants to select the most promising settlements to raid next, but they soon discover that Greg's notes are in Norwegian. They set off towards Sloton to compel Agnes to translate. When one of the gang returns to Greg's body, he discovers, to his cost, that Greg is still alive. With his last reserve of energy, Greg mounts the dead man's horse and sets off towards the community run by Dr Adams – the apparently thriving settlement that had been his next destination. He awakes to find himself a prisoner as well as a patient at Adams' settlement. Breaking free, he discovers that the community has been decimated by a disease resembling smallpox, and that Adams himself is a victim. Greg is forced to accept that he has contracted the illness, and he decides on a final act of revenge – on Mason and his leader, the Captain – before his now-inevitable death. Returning to Sloton, Greg evades an ambush set by Mason's men. Keeping Agnes, Pet, Jack and the children at a safe distance, Greg pretends to have lost all concern for their well-being, and to consider his own plans worthless. He asks to join Mason's gang and, as he leaves, offers Agnes a 'special Norwegian goodbye'. Agnes quietly reveals the truth of Greg's message. Arriving back at the 'smallpox'-infested farm, Greg is afflicted by a nosebleed – a clear sign that his own time is running out. Calmly he leads the gang on into the farm, and towards their deaths.

ANALYSIS: "The Last Laugh" is arguably the finest of Ian McCulloch's three *Survivors* scripts. It contains the signature elements of McCulloch's scriptwriting style – high adventure and peril, lots of plot shifts and twists, mixed in with some interesting observations about the nature of life in the post-Death world. Here though there is the added *frisson* of Greg's own demise – and this brings a darkness and sense of foreboding to events that have not been encountered before. Throughout, Greg appears as a haggard and exhausted figure, but never less than fully committed to seeing through his increasingly desperate plans. The result is a storyline that is both compelling and frequently surprising. There are also some excellent guest characters, and convincing dialogue, which reinforce the tightly plotted narrative.

The opening sequences involving the apparently hospitable Mason are well-realised and effectively played. Mason feigns interest in Greg's plans to revive trade and federation, and reveals that he and his men have heard of the 'Quetzalcoatl' figure (an Aztec god, who returned from the sky to usher in a new 'golden era' in the world) roaming the countryside with tales of his exploits in Norway. When Greg is – quite literally – stabbed in the back by the gang, the moment is both horrible and unexpected: the ever-wily Greg is finally and fatefully tricked when he lets down his guard and relaxes for just a second. As Mason mocks: 'You were careful, but you weren't careful enough.' Given all that the viewer has experienced, it is easy to believe that this is the end of Greg, as his body is plunged, lifeless, into the water – and McCulloch is prepared to get dirty and soaked (and probably bruised and battered) to invest the scene with some welcome realism. The later sequences in which he beats unconscious and drowns his assailant are appropriately unpleasant. After the first ten minutes of screen time, there is no doubt whatever that this is to be an unwaveringly bleak storyline. When it becomes clear that they have already lost two of their number to internal feuding, and that they are in fact just the raiding party for the mysterious and avaricious Captain, Mason's gang are revealed as both ruthless and unpredictable.

The 'mystery' of Cawston Farm is also well-handled – with Greg as both captive and invalid, babbling his secrets incoherently in his feverish sleep, and raging against the insistence of his jailers that the settlement is empty and derelict. McCulloch recalls that he drew inspiration for this element of the story from the 1950 Dirk Bogarde film *So Long at the Fair*: set against the background of the 1889 Paris Exhibition, a young man who contracts the plague is hidden away from his family, and those keeping him in quarantine deny all knowledge of his whereabouts. Adams's 'smallpox' make-up might be basic – but the revelation about the doctor's condition is shocking (and how appropriate that Greg's own bullish determination and misplaced bravery seals his own fate). In McCulloch's initial script, Greg – still convinced that Adams is a prisoner – grabs hold of him, with Adams revealing his illness only after screaming and wriggling free of Greg's grasp. In many ways, this would have made for a more shocking and effective revelation than is apparent in the episode – in which the two men never make physical contact. Perhaps director Peter Jefferies judged that keeping the characters at a distance made it more possible that Greg might have escaped infection. When, the following morning, Greg vomits over his horse as he prepares to depart, his lifeline is unexpectedly withdrawn. Although this signals the impending death of a single character, the sequence is in many respects as stomach-turning as any of the events glimpsed or described in "The Fourth Horseman". Clifton Jones's portrayal of Dr Stephen Adams is superb. He invests McCulloch's electrifying dialogue with real emotional conviction – from his anguished warning that he has smallpox, through his insistence on a rejection of self-pity, to his pained acceptance of Greg's plan to exact vengeance on Mason and his men. Some excellent exchanges follow – as Greg is overcome by remorse, regret and self-doubt over his relationship with Jenny, and all the things left undone and unsaid. This all dovetails extremely well with Jenny's own anguish over the pain of separation, although Greg certainly overplays how rotten he has been. The fact that Greg cannot recall 'one moment of gentle tenderness' with his wife says more about the depths of his despair than it does about the history of their relationship – the on-screen record tells a very different story. As this scene unfolds, viewers still cannot quite believe that Greg will die, or that Jenny and he will be denied their own reunion. When he learns of the outbreak that has wiped out all but two of the settlement, Greg agonises about the grim realities of the 'brave new world' he has been working to engineer. How cruelly ironic it is that Cawston Farm should have been wiped out precisely because of their commitment to the Norwegian plan: it is their willingness to exchange goods and people with other communities that has made them so vulnerable to a disease spread by 'breath, touch, [and] clothing.' Here, trade and federation has delivered not a better life, only more death. The deal that he finally strikes with the Cawston survivors – to lure the Captain's men to their deaths – is impossibly grim, despite its practicality.

When Mason's gang arrive at Sloton, Jack, Pet, John and Lizzie are afforded some rare and welcome screen time, as the threatening undercurrents beneath Mason's requests break through the polite veneer. Sloton was originally conceived as a much busier and more bustling settlement than the one apparent on screen. As Mason arrives, viewers were to see groups of residents 'going about their everyday business.' When Mason quizzes John on the numbers living at the settlement, he was to reply: '22 – 23 with my mother, but she's not here today. She's vetting somebody.' Agnes has the good sense to hide herself away, until she is finally flushed out and Mason discards his thin deception in favour of naked threats. The exchanges around the kitchen table become explosively aggressive.

The final sequences here, in which Greg renounces his family and injures Jack, are powerfully played and distressing to watch. Apart from the events of "Manhunt", "The Last Laugh" comprises Jack's only really significant contribution to the events of the series (although in the camera script it was not Jack who was to take the bullet, but another unconfirmed victim!) Greg condemns his eldest son John as 'a stupid, useless kid … I haven't got the time to waste on him.' As far as his friends from Whitecross are concerned, they 'can all rot in hell.' Appalled by what she is hearing, Pet is unable to spot the hidden message of self-sacrifice in Greg's message to Jenny: 'You can tell her that I love her, and say that I'm following in the footsteps of Paul.'

It does seem a shame that the settlement's hosts, Janet and Philip (introduced in "Reunion"), are not present to hear Greg's outburst. How horrified would Janet have been at Greg's description of his relationship with her son, especially as she would be so eager to thank him for all that he has done to look after John? It is also striking that none of the other Whitecross residents who were described as having moved to Sloton Spencer in "The Peacemaker" are depicted here.

Apart from the physical absence of characters, the other frustrating omission is that none of the characters – John, Lizzie, Pet or Jack – are given screen time in which to react or come to terms with the shocking truth that Greg reveals in his 'special Norwegian farewell' to Agnes. Although John is allowed a bewildered reaction shot as Greg departs, none of these characters – who have all played a significant role in *Survivors* – is afforded a proper exit from the series. They simply walk out of frame never to be seen again.

However, the most significant absentee is Jenny herself. It is not entirely clear if the decision to deny them a reunion was one taken by Dudley or by McCulloch himself. Greg's denunciations of his past connections with friends and family would have had an almost unbearable dramatic power had Jenny been present on the steps of the settlement, but her absence invests Greg's demise with an agonisingly strong sense of pathos, regret and loss. If Abby's imminent reunion with her son Peter provides an unexpected and welcome conclusion to the events of "A Beginning" in series one, the *lack* of a similar resolution for Greg and Jenny is – for the opposite reason – just as surprising. Their unresolved separation sets up some tense interactions between Jenny and Agnes in "Long Live the King", in which Agnes's shifting tales of Greg's fate are listened to with great scepticism by Jenny.

It is however a testament to the maturity of the drama that Mason is *not* convinced by Greg's recantation of his past, but is willing to go along with it to discover what Greg is really plotting. There follows a brilliantly underplayed finale, with McCulloch giving a fine performance as he delivers his last line – much more effective than some extended deathbed scene. The cold revenge served up in the episode's final scene is a one of the series' most jaw-dropping denouements. Greg's demise is brilliantly, if harshly, conceived – he dies separated from Jenny and their young son, having terrified his two older children, with the Norwegian plan short of fruition, and with no chance to make amends (and unaware of the mythical status he is soon to be afforded courtesy of Agnes).

McCulloch provides an exemplary send-off for his own character, and with it one of the strongest closing sequences in the entire series. Surprisingly, this was not the final scene in McCulloch's submitted script. As originally conceived, the episode was to end on the earlier image of the bereft and saddened face of John as he watches Greg depart, before turning back to the main house.

Despite the fact that he is not seen to perish on screen, McCulloch insists that there is no question whatsoever that Greg subsequently succumbs to the 'smallpox' infection. Greg, whose memorable return home by helicopter opened the series' second episode "Genesis", here dies an unseen hero's death – trying to find absolution for his neglect of his family, and exacting a terrible revenge on those who tried to kill him. Almost unheard as the closing theme soars is Mason's final observation to Greg (who is smiling wryly) that a nosebleed is 'nothing to laugh about.' As he enters the farm, taking those murderers and villains to their death, that last – very bitter – laugh belongs to Greg. *RC*

3.11 LONG LIVE THE KING

UK TRANSMISSION: 1 June 1977: 8.10pm – 9.00pm
VIEWING FIGURE: 5.71m
WRITER: Martin Worth
DIRECTOR: Tristan de Vere Cole
REGULAR CAST: Denis Lill (Charles Vaughan); Lucy Fleming (Jenny Richards); John Abineri (Hubert Goss); Anna Pitt (Agnes Carlsson); William Dysart (Alec Campbell); Robert Gillespie (Sam Mead)
GUEST CAST: Roy Marsden (The Captain); Frank Vincent (Mitch); Gabrielle Daye (Mrs Hicks); John Comer (Les Norton); Barry Stokes (Tom Walter); Sean Matthias (Mike); Ray Mort (Joe Briggs); Denis Holmes (Albert Banks)
UNCREDITED CAST: Constance Reason (Alice Briggs)
OB RECORDING: 6 - 11 May 1977
LOCATION: Piddlehinton Army Camp, Piddlehinton, Dorset

SYNOPSIS: While *en route* to Scotland, Charles, Jenny and Hubert discover messages from Greg asking Charles to come to a place called Felbridge Camp where he is needed urgently. Jenny is not convinced that Greg is there, so Charles sets off alone. A man calling himself 'the Captain', who is the only survivor of Greg's trap at Cawston Farm, is also on his way to the camp, accompanied by his new associate, Mitch. Jenny meets Les – the man who left Greg's message – and travels with him to a brick-making centre where she is reunited with Tom Walter. Les seeks to trade with Tom using a 'petrol note' that bears Greg's name. Charles arrives at Felbridge, where Agnes is waiting for him. She tells him that Greg has smallpox and is still at Cawston, and explains that Greg has asked her to continue his work. She talks about forming a government and tells Charles about Greg's achievements. Jenny and Hubert decide to join Charles, while Alec and Sam continue north. Les arrives at Felbridge to claim his petrol. Agnes reveals to Charles that they do not actually have the million gallons of petrol on which the notes are based and that they are using Greg's name as a symbol of trust and central authority. Jenny arrives and is livid that Greg is not there after all. Charles explains to her that Greg has smallpox, and he and

Jenny decide to go to Cawston. Agnes – who now openly claims to love Greg – prevents them from leaving and reveals that she has summoned everyone there to form a council to enforce peace and order. The Captain, who has gained entry to the camp, attempts to access the armoury, but is overpowered by Hubert. Agnes finally admits that Greg is dead and that she lied so that the council could be established before this news leaked out. Agnes believes that Greg would have achieved much more if it had not been for his love for Jenny.

ANALYSIS: The valiant efforts of Martin Worth's "Long Live the King" to bring many disparate and long-running storylines to conclusion make this penultimate episode of *Survivors* feel like its last. The episode bravely attempts to dramatise the fruits of Greg's and Agnes's largely off-screen labours through the depiction of the birth of a nation, which is shown to consist of: a safe transport system; a phone network; a currency; and – if Agnes gets her way – a government and king.

The third series in particular would have benefited hugely from a more worked and controlled story arc. This in turn would have abrogated the need for scriptwriters to have to both introduce and play out major plot developments within the space of a single episode. This is nowhere more true than in "Long Live the King" and specifically in the characterisation, actions and motivations of Agnes. The Norwegian, who has undergone a significant transformation since her appearance in the previous episode, is suddenly the central protagonist here. Decked out in what can only be described as 'combat chic' she strides about Felbridge Camp barking orders, propagating lies and manipulating events. As her true aims remain hidden for the majority of the episode – and as she has never come across as the most sympathetic of characters – her motives immediately appear to be self-serving. It is a clever but perhaps too well-disguised irony that her actions are ultimately revealed to be in the interests of all the survivors of The Death. However, her new 'persona' is problematic, because – as Anna Pitt has said – 'In this episode she becomes a different person, without there ever having been any natural progression'. This is also the trouble with Agnes's admission that she has always loved Greg. Although this love is used to explain her lofty ambitions after his death ('I didn't want him to die for nothing'), her feelings should have been revealed earlier in the series in order to lend some much-needed coherence to the continuing narrative, by providing a plausible explanation for the failure of Jenny's repeated attempts to be reunited with Greg ('He'd have come back to you sooner, if I'd let him').

The scale of what Greg has achieved and what Agnes is now trying to achieve in his name also feels like too much too late. Although we have witnessed a few examples of Greg's recent achievements – such as a working steam train ("Mad Dog") and a methane-powered car ("Bridgehead") – the sudden news that he has also been behind the location of twenty-eight different communities (numbering some eight thousand people), the opening of three railway lines and the regular sailing of barges down the east coast, does seem somewhat unlikely. However, even more far-fetched is the advanced set-up at Felbridge with a view to government, especially as this development is supposed to have taken place since the previous episode. The exposition that describes Greg's achievements and Agnes's demonstration of her own endeavours also have the unfortunate effect of making the concurrent activities of Charles and Jenny seem rather dull in comparison, inevitably begging the question: why have we been following their uninspiring exploits (particularly during the Roger Parkes trilogy of episodes) rather than these more successful attempts to make the country into a nation again?

Far too much attention has already been paid to McCulloch's obvious absence from the series through the 'search for Greg' narrative, so it is unfortunate that it is made to seem like even more of a loss, by alluding to events involving his character that sound far more interesting than those we have actually been watching!

Despite these failings, there is much to be enjoyed in "Long Live the King" and, in line with its predecessor, the episode feels like an upturn in the series' fortunes. One of the definite plus points is Lucy Fleming's strong performance as Jenny, a character who engenders much sympathy here as she displays a range of emotions, including: frustration ('By the time we get there, he'll be somewhere else; he always is!'); anger that, as she initially suspected, Greg isn't at Felbridge after all; defiance in response to Agnes's high-handed orders; and grief as she learns that Greg is in fact dead. The

Denis Lill (Charles Vaughan). © Denis Lill

episode provides a bittersweet conclusion to Jenny's long-held doubts about Greg's love for her. Although she has to endure Agnes's harsh tongue, her love rival does provide her with the comforting fact that what Jenny wanted of Greg ('To hold your hand, tell bedtime stories to the children, dangle the baby on his knee') did actually mean more to him than his work towards federation and the birth of the nation. This is a sensitive touch that feels like a fitting end to this particular plotline. It also precipitates the resolution of the feud between Jenny and Agnes; as they discuss Greg at the episode's close, the anger between them is replaced with a new-found honesty.

Charles adopts a defeated look for much of the proceedings as he is forced to accept that Greg has achieved a great deal, effectively eclipsing his similar ambitions. Despite the obvious knock to his pride caused by what he learns at Felbridge, it does seem a little out of character that he does not defend himself when Agnes goads him by describing his own venture to restore power to the whole country merely as 'pushing off to Scotland.' However, Alec's point to Jenny about how they have been working on the national power line, rather than on individual generators like Greg, does redress the balance somewhat. Unlike the ill-fated Greg, Charles does of course receive the pay-off for his recent endeavours through an assured place in the new government at Felbridge.

In the case of both the Captain and Agnes, the matter of smallpox (or whatever the infection actually is – Adams previously stated that it was not smallpox) is handled a little too casually and without enough import to be convincing. A note in Worth's original script states that the Captain has 'a pockmarked face' and that he is recovering from infection, but on screen Roy Marsden has been made up to have sores that seem to indicate that the Captain still has the disease and may still be infectious. When it comes to Agnes, Worth struggles to justify her convenient immunity to the smallpox by deciding to have her come out with a startlingly flip piece of dialogue – delivered too cheerfully by Anna Pitt – about how the brucellosis infection she picked up (in Worth's own "Bridgehead") may have protected her while she nursed Greg; while her brave (or stupid) decision to walk into certain death by following Greg into Cawston Farm in the first place is glossed over altogether. Love conquers all?

The idea of presenting Greg as the nation's new figurehead and king is an interesting development. However, questions of the late engineer's suitability for the role aside, the industrious branding of the GP logo through hand-painted signs, sewn badges and the Union Jack GP flag does initially seem a little silly, even if the serious objectives behind their propagation and invention do not. Nevertheless, the GP flag eventually emerges as a powerful *Survivors* image – aided by its prominence in the closing titles – serving both as an epitaph for Greg's achievements and as a hopeful icon of a new age. The introduction of the GP petrol notes does feel like a natural consequence of the increasingly joined-up nation that is described here. That the inevitable return of money and the value of petrol as 'the new gold' are ideas that have peppered the entire series also makes the new currency seem entirely appropriate and believable. What is perhaps most surprising about the scripting of Greg's new role as a trusted figurehead and king and the dependent formation of a new parliamentary democracy, is that Worth does not indulge in any political allegories or references to historical antecedents in British history, especially as such an approach could have successfully underscored the magnitude of exactly what is being attempted at Felbridge.

The recurrent *Survivors* theme of law and order is explored for the last time in "Long Live the King"; however, the difference here is that a consensus on the subject is finally reached. The events of this and previous episodes – Brod and Mason are both cited by Agnes – add up to a compelling argument that 'enforced peace' is the only way forward. The Captain (convincingly played by Roy Marsden) is used to fulfil an important narrative function as an antithetical predator, representing exactly the sort of threat the survivors face if they don't ensure 'the safety of the state.' His callous and gruesome murder of Mrs Hicks and Joe's wife is concrete and timely proof that 'the strongest take over the weakest' and that Charles's vision of 'a loose federation of communities peacefully trading with each other' can only ever be an idealistic dream. The airing of Agnes's view that, with Charles's approach, 'any unscrupulous gangster can prey on anyone he likes' is deliberately followed by a scene in which the Captain eulogises about protection rackets, fitting Agnes's description perfectly and thus further emphasising her point. Although Agnes's execution of the ideals of law and order may differ from those of Arthur Wormley way back in "Genesis" – she elects not to kill the Captain straight away, but to try him in front of the new council – the point is soundly made that without their enforcement the survivors will, as Wormley said, 'never get anywhere.'

For its fifty minute length, "Long Live the King" covers an incredible amount of ground in plot terms, and thankfully brings some crucial cohesion to a third series which, for the most part, has felt disjointed and confusing. The arrival of the councillors of the new government and the flying of the GP flag overhead – Greg's position as figurehead being assured – signals the end of the road for *Survivors* as the series advances towards a natural conclusion. All that remains is for Charles to 'push off to Scotland' to switch the power on … *AP*

3.12 POWER

UK TRANSMISSION: 8 June 1977: 8.10pm – 9.00pm
VIEWING FIGURE: 7.52m
WRITER: Martin Worth
DIRECTOR: George Spenton-Foster
REGULAR CAST: Denis Lill (Charles Vaughan); Lucy Fleming (Jenny Richards); John Abineri (Hubert Goss); William Dysart (Alec Campbell); Robert Gillespie (Sam Mead)
GUEST CAST: Iain Cuthbertson (McAlister); William Armour (Davey); Brian Carey (Hamish); Dorothy Dean (Mrs Crombie); Ray Jeffries (Rob)
OB RECORDING: 17 - 22 May 1977
LOCATIONS: Taymouth Castle and grounds, Kenmore, Perth and Kinross; Lochay Hydroelectric Power Station, Glen Lochay, Nr. Killin, Stirling; Switching Station, Killin, Stirling; Stronuich Reservoir, Nr. Killin, Stirling

SYNOPSIS: Alec and Sam are nearing the end of their journey northwards towards the hydroelectric power plants of Scotland. At the last of the switching stations, Sam pretends to turn off the connection, but instead switches it on – knowing that this will thwart Alec's plan to bring the supply back on line. The train carrying Jenny and Charles has broken down, and in search of a replacement part they meet the local Scottish Laird, who agrees to help, and who is intrigued by their plans. Arriving at the first station, Alec begins the complex process of restarting the machinery. Sam finally reveals his true intentions, and when Alec refuses to stop work, he knocks him unconscious and drags his body beneath a grating, before fleeing. Alec comes round to hear Charles and the Laird arguing over the ownership of the electricity, and decides to keep the truth from them all. However, the Laird reveals that one of his men saw the assault, and he despatches word to guard all the nearby power stations from sabotage by Sam. Alec is persuaded to try to start up the station, but discovers that the supply keeps 'tripping out' because of an overload. He realises that Sam deceived him at the last substation. Meanwhile, Sam sets a trap, hoping to lure Alec to his death in the inlet pipe running from the reservoir. He fails, but escapes once more. Alec returns to the last substation to reset the vital switch. Jenny declines Alec's offer that she and the children settle with him for a simple life in the Highlands, and tells him that he must switch on the power. As the station becomes active once more, Sam attempts a futile final act of sabotage, but as he runs away he collides with Hubert, plunges into the raging waters below and drowns. As Charles and the Laird reconcile their differences, Alec insists that he alone will be responsible for the upkeep of the station and the training of new technicians. Jenny, Charles and Hubert set off for England – towards the brighter future that now awaits them.

ANALYSIS: The series finale – and the final episode of *Survivors* – is a solid 'procedural' drama from scriptwriter Martin Worth, who had done extensive on-site research to make the process of reviving the first hydroelectric power plant appear credible. "Power" offers a satisfying sense of closure to the quest to 'bring the lights back on'. It is however far less effective in drawing together the other strands of the series' story arc, and in particular in giving Jenny, Hubert and above all Charles the dramatic payoffs that – after their exhaustive

211

travels – they so evidently deserve.

The Scottish counties of Stirling and Perth and Kinross were the furthest that the production had decamped from its London base, and the settings for the episode are uniformly superb, showcasing what Denis Lill acknowledges were some 'stunning locations' to great effect for one last time – the Laird's impressive castle and estate, the flowing rivers and deep reservoirs that surround the hydroelectric plant, and the 'mothballed' interiors of the power station all help to reinforce the sense of realism of the on-screen drama. The story begins with some footage of a steam railway engine in motion, shot during the recording of "Bridgehead", but reserved for use in this final episode.

Social organisation in rural Scotland does not seem to have been overturned in quite the same way as elsewhere in the aftermath of The Death. In "Genesis", Arthur Wormley claimed legal authority for the regime he sought to establish in the immediate aftermath of the plague. In "Garland's War", Jimmy Garland fought a one-man guerrilla campaign to win back control of the family estate from the usurper Knox. Yet at the Laird's castle, the old paternal structures seem to persist, and apparently without a fight. The reach of the Laird's organisation is impressive, and when he commands something, it is done. Hubert, as ever, is despatched to the stables and then below stairs, while Jenny and Charles absorb the hospitality of their host, and enjoy all the luxuries on offer. The resilience of those traditional class distinctions has unexpected repercussions for Hubert, who seems to lose his place as an equal member of the company: throughout the episode, he is ordered about and sent hither and thither at the whim of either Charles or the Laird. Despite the loyalty and bravery he demonstrates in trying to thwart Sam's attempts at sabotage, "Power" sees the faltering evolution in Hubert's character again thrown largely into reverse at the hands of another scriptwriter. Several short scenes that focused on Hubert's relationship with the quietly reserved Hamish – which would have afforded Hubert a modest subplot of his own – were excised from the original script before recording.

Lill was frustrated that Worth's script seemed to ignore Charles's Welsh origins. He remembers that he and Lucy Fleming 'fetched upon Iain Cuthbertson, who played the Laird of the manor absolutely beautifully, and I was holding up this piece of metal and saying [*in a fine Welsh accent*]: "We've broken down. Do you have anything that looks like this!" To which Iain Cuthbertson's response was: "I wondered how long it would take the English to come up here." [*Laughs*]. There I was, having for the previous twenty-whatever-it-was episodes knocked myself out being Welsh!' He does, however, acknowledge that the Laird's ignorance or indifference may have been intended as a way to highlight his lack of interest in the distinctions between the various 'people of the south.' 'I'm sure there was a certain amount of "Celtic irony" involved – absolutely!' Worth does imply that the Laird's view of the world is marked by both arrogance and self-importance. This is, it becomes clear, a character who has already broken into the power plant, flicked a few switches and then left the vital batteries to run flat, with hardly a thought as to the consequences of his reckless and ill-informed behaviour. That sense of pomposity is in many ways reinforced by the rather traditional (or hackneyed, depending on your view) sense of Scottish culture that Worth evokes: this is a Scotland defined by whisky, haggis, tartan and tweed, oatcakes, distilleries, and salmon fishing – where the taciturn gamekeeper waits by the loch side for the Laird's instruction. It is also an entirely rural Scotland: the fate of the conurbations of Glasgow, Edinburgh or Dundee is never once mentioned in the Laird's account of the country's resilience.

As Sam and Alec explore the abandoned plant, Sam's subterfuge is abandoned and he confronts Alec with the enormity of their responsibility. Sam is convinced that the revival of electric power will mark the return of industrial tyranny, and the enslavement once again of those that The Death has 'freed' from exploitation. When Alec dismisses these concerns, Sam attacks him, knocking him unconscious and dragging him beneath a grating. Fired up by his own missionary zeal (which has goals diametrically opposed to Charles's own), Sam prepares to wreck the facility. Lill has also expressed his disappointment that, for reasons of dramatic excitement: 'We had to have the saboteur, and we had to have that saboteur dying, which I felt rather spoilt things. I would far rather we had concentrated on the technology side of things, to see if it was possible that we could do it and actually restore power.' It is certainly arguable that Sam's escape to become a roaming Luddite menace, threatening to destroy all Alec's efforts, would have been a more interesting and thought-provoking payoff for his character. But Sam remains, without doubt, the necessary 'spanner in the works' of "Power". His determination to wreck proceedings, and the group's initial unawareness of the presence of an enemy within, is vital to the narrative tension. Without Sam as the project's nemesis, the battle is simply one to fix a broken machine – and the dramatic obstacle they face does need to be more challenging than a rusted handle or a congealed valve.

"Power" also reveals the more conceited sides of Alec's nature. As he instructs others in the operation of the plant, his tone is decidedly patronising. When he announces, at the episode's conclusion, that he will train up a new generation of technicians only if he remains 'answerable to no-one', his terms seem both unreasonable and more than a little egotistical. It might be thought that his debt of gratitude to Charles's company would temper such self-aggrandisement. More generously, it can be acknowledged that Alec is likely to still be reeling from Jenny's decision to leave him behind. However gruff his manner, he is at least willing to commit himself to the hydroelectric project: moments earlier, he had pictured himself in the guise of the happily-married crofter, living free of responsibilities in the Scottish hills, until Jenny had dashed his dreams.

Despite the strong narrative, there are some significant misfires along the way: Worth changes at a stroke one of the premises under which our heroes have laboured since the earliest episodes of the first series – the survival rate. En route to his castle, he explains that overall Scotland: '... lost 9 out of 10 in the plague ... But in the Highlands the plague couldn't spread that much through the hills, and most of the Isles weren't affected by it.' As a consequence, he announces to the complete surprise of Jenny and Charles that there could be up to '150,000 people left alive' in Scotland – a figure that Jenny acknowledges dwarfs the estimated English population of 10,000. The idea that Scotland has retained this secret survival rate to become the 'most densely populated' area of the UK is an intriguing one, but the notion that The Death simply failed to reach large areas is hugely problematic. In series one stories such as "Gone to the Angels", great emphasis is laid on the fact that survivors of the plague remain carriers, destined to infect those they encounter as yet untouched by the contagion. This notion comes under strain in the series two episode "Over the Hills", in which Melanie is convinced that the survivors might yet discover an enclave of civilisation that The Death overlooked. Yet in "Power", the premise collapses completely. If those in the Scottish hills have truly escaped The Death, then their continued survival rests on their continued separation from the world. It could be argued that the survivors are infectious as plague carriers only for a short time, but there is no acknowledgement here that this is a critical issue. Also, although Charles makes no reference to it, the simple fact of the size of the population living in the Highlands means that the London community's preoccupation with its burden of

Iain Cuthbertson (McAlister). © Denis Lill

keeping the human race going ("Lights of London") is entirely unwarranted. The size of the gene pool in the hills and valleys of the Scottish Highlands completely outstrips anything that those in England's capital city can put forward. (As a flippant side point, it also suggests that – had they kept to their original plan to travel towards the Scottish islands – Charmian and Arthur might have discovered a more familiar and prosperous fate than they settled for in

Herefordshire.) There is some much better continuity with the developments of "Long Live the King", as the (ever-modest) Laird seeks to appoint Charles as his 'Secretary of State for England' who can negotiate terms on behalf of Agnes's new governing council for continued access to 'Scottish power'. The story hints at future trade and greater integration between Scottish and English survivors (although, as Charles might well complain, the Welsh appear to be left out of the equation once again).

It must be conceded however that the final denouement is, in dramatic terms, a missed opportunity. Jenny is given a nicely rendered resolution with Alec Campbell, in some touchingly played scenes in which Alec tries to persuade her to come and settle with the children on a Scottish farmstead, and she gently but firmly declines. However, Charles is left without any payoff at all for twelve episodes of 'federation' rhetoric. Charles's final line in *Survivors* is not a reflection on future possibilities now opening up, or on the rights and responsibilities of the next generation, or even on the next stages in the battle to found a functioning new society. Rather, it is the lamentable (if suitably polite) farewell to the Laird: 'Thank you for your hospitality.'

Instead, it is the guest characters who have the final screen time of the series as they sit down to their supper. Lill certainly liked the fact that: 'When the power was restored, it was the Laird who decided he'd far rather go back to the original – and sit down with his housekeeper in the candlelight. It seemed a much more romantic idea.' But while this closing scene provides an atmospheric, if understated, send-off, it also skews the final moments of the series. While the Laird can now exercise a choice previously denied him, it remains somewhat deflating to see Alec's triumph immediately dispensed with – especially as the Laird has earlier asked for the restoration of electric power and made much of Scotland's greater claim to the resource. Compared with the uplifting finale to the first series (in which Abby learns of her son Peter's survival, and the Grange community is shown to be thriving), or the unexpected conclusion to series two (in which Greg, Jack and Agnes soar into the sky on their way to Norway), this is an off-centre ending that takes the focus away from the central characters and in doing so leaves too much unresolved and unsaid. Lill wryly suggests that it is: '… tempting to extrapolate as to what Charles would then go on to do, and I think he becomes rather bitter and disillusioned about the whole thing, and finds a mountain to live on somewhere in Wales.'

That said, those final moments do retain a poignancy of their own: the lights that failed so dramatically in "The Fourth Horseman" flicker back on at the conclusion of "Power". What had signalled the collapse of civilisation then, is here a symbol for its rebirth.

Yet the over-riding question remains whether *Survivors* should have arrived at this destination at all, and whether switching on the lights effectively switched off any prospect of a fourth series for the show. With the government formed, money and trade revived, electric power now flowing, and the size of Britain's population suddenly increased 16-fold, the post-Death world is evolving into an increasingly familiar and recognisable place. The more the new world resembles the old, the less distinctive and compelling the dramatic premise of *Survivors* becomes. *RC*

SERIES 3: REVIEW

The drama of *Survivors'* third series came to be based on an unexpected inversion of the original premise – concerned, as it was, not with the settled life of a communal smallholding but with the restless travels of a roving band of survivors; and not with the acceptance of civilisation's loss, but with the struggle to secure its return.

Series one was dominated by the impact of The Death, the hunt for Peter Grant and the struggles of the fledging Grange settlement. Series two focused on the travails of the Whitecross community, and the adventures triggered by visitors or by the settlers' own forays into the outside world. Through the combined quest to reunite with Greg and spark the rebirth of an industrial society, series three came to be dominated by the twins themes of 'loss' and 'recovery'. There are numerous sacrifices evident in the storylines of series three – the Whitecross haven is abandoned, the better to pursue the Norwegian plan; Greg and Jenny remain painfully separated; and Charles and his travelling band forgo safety and security in the multiple, cumulative dangers posed by their mission on the road. Such 'losses' are at least partly offset by the hope of that imminent 'recovery': the longed-for revival of industry and social order. Largely as a result of this, the ambience and mood of *Survivors'* final series are markedly different from those of the two that have preceded it. It remains a persistent paradox that the atmosphere of series three is frequently the bleakest and darkest ever seen in the show, while its finale is unquestionably the most optimistic in tone.

The core trio of characters at the heart of the series' drama had been revised for a second time, as Hubert joined Jenny and Charles as the recurring leads. One of the things that distinguished the third series from the previous two was an increased reliance on guest actors of the week, many of whom enjoyed significant screen time. It was also an innovation to have two separate storylines unfolding in parallel across the series – as the events of "A Little Learning" and "The Last Laugh", which focused on Greg, unfolded largely in isolation from the exploits of Charles, Jenny and Hubert. Although some secondary characters appeared in both these separate story arcs, Charles's group and Greg are never reunited on screen. Taken together, these structural changes mean that the series' leads are not so dominant as before.

In the third series, *Survivors'* main characters also all face huge risks in their efforts to kick-start a social, political and economic revival: Charles is nearly killed by the events of "Mad Dog"; all his party are put at risk by the drama of "Law of the Jungle"; Greg finds unexpected danger in the events of "A Little Learning", and succumbs to certain death in "The Last Laugh". Agnes, meanwhile, pushes herself beyond what she considers her limits of ability and competence to see through Greg's reconstruction plans. The demands of the struggle to forge a new civilisation remain high.

At the same time, the protagonists gain greatly from their commitment to this struggle – Charles finds his evangelism endorsed; Greg is heralded as an inspiring organiser and enabler (albeit a sometimes over-eager one); Jenny finds new resources of self-belief and a resilience of spirit that appeared beyond her reach in the closing episodes of series two (proving that life without Greg might yet be worth living). Jenny is frustrated and unnerved by Greg's continued absence, and later mourns his loss, yet her confidence ultimately emerges strengthened by the challenges she has overcome. Although his own evolution is uneven and halting, Hubert also finds renewed self-efficacy and confidence in this new role, less often the grumbler and the fumbler, more often the doggedly heroic ally. Had news of the Norwegian plan not reached Whitecross, or been rejected as impractical or unwelcome, all four of them could have settled for the more predictable demands of the smallholder's pastoral life, drawing down the shutters on the world outside. It was, of course, producer Terence Dudley's conviction that such a decision would have been disastrous for the show. He remained convinced that change was an essential component of its continuing success, and that a similar upheaval to that which had occurred between series one and two was again needed if *Survivors* was to remain fresh and engaging.

The contrasts that this dramatic upheaval introduces are striking. If life at Whitecross had frequently been introspective, the storylines of the final series are consistently outgoing and outward-looking. If the setting for series two was predominantly static; series three remains mobile and restive throughout (with even the new Sloton Spencer homestead rarely in view). In some respects, the latter episodes of the third series are reminiscent of the opening episodes of the first: in both cases, a rootless group of survivors encounter diverse communities as they pursue their quest. In series one, such settlements include: Arthur Wormley's putative militia headquarters; Charles Vaughan's own Maredell community; and the ousted Jimmy Garland's Waterhouse estate. In the final series, those communities include: Colonel Clifford's military pharmacy; Brod's ramshackle outlaw outpost; and Leonard's Woollen's hospitable Toll Bar. What distinguishes their travels is the trajectory and context in which this mission takes place. These wanderers are not preoccupied with how to cope with the collapse of civilisation, but how to prepare for and hasten its return.

In series two, Charles and Greg had remained equally prominent in the storylines. McCulloch's desire to extricate himself from the show, and Dudley's interest in giving Lill top billing, changed the narrative balance between them significantly in series three. The result of this did not fully become clear until the closing episodes. Throughout the first nine episodes of series three, Charles repeatedly finds that Greg is several steps ahead of him, a restless emissary for the Norwegian plan, whose compound successes in recruiting and inspiring others far outstrip anything that Charles appears capable of. Yet with McCulloch's insistence on killing off his own character in his third and final script, the situation is overturned. Greg falls victim to the Captain's predators and dies, alone and embittered, while Charles goes on to secure the revival of the first electric power plant in the British Isles (a feat that had eluded Greg) before returning to Sloton vindicated and triumphant. Agnes may use Greg as the symbolic figurehead of the new governing council, but this near-mythical status is of little consequence to him: he dies without ever having laid eyes on a 'GP' Union Jack. It is ironic that a character who returned to Britain in the days following The Death determined not to take on any further responsibilities in the life that remained to him should, after his own demise, become the appointed leader of a country now beginning to emerge from the ruins.

Making the struggle to refound civilisation a central driving narrative certainly helped to give the third series a greater sense of purpose than its wandering adventures would have had without it. Allowing the series' heroes to win the first symbolic victories in the struggle to rebuild society gave *Survivors* an evocative and upbeat finale, completing the series' dramatic journey by pointing its characters back to their original point of departure – a country with government, trade and industry. Inevitably, viewers at the time and since have divided between those who thought the return of electric power provided an uplifting and hopeful denouement for *Survivors*, and those who saw it as an artificial payoff that frittered away the power of the drama that had gone before.

Certainly, in the latter episodes of the third series, the journey towards Scotland does come to dominate the drama, as plots are obliged to move the expedition storyline along to its next location, in the company of Charles's newest recruits. The destination at which the series' heroes arrive in "Power" – with its new governing council, its petrol promissory notes and its electric power plants – seems a world away from the show's origins in "The Fourth Horseman". It is certainly the case that, as the context and setting of the series became more recognisable and familiar, the distinctiveness that made it such compelling viewing would have dissipated. Lill concedes that, towards the end, the series was 'no longer wrestling with 18th Century technology any more, but travelling back through the centuries again … I suppose there was only so much mileage to be got out of the situation as it was.' Yet there are important continuities that connect *Survivors'* first and final episodes. One of the clearest themes of "The Fourth Horseman" is the resilience of the human spirit in conditions of unimaginable calamity. The events of "Power" suggest that conviction, perseverance and collective effort can produce near-impossible results in the most difficult and dangerous of circumstances. In very different ways, both can be seen as a vindication of the fortitude and adaptability of humankind.

It is also in series three that a disparity present since the very first episode of *Survivors* becomes most acutely apparent. Although *Survivors* is about the complete devastation of human society across the entire planet – a fact of which the title sequence of every episode reminds viewers so effectively – its storylines all focus on the struggles of a small group of British plague survivors. As the third series opens up the show's field of vision, it paradoxically reinforces the sense of how limited a picture of life beyond the Grange and Whitecross has been visible until now. This is something that reaches its apex in "Power" – with the revelation of the existence of some 150,000 hitherto unknown survivors in the Scottish countryside, a single fact that will alter the social and economic landscape of the new Britain beyond recognition. It remains the case, however, that aside from the position in the Nordic countries, our British survivors still have only the most fragmentary information about the fate of humanity in the wider world. A further persistent frustration of series three is that Greg's ambitious successes at reconstruction (which occur largely off-screen) so often outclass the more modest efforts of Charles's group, whose work is followed so closely on-camera. Even as series three depicts the revival of human society, important elements of that emerging new world evolve 'unseen'.

One of the most intriguing counterfactuals of *Survivors'* third series is the question of possible alternatives to the plots and storylines that made their way on screen. There is, however, no simple unanimity about what the 'lost opportunities' of *Survivors* might have been. Nation remained convinced that Dudley had never grasped the true potential of the series, and that the first series was less successful than it should have been as a result. Carolyn Seymour was equally adamant that the triumph of the first series was frittered away, once the original triumvirate of characters had been broken up after the events of "A Beginning". Ian McCulloch has long argued that the series 'lost its way' when it surrendered its adventurous sensibility and became preoccupied with the mechanics of self-sufficiency. Christopher Tranchell left for almost exactly the opposite reason – convinced that *Survivors* was too little concerned with the business of survival and communal living. Others who contributed in one way or another to the series have suggested that *Survivors* could successfully have evolved along different lines to the ones that it did. Yet there was no single alternative consensus able to match the forceful clarity of Dudley's own vision.

Overall, Dudley seems to have approached his own work on the third series in a notably different way than before. Between the first and second series, Dudley's command and control had become less absolute. In the course of series three, he became an even less prominent fixture in the production process, more content now to work in the background and allow his production units the latitude his writers and directors clearly relished. Confident in the skills of his team, Dudley was able to step back sufficiently to enjoy his own first outings as a writer ("Manhunt") and as a director ("Reunion") on the series. Prior to *Survivors*, Dudley's writing, producing and directing credits had been impressive, but this would prove to be the last opportunity he had to exercise such broad executive control over a major BBC series. The year after *Survivors* concluded, Dudley's worked as a director on four episodes of the second series of the BBC's wartime serial *Secret Army*, which was being produced by Gerard Glaister. The role of lead director was a significant one, but it still meant that Dudley was now having to work under the stewardship of a producer of his own. It is not clear if Dudley was becoming a less fashionable figure amongst the commissioning editors of the Drama Department, or if he simply never again sought to take on the mantle of a series' producer.

Long before the cast and crew held their final 'wrap party' after the end of production on "Power", it became clear to all involved that there would be no fourth series of *Survivors* – although memories amongst cast and crew are hazy over exactly when this news reached the production team. Scriptwriter Don Shaw argues that, as an intelligent and reflective series, *Survivors*: '… could have gone on; I'm absolutely convinced of it.' What is even less certain is whether, some nine months earlier, as Dudley put together his outline for the third series for BBC approval, he himself was reconciled to the fact that this would be *Survivors*' final run, or whether he had entertained notions of how a fourth series might develop.

Whatever the precise reasons for its non-renewal, *Survivors*' third series is emphatically more than a simple postscript to the events of its two predecessors – as some commentators have claimed over the intervening years. Indeed it contains several of the strongest episodes. Shaw recalls that, in his work on the second and third series, producer Terence Dudley: '… gave me the great opportunity to write the stuff that I wanted to write … It just sort of poured out of me! In terms of all the millions of words I've written, I would say that *Survivors* came the easiest, mainly because I was at my most inspired.' At times, the third series was certainly more disjointed and less sure-footed than its predecessors, yet it remained replete with standout moments – the mystery of Jack's feverish return in "Manhunt"; the shock of Fenton succumbing to rabies in "Mad Dog"; John's emotional reconciliation with his mother in "Reunion"; Greg's fate in "The Last Laugh"; and, ultimately, the triumph of electric light in "Power". These highlights equal – and at times surpass – anything seen in the show previously. At the same time, there can be little doubt that the experimental, mobile format of the third series falters at times; and no question that it lacks some of the cohesion and clarity of the previous two series.

Survivors' upbeat conclusion may draw the series to a close in optimistic mood, yet the settlement that it offers is far from complete, and a potent sense of melancholy still pervades proceedings. The remaining survivors face an almost insurmountable matrix of challenges and obstacles if the goal to rebuild civilisation is to advance beyond their modest beginnings. Moreover, the conclusion inevitably draws viewers' attention back to the seemingly endless list of those who have perished in the struggle for survival since The Death. It is hard to think of a television drama in which the life expectancy of both leading and supporting characters is so brutally short. Of the adults that assembled to find collective safety in the events of the series one stories "Starvation" and "Spoil of War", only Jenny is definitely still alive at the close of "Power". Whatever the controversies of its final destination, *Survivors*' conclusion remained true to the stark and unflinching view of the human predicament with which Terry Nation had begun.

LIFE AFTER DEATH:
REPEATS, MERCHANDISE AND FANDOM

OVERSEAS SALES

The BBC sold *Survivors* around the world to networks in Canada, Denmark, New Zealand, Sweden, Switzerland and the United States, but it was nowhere more popular overseas than in Italy, where the first two series were broadcast – as *I Sopravvissuti* – by RAI (1979-82) and TMC (1983). The episodes were re-dubbed and featured the addition of rather intrusive incidental music. Ian McCulloch, who visited Italy in 1979 to play the lead role in the cult horror film *Zombie Flesh Eaters* – a part he was cast in as a direct result of *Survivors* being broadcast there – recalls that the Italian public's enthusiasm for the series was such that he was regularly mobbed in the streets during his time there. But despite this initial fervour for the show, the final series was never purchased. The series is still sold by the BBC for broadcast, with the San Diego-based KGTV and the Australian station UK-TV both airing the series in recent years.

THE NOVELS

Terry Nation penned a novel based on the series during 1975. It was published the following year in paperback by Futura and in hardback by Weidenfeld and Nicholson. Its title was simply *Survivors,* and the cover featured a portrait of Abby Grant behind a pane of smashed glass. Freed from the constraints of a BBC budget, Nation took the opportunity to rework the storyline of the first series on a more epic scale. Although most of the events of his first four scripts ("The Fourth Horseman", "Genesis", "Gone Away" and "Garland's War") are retained, beyond this point Nation elected to leave the action of the TV series behind altogether. In place of the founding of the Grange community, the survivors first settle in a village before embarking on a hazardous journey across the English Channel towards a new existence in the more hospitable climate of the Mediterranean. Other notable differences include: Greg returning to the quarry to find Vic dead; Anne Tranter – renamed Sarah Boyer – joining up with Arthur Wormley; John Carroll ("Garland's War") becoming a central character; and the continued survival of Tom Price. The book's conclusion sees Abby reunited with her son Peter, only for him to then gun his mother down. Years later, Nation commented: 'It was always intended – almost in a huge operatic form – that Peter, the boy she had looked for for so long, should destroy his mother.' As the *Survivors* novel is far more than a mere adaptation of the TV series, it gives a fascinating insight into how Nation would have liked to see his creation develop. The book was also published in the USA (with illustrations by Richard Hefter) by Coward, McCann & Geoghegan (1976) and in Italy by Sperling Kupfer (1978), Euro Club (1979) and Biblioteca Universale Rizzoli (1980).

Survivors: Genesis of a Hero, a sequel to Nation's novel, was published in the UK in 1977. Written by John Eyers (a pen-name for an unknown author), the book's narrative was almost entirely divorced from the events of the TV series, concentrating on Peter's adventures after the death of his mother. The post-Death Britain in Eyers' novel is a war-torn and bloody place that is being fought over by Arthur Wormley's National Unity Force (NUF) and the Red Dragons (guerrilla fighters based in Wales). Peter initially enlists with the NUF and builds up a reputation as a brave and skilled fighter during the group's invasions of Wales and the North, where there is a primitive capitalist community. Along the way, Peter murders Tom Price, the only witness to Abby's death. The narrative draws an obvious parallel with "Lights of London" by also depicting a London Underground-based group who call themselves the Rat Pack. Ultimately, while guarding Wormley at his new home – Windsor Castle – Peter sleeps with his wife, the aforementioned Sarah Boyer, and fathers a son before eventually becoming King. The tone and action-romp style of Eyers' novel sets it apart from both the TV series and Nation's remodelling of the concept in his own novel, but it nevertheless stands as an interesting, if unlikely, alternative to the television canon.

REPEATS

To the disappointment of the series' directors and performers, *Survivors* was never repeated by the BBC, and a total of sixteen years passed before satellite station UK Gold began a run of the series in 1993. The first broadcast since 1975 of "The Fourth Horseman" managed only 8,000 viewers, but audiences soon picked up, peaking at 90,000 for "Corn Dolly". The episodes were initially shown on weekday evenings and Sunday mornings. Several minor cuts were made to these broadcasts simply in order to fit the episodes into the schedule, while some particularly violent sequences (for example Kane shooting Lewis in "Parasites") were excised completely. UK Gold continued to broadcast all thirty-eight episodes regularly for several years in different time slots, up until April 1998.

VHS RELEASES

Concurrent to the first repeat run on UK Gold, BBC Worldwide decided that the time was ripe to release the first series of *Survivors* on VHS. The release was packaged in six volumes, comprising two episodes each on the first five tapes and the concluding three on the sixth. The covers featured the (deliberately pixellated) scientist from the title sequence, several small BBC stills of the principal characters and an approximation of the *Survivors* font. Due to limited promotion and distribution issues, sales of the tapes were relatively poor, and if there were any plans to move on to a release of the second series, they were soon shelved.

In 1998, an independent video label called Sovereign decided to re-release the first series on VHS under license from BBC Worldwide. The tapes were packaged in a similar six volume format, but this time featured original cover artwork by Pete Wallbank. Later that year, Sovereign announced that they were due to release the second series over a further six volumes. Wallbank was commissioned to produce the covers, colour advertising appeared in the genre press and the episodes were reviewed in *SFX* magazine; however, the tapes themselves never materialised. The art that Wallbank had already completed was never used and, after the releases were cancelled, Sovereign soon ceased trading.

THE MAKING OF TERRY NATION'S SURVIVORS

In 1995, Kevin Marshall independently wrote and published a book on *Survivors*, in which he intended to explain how the series was made and developed. Two years in the making and mainly comprised of fascinating and frank interviews with principal cast and crew rather than in-depth analysis and criticism, the book told the behind-the-scenes story of *Survivors*

Denis Lill, Lorna Lewis, Pennant Roberts and Heather Wright together again for the Series 2 DVD studio day. ©
Rich Cross

for the very first time. Marshall introduced the text as a source book 'in which a treasure of information and anecdotes are to be found' and instructed that the order in which it was read was of no consequence. In addition to the interview testimony (gathered by Marshall and his partner Consuelo by travelling the length and breadth of Britain), episode reviews were provided by Tanya Ronder (Lizzie), Anne Christie (wife of the late Jack Ronder, who had chaperoned her daughter Tanya while the series was being made), Julie Neubert (Wendy), writer on cult TV Paul Mount and Anna Pitt (Agnes), whose obvious dislike of *Survivors*, and of her time making it, made her a strange choice to review so many episodes. As she has also done for this book, Anne Christie generously supplied many of her own evocative photographs taken during the production of the first and second series. Published by Marshall himself as 'A Fourth Horseman Publication', the work was reviewed positively: 'The research is breathtaking, perhaps a little dry for many, *The Making of Survivors* is an impressive feat'; 'Labours of love don't come much better than this.' The tome was greeted with huge enthusiasm by both new and long-term fans of the series, who lapped up its highly original content. The book had a limited print-run and copies now exchange hands at incredible prices.

FANDOM

Although *Survivors* commanded a large and loyal audience during its initial broadcast, there was no organised fandom as such until the UK Gold broadcasts and BBC VHS releases began to generate new interest. Another important turning point was the Dreamwatch '94 convention, which featured a panel of *Survivors* luminaries (John Abineri,

Lorna Lewis, Julie Neubert, Christopher Tranchell, scriptwriters Roger Parkes and Martin Worth, and director Pennant Roberts) compered – and brought together – by Kevin Marshall, who at the time was still writing his book.

Later that year, the first fanzine devoted to the series was produced, entitled *Over the Hills*. This A4 publication, edited by Carole Stevens, was produced irregularly from December 1994 until 1998 and featured news and views on the series. Other contributors included Bob Meade, who had by that time scouted out many of the locations used in *Survivors* and reported on his travels through the pages of the fanzine, and Lynne Sweetman, who acted as 'cast liaison'. A popular contributor was 'Roo', whose cartoons sent up the series' leads. As a result of *Over the Hills*, many fans met each other for the first time through organised gatherings (7 September 1996 being the date of the very first meet) at the series' key locations, such as Hampton Court. To this day, this location remains a regular place of pilgrimage for fans, and in 2002 – thanks to the efforts of Adrian Hulme – a guided tour of the inside of the Court took place, complete with a restaging of the lot drawing scene from "Law and Order". While *Over the Hills* continued, Mark Wheatley (who had already guest edited *Over the Hills* for a time) produced a new A5 fanzine, *Whitecross Calling*, which provided a more in-depth and analytical look at the series, with lengthy articles on particular episodes. When both *Whitecross Calling* and *Over the Hills* folded, a more slim-line A4 newsletter entitled *Bridgehead* took their place. Later retitled the *Survivors Newsletter,* this publication was (in 2005) still regularly produced by long-term fans Lynne Sweetman and Steve Brailsford.

Fanzines aside, from the mid-1990s, *Survivors* devotees also began to converse via the internet, and by 1998 several websites were flourishing, including Chris Barker's image-rich *Felbridge Camp*, containing cast interviews, location photos and reports, and a US site known as *The Survivors Homepage,* incorporating behind-the-scenes trivia, an opinion section and location information. Although neither site is updated any longer, *Survivors* continues to enjoy a presence on the web thanks to: Andy Priestner's *Survivors TV Series*

A fan gathering at the entrance to Hampton Court. © Adrian Hulme

Lucy Fleming and Ian McCulloch at the Series 1 DVD studio day. © Rich Cross

(www.survivorstvseries.com); location expert Bob Meade's site (pages.zdnet.com/bobmeades/); Luca's Italian site, *I sopravvissuti* (sopravvissuti.altervista.org/); and Rich Cross's two sites, *Mad Dog* (www.survivors-mad-dog.org.uk/) – an in-depth look at the classic third series episode – and *A World Away* (www.survivors-mad-dog.org.uk/a-world-away/) – a site containing unique *Survivors* material, launched in 2004. At the time of writing, fans still meet online to debate the merits of the show via Bob Meade's message forum, Chris Herbert's *TV Gold* forum site and a *Yahoo Groups* mailing list. Adrian Hulme continues to organise location trips and produces professionally packaged DVDs (under the banner 'Brimpsfield Productions') to commemorate the events, which are dubbed 'reunions'.

DVD RELEASES

An announcement that DD Video (now DD Home Entertainment) intended to release the series on DVD and VHS was first posted on the *Zeta Minor* website in March 2003, some time before DD's own official press release. The news coincided with a fan-organised trip to the Derbyshire Dales (where "Mad Dog" was recorded) and appropriately enough was related to the attendees at the Eyam plague museum! Mindful of the previous BBC and Sovereign releases, there was some consternation at first from fans over DD's plans to release the first series yet again (its third release), although the DVD format was an obvious plus point. It was also revealed that DD had the option to release the second and third series as well, but only time would tell if sales would be strong enough to enable them to get further than their predecessors. However, when it became clear that DD intended to incorporate a wealth of extras into the Series One boxset (which it was jokingly suggested at one stage could also include a SARS mask – the spread of the virus being coincidentally the biggest news story of Spring 2003), the future for *Survivors* fans suddenly looked very bright indeed.

Charged with helping to compile the first release was fan Andy Priestner, who on the strength of his *Survivors* website was commissioned to write a behind-the-scenes booklet and text for the packaging and, most importantly, to assemble a number of the show's cast and crew for a studio day on 5 June 2003. Luck was on his side as Carolyn Seymour, Ian McCulloch and Lucy Fleming all proved to be available, as did director Pennant Roberts. Late in the day, Tanya Ronder also agreed to take part as a surprise guest. Prior to the studio day, the stars re-watched the first series; indeed Seymour – who flew over from her home in the States especially for the event – did so much *Survivors* homework that she found herself inadvertently calling McCulloch, with whom she was staying, 'Greg'! After the inevitably emotional reunion at the start of the day, two audio commentaries were recorded during the morning session. Seymour and Roberts teamed up for "The Fourth Horseman", while Fleming and McCulloch watched "Law and Order". While Seymour was finding it 'scary' watching herself again, she was nevertheless pleased that 'the acting is quite amazing and it grips you.' McCulloch in particular found the commentaries a difficult experience: 'It's a slog. One is constantly being surprised by: a) what you look like, b) what you say, c) who's in it with you, and then probably the worst thing of all, realising that half the people in it aren't around anymore!' Proceedings continued with camera interviews, which were briefly interrupted by a mid-afternoon reunion with Tanya Ronder, who also brought along her mother's photographs – bringing back further happy memories of the summer of '75. While not catching up with each other or being needed on set, the five attendees were also interviewed by representatives from *TV Zone*, *Ultimate DVD* and *Dreamwatch* magazines in order to publicise the release. The day had been a great success and Lucy Fleming commented that 'it felt like old times.' A little while after the studio day, a Herefordshire resident responded to Priestner's newspaper appeals for home movie footage and photographs with the news that

Tristan de Vere Cole and Morris Perry at the Series 3 studio day. © Rich Cross

she had a reel of film containing footage of *Survivors* being recorded, which she herself had taken while her horses were being used in the series. The 16mm film turned out to feature the recording of one of the very last scenes of "A Beginning" on 16 June 1975, and became a worthy addition to the boxset. The Series One DVD was released on 6 October 2003 and healthy sales soon assured DD's release of the second series for the very first time.

Scheduled for a year later, the Series Two DVD was set to comprise once again a behind-the-scenes booklet and special features. This time around, Denis Lill, Lorna Lewis and Heather Wright were chosen to join a returning Pennant Roberts to share their memories of the unforgettable shoot at Callow Hill back in 1976. The studio day took place on 3 June 2004. First up was an audio commentary on Jack Ronder's "Lights of London Part 2" with Roberts and Lill (whose involvement had been confirmed only the previous day due to his intensive filming schedule on *The Royal*). After that came a happy reunion with Lewis and Wright and a friendly lunch, then it was back to the studio to record camera interviews and meet the gathered press. Released in October 2004, the DVD once again sold strongly in the high street and online, entering *amazon.co.uk*'s Top 100 chart.

On 4 August 2005, *Survivors* actors Lucy Fleming, Stephen Dudley and Morris Perry were joined by directors Tristan de Vere Cole and Peter Jefferies to record the special features for the series three *Survivors* DVD, ahead of its November 2005 release. In the morning, two episode commentaries were recorded, with Perry and de Vere Cole reviewing "Mad Dog", and Jefferies and Fleming discussing "Law of the Jungle". In the afternoon, individual on-camera interviews were held with de Vere Cole, Dudley, Jefferies and Fleming. Co-author of *The End of the World?* Rich Cross was also interviewed discussing the production process on series three. For this final DVD release, these interviews were then edited into an original documentary feature on the making of *Survivors'* third series "New World Rising". By the close of 2005, all thirty-eight unedited and digitally remastered episodes of *Survivors* had been made accessible for the first time on DVD.

AFTERMATH:
REVIVAL PLANS AND INFLUENCE ON THE POST-APOCALYPSE GENRE

AFTERMATH

The disappearance of *Survivors* from British TV screens in 1977 marked the beginning of a long period of stasis for the series – one from which it began to re-emerge only with the first repeat showings on UK Gold, and the BBC Worldwide video release of the first series that followed, in the early 1990s. But even in those years in which it remain locked in the BBC's archives, the influence that *Survivors* continued to exert over the calculations of both filmmakers and television executives was still clearly in evidence. Though unseen and inaccessible, *Survivors* remained a continual point of reference for those concerned with post-apocalyptic dramas of all kinds. In fact, it became all but inconceivable that writers and producers would devise an end-of-the-world drama without first scrutinising Nation's own genre-redefining adventures.

In the early 1990s, as *Survivors* emerged from its enforced hibernation, it even appeared possible that a new 'fourth' series of the show might be given the go-ahead, following the efforts of one of the original stars. Now living in the US, Nation had himself been thinking about the possibility of pitching an outline for a new series of *Survivors* to an American TV network. This would have gone back to the onset of The Death, to explore the struggles of a disparate group of American survivors. He told the US *Liberator's Log* fanzine in 1992: 'I want the story to start in the north-east of the United States, just before the winter sets in. We start there, and we do our first terrible winter there' before the storyline follows the adventures of a 'very bizarre wagon train of strange vehicles crossing empty America, where there are little pockets of survivors here and there.' It was a format that Nation thought opened up interesting possibilities 'because you could stop in a place for maybe four or five episodes' before the drama moved on to new surroundings. There is no evidence that Nation developed his initial ideas further, but he did give his support to efforts being made to revive the series on the other side of the Atlantic by Ian McCulloch.

Despite his own criticisms of the direction that the show took after the series one finale "A Beginning", and his withdrawal from all but two episodes of the final series, McCulloch remained convinced that there was still unrealised potential in the premise, and that – if conditions proved conducive – a *Survivors* revival was a real possibility. McCulloch recalls: 'I talked to Terry Nation and I talked to Terry Dudley, and I said that I had this idea of doing another lot [*of episodes*]. They were both keen, including Dudley, who had some ideas about it.' McCulloch's approach reflected his keen interest in the adventure elements of the show, as well as his conviction that series two and three had rarely realised its true potential. The premise for the new series was that British survivors would face: '... an invasion by a black African country, which had still managed to hang on to all the hardware of civilisation that everyone else had lost, and so still had, and could use, planes and warships.' In effect, it was going to 'be like "colonisation in reverse", and we were going to suffer what they had all suffered' as these invaders sought to seize control of the country, its resources and its population. Their leader was to be modelled on the infamous and brutal then-dictator of Uganda, Idi Amin. The series' storylines were intended to be 'really pretty terrifying and scary.'

Although McCulloch was keen to preserve and extend the existing *Survivors* canon, he did not propose to follow on directly from the concluding events of series three. He has chosen never to watch the final episodes of the series, and acknowledges: 'I'm afraid I don't know how it ended. I haven't seen them – didn't want to see them.' He remained convinced that *Survivors* had come to a premature end 'because too many of the things that were important to its success had gone.' McCulloch drew up a full pilot script and outlines for a further twelve episodes, and pitched his plans to the BBC. The series' controversial premise raised immediate objections. McCulloch recalls that his proposals 'were spurned because they thought it was "racist."' It was an accusation that McCulloch rejected outright. He readily acknowledges that his proposal was deliberately contentious: 'The fact that here are people doing to you what they claim you've been doing to them for the past three hundred, four hundred years – as the British Empire got set up' meant that the new series would have a provocative premise. But the fact that the idea inverted the historical experience of imperialism, confronting British survivors with the threat of colonisation, meant that for McCulloch it remained 'exactly the opposite of racist.' McCulloch also stressed to the BBC that the new production would provide television work for a large number of black actors and performers. To McCulloch's frustration, neither of these arguments won over BBC producers, who he felt remained convinced 'that it was racist – and it just died a death.'

McCulloch's approach would certainly have provided *Survivors'* fourth series with a strong narrative arc. His plan also implied a larger sense of scale than the show had attempted before, as the invading forces met the armed opposition of the network of British settlements. This was something McCulloch felt could be addressed by a more sophisticated use of technology and visual effects than had previously been used on *Survivors* and would not have required an uneconomic increase in the production budget. In terms of the cast, he was also intending to bring back 'as many people whose characters were still alive [as possible].' Although others have since debated the precise nature of Greg's fate in between the events of "The Last Laugh" and "Long Live the King" (and have pointed to the duplicity and deceit carried out by Agnes, who is repeatedly revealed to be lying about Greg), McCulloch is reconciled to the fact that Greg perished as a result of his act of revenge and absolution at Cawston Farm. McCulloch was: '... quite sure I was dead.' He had, however, 'worked out a way of bringing my own self back' in the opening segment of the revival.

Over the next few years, McCulloch returned to the question of a *Survivors* revival, looking afresh at his own premise. With the support of Nation and director Pennant Roberts, he drew up a new set of script outlines – this time around a revised set of core themes (ones that McCulloch is understandably reluctant to reveal in detail while the project remains commercially sensitive). In one early treatment, McCulloch had explored the idea of bringing back the Captain (introduced in McCulloch's own third series script "The Last Laugh" – at least in name, if not in person) as a recurring villain, and of reworking his original idea of a foreign invading force. Roberts suggested to McCulloch that: '... it was something BBC Wales might be interested in. I also thought that it would be wonderful if it was done near where I lived in Scotland, because it's as wild as where we did the first series – the planes don't go overhead; it would be nice to do it at home; and, it would be good publicity for an area of Scotland that badly needs it.'

In 1994, whilst working on an episode from the first series of *The Tales of Para Handy* entitled "The Poacher" (in which he played the role of Laird Ferguson), McCulloch had discussed his latest ideas for a *Survivors* revival with the programme's producer Colin Gilbert: 'He said, "What are you doing, have you got some script on the go," and I said "I'm thinking of doing this." And that was the end of the conversation, and we finished filming. Then, afterwards, back in London, I got a phone call saying, "Were you serious?" I said, "Yeah, of course I am," and he said, "Well, we'd like to do it. Show me what you've got. We've got a big meeting in London with Alan Yentob." And he had the meeting, and the word came back that Yentob had said, "We don't want to resurrect some seventies series that's gone cold." And that was the end of it ... I certainly wasn't alone, or BBC Scotland wasn't alone, in getting these sort of rejections.'

McCulloch has certainly not given up on the possibility of a future revival of the show. He continues to maintain his manuscripts and he 'keeps on adding little bits, nice little twists and things' and remains committed to involving 'all the actors who had been reasonably prominent in the seventies series.' He is also certain that the latest advances in digital technology increasingly 'make filming on some larger "scale" financially acceptable.' As McCulloch says, any new version of *Survivors* would need to win the renewed approval both of the estate of Terry Nation and of the BBC before it could proceed. McCulloch has also not dismissed the idea of acting as a producer and consultant for an independently licensed production, provided he retains sufficient control 'to see that it goes in the right way.'

There are an increasing number of precedents for a potential *Survivors* revival, with a number of classic 1970s shows having become the subject of revival bids. Of immediate relevance to *Survivors* was a new one-off instalment (and potential new series pilot) of the eco-thriller *Doomwatch*, that aired on Channel 5 in 1999. The original *Doomwatch* had been *Survivors'* clearest small-screen antecedent, both thematically and in terms of overlapping cast and crew members, and a successful *Doomwatch* revival would doubtless have increased *Survivors'* own chances of being recommissioned. The contemporary resonance of *Doomwatch*'s key themes can hardly be in doubt: scepticism at the 'reckless indifference' of scientists and big business is arguably more pronounced amongst the viewing public today than it was in the 1970s. There would be no shortage of new concerns for *Doomwatch* to address: genetically modified food; 'designer babies'; the new technologies of surveillance; computer 'hackers' and virus writers; and the 'black economy' of arms proliferation around the world, to name but a few. The new *Doomwatch* drama "Winter Angel" remained faithful to the themes of its predecessor, exploring a conspiracy surrounding the storage of Soviet nuclear waste at a British facility. "Winter Angel" also took some care to preserve the *Doomwatch* canon, and briefly featured the earlier series' lead character Dr Spencer Quist (here played by Philip Stone). Yet despite boasting some strong production values, a robust and intelligent plot and a convincing new central character in the guise of university lecturer Neil Tannahill (played with some panache by Trevor Eve), this remount garnered decidedly mixed reviews and only middling viewing figures, so no further instalments were ordered.

Survivors could, of course, claim an equally strong present-day relevance, with outbreaks of SARS and other deadly diseases, and the threat of biological and chemical attack, repeatedly dominating today's news headlines. In more recent years, the single strongest boost to a potential *Survivors* revival was the BBC's decision to commission a new series of *Doctor Who*, produced by BBC Wales and broadcast in 2005. Although the profile of *Doctor Who* dwarfs that of *Survivors*, it remains significant that the BBC is willing to consider giving new life to 'classic' genre drama series from an earlier era.

However, it is evident that any revival of *Survivors* would need to overcome a number of narrative and dramatic challenges. Neither of McCulloch's proposals are premised on a 're-telling' of the original story in the present day. This is not a 're-imagining' of *Survivors*, but a return to its fictional setting some thirty years on from the time of The Death.

This means that the programme makers would face the challenge of a present-day television audience who would have to accept a lost version of civilisation that was thirty years old – so that the series would have an historic as well as a post-apocalyptic premise. None of the series' characters could mourn the loss of the laptop PC, the mobile phone, keyhole surgery, the digital camera or any of hundreds of other technological and scientific advances. The survivors of a 1975 catastrophe would also have lost all connection with a future in which popular concern with the rise of global instability, the depletion of the rainforests, the risks of genetic modification, the loss of deference to traditional institutions, the remaking of the workforce, or the 'pensions time bomb' have all become of prime importance.

It could, of course, be countered that the series' medieval setting would give it a clear sense of time and of place, and one in which the series' historical discontinuity would be of little relevance. Viewers could still picture, it could be argued, a global calamity in which the loss of technology and social organisation remained total, and that the distance from which humanity had fallen backwards into the past would not be of much importance. Yet viewers might still be puzzled by the survivors' ignorance of the Ebola virus, the Channel Tunnel or artificial insemination, and make audience identification with their plight more difficult.

What drew viewers to the series in the 1970s was that the catastrophe befell a world that was familiar and instantly recognizable. Any revival of *Survivors* would need to bridge that conceptual and emotional gap.

A further potential obstacle is that of the passage of time itself. The principal adult characters of the original series were played by actors now in their fifties and sixties. The all important 'audience demographic' that producers are compelled to build into their proposals would seem to demand that many of the series' leads would need to be in their twenties and thirties – effectively the children of Charles's and Jenny's generation. And yet, those characters would have to have grown up in the post-apocalyptic environment and have no real perception of what the old world would have been like. They would not act, as Greg eloquently describes it in the events of "Parasites", as 'rear-mirror drivers,

Ian McCulloch at Callow Hill. © Lucy Fleming

233

forever looking backwards.' This post-Death generation would have a completely different sense of the 'loss' that Abby and her cohorts feel. These younger characters' detachment from the 'old world' in which their parents had lived until the calamity of the plague might make it still more difficult for a modern-day audience to connect with.

Associated with this is the question of the passage of narrative time in the series. Several key post-apocalyptic novels, including the seminal *Earth Abides* (1949) by George R Stewart, are constructed around a narrative thread that stretches over decades and generations. Although not quite the phenomenon of 'real time', events in the original three series of *Survivors* unfolded over the course of three years, and concluded with the switching on of the first electricity supplies and the formation of a new ruling council in the events of "Long Live the King" and "Power". *Survivors* retained a tight focus on the 36 months immediately following the plague. Any new series would need to return to the drama a generation on. Even if Charles's and Greg's efforts at regeneration had come to naught, it is inconceivable that social and economic organisation would have stood still over the intervening years – whichever philosophies and lifestyles had triumphed over the aspirations of the Norwegian Plan. Whether a descent into barbarism and banditry or the rise of new agrarian communalism had succeeded, the context in which new *Survivors* drama would have to unfold would need to be profoundly different. While this could be seen as an opportunity, it would also serve as a challenge to the new programme makers.

Finally, it seems inevitable that any new series of *Survivors* would of necessity be dramatically different from the original, in terms of production methods and on-screen tempo. Ian McCulloch acknowledges that the original series had none of the fast-cutting, restless style that is today's TV standard, and that modern audiences would struggle with the 'slowness and [the] waiting for people to react and to say their lines.' Lucy Fleming half-seriously suggests that 'somebody could re-edit' the original series to 'make it a bit faster' in order to accommodate the impatient viewer of today. Any new series of *Survivors* would undoubtedly need to adopt a contemporary televisual sensibility, and as a result would look and feel very different from its 1970s predecessor.

There are, of course, a number of advantages that a present-day *Survivors* production would enjoy over its forerunner. McCulloch has observed that developments in camera and lighting design, and the increased mobility and versatility that these bring, would provide huge potential benefits to a cost-conscious production. So too would the development of modern digital editing techniques and the economy with which state-of-the-art special effects can be woven into the on-screen action. Certainly, none of these were available in Terence Dudley's day, and all would enhance the production values of any revival of the show.

With the successful release of *Survivors* on DVD, growing public interest in the 'golden age' of genre television, the persistent popularity of post-apocalyptic drama, and the increasing number of remakes and revivals of classic TV shows, it would certainly be premature to suggest that the idea of a new, fourth series of *Survivors* will never again attract the interest of an enterprising commissioning editor.

Whatever the immediate potential for a revival, there can be little question about the influence that *Survivors* continues to exert over the thinking of present-day television and film makers. Its imprint is clearly visible in some of the most successful contemporary 'post-apocalyptic' screen dramas, notably: Granada's time-shift end-of-the-world mini-series *The Last Train*; the generation-premised apocalyptic TV shows *The Tribe* (Australia-UK) and *Jeremiah* (US); and, on the big screen, the hugely successful British horror film *28 Days Later*, and the US blockbuster *The Day After Tomorrow*.

Filmed in 1998 (and first broadcast in April 1999), *The Last Train* was an expensive sci-fi-premised six-part drama series (with an estimated budget of around £4 million), which flung a disparate group of cryogenically frozen protagonists into a future Britain in which a meteorite collision with the Earth had wreaked catastrophe, destroying civilisation and re-engineering the country's ecosystem. It was the first major foray into the genre to hit British TV screens since the more scientifically-based docu-drama *Threads*, and *Survivors* provided a clear source of reference for the series' creators. The producer Sita Williams conceded to *SFX* magazine in February 1999: 'The original *Survivors* was, in a sense, the genesis for this. But now we can do it differently.' Alongside its strong British setting and reliance on on-location filming, there were a number of clear similarities between the two shows, although as a mini-series *The Last Train* was inevitably more focused around a single overarching storyline: the search for the salvation promised by Ark (a repository of technology and resources thought by survivor Harriet Ambrose to have survived the impact). *The Last Train* shared with *Survivors* a focus on a key strong female protagonist – Harriet (Nicola Walker) – who tries to rally a disparate ensemble of 'survivors' flung together in their shared plight. Like Abby Grant's search for her son Peter in the early episodes of *Survivors*, the 'quest narrative' (the hunt for Ark) in *The Last Train* provides the rationale for keeping the drama on the move. The landscape of *The Last Train* is, as in *Survivors*, filled with marauding wild animals and roaming gangs of armed militia, and scattered settlements attempting different solutions to the struggle for survival. As a key member of *The Last Train* group is fatally injured, their desperate need for medical equipment and know-how is brought into sharp relief – a recurrent theme in several *Survivors* stories. With its reliance on the 'cryogenic suspension' of its main characters and the impact of the devastating asteroid, *The Last Train* initially exhibits many of the characteristics of 'high concept' science fiction. However, it soon develops into something much more recognisable as a drama series, as its main characters engage with the battle for immediate and long-term survival. As the series' writer Matthew Graham (who also worked on the contemporary drama series *This Life*) explained to *Dreamwatch* in May 1999: 'This was to be a show about pulling together and having faith. It was to be a show about learning to let go of the past and look to the future. About adapting, and of course about surviving at all costs. And it was also going to involve a journey. An epic journey across half the country toward that faint flickering candle flame of hope burning in the darkness; the chance to find others like themselves.' Some observers suggested that *The Last Train* was not quite as sophisticated as its creators suggested – Richard Jordan in *The Guardian*, for example, concluding that it was: 'Predictable, but a lot of fun, and the devastation looks wonderful.' *The Last Train*'s pre-broadcast title (*Cruel Earth*) was changed to avoid confusion with an impending documentary series of the same name that focused on the real-life unpredictability of the world's ecosystem (although the show was transmitted under its original title in Canada). The reception for *The Last Train* was mixed, and several reviewers took the opportunity to make illuminating comparisons with *Survivors*, with Robert Hanks in *The Independent* pointing out how 'pervasively' the series recalled 'Terry Nation's 1970s apocalypse drama … in which a similarly ill-assorted group was left to struggle after mankind had been all but wiped out'. Although repeated on both terrestrial ITV and the satellite Sci-Fi Channel, *The Last Train* does not yet appear to have secured much of a lasting reputation.

The long-running end-of-the-world drama *The Tribe* shares many of the same assumptions about the loss of innocence and the fight to reclaim a more civilised future as *Survivors*. The premise of *The Tribe* is that an unexplained virus, the origins of which remain unknown, decimates the world's population. As the contagion spreads, families in Australia arrange for their children to be evacuated from the danger area until the infectious period has passed. When those children return, they discover – as the *Tribeworld* website explains – the awful truth: 'With no adults to guide, rule or protect them, the children of the world are on their own. Their task: to build a New World in their own image.' A hugely successful Australian-British co-production, more than 250 episodes of the show were filmed across five seasons between 1999 and 2003, with a 26-part spin-off sequel *A New Tomorrow* in development in 2004. *The Tribe* combines many familiar elements from children's fantasy drama with elements of soap opera to construct a complex serial following the adventures of a large ensemble cast of young characters. It is distinguished by its combination of impressive urban and rural locations with in-studio interior sets, and by the 'tribal' make-up and attire that all the characters adopt and through which they identify their allegiance (or assert their independence). Designed to appeal to a young adult audience of a similar age to the series' cast, the conflicts between good and evil that are explored are – inevitably – of a much less sophisticated nature than those seen in *Survivors*. *The Tribe*'s narrative palette is in every respect lighter and gentler in tone, although character conflicts and human relationships remain at the core of its post-apocalyptic drama.

Jeremiah also has a generationally based premise, although this adaptation of a series of graphic novels by Hermann Huppen is an altogether darker and more mature drama than *The Tribe*. Brought to the small screen by J Michael Straczynski, creator of the space-epic *Babylon 5* (1993-98), *Jeremiah* is set fifteen years after a devastating plague (known as 'The Big Death') has wiped out everyone in the world over the age of puberty. Those children who emerged unscathed from the catastrophe have now grown up into adults, inheriting a medieval world comprised of scattered settlements and communities. For the survivors, life in this new world has become – as the series' official website explains – 'a bleak and seemingly soulless attempt to stay alive – to plunder, forage or barter for food and clothes and to seek out the sordid and fleeting pleasures that briefly distract them from their lives of terror and savage desperation.' The series is structured around the efforts of Jeremiah and his companion Kurdy to seek out what they hope is the salvation to be found in the mysterious 'Valhalla Sector' (an area in which civilisation is initially thought to have survived unscathed). Fulfilling a similar role to the search for Ark in *The Last Train*, the hunt for Valhalla enables the two leading characters to travel far and wide, encountering different communities as their quest unfolds. When the series was first broadcast in the US in March 2002, many reviewers focused on the occasional nudity and strong language found in it – in the process missing many of the less controversial but far more important elements that revealed its status as a morally sophisticated adult drama. A number of recent high quality US genre shows have suffered as a result of their attempts to mix 'grown-up drama' and 'science fiction' elements within the confines of a single programme. Shows such as *Now and Again* (1999-2000), *Good vs Evil* (1999-2000) and *Dead Like Me* (2003-4) have all struggled to find a stable 'audience demographic' and been prematurely cancelled as a result. Despite some strong reviews, *Jeremiah* suffered a similar fate. Although the show was renewed, broadcast of its second season was suspended in November 2003 for over twelve months, with the concluding episodes shown only in late 2004, with no prospect of a resolution for its cliffhanger season finale. To date, in the UK, *Jeremiah* has been broadcast only on satellite station Sky One.

In particular, since '9/11', television has seen the revival of the 'what-if' catastrophe genre.

Drawing their dramatic approaches from such classics as *Threads* (1984) and *The War Game* (1985), these narrator-led docu-dramas have explored such themes as: a smallpox outbreak (*Smallpox 2002*); the collapse of the travel system (*The Day Britain Stopped* (2003)); the failure of the electricity supply (*If... The Lights Go Out* (2004)); and – in several different manifestations – the impact of a terrorist strike and its bloody aftermath. Although these pieces are wholly unlike a serial drama such as *Survivors*, they do illustrate clearly the interest of TV producers in reflecting the viewing public's anxieties about the fragility of civilisation and the numerous menaces that threaten it.

Perhaps the clearest indication of the imprint of *Survivors* on another drama can be found in the 2002 British horror film *28 Days Later*. Brought to the screen by the creative talents responsible for *Shallow Grave* (1994) and *Trainspotting* (1996), *28 Days Later* depicts a world in which a contagion of psychotic 'Rage' has reduced humankind to a race of zombies determined to prey on the few remaining survivors who have escaped infection. Describing the genesis of the project, director Danny Boyle told *Dreamwatch* in December 2002 that his production team had become interested in developing: '.. something that was kind of stolen from John Wyndham and J G Ballard and that TV show *Survivors* – we borrowed from all that, really.' Although the single biggest influence on the screenplay must be recognised as the BBC's 1981 adaptation of *The Day of the Triffids* (from which the early hospital sequences draw direct inspiration), the presence of *Survivors* is evident in both general themes and particular scenes – for instance, in the centrality of a strong and independent female lead character (Naomie Harris as Selena); in her convoy's visit to pick up supplies from a supermarket during which she instructs her companions on how to 'shop' effectively (in a direct parallel with Abby's own instructions to Greg and Jenny in "Gone Away"); in the plague of rats that overwhelms London (as depicted in "Lights of London"); and in the image of the isolated survivor signalling to others with a light in the dark of night (as Abby succeeds in doing in "Genesis"). In *28 Days Later*, the calamitous plague is also unwittingly unleashed from a laboratory – although in this case as the unintended by-product of a raid by animal liberationists rather than as the consequence of an unforeseen accident. Although the very different second half of *28 Days Later* has more in common with the horror flick than with post-apocalyptic drama, there is much in the ambience and mood of the early set-pieces that is reminiscent of *Survivors*. Even though the film-makers' rendition of deserted London streets is far more expansive and expensive than was ever available to the BBC's directors, the echoes of earlier television dramas in the atmosphere of *28 Days Later* were observed by several reviewers. *The Independent* noted: 'The desolate environs of Whitehall and Westminster make a thrillingly eerie sight, reminiscent of 1960s episodes of *Doctor Who* and 1970s what-if dramas like *Survivors*.'

The popularity of the post-apocalyptic genre is again proved by the success of the 2004 eco-catastrophe movie *The Day After Tomorrow*, which itself followed on from the 1998 'asteroid-threatening-Earth' flicks *Deep Impact* and *Armageddon*, and the alien-invasion blockbuster *Independence Day* (1996). As with the first series of *Survivors*, *The Day After Tomorrow* does make a parent's efforts to reunite with a son following the apocalypse the driving narrative of the story, yet the central reference points here – not only for the special effects-driven storyline, but for the emotional sophistication and plot structure – are more the disaster movies of the 1970s than the post-apocalyptic genre itself. Again, however, filmmakers are reflecting what they see as an audience-attracting premise – that of the ecosystem's fragility and humanity's impermanence.

AFTERMATH

The relevance of *Survivors'* terrifying premise has scarcely changed in the decades that followed its original transmission. Global society today is more interconnected and cross-reliant than ever before. Trade in foodstuffs, medicines and livestock now occurs at record-breaking volumes across the planet. The world's population is now more mobile than at any time in human history. Despite huge technological advances, there is greater concern than ever at the state of the global ecosystem, and the cutting-edge sciences of genetic modification and cloning are mired in controversy. Widespread panic ensues over each new outbreak of disease, whether it be SARS or Ebola, and fears are growing at the alarmingly common cross-species transfer of animal contagions. There is certainly little evidence to suggest that – in the event of a calamitous accident in some secret research laboratory – 21st Century men and women would find themselves any better equipped to survive the fall of civilisation than the heroes of Terry Nation's electrifying 'speculative' drama set some thirty years earlier.

CHARACTERS
(IN ORDER OF APPEARANCE)

CHARACTERS

ABBY GRANT

Abby Grant lived the comfortable and cosseted life of the Home Counties 'commuter wife' until The Death swept away all the privileges and protections of the old world. Refusing to give in to the sense of hopelessness she at first feels, Abby discovers reserves of strength and perseverance that she has not had cause to

Abby Grant. © Hereford Times

call upon before. Her determination to discover the fate of her young son Peter, away at boarding school at the time of the plague, gives her a sense of purpose and a reason to go on in the first weeks after the catastrophe. At the same time, Abby is aware of the need to find like-minded souls who can help her establish a new, viable community in the relative safety of the countryside. She is surprised to discover that her pragmatism, bravery and intelligence make her a natural leader in the eyes of others. She quickly wins the friendship and loyalty of both Greg and Jenny, who help her in her search for Peter and in setting up the Grange commune. Throughout all the privations and dangers that the community face, Abby remains committed to securing their collective survival. When the burdens of leadership become exhausting, Abby finds solace and intimacy in the arms of Jimmy Garland; and with it a renewal of energy and confidence. Returning to the Grange, Abby learns that her son Peter is alive and well, and she leaves the community to reunite with him. Although she never returns, in the months that follow, Greg and Jenny learn of her movements through their encounters with other survivors. Abby visited Manny's community in London in pursuit of a lead on Peter, but left disappointed to head north through the city. Manny insists that she will not have made it out alive, but he would not be the first to underestimate Abby's tenacity. In the spring, Alistair McFadden brings news to Whitecross that Jimmy Garland was following in her trail, hoping to catch up with Abby – and Peter.

JENNY RICHARDS

Working as a temporary secretary before The Death, Jenny initially appears to be an unlikely candidate for survival. However, she ultimately proves to have a reserve of strength and resilience that help her to adapt successfully to the rigorous demands of her new way of life.

In Abby she finds a kindred spirit with similar views on the way forward, while in Greg she finds a man she loves, until his untimely death two years later. Her relationship with Greg is further cemented by their joint adoption by John and Lizzie, who treat them as 'mummy' and 'daddy'. As her affection for the children steadily grows, her initial unwillingness to take on the maternal role quickly subsides. Jenny's later pregnancy causes her much distress, especially as it coincides with the destruction of the Grange by fire and the prolonged absence of medically-trained Ruth, and results in an afterbirth infection that ultimately leads to Paul's sacrifice on her behalf. Jenny ensures that his heroic act will never be forgotten by naming her son after him. Her long-held fears over Greg's possible future absence from her life are eventually justified by his decision to go with Agnes to Norway – a trip from which he will return, but never to her side. Desperate to see him again, Jenny sets out with Charles and Hubert on a long and fruitless quest to be reunited with her 'husband'. During this time, she is thwarted by bad luck and by Agnes's deliberate – and secret – attempts to prevent Greg from returning to her, as well as suffering from her own paranoia that he no longer loves her. However wearying she finds her

Jenny Richards. © Anne Christie

experiences during this search, they do afford her a new level of independence and composure that ironically prepares her for the eventual news of Greg's death. Although she never sees Greg again, she is at least comforted by the knowledge that his love for her and their children was far more important to him than his attempts to rebuild the nation. Though flattered by the attentions of Alec Campbell, she declines the romantic existence he offers her in Scotland and crucially asks him to switch the power back on, before returning to England to be with her children.

TOM PRICE

Before The Death, the itinerant Tom Price lived on the margins of society, working as a fruits and hops picker in the summer and turning his hand to odd jobs in the building trade in the winter. Despite his fondness for storytelling and exaggeration, his life was marked by poverty and exclusion. Not over-bright, he has more than his share of native cunning. When the catastrophe struck, Tom sought shelter in a makeshift hilltop shelter that he lashed together himself. He shuns Jenny when they first meet, urging her to 'keep away from people,' until his own curiosity gets the better of him and he ventures back towards civilisation. It takes time for

Tom Price and Barney. © Hereford Times

Tom to absorb the reality of the plague's horrific legacy. At first he is willing to strike whichever temporary alliances he thinks will secure him a full belly and a warm fireside – telling whatever stories are necessary in the process. He joins up with Abby's group, and then quickly defects to Wormley's militia. Stealing a cache of rifles, he deserts once more and sets out for an independent life on the road, although he soon finds the responsibilities and burdens of the solitary life harder than he cares to admit. When his wafer-thin bravado is crushed, he throws in his lot with the Grange settlers – and delights to find in Barney a doting dependent. At the same time, Tom resents Abby's and Greg's efforts to make him work for a living, and there are frequent clashes over his lazy and slipshod contributions to settlement life. The darkest depths of Tom's personality are finally revealed in his drunken and brutal murder of Wendy on the night of the May Day party, and by his efforts to implicate Barney as the killer. When Barney is executed for the crime, Tom's deceit collapses and he reveals his guilt to Abby and Greg. Soon afterwards, wounded in the gun battle with Huxley's men, Tom manages to shoot Huxley dead, before being killed himself. When Tom is buried, only the two leaders of the Grange settlement know of the desire for absolution that might have inspired Tom's act of self-sacrifice.

GREG PRESTON

When the plague struck, Greg Preston, a skilled civil engineer, was working on a major construction project in mainland Europe. Returning home by helicopter, he finds his wife Jeannie – his partner in a troubled and childless marriage – dead. Determined that he must

Greg Preston. © Lucy Fleming

control his own fate and be free of obligation, he initially resists the efforts of other survivors to tie him into their plans. Yet after meeting Jenny and then Abby, and later the children John and Lizzie, his view softens and he comes to accept new commitments – becoming a partner for Jenny, a surrogate father for the children, and the hard-working manager of Abby's settlement. Greg repeatedly risks his life to protect the community and its members, and shoulders some awesome responsibilities – acting as the executioner of one of the settlement's own members following the guilty verdict of a murder trial. With Abby gone, it is Greg's strength and resolve that ensures that the survivors of the Grange fire make their way to the shelter of Whitecross. With Jenny pregnant with his child, Greg recognises that he must settle and commit himself to Charles's community, and again take on a joint leadership role. Despite the many challenges he confronts in the months that follow, Greg finds himself torn by the news that Agnes brings to Whitecross about the desperate lack of technicians in Norway. His loyalty to his family and to the community require him to stay, but both his curiosity and his sense of frustration demand that he go. Although they share the pain of separation, Jenny concedes that he must be allowed to travel to Norway and investigate. When he and Agnes return, Greg becomes a roving ambassador for the Norwegian plan, visiting settlements to secure their co-operation before moving on to recruit others. In the process, he inspires an impressive degree of organisation and industry across the country. Efforts to rendezvous with Jenny and Charles are repeatedly thwarted, and when Greg contracts a fatal infection, he knows that any hope of reuniting with his wife and family has been lost. To exact retribution on the gang who tried to kill him and who are now threatening his loved ones, Greg tricks them into a deadly ambush, before his own infection reaches crisis point.

Anne Tranter. © Anne Christie

ANNE TRANTER

Anne Tranter lived a life of luxury before The Death and, although totally unprepared for the practicalities of the world the plague has left behind, still proves to be a born survivor due to her keen sense of self-preservation at all costs. She initially forms a partnership with Vic Thatcher, but after accidentally crippling him, quickly transfers her attentions to Greg, whom she views as a better option for survival than Vic. Anne fails to realise that her self-serving concerns and lack of compassion have done little to endear her to the engineer, and she is both stunned and angry when he elects to leave her behind. Her horrendous decision to do the same to Vic underlines just how little remorse she feels for her actions and how callous she is prepared to be in order to live her life in the way she chooses. Anne eventually finds herself back in Vic's vicinity at the Grange community after causing trouble at another settlement; she appears to have changed little and is accompanied by a new partner named Donny. On discovering that Vic is alive, she wisely fears for her safety, but on seeing him again still stands by her decision to leave him behind. Later forced to plead to Vic for her life, Anne reveals that her survival means everything to her; once she has secured his understanding, she drops her cold façade for the first time, admitting her true selfish nature. The following morning she leaves the Grange alone, and although she is never seen again it is clear that she will have no trouble surviving.

VIC THATCHER

Before The Death, Vic worked heavy machinery on a timber wharf. As a survivor, he immediately demonstrates a practical streak by electing to scavenge for food to store in a Portakabin in an isolated quarry. However, he is joined in his endeavours by spoilt rich girl

Anne Tranter, who views Vic as a ticket to relative luxury in the new world. After Anne accidentally overturns a tractor on Vic's legs, his prospects look bad. Although Greg tries his best to set his legs with splints, Vic soon faces the future as a cripple. Worse still, Anne makes the incredibly callous decision to leave her former partner behind to die. During the lonely and harrowing months that follow, Vic is driven to the edge of insanity and despair. When he is eventually discovered by Greg, he is dishevelled and desperate and, on learning of Anne's solo contribution to his terrible experience, is consumed by thoughts of revenge. As a recruit to the community at the Grange, Vic is frustrated by his perceived lack of ability to contribute, and eventually makes a suicide attempt. Vic takes little interest in Greg's subsequent idea that he could play an important role as teacher to John and Lizzie, as

Vic Thatcher and Lizzie. © Anne Christie

he is still too preoccupied by his crippled condition and thoughts of Anne. When fate brings Anne to the Grange, Vic is initially determined to exact a very final sort of revenge on her. However, he ultimately relents when he identifies with Anne's plea that life is more important than anything else. Freed from his all-consuming thoughts of revenge, Vic is able to contribute to the day-to-day life of the community. Despite his efforts to escape, Vic dies in the tragic winter fire that destroys the Grange.

CHARLES VAUGHAN

Charming and charismatic Welshman Charles Vaughan is a resourceful, resilient and highly motivated organiser. A skilled architect with a passion for restoring old buildings, his life before The Death reflected a devotion to the ideals of self-sufficiency. In reaction to the

Charles Vaughan. © Anne Christie

plague, he causes several women at his newly-founded Maredell settlement to fall pregnant, firmly believing in the necessity to plan ahead to the next generation and so ensure the future of the human race. His insistence that all women of child-bearing age should accept this responsibility is a view that brings him into conflict with women whenever the subject is raised. After his first settlement is devastated by a poisoning accident, Charles establishes the Whitecross community, becoming its effective leader and manager. There, he soon settles down to a monogamous relationship with Pet Simpson, whom he loves deeply. After the Grange residents are forced to relocate to Whitecross, Charles is willing to share leadership responsibilities with Greg, despite the tensions that this generates for both of them. Although it is Greg who eventually leaves for Norway, Charles is no less enthusiastic about Agnes's plans for reconstruction and trade. As he travels the country, persuading and cajoling others to join the struggle to create a new social order, his commitment never falters, despite the many dangers he encounters. His efforts, alongside those of Greg and Agnes, produce some remarkable results, but the return of electricity, the birth of a new economy, and the formation of a new governing council remain, for Charles, only the first steps in the long journey back to civilisation.

JOHN AND LIZZIE

John and Lizzie are two ebullient children who seem largely unfazed by the horror of The Death. As their adoptive parents, Greg and Jenny quickly become protective and loving towards their new charges, hoping to ensure that they grow up as well-adjusted, happy and bright children, despite what they have experienced. Although the children suffer the loss of many fellow survivors and often find themselves in danger from unstable individuals – such as Lincoln and Kane – their enthusiasm for the new world around them never appears to be diminished. The children cope well with Greg's departure for Norway, but begin to show some understandable concern when Jenny also leaves them behind while she searches for their adoptive father. Although their closeness to surrogate parents Pet and Jack gives them some security, their playing of 'mothers and fathers' would seem to be indicative of subconscious compensation on their part. When, against the odds, John is reunited with his real mother, it is revealed that he has always harboured fears that she did not send for him before The Death because she did not want to see him; however, he and his mother are eventually reconciled. When Greg finally returns, John in particular suffers as a result of his adoptive father's verbal rejection, from which it can only be hoped he recovers. After Jenny's trek to Scotland – during which she chooses to give the children a life with electric power and therefore a potentially

John Millon. © Anne Christie

Lizzie Willoughby. © Lucy Fleming

better existence with greater opportunities – she returns to Sloton to be with them. John and Lizzie are undoubtedly set to face many new challenges if they are to reach adulthood in the dangerous post-Death world.

JIMMY GARLAND

Jimmy Garland, who considered himself to be a misfit in the old world, is thrilled to be alive at a time when the skills he learned through his military and expeditionary experiences can be put to practical use. By the time Abby meets Garland, he has long since set his sights on regaining control of the Waterhouse estate that – as the seventeenth Earl of Waterhouse – is his by hereditary right. Garland sees himself as a natural leader and is determined to oppose the estate's current manager, Knox, especially as the man does not have the requisite knowledge to run the estate effectively. In securing his aim, Garland shows immense bravery and ability, risking his life for what he believes is right. The former soldier falls for Abby and she for him, but he sees his war with Knox – and

Jimmy Garland. © Anne Christie

the subsequent reclamation of his estate when Knox dies – as his priority. However, when Abby later comes looking for him, the pair finally consummate their relationship, and by this point are able to share their experiences of leading their respective communities. Garland shows true sensitivity to Abby's feelings, and she values both his listening ear and his promise that he will help her to find Peter; however, she is not willing to give up her community just yet. When Abby later leaves the Grange to follow a lead on Peter, Garland sets off to track her down. The last we hear of Garland is from Alistair McFadden, who relates that he was heading for the coast to look for his wife and child.

WENDY

Fleeing from the city as the plague spreads, the young Wendy meets up with the elderly grandmother Emma Cohen at her family's weekend cottage. Both are relieved to end their isolation, and despite their differences of age, experience and temperament, they quickly settle

Wendy. © Anne Christie

into a mother-daughter relationship that both appear to be comfortable with. The results of Wendy's foraging trips prove meagre, and the couple's hunger becomes acute. Despite the dangers, Wendy decides to widen the search for food. As she sets off, she seems uncertain whether or not she will return, and if she really needs Emma as much as Emma confesses that she needs her. But the outside world soon proves a threatening place – as both marauding dogs and the unwelcome propositioning of Tom Price cause Wendy to reconsider her options. Although often naïve in her dealings with others, Wendy is still capable of acting with both intelligence and guile. She steals Tom's fish and escapes from him despite the risks this involves, and later helps Abby to trap the witless tramp in his own van. Wendy clearly finds reassurance and relief in the founding of the Grange settlement. Content to work in the background under Emma's guidance, Wendy recognises only when it is too late what Tom is capable of. After the May Day party he drunkenly pursues her to her room, where she meets a bloody end. Wendy is buried in the grounds of the Grange, next to Barney – who was wrongly convicted of her murder and executed.

EMMA COHEN

Before the plague, Emma Cohen was the matriarchal grandmother of a large Jewish family.

When The Death struck, Emma was alone at her son's weekend cottage, preparing for the arrival of family guests who would never come. Emma was relieved of her isolation by the unexpected arrival of Wendy, and together the two women tried to eke out a scavenger existence. Emma is naturally maternal to the young and inexperienced Wendy, encouraging her in her foraging efforts and warning her of the dangers she faces. When Emma is rescued from an attack by a dog pack, as Jenny and Greg lure the animals away, she confides to Abby her frustration with her age and frailty, but concedes that she has already discovered reserves of strength she was unaware that she had. Emma is delighted by the formation of the Grange community, and by the opportunity it affords her to take on the role of cook and housekeeper for a new extended 'family'. Emma is also a keen advocate for all those

Emma Cohen. © Anne Christie

in the community she sees as in need of support – who at different times include Vic, Barney, Laura and her baby, as well as Wendy and the children. Her role as carer and nurturer does not preclude Emma from challenging those in authority or who threaten her community – she questions Abby's right to rule by decree; she demands that Vic's needs be taken more seriously; she rejects Greg's and Abby's assumption of Barney's guilt; and she stands up to Huxley's armed raiding party with nothing more than her knitting to protect her. Her compassion and determination remain intact until Emma falls victim to the fire that decimates the Grange.

BARNEY

Barney is sheltering in the Grange after being attacked by dogs, when he is discovered there by Lizzie. At first, Greg and Jenny regard the simple man as gentle and harmless, and John and Lizzie consider him as a playmate. Tom Price, meanwhile, takes Barney under his wing and the pair become inseparable. Barney is pleased to have Tom's friendship, while Tom – though fond of Barney – undoubtedly sees him as someone over whom he can assert his authority. After he murders Wendy, Tom ruthlessly decides to use his friend as a scapegoat, knowing that Barney will be incapable of defending himself; his advice to Barney that he should flee sealing the simple man's fate. Throughout his subsequent trial, Barney is eager to help but entirely confused by the proceedings, although he does manage to profess that he did not kill Wendy. Circumstantial evidence brings the community members to find him guilty, while Greg's argument that it wouldn't be right to simply banish a murderer who could strike again leads to a terrible sentence of execution. Greg literally draws the short straw and executes Barney, who is buried in the grounds of the Grange alongside the equally innocent Wendy.

When Greg is faced with another possible murderer at Whitecross, the memory of Barney's tragically unnecessary fate leads him to rule out the possibility of execution.

PAUL PITMAN

Paul is an open, cheerful and optimistic man whose agricultural expertise proves vital when he arrives at the fledgling Grange settlement. Before The Death he had lived at a commune

with his young daughter and learned a great deal about working the land. His almost cowboy-like appearance – Montana-style hat decorated with wampum, long fleecy coat and tall boots over his jeans – accurately conveys his laid-back, unassuming nature. However, he does become urgent and quite tactless – a failing he willingly admits – when it comes to his assessment of the community's farming achievements. Paul is able to advise where they are going wrong and is quickly accepted as an important member of the settlement, with Greg regularly choosing him as a second for expeditions and recces, despite his inexperience with armaments. Although happy at the Grange, he becomes keen to find a partner and unknowingly catches Ruth's eye some time before they finally commit to each other after resettling at Whitecross. Fate is cruel to the couple: soon after, Paul

Paul Pitman. © Anne Christie

volunteers to carry out a dangerous trip into Birmingham to retrieve medical supplies with which Ruth can save Jenny's life, but he returns sick and has to be isolated. Clothed in protective plastic sacks, Ruth is with Paul when he dies. Although theirs was a relatively new relationship, Ruth is nevertheless beside herself with grief and considers suicide. Jenny decides to name her baby son after Paul so that he will never be forgotten and remains forever grateful to him, regularly referring to the heroic sacrifice he made.

CHARMIAN WENTWORTH

Charmian was Arthur Russell's personal secretary before The Death. Bizarrely, during the initial aftermath and their first few weeks at the Grange community, she and Arthur continue to assume the same roles, and for some time she still addresses her ex-boss as Mr Russell.

Despite Arthur's misgivings, it is Charmian who decides that she likes the set-up at the Grange and wants to stay on. Charmian gradually assumes a more equal status with her former employer, crucially taking an opposing view to him over the verdict on Barney after Wendy's death. During the months that follow, Charmian's considerate and dependable nature make her a valuable asset to the community. However, alongside several of her new friends, Charmian is tragically killed during the fire at the Grange.

ARTHUR RUSSELL

As a manager and financier who lived a comfortable life even more privileged than Abby Grant's, Arthur Russell is reluctant to face the true reality of the catastrophe that has befallen the world. Arriving at the Grange in the care of his faithful secretary Charmian, Arthur seems scarcely to have acknowledged that the old order of things has gone forever. He expects Charmian to carry on in her role as his employee, and greets his hosts as if they were neighbours at an upmarket caravan site. Arthur is also profoundly unrealistic – he remains committed to his plan to travel to an uninhabited Scottish island to which he holds the legal deeds, to live the life of a fisherman hermit. It is not a plan about which he has sought his companion Charmian's opinion. Life at the Grange quickly begins to exert its influence over Arthur, and once he has agreed to share his supply of hidden contraband, he comes to accept his role within the settlement under Abby's and Greg's leadership. He finds farm labouring hard, but relishes the opportunity to use his negotiating and organisational skills. Arthur's plain-speaking temperament and apparently fixed opinions often hide a more complex emotional make-up. Arthur is at first devastated by the fire at the Grange, and mourns the death of Charmian and the others acutely. He soon finds renewed purpose at Whitecross,

Arthur Russell and Charmian Wentworth. © Anne Christie

compiling a census, helping with the teaching of the children, and running the community's stores. When Arthur contracts a serious virus from Mark Carter's failed settlement, his morale gives way completely and – seemingly unwilling to fight the infection – he quietly succumbs to it.

RUTH ANDERSON

Ruth arrives at the Grange community in a state of ill-health, having been abandoned there by another group of survivors. When she recovers, she reveals that she was studying to be a doctor before The Death and has three years of vital medical training under her belt. News of Ruth's presence in the area soon spreads; her skills and devotion to her profession prove

invaluable in advising and healing the sick. Ruth falls in love with Paul just as she learns that Jenny has an afterbirth infection. When he dies after risking his life to retrieve the drugs his new love needs in order to operate on Jenny, Ruth is utterly devastated and considers taking her own life. Soon after, she is taken to London against her will and there finds herself torn between her duty to her new patients and that to her friends back home. Her impartial code of professional ethics proves to be so unshakeable that Charles and Greg have difficulty persuading her to leave the five-hundred-strong London settlement behind. On her return to Whitecross, Ruth's diagnostic skills continue to prove invaluable to the community, especially when it is threatened by a flu-like illness; she wisely counsels that the morale of those who have succumbed is the key to the matter, believing that its victims are suffering from a delayed depressive reaction to The Death. By now, Ruth is adamant that her

Ruth Anderson. © Anne Christie

position as the 'only known doctor' leaves her totally fulfilled; however, she sensibly realises that the new world is not to everyone's taste and that many of her fellow survivors long for their old lives. This is most apparent through her opposition to Charles's longed-for 'baby boom'; Ruth fears that, without contraception, the female survivors face a new dark age in which they will lose the independence that women had only recently gained before The Death. Ruth remains behind when Charles and Pet move on to Challenor, her unique skills ensuring that she will remain in great demand for the rest of her days.

PET SIMPSON

Pet Simpson is optimistic and caring by nature, an outlook she claims to derive from a happy upbringing as the youngest child of a large family. She enthusiastically welcomes the survivors of the Grange fire to Whitecross, offering them the friendship, support and comfort they sorely need. As Charles's common-law wife, Pet always supports him in his endeavours to lead the community, but has no trouble speaking her own mind. Her fierce loyalty to Charles and Whitecross is most obvious when either his leadership or their way of life is directly threatened; she relies heavily on her instincts in such situations. When Greg reveals that Charles fathered children at Maredell, Pet's fears that she could be infertile are confirmed. However, the situation strengthens rather than damages her relationship with Charles, who admits that he loves her as he would a wife. When the future of the community is threatened by news of the world beyond Whitecross, Pet is vociferous in her criticism of Charles's and Greg's plans, but her protests fall on deaf ears. She begins a new life at Challenor, where she is literally left holding the baby – Jenny's Paul – and together with Jack helps to look after John and Lizzie while

Pet Simpson. © Anne Christie

their adoptive parents are away; Jenny having total faith in Pet's ability to care for her children. Pet is later reunited with Charles at Sloton Spencer and remains in contact with him by telephone after his subsequent departure, patiently waiting for her loved one to return. She is certain to require a great deal more tolerance if Charles continues to pursue both his national and his political ambitions.

HUBERT GOSS

To many in the Whitecross community, Hubert is a source of constant irritation and exasperation. A grizzled former farm hand, he is seen by some as little more than a grumbler and a malcontent, whose efforts to avoid work and freeload off others are as transparent as his tall stories. Hubert certainly does little to ingratiate himself with those who know him well – his clothes are as grubby as he is; his manner is gruff and direct; and his prejudices are numerous. Hubert is a source of rumours and ill-founded gossip, and yet he constantly complains that he is undervalued and underappreciated. He alerts Charles to the terrible truth about Alistair McFadden's past, offering to keep quiet about it in return for a better life for himself. To Mina, who rebuffs his romantic approaches, he is a menace. However, despite his recurrent moaning, he does at least usually take his shepherding duties seriously. It is when Hubert leaves Whitecross behind and joins Jenny and Charles in their quest for Greg and for civilisation, that his own nature begins to change. His old antics persist, but alongside them there is growing evidence of Hubert's loyalty and sense of commitment to his friends. When the group become trapped in Brod's settlement, it is Hubert who shoulders the responsibility to fire the fatal crossbow arrow; and when gunfire breaks out at the peaceful windmill community, he grabs his rifle and runs towards the shoot-out. Hubert is trusted to act as the group's scout, and it is he who finds Alec Campbell first. And at many of the communities

Hubert Goss. © Anne Christie

they visit, it is Hubert who tends to the horses and guards them through the night, or volunteers his labour behind the scenes. And, whatever his own views on the plan, Hubert does all he can to frustrate Sam Mead's efforts to wreck Charles's hopes of hydroelectric power, at no little risk to himself. As Hubert journeys southwards, back towards the comforting arms of his new lover Blossom, it is certain that his own 'heroic deeds' will feature prominently in the fireside tales he will tell of his adventures.

JACK WOOD

Jack, who worked at the Liverpool docks before The Death, found himself employed at the Whitecross settlement in the role of carpenter and handyman. Generally cheerful and outgoing, he is content with his new, simple way of life and has no desire to go back to the old world order, as depicted in his cynical attitude towards Arthur's census. After Paul dies, he uses his carpentry skills to build a serviceable and vital quarantine house, which is to be used by new visitors and community members returning to Whitecross. Jack quietly longs for a partner, and it is perhaps the absence of such a person that causes him later to contract what Ruth describes as 'broken heart syndrome'. After Agnes arrives and relates the problems facing her countrymen back in Norway, Charles persuades an uncertain Jack to accompany her and Greg there by balloon. Six months later, Jack returns with Greg and Agnes and takes news of their return back to Charles and Jenny. After recovering from a fever, Jack joins Pet at Challenor and takes on a new role as a dependable and loving surrogate father to John, Lizzie and baby Paul; a responsibility he will continue to accept after the move to Sloton Spencer.

MANNY

Before The Death, cockney Manny was a 'fruit and veg' man. Now, force of circumstance (together with some wily political manoeuvring) has propelled him to a position of power and influence beyond anything he was ever likely to have attained before. With the support of some able organisers, he has moulded the remains of London's population into a viable functioning community, in which many of the luxuries of the old world persist – although it is one based almost entirely on scavenging upon diminishing resources. Manny has secured his position through a combination of charisma, bribery, duplicity and – in all likelihood – bloodshed. But the avuncular and paternal personality he projects to those around him hides a darker and more sinister nature. In truth, Manny is both in denial and out of his depth. He asserts that the responsibility for the fate of the human race rests within the community he governs, yet he refuses to face up to the seriousness of the 'London sickness', and continues to prevaricate over the 'Big Move' to the Isle of Wight that might save his followers. He also responds angrily to any challenges to his authority. As things become more grave, Manny opts to do everything in his power to protect his position at the top of his failing empire – including the murder of both opponents and allies. When Manny attempts to stop Greg, Charles and Ruth leaving London, he is willing to risk the deaths of all three – including the doctor he claims is so vital to his community's survival. It seems that Manny is more angered by Ruth's defiance of his instructions than he is concerned for the well-being of those in his care. Manny falls victim to one of his own botched attempts to protect his rule – as the wounded Wally intervenes to protect the Whitecross travellers and shoots him dead.

CHARACTERS

NESSIE

As formidable as she is warm-hearted, Nessie is a resilient and wily character, and a more than capable nurse. Serving diligently as the effective ward sister of the London hospital, she initially supports the kidnapping of Ruth, due to her concern about the ailing health of the community's existing doctor. When Ruth arrives, she provides support, encouragement and reassurance, urging Nessie to recognise her talents to the fullest. When the doctor collapses and dies, Nessie takes a critical decision to face up to Manny and to urge Ruth to leave while she still can. It is a momentous decision, and demonstrates Nessie's acceptance of the responsibilities she has inherited. Her squaring up to Manny is a turning point, showing her determination to resist his bullying manner – and evidence of what he can expect in future. Anticipating Manny's ban, she gives a bag full of vital medical supplies to Ruth to take back to Whitecross. With Manny dead, Nessie would be a prime candidate for the new ruling council for the London community that Wally is likely to recommend.

WALLY

Wally is a dissident figure who finds unjust and unreasonable authority intolerable. His age, his political beliefs and his temperament make his recurrent conflict with Manny inevitable. He is hot-headed and impatient, and the competition between them is uneven – Manny is more skilled as a political manipulator and public negotiator than Wally, something the results of their electoral competition prove all too well. Exiled from the community because of his intransigence, Wally haunts the settlement from the outside. He intervenes to save Charles and Greg from the rat attack, and realises the importance of getting Charles to the centre for medical attention. Tricked and expelled once more, Wally is rightly suspicious of Manny's motives, but nevertheless agrees to go to Whitecross to send word of the movements of Charles, Greg and Ruth. On his return – and probably against his better judgment – he agrees to help Manny on a foraging trip, which proves to be a trap: he is shot and left for dead. Wally survives and returns to exact retribution on Manny, and to save the Whitecross trio at the same time. Rather than flee London after the killing, he intends to return to the community – potentially as its new leader. He also pledges to continue the search for the replacement doctor the Oval settlement needs more now than ever.

MINA

Of all the Whitecross settlers, Mina is both the most solitary and the most self-possessed. By choice she lives separately from the rest of the Whitecross community with her baby, Matthew, and – although happy to live on the fringes of the group – she does not welcome the excessive intrusion of others. Mina's position at one remove from the settlement is reinforced by what others see as her eccentricities – her interest in collecting herbs and wild plants, enthusiasm for art and nature, and sometimes unsettlingly odd behaviour. When anxieties at Whitecross are running high, Mina becomes branded as a witch by some – one whose curses have brought bad luck to the settlement. It is a myth that Hubert, whose clumsy lecherous advances Mina has rebuffed, does much to encourage. When the situation has blown over, Mina agrees to stay on at the settlement. While collecting plants by the canal, she finds herself drawn to the bargee John Millen. His gentle good humour and quiet intelligence make him an engaging figure, and his clear interest in Mina is immediately reciprocated. When the barge arrives at Whitecross the next day, she is shocked to find it in the hands of two much younger and uncouth men, and determines to discover John's true fate. Horrified to find his corpse floating in the canal, she finds the courage to physically confront his killers before being restrained by Charles. Still mournful and depressed, Mina later contracts the 'flu brought to Whitecross from Mark Carter's settlement.

LEWIS FEARNS

Lewis is a sensitive Christian, who was curate of a quiet country parish before The Death. Although the plague initially caused him to reject his faith in God, his experience of nature's buoyant survival in the new world leads him back to his former belief system; a brave decision to wear his shirt back-to-front as a makeshift dog collar signalling to others his return to his faith. Lewis's words about spiritual nourishment influence new arrivals Judy and Philip to abandon the Whitecross set-up, whereas news of his status leads Daniella and Jack to abandon their regular work in order to make clerical accoutrements for him. In such a way, Lewis's presence has a significant and – from Greg's and Charles's point of view – worrying effect upon the community. Jenny is quite indignant at Lewis's sudden reaffirmation of faith, unable to comprehend his belief in God; however, their conflict proves to be indirectly responsible for alleviating her post-natal depression, and the pair reach an understanding. Although Lewis becomes plagued by self-doubt over his worth to the community as its parson, he does ultimately preside over a harvest festival service. Lewis's life is cut tragically short when he attempts to reason with Kane and Grice during their kidnap of John and Lizzie. Ironically, it is Kane's reaction to his dog collar that causes the curate to be shot in cold blood.

ALAN

Alan is one of few strong young men at Whitecross and is therefore initially employed to undertake much of the heavy labour at the settlement. Before The Death, Alan's father was in the army, an experience that leads Alan to make direct comparisons with his new existence, viewing Charles as the equivalent of a commanding officer. Alan's simplistic take on the new world is evidenced by the fact that he sees Lewis Fearns' reclamation of faith as merely an opportunity to shirk his responsibilities. The arrival of several female recruits at Whitecross gives Alan the perfect opportunity to behave like a red-blooded male. It is Melanie who principally catches his eye and is responsible for his move to join the younger group at the mill. He is soon sleeping with Melanie. He realises that he is no match for her intellectually or in terms of background, but is nevertheless quite happy to remain her 'bit of rough' when required. His effect upon Sally is very different: as well as falling pregnant by him, she has also fallen in love with him. However, Charles's views protect Alan's independence – he is not expected to stand

Alan and Sally. © Lucy Fleming

257

by Sally – and his promiscuous behaviour is condoned rather than criticised. Alan begins to follow Melanie's lead as far as the pull of the outside world is concerned, and is only too pleased to join her on an expedition away from Whitecross to find out more about Lars Carlsson's endeavours. If Melanie will let him, it seems likely that he will join her in an exploration of the new world.

DANIELLA

Daniella is a loud, single-minded Italian woman who arrives at Whitecross at the time of the sniper scare. Relieved to be with people again after some time alone, she quickly slots into the daily life at Whitecross, taking on domestic chores and supervising new arrivals. Lewis's revelation that he is a priest delights Daniella, who is also a devout Catholic. She believes that she can now be relieved of her burden of sin through confession. Both her unwillingness to understand that he is unable to take her confession as a Church of England priest and her subsequent refusal to stop spending her time creating clerical vestments for him are typical of her tendency to hear only what she wants to hear. This is further exemplified by her inability to see the Midsummer party as anything but a wedding breakfast for Sally and Alan, despite Charles's protestations otherwise.

MELANIE

Melanie's flirtatious and confident approach ruffles several feathers after her arrival at Whitecross. Before The Death, she lived an exciting life with a film director boyfriend, a whirlwind of movies, parties, shopping, fine clothes and weekend trips to Cannes by Lamborghini. Given this existence, it is little wonder that she is bored rigid by her new, rustic life and looks for alternative excitement whenever the opportunity arises, be it through the

Heather Wright. © Lucy Fleming

dangerous rope game, teasing Whitecross's men-folk or the trip to Linden. Last on Mel's list is the prospect of motherhood, an issue that leads her to encourage Ruth to find a decent contraceptive and thus places her in direct opposition to Charles, who is desperate to see a baby boom at Whitecross. She is aware that all the men at the settlement have eyes for her and enjoys their attention, but is sleeping only with Alan, whose attentions she wisely refuses at certain times of the month. Her fiercely independent spirit leads her to be protective not only of her own freedom, but also of that of her followers at the mill, as demonstrated by her assertion that Sally has the right to play the rope game, despite the inherent dangers of miscarriage. Melanie is desperate to leave Whitecross, as evidenced by her description of Greg's methane-powered motorbike engine as 'the best thing that's ever happened here' and her interest in the implications of Carlsson's activities. Despite the fact that she does not leave Whitecross via the balloon, there can be little doubt that Melanie will decide to move on soon, following in Judy's and Philip's optimistic footsteps.

SALLY

Sally is a traditional-minded girl who, along with Melanie, arrived at Whitecross as one of a group of new arrivals from a failed settlement. Although young and inexperienced, she is still cynical enough to recognise Mark Carter's failings and self-serving motivation. After sleeping with Alan, for whom she quickly develops feelings, she finds herself pregnant. She is distressed at this news as she realises that there is no chance of Alan agreeing to live with her as if they were husband and wife. At the Midsummer party held in her honour, Charles states that the whole community will be responsible for her baby, exacerbating Sally's concerns over ownership of the child, which she is beginning to feel is no longer her own. That night, much to Charles's dismay, Sally loses the baby after insisting on playing the rope game at the mill. However, when it later becomes clear that Greg is leaving for Norway, Sally does offer to help Jenny with baby Paul.

AGNES CARLSSON

Agnes grew up in Skaggerund, Norway, where she found it difficult to make friends, always being closer to her father Lars. When The Death struck and both she and her father were spared, they were prompted by the plight of their starving countrymen to seek help elsewhere and bravely travelled to England by boat. While at a place called Felbridge, Agnes hit on the idea of taking a hot-air balloon around England and recording information on settlements as they travelled. Agnes arrives at Whitecross soon after her father is killed when their balloon crashes nearby; as she explains the purpose of their ballooning expedition, the Norwegian predicament and her radical view that they should abandon Whitecross, she comes over as a determined and persuasive character. So effective are her arguments that she soon finds herself accompanied by Jack and Greg – to whom she is immediately attracted – and on her way back to Norway. Returning six months later, she remains intent on talking to as many people as she can about the problems back in Norway and helping Greg in his efforts to restore the English nation; however, she is frustrated by his love for Jenny, from whom she attempts to keep him. Her absolute devotion to Greg is later demonstrated by her brave decision to follow him to Cawston Farm despite the potentially fatal danger of infection; and, after his death, by her attempts to continue his work in his name. Through her endeavours back at Felbridge Camp, Agnes displays a great deal of ingenuity – setting up a façade of order and stability and utilising Greg as a figurehead of a new government and currency, despite the engineer's death. Although Charles and Jenny do not trust her attempts to convince everyone that they must now unite in Greg's name to establish both a system of law and order and a council of representatives, her objectives are ultimately revealed to be creditable – a fact that is initially belied by her secrecy and unsympathetic nature. Agnes is presumably set to play an important role in the new government that she almost single-handedly founds.

EDITH WALTER

Edith Walter is a strong maternal figure whose hold over her young sons is slipping in the frightening new world in which she and her family find themselves. Since her eldest son Tom left, she has been battling against the odds to keep the family farm going – grateful that the plague has spared so many of her family. Greg and Agnes had been impressed by the thriving Walters' smallholding, but after the departure of Tom, Brod arrived to uproot the settlement and seduce her two younger sons, Steve and Owen, with tales of the brigand life. Forced to join Brod's settlement, Edith endures her new lot, hoping that the return of Tom will be the catalyst for a revival of the farm. She is encouraged by the arrival of Charles, but fears that he has overplayed his hand when his attempt to break apart Brod's settlement fails. When Brod is killed, Edith returns to the farm, and after Charles leaves in search of Tom, she attempts to revive her settlement – against the odds, with minimal resources, and in the face of the surly apathy of her sons. In her desperation, she even urges Agnes to use her charms to keep the boys from leaving. When Charles returns, Edith supports his efforts to found a new market at the railway station. Her disappointment at Charles's failure to find Tom is replaced by delight when the latter arrives by steam train.

Edith Walter. © Denis Lill

FRANK GARNER

Frank Garner was a 'head-hunter' before The Death, working for a personnel selection firm. He therefore has a keen grasp of human psychology and an ability to manipulate both events and people to his own advantage. However, he is also kind-hearted, and when Charles and Jenny first meet him they discover that it is this attribute that has trapped him as a leader of a settlement, which he helped to get on its feet by instituting therapy sessions. Frank believes that an Indian girl named Rutna – who considers him to be the reincarnation of the guru Maharajah G – is the real reason for the settlement's success. Although he is not sold on her ideas of fatalism and pre-destiny, his principal reason for deciding to leave the community is that he has a pacemaker with a five-year battery and may not have much longer to live. When he encounters the severely depressed Alec Campbell, Frank proves that the measures he is willing to adopt as a means to an end can sometimes be dangerously extreme. He adopts a cathartic therapy that almost causes Alec's suicide; however, his techniques ultimately meet with success. Frank continues to manipulate his fellow travellers at their next stopping place, the Toll Bar, but does so from the confines of his bed, as his pacemaker begins to fail. Frank dies shortly after he is traumatised by former junkie Sam Mead, before he can warn his friends of Sam's desire to prevent a new industrial revolution.

ALEC CAMPBELL

Sensitive Scottish engineer Alec Campbell spiralled into a guilt-ridden deep depression when he failed to get back to his wife Rita before The Death took her from him. Two years on, he has become a shadow of his former self, spending all his days sat by a woodpile staring at her photograph. However, the importance of his expertise to the quest of Charles, Frank and Jenny to restore power to the nation prompts them to try to bring him out of his reverie. This is achieved by causing him to confront his past while in a state of delirium, during which he focuses on Jenny as a substitute for his dead wife. Despite an abortive suicide attempt, Alec

Frank Garner. © Denis Lill

eventually emerges from the experience as a new man, who is not only ready to assist with Charles's mission, but actually suggests a long trek north to a hydro-electric plant in Scotland. Alec is angered by Charles's subsequent attempts to pair him up with Jenny in order to secure his assistance with the mine generator at The Toll Bar, but admits to Jenny that he does indeed harbour feelings for her; however, she rebuffs him due to her feelings for Greg. Back in his homeland – a short time after Greg's death – Alec makes one further attempt to win Jenny's heart, suggesting that if he didn't turn the power back on she could bring the children up and live a simple life with him in Scotland; however, she declines. After the power is turned on, Alec does not underestimate his indispensable engineering knowledge and informs Charles and McAllister that he will stay at the Loch Mannoch power station to train technicians who will be responsible to him alone, and that he himself will be answerable to no-one. He also threatens that if they do not agree to his terms, he will close the place down in such a way that they will never get it started again.

SAM MEAD

In the old world, Sam Mead was a tragic figure – a heroin addict who had lost both self-respect and purpose, and who was locked in a downward spiral. Sam found a kind of absolution in The Death, a means to break completely from the constraints of his former life and to start afresh. Settling down in a community and fathering a child with his wife Mary-Jean, Sam remains obsessed by the nature of his own 'rebirth'. In Sam's mind, it was the alienation and moral corruption of 'the supermarket society' that led him down the path towards self-destruction. He is evangelical in his belief that technology and human organisation must never again take the form that they did before. For Sam, if Charles succeeds in his plan to restore electric power, then the plague's survivors will again lose their freedom and become enslaved and degraded once more. Despite the efforts of his wife to dissuade him, Sam decides that he must thwart Charles's plans from the inside – joining his troupe in order to prevent them from bringing hydroelectric power back on line. Driven by his conviction, Sam hides the truth from the rest of the company, and shares the last leg of the journey northwards alongside Alec. Sam considers himself a missionary, motivated by a desire to save humankind from the 'tyranny' of a new industrial age. Yet Sam proves to be an ineffective saboteur, and his plans to stop Alec from switching the power back on are repeatedly thwarted. He meets his end in a struggle with Hubert, plunging into the inlet stream and drowning – dying what he would doubtless consider a martyr's death.

LOCATION GUIDE

The village of Elmley Castle, Worcs.   © Marisa Priestman
The Fourth Horseman | 1.1 The Grants' house and village

St Mary the Virgin church, Elmley Castle, Worcs.   © Marisa Priestman
The Fourth Horseman | 1.1 The Church where Abby delivers her famous line – 'Oh God, please don't let me be the only one!'

© Marisa Priestner

House and driveway in Little Comberton, Worcs.
The Fourth Horseman | 1.1 The back of the Grants' house

© Rich Cross

Great Malvern train station, Worcs.
The Fourth Horseman, Gone to the Angels | 1.1, 1.5 Brimpsfield station

Llanarth Court, Raglan, Mons. © Rich Cross
The Fourth Horseman, Gone to the Angels | 1.1, 1.5 Peter Grant's boarding school

Clenchers Mill Ford, Bromsberrow, Nr. Ledbury, Herefs. © Rich Cross
Genesis | 1.2 The ford where Abby camps for the night and where Jenny, spotting the wood-smoke, arrives only after she's gone

© Marisa Priestner

Harewood End church, Harewood End, Herefs.
Genesis, Gone Away | 1.2, 1.3 The church which becomes a temporary base for Abby, Jenny and Greg

© Rich Cross

Suspension bridge, Hole-in-the-Wall, Nr. Ross-on-Wye, Herefs.
Gone Away | 1.3 The footbridge where Abby suffers her crisis of confidence after escaping from Wormley's men at the supermarket

Llangarron, Herefs. © Marisa Priestner

Corn Dolly | 1.4 The village where Lorraine and Charles are putting up Maredell notices and preparing an inventory of local dwellings

Broad Oak, Herefs. © Marisa Priestner

Gone to the Angels | 1.5 The petrol station where Abby refuels and where Greg and Jenny first meet John and Lizzie

© Marisa Priestner

Railway House, Ripple, Worcs.
Gone to the Angels | 1.5 The house where Abby, Jenny, Greg and the children stay and meet Lincoln

© Marisa Priestner

Brockhampton Court, Brockhampton, Herefs.
Garland's War | 1.6 Waterhouse, Jimmy Garland's estate

269

Hampton Court, Hope-under-Dinmore, Herefs.
© Rich Cross

Starvation – A Beginning | 1.7-1.13 The Grange, the location of the first community

Hampton Court, Hope-under-Dinmore, Herefs.
© Rich Cross

Starvation – A Beginning | 1.7-1.13 The Grange, the location of the first community

Hampton Court, Hope-under-Dinmore, Herefs.
© Rich Cross
Starvation – A Beginning | 1.7-1.13 The library where the community decide Barney's fate

Hampton Court, Hope-under-Dinmore, Herefs.
© Rich Cross
Starvation – A Beginning | 1.7-1.13 The main stairway

Vauld House Farm, Marden, Herefs.   © Rich Cross

A Beginning | 1.13 The cottage where Garland took Abby when she took a break from life at the Grange

Michaelchurch Court, Michaelchurch Escley, Herefs.   © Rich Cross

Birth of a Hope | 2.1 The house which doubled for the burning Grange

© Rich Cross

Michaelchurch Court, Michaelchurch Escley, Herefs.
Birth of a Hope | 2.1 The barn where the survivors of the fire took shelter

© Andy Priestner

Callow Hill Farm, Monmouth, Mons.
Birth of a Hope – New World | 2.1-2.13 Charles, Pet and Ruth's house at Whitecross

Callow Hill Farm, Monmouth, Mons.
© Marisa Priestner
Birth of a Hope – New World | 2.1-2.13 Pet's kitchen, scene of many councils of war

Callow Hill Farm, Monmouth, Mons.
© Andy Priestner
Birth of a Hope – New World | 2.1-2.13 The main farmyard

© Marisa Priestner

Callow Hill Farm, Monmouth, Mons
Birth of a Hope – New World | 2.1-2.13 Daniella's kitchen

© Marisa Priestner

Callow Hill Farm, Monmouth, Mons
Birth of a Hope – New World | 2.1-2.13 The White House where Arthur and others lived

Callow Hill Farm, Monmouth, Mons. © Marisa Priestner
Birth of a Hope – New World | 2.1-2.13 The lawn where the Midsummer Party was held and the tennis court where the *Survivors* production crew parked their vehicles

Welsh Newton Common, Herefs. © Rich Cross
Greater Love | 2.2 The barn where Paul was quarantined when he returned from Birmingham

© Rich Cross

Bridge 76, Brecon and Monmouthshire Canal, Pen-groes-oped, Mons.
Parasites | 2.10 The bridge where Greg is teaching the children to fish and where Kane and Grice moor the barge

© Marisa Priestner

The Mill, Skenfrith, Mons.
The Witch, New Arrivals, Over the Hills | 2.6, 2.11, 2.12 The mill which Greg and Charles attempt to restore, which is later taken over by Melanie and the other new arrivals to Whitecross

Wolverley Court, Wolverley, Kidderminster, Worcs.   © Adrian Hulme

A Little Learning | 3.2 The school where Eagle's community of children lived

Viaduct, Monsal Dale, Derbys   © Rich Cross

Mad Dog | 3.4 The viaduct beneath which the dog pack attacks Charles and where he first encounters Fenton

© Marisa Priestner

Air Cottage, Nr. Ilam, Derbys
Mad Dog | 3.4 Fenton's halfway house

© Rich Cross

Highley station, Bridgnorth to Kidderminster Severn Valley Railway, Shrops.
Bridgehead | 3.5 The station where Charles attempted to set up a regular market day

Ffrwdgrech House, Ffrwdgrech, Brecon, Powys
© Rich Cross
Reunion | 3.6 Sloton Spencer

Imber, Salisbury Plain, Wilts.
© Adrian Hulme
Sparks | 3.8 The church where Queenie's community lived

© Rich Cross

Penoyre House, Cradoc, Nr. Brecon, Powys
The Enemy | 3.9 The main staircase inside the Toll Bar

© Adrian Hulme

Taymouth Castle, Kenmore, Perth and Kinross
Power | 3.12 The Laird's castle

281

Lochay Hydroelectric Power Station, Glen Lochay, Nr. Killin, Stirling © Adrian Hulme
Power | 3.12 The hydroelectric power station which Alec starts up again

APPENDIX:
DOOMWATCH AND SURVIVORS
CONNECTIONS AND CONTINUITIES

APPENDIX

I t is difficult to overstate the significance of *Doomwatch* in the genesis of *Survivors* – both in terms of the narrative preoccupations that the two series share, and in the significant overlap of personnel responsible for bringing them to the screen. *Doomwatch* certainly anticipated *Survivors'* sense of scepticism about the consequences of unconstrained scientific 'progress'. The world never actually comes crashing down in *Doomwatch*, but on many occasions in the series' frequently doom-laden storylines, foolhardy scientists and inattentive politicians push things to the very brink – and the future of the planet hangs in the balance.

The name 'Doomwatch' was a shorthand for the fictional Department of Measurement of Scientific Work (and also its super-computer), run by the dogged and sometimes irascible Dr Spencer Quist (John Paul) – with the aid of his assistants, the bright young Tobias 'Toby' Wren (Robert Powell) and the dashing and wily John Ridge (Simon Oates). The premise of the series involves the team being called in to investigate instances of commercial, scientific and governmental wrong-doing.

Doomwatch (1970-72) was the brainchild of Kit Pedler and Gerry Davis, scriptwriters long fascinated with green and environmental issues, who saw great dramatic potential in a prophetic series that took cutting-edge scientific developments and extended them into the realm of imaginative fiction. As one-time head of the Department of Anatomy at University College, London, Pedler was a proven real-world scientific specialist. Davis had a track record as an effective television script editor. In 1969, Pedler and Davis, who had previously worked together on *Doctor Who* and devised the first Cybermen story, won a commission for an initial thirteen episode *Doomwatch* series, to be broadcast in a primetime BBC1 slot the following year. It was agreed that between them they would script four episodes, and that seasoned BBC producer Terence Dudley would act as a producer-scriptwriter for the series.

In their suspicious and often cynical view of industrial science and technology, the three series of *Doomwatch* would go on to explore themes that would resurface in various guises in *Survivors* – "The Web of Fear" focused on an outbreak of a 'Yellow Fever' epidemic in the Scilly Isles, while "Fire and Brimstone" looked at the threat of an anthrax outbreak (both foreshadowing *Survivors'* own concern with an unstoppable pandemic); "Tomorrow, the Rat" examined the dangers of a supercharged rat infestation of London (a theme taken up in *Survivors* in the two-part second series story "Lights of London"); while "The Inquest" explored the authorities' response to a rabies outbreak (an issue that dominates the series three *Survivors* episode "Mad Dog").

But what connects the two series just as strongly as their shared sense of cynicism about the 'modern' world around them, is the fact that so many cast and crew members would go on to work on *Survivors* following their earlier involvement with *Doomwatch*.

Fifteen out of the total of thirty-eight episodes of *Doomwatch* were written by scriptwriters who subsequently wrote for *Survivors*. Producer Terence Dudley wrote five *Doomwatch* scripts in all, including the classics "Tomorrow, the Rat" and "You Killed Toby Wren". Don Shaw, Martin Worth and Roger Parkes – each of whom wrote episodes for the second and third series of *Survivors* – all contributed scripts for *Doomwatch*. Shaw wrote the pesticide thriller "Train and De-Train"; the space drama "Re-entry Forbidden"; and "The Devil's Sweets", which looked at the manipulative psychology of subliminal advertising. Parkes meanwhile supplied "No Room for Error", the story of a flawed 'super-drug' (which threatened a mass epidemic); and "Without the Bomb", which looked at the ethics of enforced behaviour modification. Worth's scripts included "Invasion", which imagined the consequences of a chemical weapons leak; "Say Knife, Fat Man"; and the jet-lag disorientation story "Flight into Yesterday". Worth also worked as an uncredited script editor on a number of series three *Doomwatch* episodes. (In addition, the screenplay for the 1972 spin-off *Doomwatch* movie – in which the TV cast have only limited or cameo roles – was written by *Survivors* scriptwriter Clive Exton.)

Three of the directors on *Survivors* – Terence Dudley himself, Eric Hills and Pennant Roberts – had all earlier helmed episodes of *Doomwatch*. Dudley had directed two of his own scripts, "You Killed Toby Wren", which opened series two, and "Fire and Brimstone", the first episode of the third series. Hills, whose *Survivors* episodes would include "Birth of a Hope" and "Over the Hills", directed four *Doomwatch* stories in total, including the memorable "Say Knife, Fat Man", which focused on the efforts of a radical student group to build an atomic bomb, and the Dudley-scripted poison-scare "Spectre at the Feast". Roberts, who would direct a total of nine *Survivors* episodes, had been responsible for the third series *Doomwatch* stories "Waiting for a Knighthood" (also written by Dudley) and "Enquiry", a military weapons thriller.

Amongst the production crew who worked on both series were designers Ian Watson and Ray London. Watson, who served as the principal designer on *Survivors*' second series, was responsible for the design of five episodes of *Doomwatch*, including the shocking series one finale "Survival Code" (in which one of the lead characters, Wren, is blown up attempting to defuse an explosive device). London, who worked on two *Doomwatch* episodes, went on to design the first series *Survivors* episodes "Genesis" and "Gone to the Angels".

In addition to the behind-the-camera connections, it is also significant how many cast members appear in both shows. No fewer than twenty-three of the actors who are in the cast credits for *Doomwatch* go on to appear in one or more episodes of *Survivors*.

Talfryn Thomas, who made appearances in the *Doomwatch* episodes "The Human Timebomb" and "Fire and Brimstone", would appear as the recurring character Tom Price. Other *Survivors* regulars who earlier made guest appearances in *Doomwatch* include Stephen Dudley (John Millon), Eileen Helsby (Charmian Wentworth), Michael Gover (Arthur Russell), Julie Neubert (Wendy), Lorna Lewis (Pet Simpson), Delia Paton (Mina), and Peter Duncan (Dave). Edward Underdown (Frank Garner) and Robert Gillespie (John Milner/Sam Mead), appeared together in the series two *Doomwatch* story "You Killed Toby Wren". Other notable *Survivors* guest stars who had earlier appeared in *Doomwatch* include Glyn Owen (Bernard Huxley in "The Future Hour"); Patrick Troughton (John Millen in "Parasites"), and Morris Perry (Richard Fenton in "Mad Dog"). June Brown (Susan in "Manhunt") appeared in the controversial *Doomwatch* episode "Sex and Violence", which focused on the issues of public morality and state censorship, and which was never broadcast due to the inclusion of documentary footage of a real-life military execution.

Although many BBC programmes of this era shared the same experience, it still remains notable that both *Doomwatch* and *Survivors* underwent a significant turnover of central cast members in the course of three series. Toby Wren, played by Robert Powell, was killed off at the end of the first series of *Doomwatch*. On *Survivors*, the lead character Abby Grant was similarly written out at the end of series one. Simon Oates, who had starred as Dr John Ridge throughout series one and two of *Doomwatch*, opted to appear in just four episodes of its third series. Ian McCulloch, who had starred as Greg in the first two series of *Survivors*, asked to appear in just two episodes of series three. The recurring characters Geoff Hardcastle (John

Nolan) and Dr Fay Chantry (Jean Trend) appeared only in series two of *Doomwatch*. Similarly, on *Survivors*, there were numerous returning characters, such as Tom Price (Talfryn Thomas), Ruth Anderson (Celia Gregory) and Agnes Carlsson (Anna Pitt), who appeared in only one of the three series (although in the case of both Ruth and Agnes, the characters – played by different actresses – did graduate from one-off guest-starring roles in the closing episode of the previous series). On *Doomwatch*, the negligent and officious government minister played by John Barron, who had made earlier guest appearances on the show, became a recurring character in series three. On *Survivors*, Charles Vaughan, played by Denis Lill, became one of the leads on the second and third series, after a one-off guest appearance in the first.

From a production point of view, both shows broke new ground: while *Survivors* set a new benchmark for the process of Outside Broadcast recording, *Doomwatch* made television history as the first BBC series to be shown entirely in colour on BBC1. There were, however, marked differences in visual appearance and narrative feel between the two series. *Doomwatch* was principally recorded on video in BBC studios, though small on-location film segments (and occasional 'stock footage') were included in many episodes. Scriptwriter Don Shaw recalls that in contributing to BBC series up until 1974-75, writers had always to remember: 'We were normally only allowed around two minutes of film per episode of fifty minutes ... So you could go out with a film camera and do just a couple of minutes on location and then have it slotted in to the studio-recorded pieces.' As a direct result of this restriction, *Doomwatch* was much more static and studio-bound than *Survivors* was required to be. Although there were exceptions (like the more extensive film sequences of the army's evacuation of a village in "Invasion"), many of *Doomwatch*'s dramatic conflicts were played out in the studio settings of a ministerial office, company boardroom or scientific laboratory. The first six episodes of *Survivors*, which share a similar reliance on a mixture of studio video recording and on-location filming, are the most visually reminiscent of *Doomwatch* – although the budget for *Survivors* afforded a far more extensive film component, which immediately 'opened up' the dramatic context. From the seventh episode of *Survivors* onwards, when the switch to Outside Broadcast recording is introduced, the visual appearances of the two shows diverge markedly.

There is one further important element of continuity that, in hindsight, can be seen to link the two series in a very significant way – that of Terence Dudley's relationship with their respective creators. *Doomwatch* was very successful for the BBC, and it was renewed in 1971 and again in 1972. At the close of the second series, however, creators Pedler and Davis left the show – angered at the direction it was taking. Pedler insisted that *Doomwatch* had lost sight of its original purpose, which was to 'make serious comment about the dangerous facts of science' so that they became the focus of public concern. He was convinced that the series was fast becoming a 'total travesty' of that intention, and that as a result he and his co-writer could no longer be party to it. Producer Dudley was equally convinced that theirs was too didactic an approach for what was, after all, intended to be a prime-time entertainment show and not a heavyweight lecture on ecological matters. He recruited new writers to replace them, and went on to steer the show through its final series. A similar conflict of approaches between Dudley and the creator of a series for which he was producer would resurface some five years later on *Survivors* – leading to a equivalent breakdown in the working relationship.

What accounts for the numerous connections linking *Doomwatch* and *Survivors*? The overriding explanation for the overlap of production and creative staff is the involvement of Terence Dudley. When the BBC Drama Department was looking for a producer for their new 'end of the world' drama *Survivors* in 1974, it was above all Dudley's experience on the recent techno-sceptic *Doomwatch* that made him such an obvious candidate. As Dudley enjoyed working with those that he had used successfully previously, it was likely that he would (as his discretion over such issues increased in series two and three), sign up familiar talents to *Survivors* – including scriptwriters Roger Parkes, Don Shaw and Martin Worth, and directors Eric Hills and Pennant Roberts. From the pool of actors who regularly worked on BBC productions of the day, Dudley, Hills and Roberts were equally likely to cast supporting and character actors that they knew and liked from previous series. The relatively high turnover of creative staff on both shows was, in large part, a reflection of Dudley's determination to keep the drama 'fresh' – a process reinforced by his firmly assertive style as a writer-producer.

BIBLIOGRAPHY AND FURTHER READING

Alsop, Neil. 1987. '*Survivors*: A Horseman Riding By'. *Timescreen*, No 10, pp.9-17.

Alsop, Neil. 1989. '*Survivors*: Birth of a Nation'. *Timescreen*, No 13, pp.4-10.

Bignell, Jonathan, and O'Day, Andrew. 2004. *Terry Nation*. Manchester: Manchester University Press.

Broe, Emma, and Simpson, Paul. 1997. 'Lucy in the Sky'. *Dreamwatch*, January, pp.48-49.

Brown, Anthony. 1993. 'Enough to Break the Glass'. *Doctor Who Bulletin*, April, pp.12-14.

Brown, Anthony. 1996. 'Doomwatch: 1970-72', *SFX*, October, pp. 68-70.

Brown, Anthony. 2004. 'Approaches to Survival'. *TV Zone Special*. No 60, pp.60-64.

Byrne, Anthony, and Smith, Nicky. 1995. '*Survivors*; 20th Anniversary Retrospective'. *Dreamwatch*, No 8, April, pp.10-13.

Clark, Simon. 1998. 'Isn't it About Time You Gave *Survivors* Another Chance?'. *SFX*, August, pp.7-9.

Cross, Rich. 2004. 'The Beginning of the End'. *Action TV*, No 10, pp.28-37.

David, Saul. 2004. 'The Hippies on the Hill', *The Sunday Times*, 10 October.

Gosling, Sharon. 2003. 'Survival Instincts'. *Dreamwatch*, No 110, November, p.18.

Greenbank, Anthony. 1976. 'Grave New World'. *Radio Times* Vol. 211, No 2740, 15-21 May.

Hari, Johann. 2004. 'Television that Told the Future', *The Independent (Review)*, 4 March.

Leigh, Gary. 1995. 'I Survived!'. *Dreamwatch*, No 11, July, pp.11-13.

Linford, Peter. 1994. 'It's the End of the World as We Know It'. *Doctor Who Bulletin*, March, pp.12-13.

Macomber, Michael. 1992. 'Terry Nation interview' *The Liberator's Log*, Vol 5, No 6, February, pp.3-6 (part one); Vol 5, No 7, March, pp.3-5 (part two).

Marshall, Kevin. 1995. *The Making of Terry Nation's Survivors*. Fourth Horseman Publications.

Nation, Terry. 1988. 'Terry Nation on *Survivors*', *Information: Newsletter of Star One*, Vol 3, Issue 5, p.14.

Nazzaro, Joe. 1992. 'Terry Nation's *Survivors*'. *TV Zone*, No 31, pp.28-31.

Perry, Chris and Richardson, Michael. 2005. 'Private Thoughts, Public Eye: Interview with Roger Marshall', *Action TV*, No 11, pp.30-37.

Pixley, Andrew, and Worth, Martin. 1989. '*Survivors*: A Writer's Tale'. *Timescreen*, Issue 14, pp.24-29.

Priestner, Andy. 2003. *Viewing Notes* [booklet accompanying series one DVD release]. London: DD Video.

Priestner, Andy. 2004. *Viewing Notes* [booklet accompanying series two DVD release]. London: DD Video.

Richardson, David. 1991. 'Lucy Fleming: Memoirs of Another Survivor'. *TV Zone*. No 24, pp.12-14.

Richardson, David. 1993.'Carolyn Seymour: Still Surviving'. *TV Zone*, No 42, pp.29-31.

Richardson, David. 1994. 'Martin Worth: Doom Merchant'. *TV Zone*, No 55, pp.17-19.

Richardson, David. 2003. 'Still Surviving'. *TV Zone*. No 169, pp.50-53.

Richardson, David. 2003. '28 Years Later'. *Ultimate DVD*, No 48, pp.92-94.

Richardson, David, and Russell, Gary. 1990. 'Ian McCulloch: Memoirs of a Survivor'. *TV Zone*, No 5, pp.12-15.

Richardson, Michael, and Pixley, Andrew. 1989, 'Doomwatch: The World in Danger',

Timescreen, No 4, pp.4-14.

Robinson, Derek. 1995. *How Did Jasper Get to Whitecross?* Self-published.

Screen, Andrew. 2004. '*Drama Playhouse*: The Incredible Robert Baldick', *The Illustrated Gazette*. http://www.the-mausoleum-club.org.uk

Russell, Gary. 1991. 'King of the Swampies'. *TV Zone*, No 21, p9-11.

Thompson, Harry. 2004. 'We All Fall Down', *Ultimate DVD*, No 59, pp.68-69.

Wyman, Mark. 1991. 'June Hudson: Universal Wear'. *TV Zone*, No 14, pp.33-38.

SURVIVORS FAN PUBLICATIONS

Over the Hills, 1994-1998, 14 issues.

Whitecross Calling, February-December 1997, 6 issues

Bridgehead / Survivors: Bridgehead, 1998-1999, 14 issues (continuing as *Survivors: The Newsletter*)

Survivors: The Newsletter, 1999-present, ongoing

ABOUT THE AUTHORS

RICH CROSS has, since 1995, written numerous *Survivors* articles, news stories and episode reviews for the fan press, including *Over the Hills*, *Whitecross Calling*, *Survivors: The Newsletter* and *Action TV*. He has moderated commentaries for "Lights of London Part 2" and "Mad Dog" for the DVD releases and maintains the *Survivors: Mad Dog* and *Survivors: A World Away* websites. He is also a regular contributor to the leading British *Planet of the Apes* fanzine *Simian Scrolls*. In his role as a political historian, he has also written for *Socialist History*, *Contemporary Politics* and the US academic journal *Science and Society*. He was awarded his doctorate from the University of Manchester in April 2003, and currently works as an academic librarian.

ANDY PRIESTNER served as consultant on the DVD releases of all three series of *Survivors*, writing the accompanying *Viewing Notes* and packaging, co-ordinating the studio days, conducting the interviews, moderating episode commentaries and directing the making of Series 3 documentary: *New World Rising*. In addition he has maintained the *survivorstvseries.com* website since 2001. He has also conducted interviews and written behind-the-scenes booklets for DD Home Entertainment's DVD releases of *All Gas and Gaiters*, *Fall of Eagles*, *Kessler*, *Oh Brother!*, *Oh Father!*, *Secret Army* and *War and Peace*. A chartered librarian, he is employed as a Senior Information Officer at Oxford University's Said Business School, where he specialises in electronic information resources.

TIME HUNTER

A range of high-quality, original paperback and limited edition hardback novellas featuring the adventures in time of Honoré Lechasseur. Part mystery, part detective story, part dark fantasy, part science fiction ... these books are guaranteed to enthral fans of good fiction everywhere, and are in the spirit of our acclaimed range of *Doctor Who* Novellas.

ALREADY AVAILABLE

THE WINNING SIDE by LANCE PARKIN

Emily is dead! Killed by an unknown assailant. Honoré and Emily find themselves caught up in a plot reaching from the future to their past, and with their very existence, not to mention the future of the entire world, at stake, can they unravel the mystery before it is too late?
An adventure in time and space.
£7.99 (+ £1.50 UK p&p) Standard p/b ISBN 1-903889-35-9 (pb)

THE TUNNEL AT THE END OF THE LIGHT by STEFAN PETRUCHA

In the heart of post-war London, a bomb is discovered lodged at a disused station between Green Park and Hyde Park Corner. The bomb detonates, and as the dust clears, it becomes apparent that *something* has been awakened. Strange half-human creatures attack the workers at the site, hungrily searching for anything containing sugar ...
Meanwhile, Honoré and Emily are contacted by eccentric poet Randolph Crest, who believes himself to be the target of these subterranean creatures. The ensuing investigation brings Honoré and Emily up against a terrifying force from deep beneath the earth, and one which even with their combined powers, they may have trouble stopping.
An adventure in time and space.
£7.99 (+ £1.50 UK p&p) Standard p/b ISBN 1-903889-37-5 (pb)
£25.00 (+ £1.50 UK p&p) Deluxe h/b ISBN 1-903889-38-3 (hb)

THE CLOCKWORK WOMAN by CLAIRE BOTT

Honoré and Emily find themselves imprisoned in the 19th Century by a celebrated inventor ... but help comes from an unexpected source – a humanoid automaton created by and to give pleasure to its owner. As the trio escape to London, they are unprepared for what awaits them, and at every turn it seems impossible to avert what fate may have in store for the Clockwork Woman.
An adventure in time and space.
£7.99 (+ £1.50 UK p&p) Standard p/b ISBN 1-903889-39-1 (pb)
£25.00 (+ £1.50 UK p&p) Deluxe h/b ISBN 1-903889-40-5 (hb)

KITSUNE by JOHN PAUL CATTON

In the year 2020, Honoré and Emily find themselves thrown into a mystery, as an ice spirit – *Yuki-Onna* – wreaks havoc during the Kyoto Festival, and a haunted funhouse proves to contain more than just paper lanterns and wax dummies. But what does all this have to do with the elegant owner of the Hide and Chic fashion chain … and to the legendary Chinese fox-spirits, the Kitsune?

An adventure in time and space.

£7.99 (+ £1.50 UK p&p) Standard p/b ISBN 1-903889-41-3 (pb)
£25.00 (+ £1.50 UK p&p) Deluxe h/b ISBN 1-903889-42-1 (hb)

THE SEVERED MAN by GEORGE MANN

What links a clutch of sinister murders in Victorian London, an angel appearing in a Staffordshire village in the 1920s and a small boy running loose around the capital in 1950? When Honoré and Emily encounter a man who appears to have been cut out of time, they think they have the answer. But soon enough they discover that the mystery is only just beginning and that nightmares can turn into reality.

An adventure in time and space.

£7.99 (+ £1.50 UK p&p) Standard p/b ISBN 1-903889-43-X (pb)
£25.00 (+ £1.50 UK p&p) Deluxe h/b ISBN 1-903889-44-8 (hb)

ECHOES by IAIN MCLAUGHLIN & CLAIRE BARTLETT

Echoes of the past … echoes of the future. Honoré Lechasseur can see the threads that bind the two together, however when he and Emily Blandish find themselves outside the imposing tower-block headquarters of Dragon Industry, both can sense something is wrong. There are ghosts in the building, and images and echoes of all times pervade the structure. But what is behind this massive contradiction in time, and can Honoré and Emily figure it out before they become trapped themselves …?

An adventure in time and space.

£7.99 (+ £1.50 UK p&p) Standard p/b ISBN 1-903889-45-6 (pb)
£25.00 (+ £1.50 UK p&p) Deluxe h/b ISBN 1-903889-46-4 (hb)

PECULIAR LIVES by PHILIP PURSER-HALLARD

Once a celebrated author of 'scientific romances', Erik Clevedon is an old man now. But his fiction conceals a dangerous truth, as Honoré Lechasseur and Emily Blandish discover after a chance encounter with a strangely gifted young pickpocket. Born between the Wars, the superhuman children known as 'the Peculiar' are reaching adulthood – and they believe that humanity is making a poor job of looking after the world they plan to inherit …

An adventure in time and space.

£7.99 (+ £1.50 UK p&p) Standard p/b ISBN 1-903889-47-2 (pb)
£25.00 (+ £1.50 UK p&p) Deluxe h/b ISBN 1-903889-48-0 (hb)

TIME HUNTER FILM

DAEMOS RISING by DAVID J HOWE, DIRECTED BY KEITH BARNFATHER

Daemos Rising is a sequel to both the *Doctor Who* adventure *The Daemons* and to *Downtime*, an earlier drama featuring the Yeti. It is also a prequel of sorts to Telos Publishing's *Time Hunter* series. It stars Miles Richardson as ex-UNIT operative Douglas Cavendish, and Beverley Cressman as Brigadier Lethbridge-Stewart's daughter Kate. Trapped in an isolated cottage, Cavendish thinks he is seeing ghosts. The only person who might understand and help is Kate Lethbridge-Stewart ... but when she arrives, she realises that Cavendish is key in a plot to summon the Daemons back to the Earth. With time running out, Kate discovers that sometimes even the familiar can turn out to be your worst nightmare. Also starring Andrew Wisher, and featuring Ian Richardson as the Narrator.
An adventure in time and space.
£14.00 (+ £2.50 UK p&p) PAL format R4 DVD
Order direct from Reeltime Pictures, PO Box 23435, London SE26 5WU

HORROR/FANTASY

CAPE WRATH by PAUL FINCH
Death and horror on a deserted Scottish island as an ancient Viking warrior chief returns to life.
£8.00 (+ £1.50 UK p&p) Standard p/b ISBN: 1-903889-60-X

KING OF ALL THE DEAD by STEVE LOCKLEY & PAUL LEWIS
The king of all the dead will have what is his.
£8.00 (+ £1.50 UK p&p) Standard p/b ISBN: 1-903889-61-8

GUARDIAN ANGEL by STEPHANIE BEDWELL-GRIME
Devilish fun as Guardian Angel Porsche Winter loses a soul to the devil ...
£9.99 (+ £2.50 UK p&p) Standard p/b ISBN: 1-903889-62-6

FALLEN ANGEL by STEPHANIE BEDWELL-GRIME
Porsche Winter battles she devils on Earth ...
£9.99 (+ £2.50 UK p&p) Standard p/b ISBN: 1-903889-69-3

ASPECTS OF A PSYCHOPATH by ALISTAIR LANGSTON
Goes deeper than ever before into the twisted psyche of a serial killer. Horrific, graphic and gripping, this book is not for the squeamish.
£8.00 (+ £1.50 UK p&p) Standard p/b ISBN: 1-903889-63-4

SPECTRE by STEPHEN LAWS
The inseparable Byker Chapter: six boys, one girl, growing up together in the back streets of Newcastle. Now memories are all that Richard Eden has left, and one treasured photograph. But suddenly, inexplicably, the images of his companions start to fade, and as they vanish, so his friends are found dead and mutilated. Something is stalking the Chapter, picking them off one by one, something connected with their past, and with the girl they used to know.
£9.99 (+ £2.50 UK p&p) Standard p/b ISBN: 1-903889-72-3

THE HUMAN ABSTRACT by GEORGE MANN
A future tale of private detectives, AIs, Nanobots, love and death.
£7.99 (+ £1.50 UK p&p) Standard p/b ISBN: 1-903889-65-0

BREATHE by CHRISTOPHER FOWLER
The Office meets *Night of the Living Dead*.
£7.99 (+ £1.50 UK p&p) Standard p/b ISBN: 1-903889-67-7
£25.00 (+ £1.50 UK p&p) Deluxe h/b ISBN: 1-903889-68-5

HOUDINI'S LAST ILLUSION by STEVE SAVILE
Can master illusionist Harry Houdini outwit the dead shades of his past?
£7.99 (+ £1.50 UK p&p) Standard p/b ISBN: 1-903889-66-9

ALICE'S JOURNEY BEYOND THE MOON by R J CARTER
A sequel to the classic Lewis Carroll tales.
£6.99 (+ £1.50 UK p&p) Standard p/b ISBN: 1-903889-76-6
£30.00 (+ £1.50 UK p&p) Deluxe h/b ISBN: 1-903889-77-4

APPROACHING OMEGA by ERIC BROWN
A colonisation mission to Earth runs into problems.
£7.99 (+ £1.50 UK p&p) Standard p/b ISBN: 1-903889-98-7
£30.00 (+ £1.50 UK p&p) Deluxe h/b ISBN: 1-903889-99-5

VALLEY OF LIGHTS by STEPHEN GALLAGHER
A cop comes up against a body-hopping murderer ...
£9.99 (+ £2.50 UK p&p) Standard p/b ISBN: 1-903889-74-X
£30.00 (+ £2.50 UK p&p) Deluxe h/b ISBN: 1-903889-75-8

TV/FILM GUIDES

A DAY IN THE LIFE: THE UNOFFICIAL AND UNAUTHORISED GUIDE TO 24 by KEITH TOPPING
Complete episode guide to the first season of the popular TV show.
£9.99 (+ £2.50 p&p) Standard p/b ISBN: 1-903889-53-7

THE TELEVISION COMPANION: THE UNOFFICIAL AND UNAUTHORISED GUIDE TO DOCTOR WHO by DAVID J HOWE & STEPHEN JAMES WALKER

Complete episode guide to the popular TV show.
£14.99 (+ £4.75 UK p&p) Standard p/b ISBN: 1-903889-51-0

LIBERATION: THE UNOFFICIAL AND UNAUTHORISED GUIDE TO BLAKE'S 7 by ALAN STEVENS & FIONA MOORE

Complete episode guide to the popular TV show.
Featuring a foreword by David Maloney
£9.99 (+ £2.50 UK p&p) Standard p/b ISBN: 1-903889-54-5

HOWE'S TRANSCENDENTAL TOYBOX: SECOND EDITION by DAVID J HOWE & ARNOLD T BLUMBERG

Complete guide to *Doctor Who* Merchandise.
£25.00 (+ £4.75 UK p&p) Standard p/b ISBN: 1-903889-56-1

HOWE'S TRANSCENDENTAL TOYBOX: UPDATE NO. 1: 2003 by DAVID J HOWE & ARNOLD T BLUMBERG

Complete guide to *Doctor Who* Merchandise released in 2003.
£7.99 (+ £1.50 UK p&p) Standard p/b ISBN: 1-903889-57-X

A VAULT OF HORROR by KEITH TOPPING

A Guide to 80 Classic (and not so classic) British Horror Films
£12.99 (+ £4.75 UK p&p) Standard p/b ISBN: 1-903889-58-8

BEAUTIFUL MONSTERS: THE UNOFFICIAL AND UNAUTHORISED GUIDE TO THE ALIEN AND PREDATOR FILMS by DAVID McINTEE

A Guide to the *Alien* and *Predator* Films
£9.99 (+ £2.50 UK p&p) Standard p/b ISBN: 1-903889-94-4

THE HANDBOOK: THE UNOFFICIAL AND UNAUTHORISED GUIDE TO THE PRODUCTION OF DOCTOR WHO by DAVID J HOWE, STEPHEN JAMES WALKER and MARK STAMMERS

Complete guide to the making of *Doctor Who*.
£14.99 (+ £4.75 UK p&p) Standard p/b ISBN: 1-903889-59-6
£30.00 (+ £4.75 UK p&p) Deluxe h/b ISBN: 1-903889-96-0

HANK JANSON

Classic pulp crime thrillers from the 1940s and 1950s.

TORMENT by HANK JANSON
£9.99 (+ £1.50 UK p&p) Standard p/b ISBN: 1-903889-80-4

WOMEN HATE TILL DEATH by HANK JANSON
£9.99 (+ £1.50 UK p&p) Standard p/b ISBN: 1-903889-81-2

SOME LOOK BETTER DEAD by HANK JANSON
£9.99 (+ £1.50 UK p&p) Standard p/b ISBN: 1-903889-82-0

SKIRTS BRING ME SORROW by HANK JANSON
£9.99 (+ £1.50 UK p&p) Standard p/b ISBN: 1-903889-83-9

WHEN DAMES GET TOUGH by HANK JANSON
£9.99 (+ £1.50 UK p&p) Standard p/b ISBN: 1-903889-85-5

ACCUSED by HANK JANSON
£9.99 (+ £1.50 UK p&p) Standard p/b ISBN: 1-903889-86-3

KILLER by HANK JANSON
£9.99 (+ £1.50 UK p&p) Standard p/b ISBN: 1-903889-87-1

FRAILS CAN BE SO TOUGH by HANK JANSON
£9.99 (+ £1.50 UK p&p) Standard p/b ISBN: 1-903889-88-X

BROADS DON'T SCARE EASY by HANK JANSON
£9.99 (+ £1.50 UK p&p) Standard p/b ISBN: 1-903889-89-8

KILL HER IF YOU CAN by HANK JANSON
£9.99 (+ £1.50 UK p&p) Standard p/b ISBN: 1-903889-90-1

Non-fiction:
THE TRIALS OF HANK JANSON by STEVE HOLLAND
£12.99 (+ £2.50 UK p&p) Standard p/b ISBN: 1-903889-84-7

The prices shown are correct at time of going to press. However, the publishers reserve the right to increase prices from those previously advertised without prior notice.

TELOS PUBLISHING
c/o Beech House, Chapel Lane, Moulton, Cheshire, CW9 8PQ, England
Email: orders@telos.co.uk
Web: www.telos.co.uk

To order copies of any Telos books, please visit our website where there are full details of all titles and facilities for worldwide credit card online ordering, or send a cheque or postal order (UK only) for the appropriate amount (including postage and packing), together with details of the book(s) you require, plus your name and address to the above address. Overseas readers please send two international reply coupons for details of prices and postage rates.